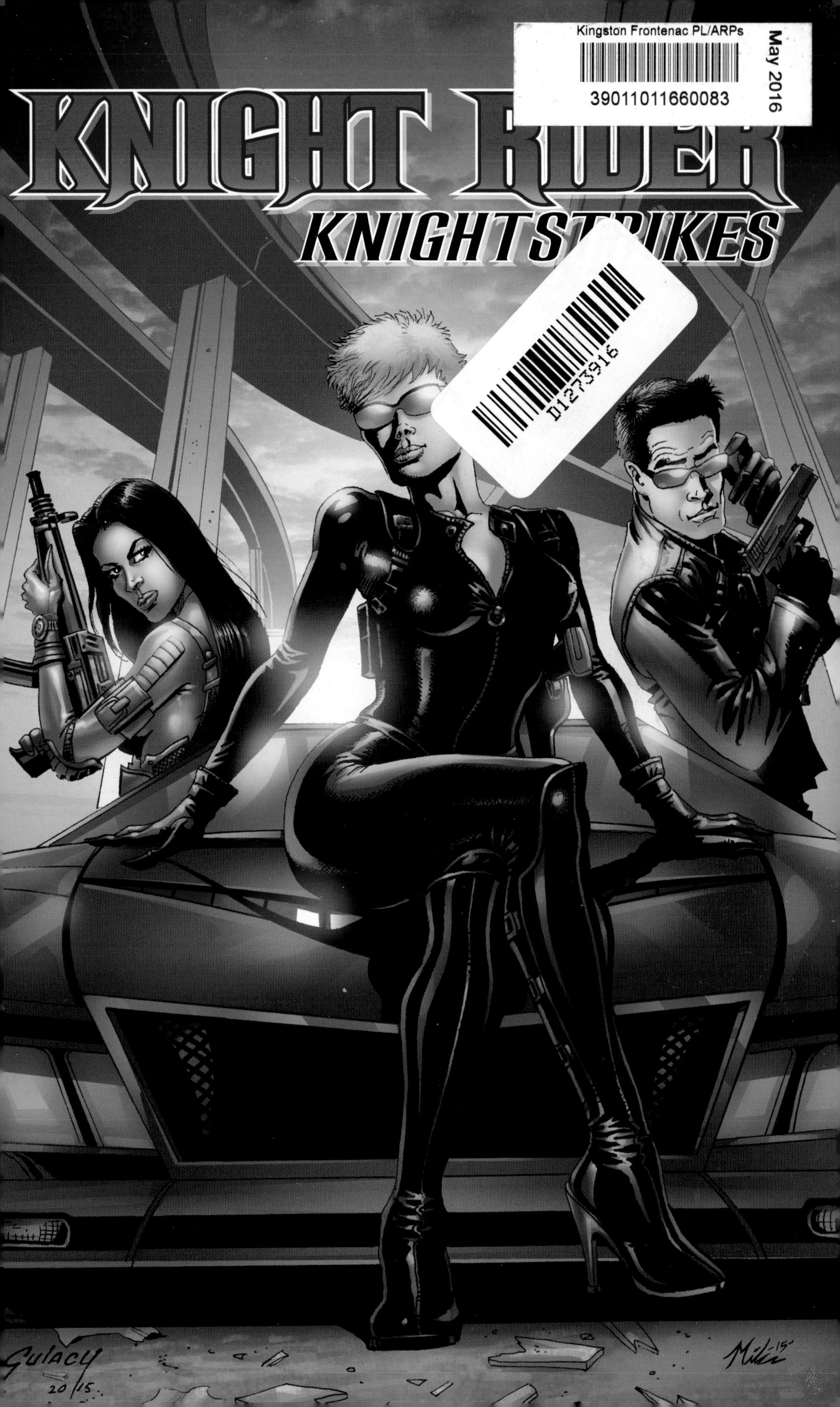
KNIGHT RIDER
KNIGHTSTRIKES
GULACY 20/15

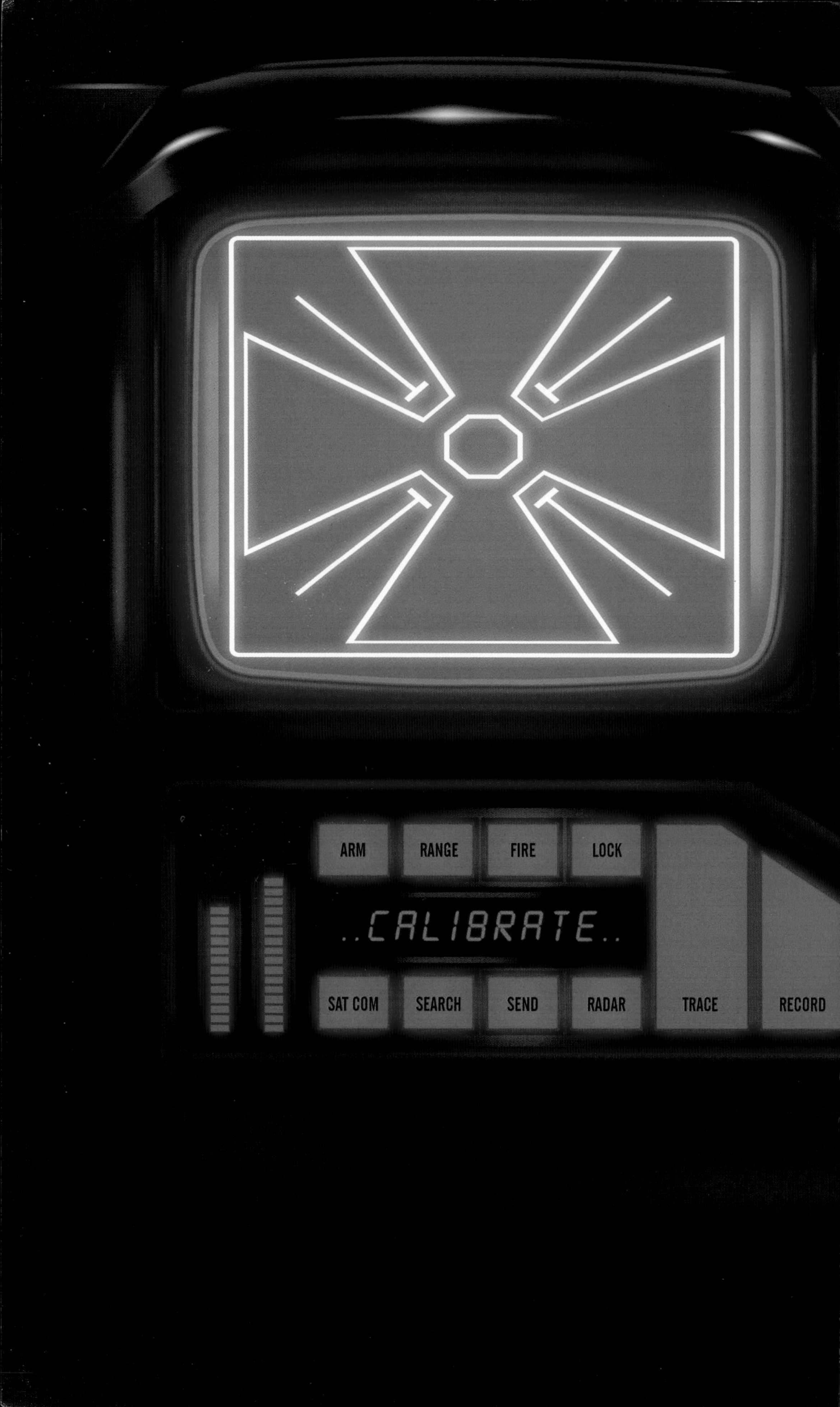

ARM
RANGE
FIRE
LOCK
..CALIBRATE..
SAT COM
SEARCH
SEND
RADAR
TRACE
RECORD

KNIGHT RIDER
KNIGHTSTRIKES

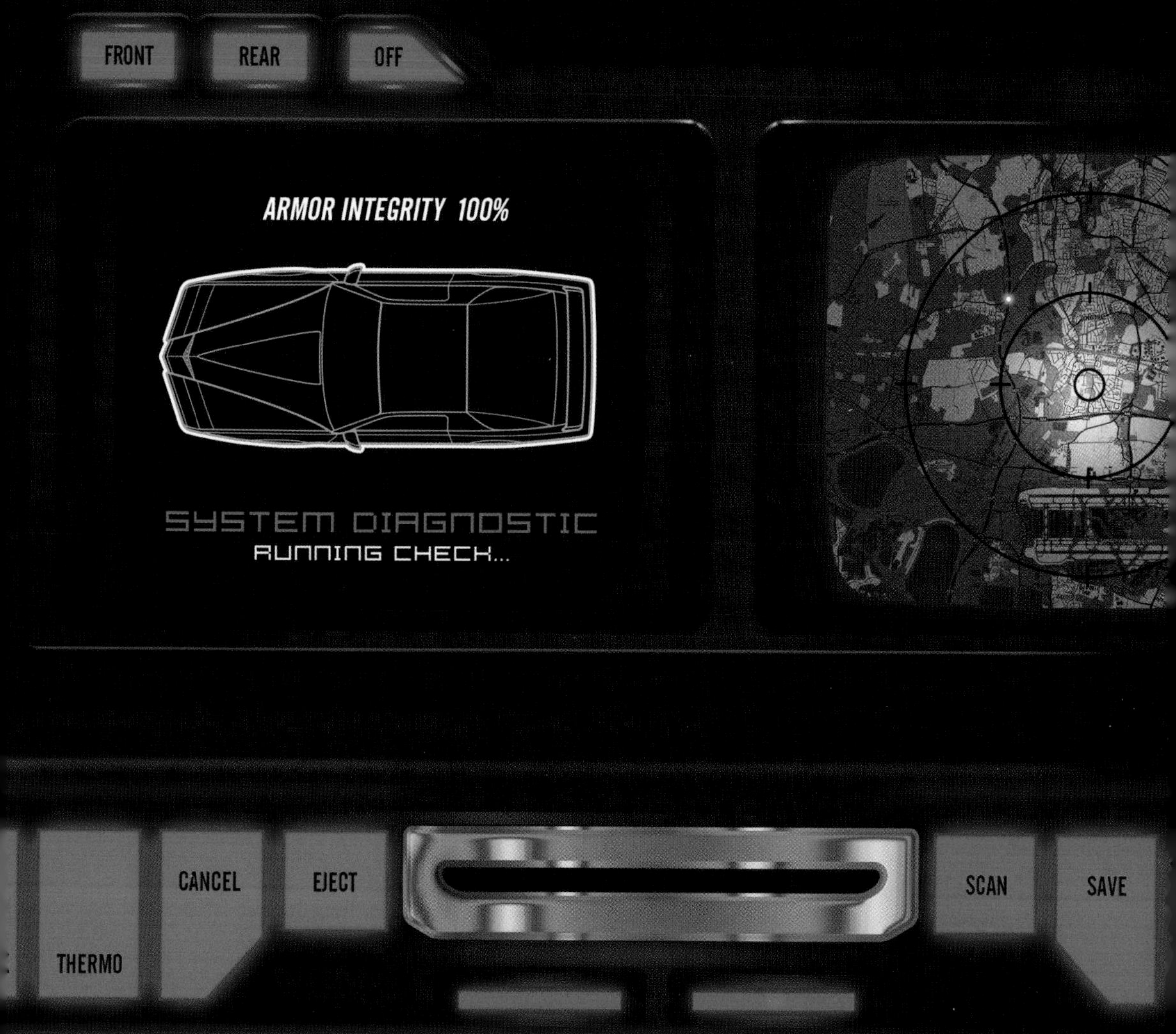
FRONT
REAR
OFF
ARMOR INTEGRITY 100%
SYSTEM DIAGNOSTIC
RUNNING CHECK...
CANCEL
EJECT
THERMO
SCAN
SAVE

LION FORGE COMICS
LIONFORGE.COM

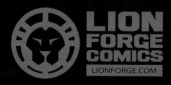

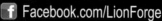

Facebook.com/LionForge
Twitter @LionForge
YouTube.com/LionForge

IDW PUBLISHING

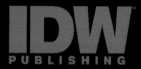

Originally published as Knight Rider #1-8 ISBN: 978-1-63140-485-6 LIONFORGE.com

DANGEROUS TERRAIN

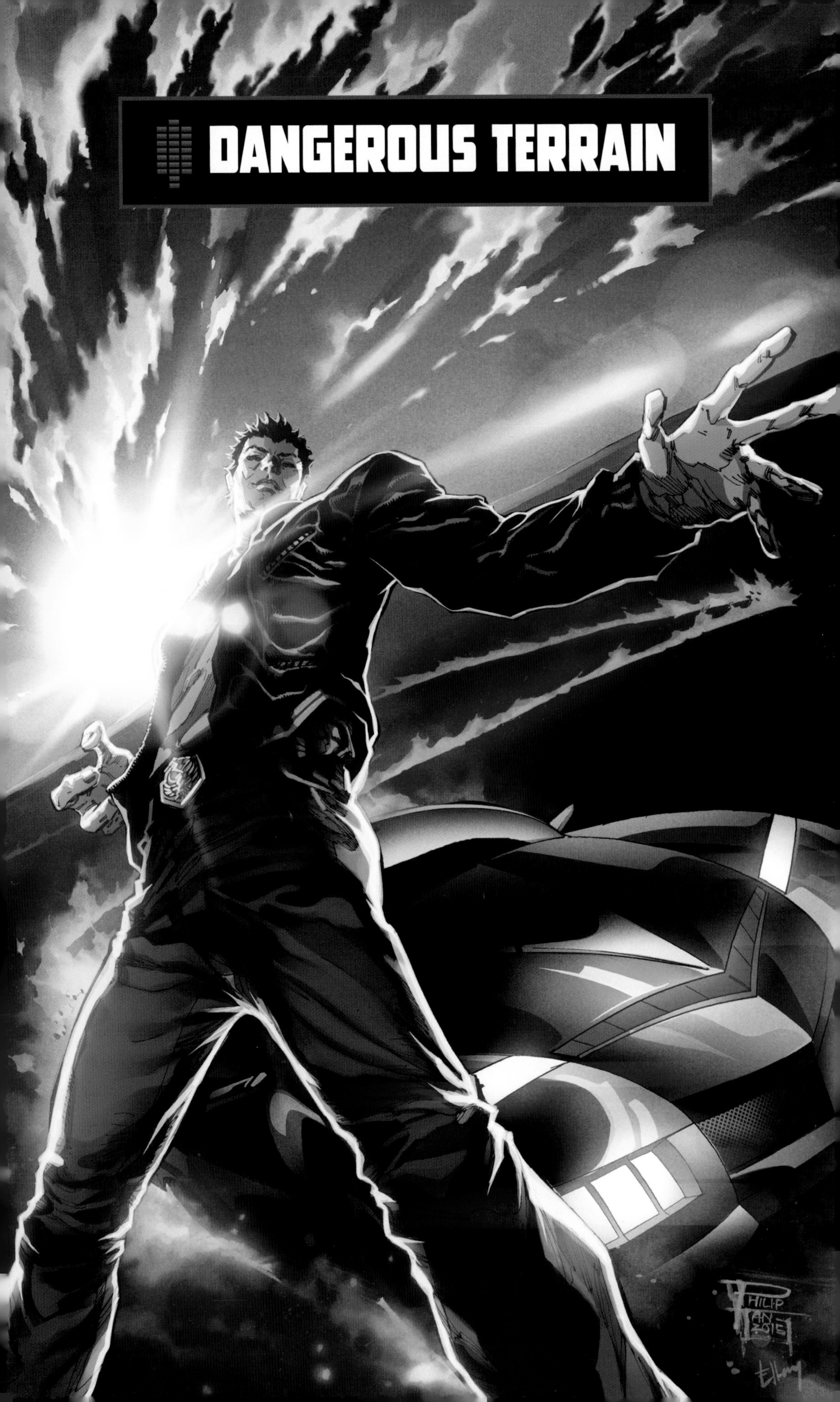
PHILIP TAN 2015

KNIGHT RIDER
KNIGHT STRIKES

WRITTEN BY
SHANNON ERIC DENTON

ILLUSTRATED BY
BRIAN DENHAM

COLORED BY
MILEN PARVANOV

LETTERED BY
STEVE WANDS

EDITED BY
SHANNON ERIC DENTON

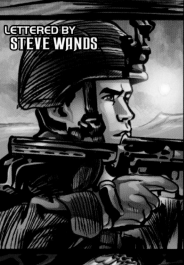

FRONT COVER BY
PHILIP TAN

KNIGHT RIDER CREATED BY
GLEN A. LARSON

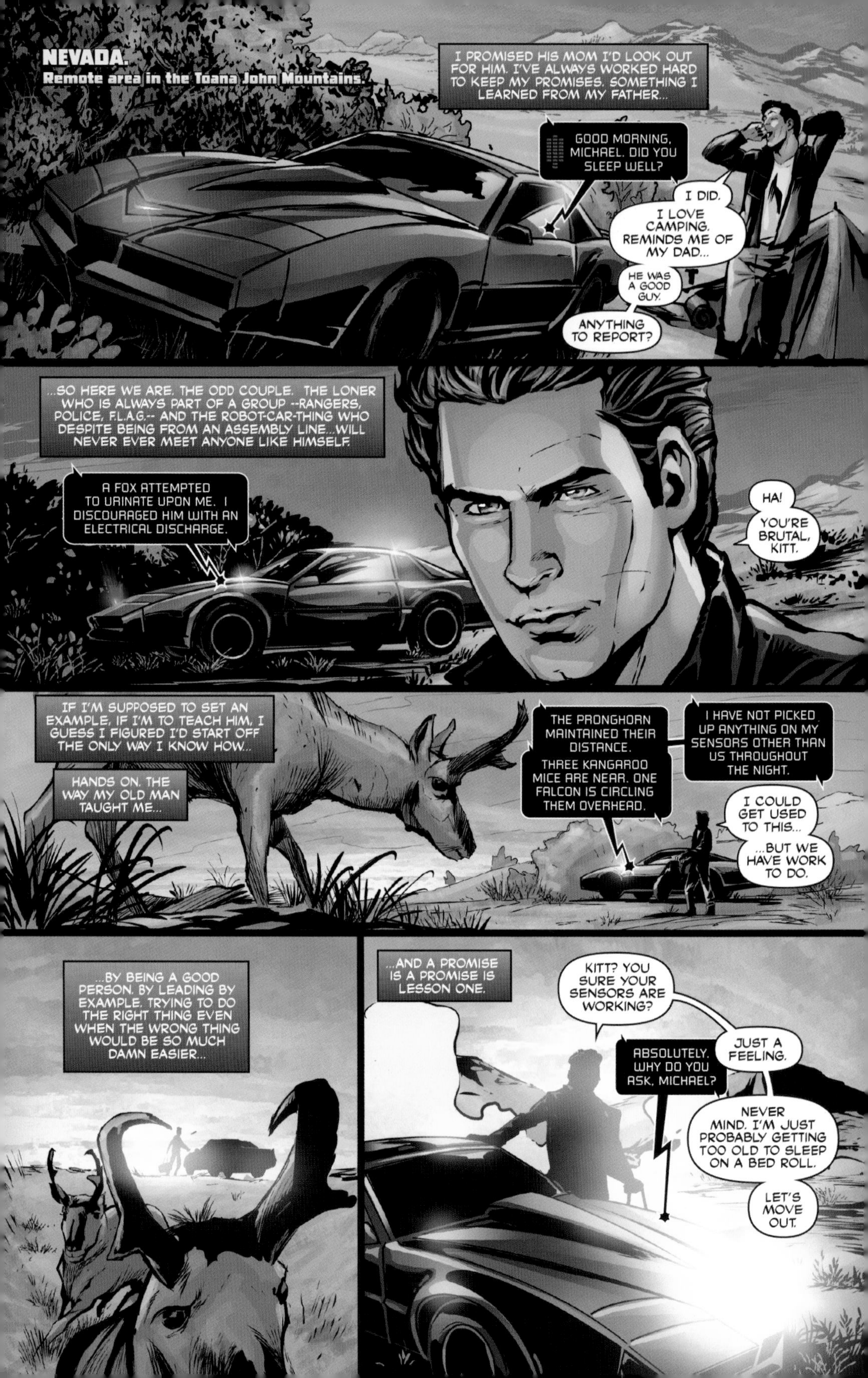

NEVADA.
Remote area in the Toana John Mountains.
I PROMISED HIS MOM I'D LOOK OUT FOR HIM. I'VE ALWAYS WORKED HARD TO KEEP MY PROMISES. SOMETHING I LEARNED FROM MY FATHER...
GOOD MORNING, MICHAEL. DID YOU SLEEP WELL?
I DID.
I LOVE CAMPING. REMINDS ME OF MY DAD...
HE WAS A GOOD GUY.
ANYTHING TO REPORT?
...SO HERE WE ARE. THE ODD COUPLE. THE LONER WHO IS ALWAYS PART OF A GROUP --RANGERS, POLICE, F.L.A.G.-- AND THE ROBOT-CAR-THING WHO DESPITE BEING FROM AN ASSEMBLY LINE...WILL NEVER EVER MEET ANYONE LIKE HIMSELF.
A FOX ATTEMPTED TO URINATE UPON ME. I DISCOURAGED HIM WITH AN ELECTRICAL DISCHARGE.
HA!
YOU'RE BRUTAL, KITT.
IF I'M SUPPOSED TO SET AN EXAMPLE, IF I'M TO TEACH HIM, I GUESS I FIGURED I'D START OFF THE ONLY WAY I KNOW HOW...
HANDS ON. THE WAY MY OLD MAN TAUGHT ME...
I HAVE NOT PICKED UP ANYTHING ON MY SENSORS OTHER THAN US THROUGHOUT THE NIGHT.
THE PRONGHORN MAINTAINED THEIR DISTANCE.
THREE KANGAROO MICE ARE NEAR. ONE FALCON IS CIRCLING THEM OVERHEAD.
I COULD GET USED TO THIS...
...BUT WE HAVE WORK TO DO.
...BY BEING A GOOD PERSON. BY LEADING BY EXAMPLE. TRYING TO DO THE RIGHT THING EVEN WHEN THE WRONG THING WOULD BE SO MUCH DAMN EASIER...
...AND A PROMISE IS A PROMISE IS LESSON ONE.
KITT? YOU SURE YOUR SENSORS ARE WORKING?
ABSOLUTELY. WHY DO YOU ASK, MICHAEL?
JUST A FEELING.
NEVER MIND. I'M JUST PROBABLY GETTING TOO OLD TO SLEEP ON A BED ROLL.
LET'S MOVE OUT.

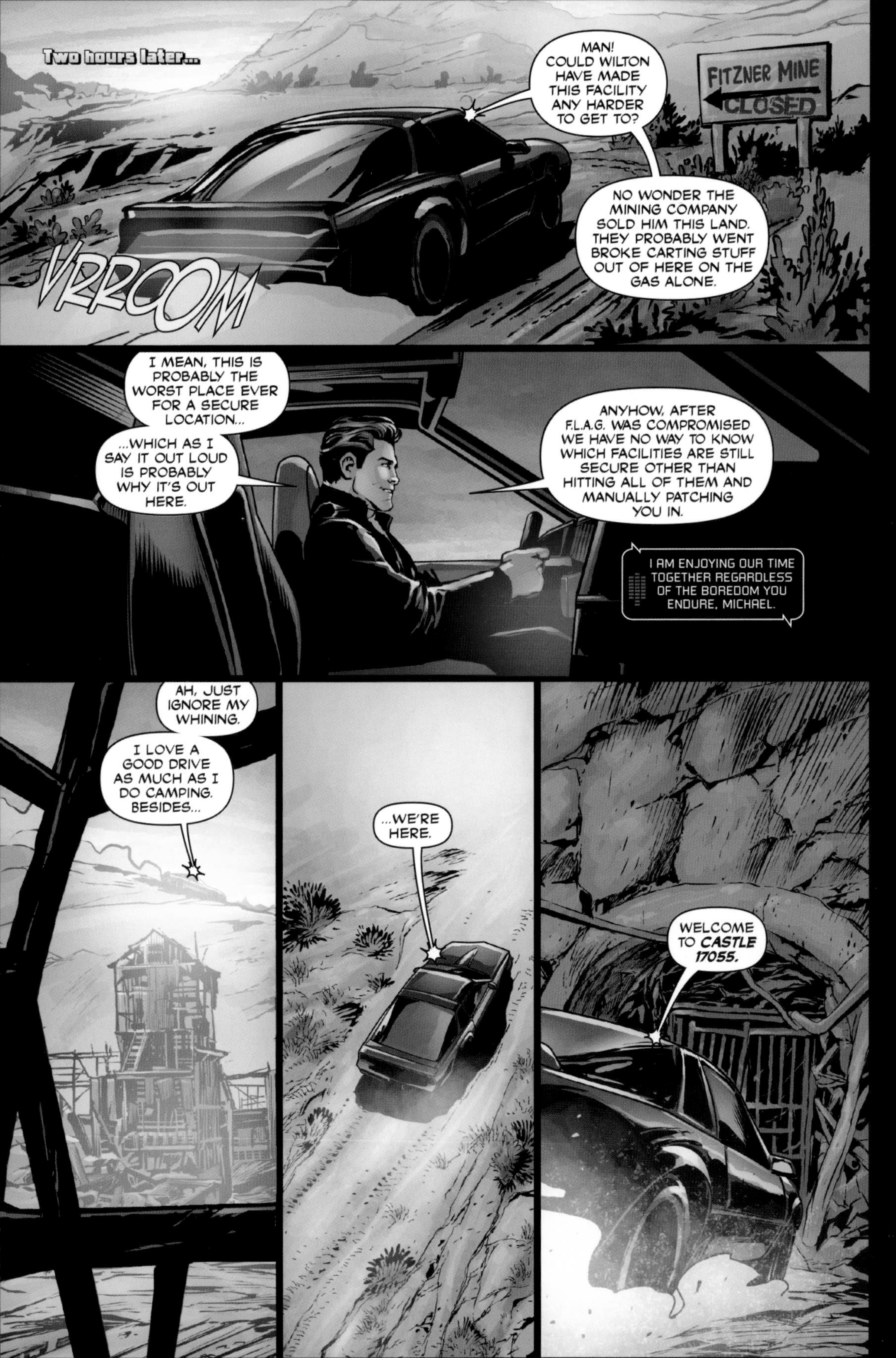
Two hours later...
MAN! COULD WILTON HAVE MADE THIS FACILITY ANY HARDER TO GET TO?
FITZNER MINE
CLOSED
NO WONDER THE MINING COMPANY SOLD HIM THIS LAND. THEY PROBABLY WENT BROKE CARTING STUFF OUT OF HERE ON THE GAS ALONE.
VRRROOM
I MEAN, THIS IS PROBABLY THE WORST PLACE EVER FOR A SECURE LOCATION...
...WHICH AS I SAY IT OUT LOUD IS PROBABLY WHY IT'S OUT HERE.
ANYHOW, AFTER F.L.A.G. WAS COMPROMISED WE HAVE NO WAY TO KNOW WHICH FACILITIES ARE STILL SECURE OTHER THAN HITTING ALL OF THEM AND MANUALLY PATCHING YOU IN.
I AM ENJOYING OUR TIME TOGETHER REGARDLESS OF THE BOREDOM YOU ENDURE, MICHAEL.
AH, JUST IGNORE MY WHINING.
I LOVE A GOOD DRIVE AS MUCH AS I DO CAMPING. BESIDES...
...WE'RE HERE.
WELCOME TO CASTLE 17055.

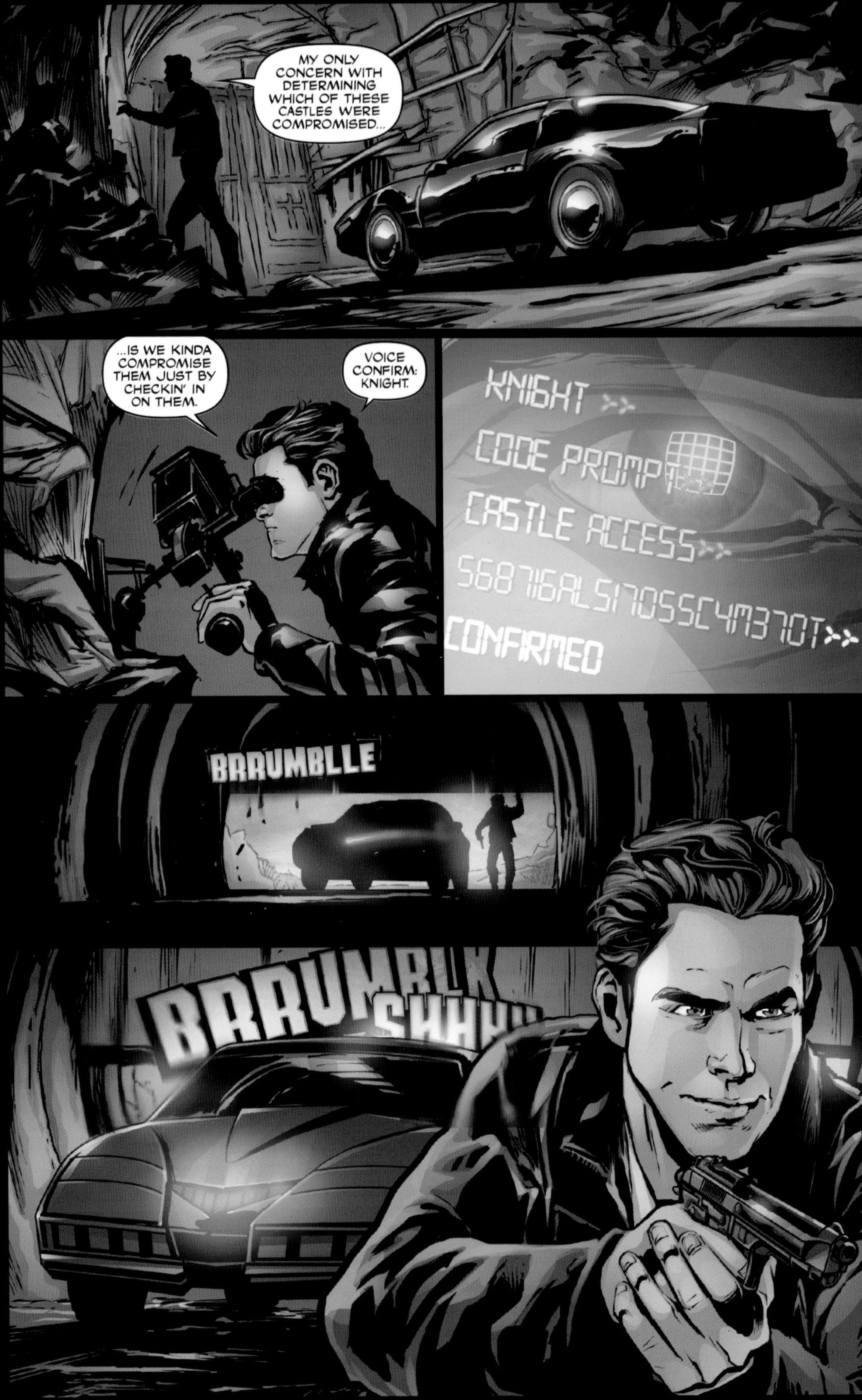

MY ONLY CONCERN WITH DETERMINING WHICH OF THESE CASTLES WERE COMPROMISED...
...IS WE KINDA COMPROMISE THEM JUST BY CHECKIN' IN ON THEM.
VOICE CONFIRM: KNIGHT.
KNIGHT
CODE PROMPT
CASTLE ACCESS
56871I6ALS1705SC4M370T
CONFIRMED
BRRUMBLLE
BRRUMBLK

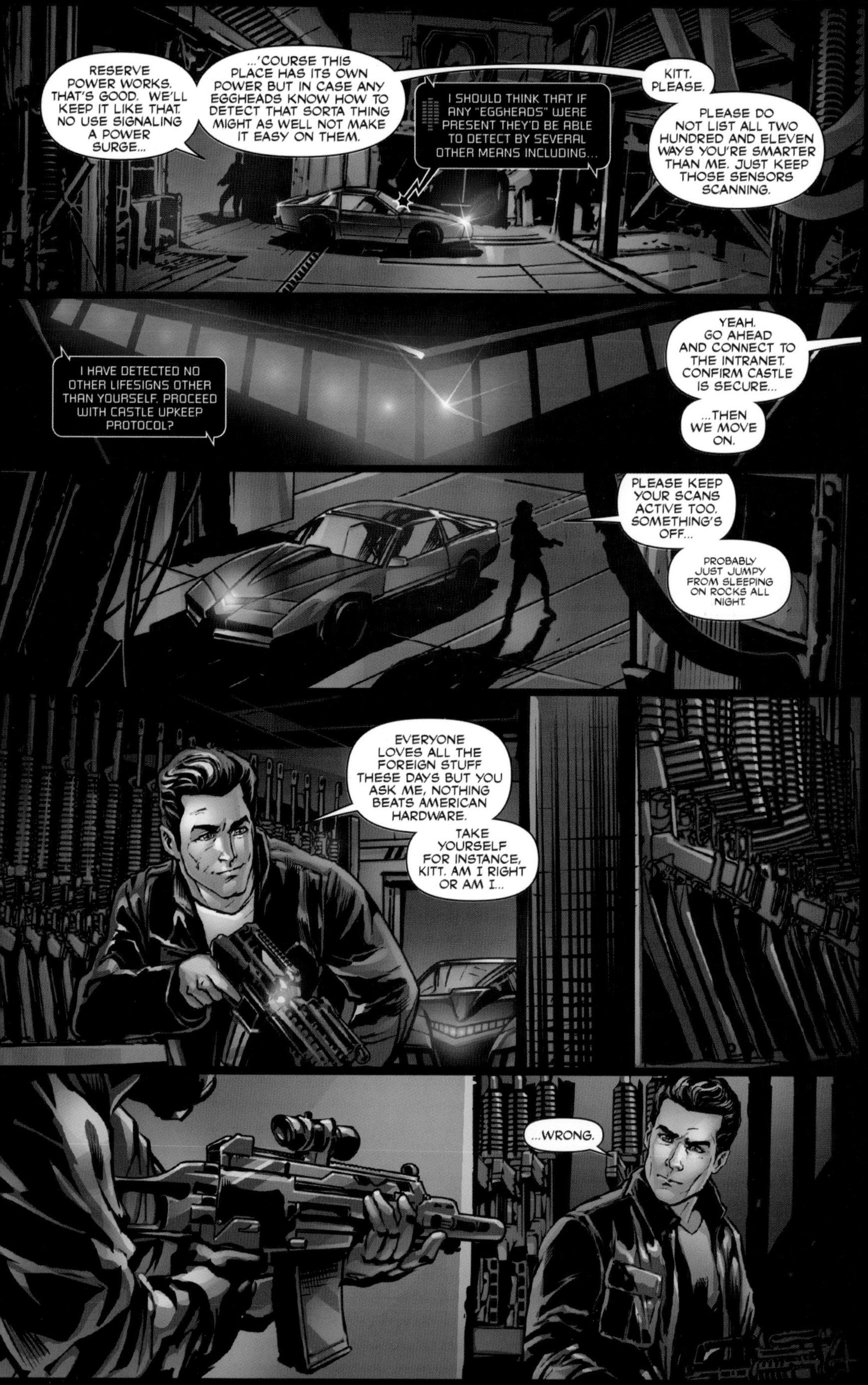
RESERVE POWER WORKS. THAT'S GOOD. WE'LL KEEP IT LIKE THAT. NO USE SIGNALING A POWER SURGE...
...'COURSE THIS PLACE HAS ITS OWN POWER BUT IN CASE ANY EGGHEADS KNOW HOW TO DETECT THAT SORTA THING MIGHT AS WELL NOT MAKE IT EASY ON THEM.
I SHOULD THINK THAT IF ANY "EGGHEADS" WERE PRESENT THEY'D BE ABLE TO DETECT BY SEVERAL OTHER MEANS INCLUDING...
KITT. PLEASE.
PLEASE DO NOT LIST ALL TWO HUNDRED AND ELEVEN WAYS YOU'RE SMARTER THAN ME. JUST KEEP THOSE SENSORS SCANNING.
I HAVE DETECTED NO OTHER LIFESIGNS OTHER THAN YOURSELF. PROCEED WITH CASTLE UPKEEP PROTOCOL?
YEAH. GO AHEAD AND CONNECT TO THE INTRANET. CONFIRM CASTLE IS SECURE...
...THEN WE MOVE ON.
PLEASE KEEP YOUR SCANS ACTIVE TOO. SOMETHING'S OFF...
PROBABLY JUST JUMPY FROM SLEEPING ON ROCKS ALL NIGHT.
EVERYONE LOVES ALL THE FOREIGN STUFF THESE DAYS BUT YOU ASK ME, NOTHING BEATS AMERICAN HARDWARE.
TAKE YOURSELF FOR INSTANCE, KITT. AM I RIGHT OR AM I...
...WRONG.

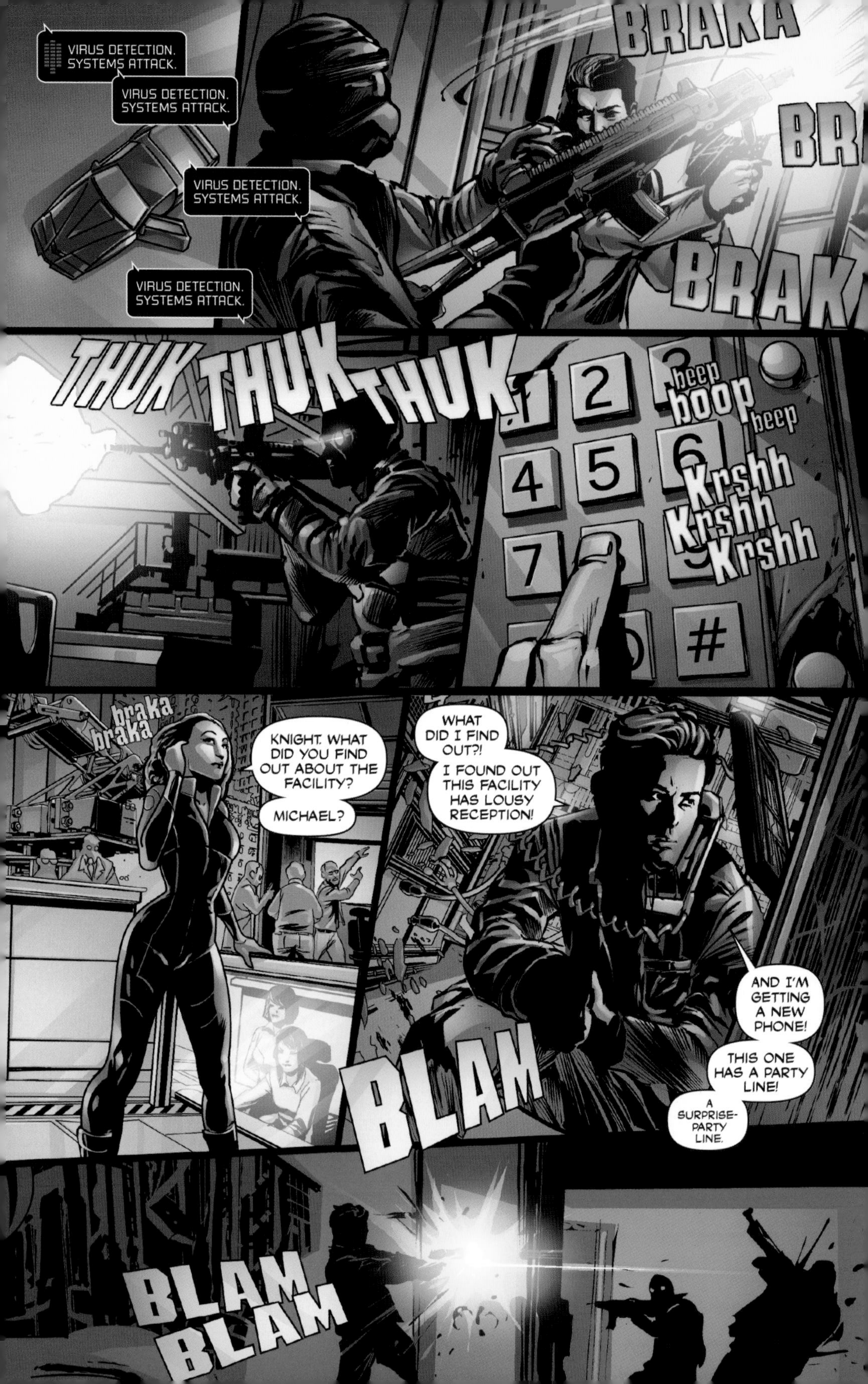
VIRUS DETECTION. SYSTEMS ATTACK.
VIRUS DETECTION. SYSTEMS ATTACK.
VIRUS DETECTION. SYSTEMS ATTACK.
VIRUS DETECTION. SYSTEMS ATTACK.
BRAKA
BR
BRAK
THUK THUK THUK
beep boop beep
Krshh Krshh Krshh
braka braka
KNIGHT. WHAT DID YOU FIND OUT ABOUT THE FACILITY?
MICHAEL?
WHAT DID I FIND OUT?!
I FOUND OUT THIS FACILITY HAS LOUSY RECEPTION!
AND I'M GETTING A NEW PHONE!
THIS ONE HAS A PARTY LINE!
A SURPRISE-PARTY LINE.
BLAM
BLAM BLAM

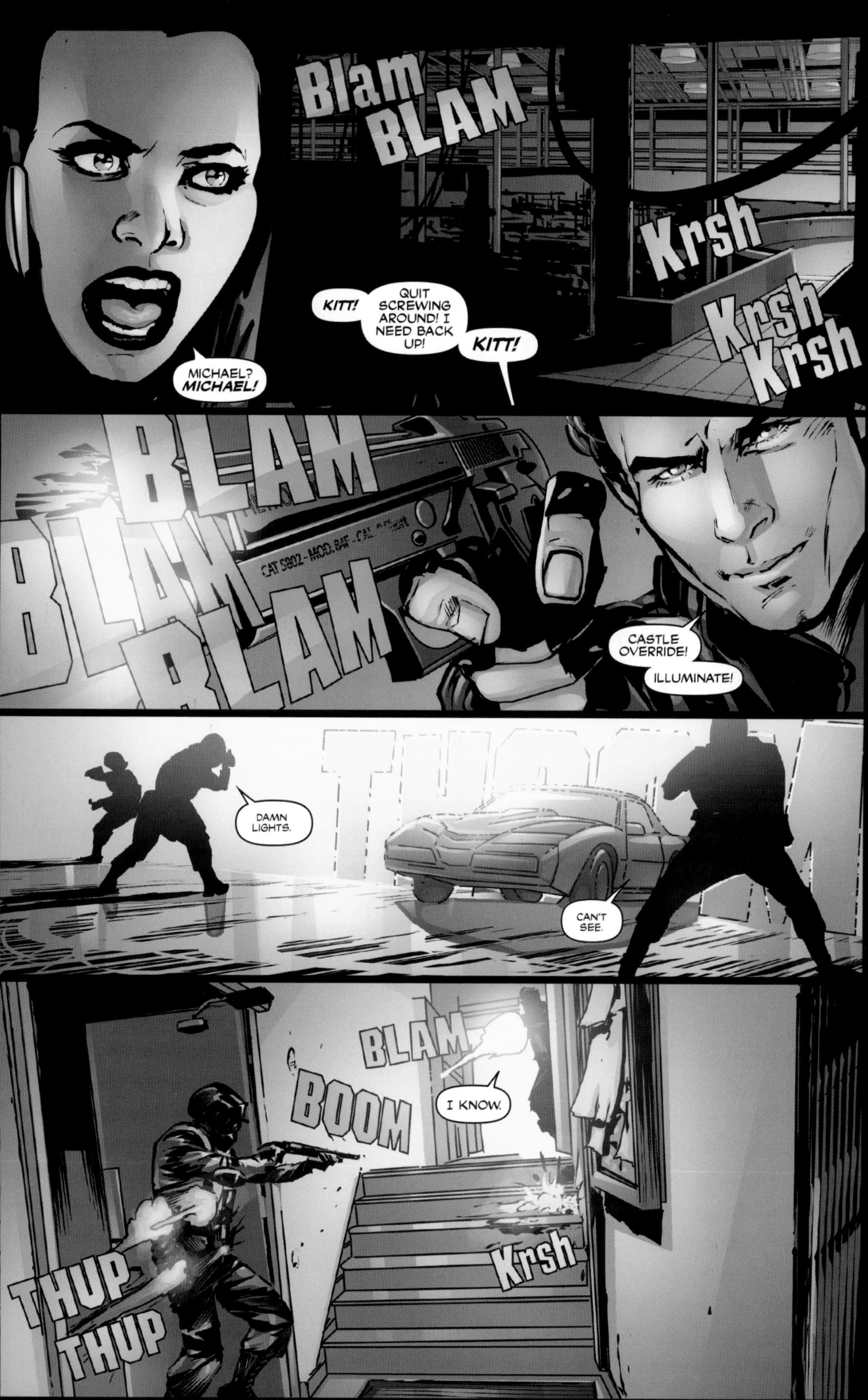
MICHAEL? MICHAEL!
Blam BLAM
KITT!
QUIT SCREWING AROUND! I NEED BACK UP!
KITT!
Krsh
Krsh Krsh
BLAM BLAM BLAM
CAT 5802 - MOD. 84F - CAL. 9 Short
CASTLE OVERRIDE!
ILLUMINATE!
DAMN LIGHTS.
CAN'T SEE.
BLAM
BOOM
I KNOW.
Krsh
THUP THUP

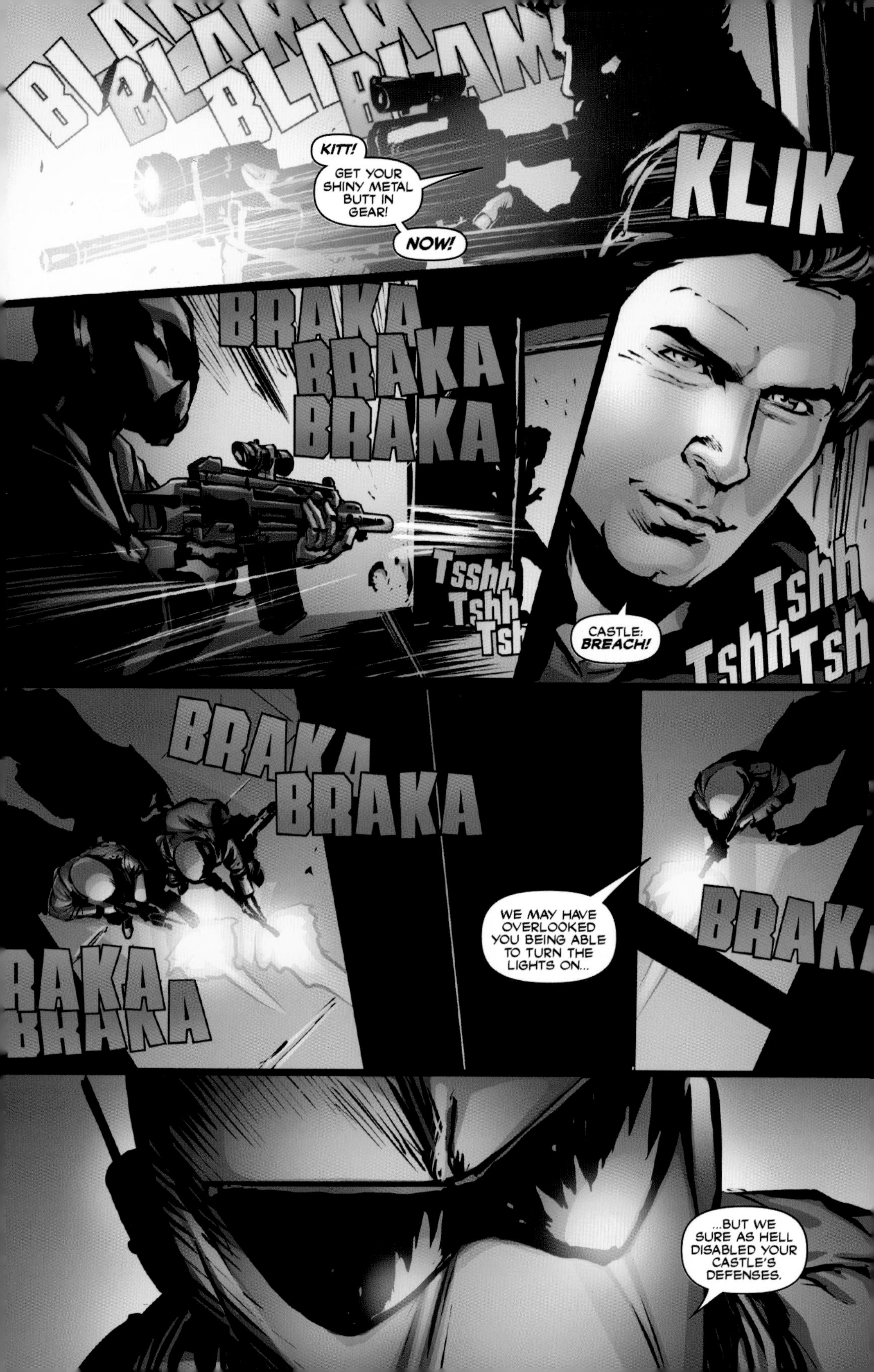
BLAMM BLAMM BLAMM!
KITT!
GET YOUR SHINY METAL BUTT IN GEAR!
NOW!
KLIK
BRAKA BRAKA BRAKA
Tsshh Tshh Tsh
CASTLE: BREACH!
Tshh Tshh Tsh
BRAKA BRAKA
BRAKA BRAKA
WE MAY HAVE OVERLOOKED YOU BEING ABLE TO TURN THE LIGHTS ON...
BRAKA
...BUT WE SURE AS HELL DISABLED YOUR CASTLE'S DEFENSES.

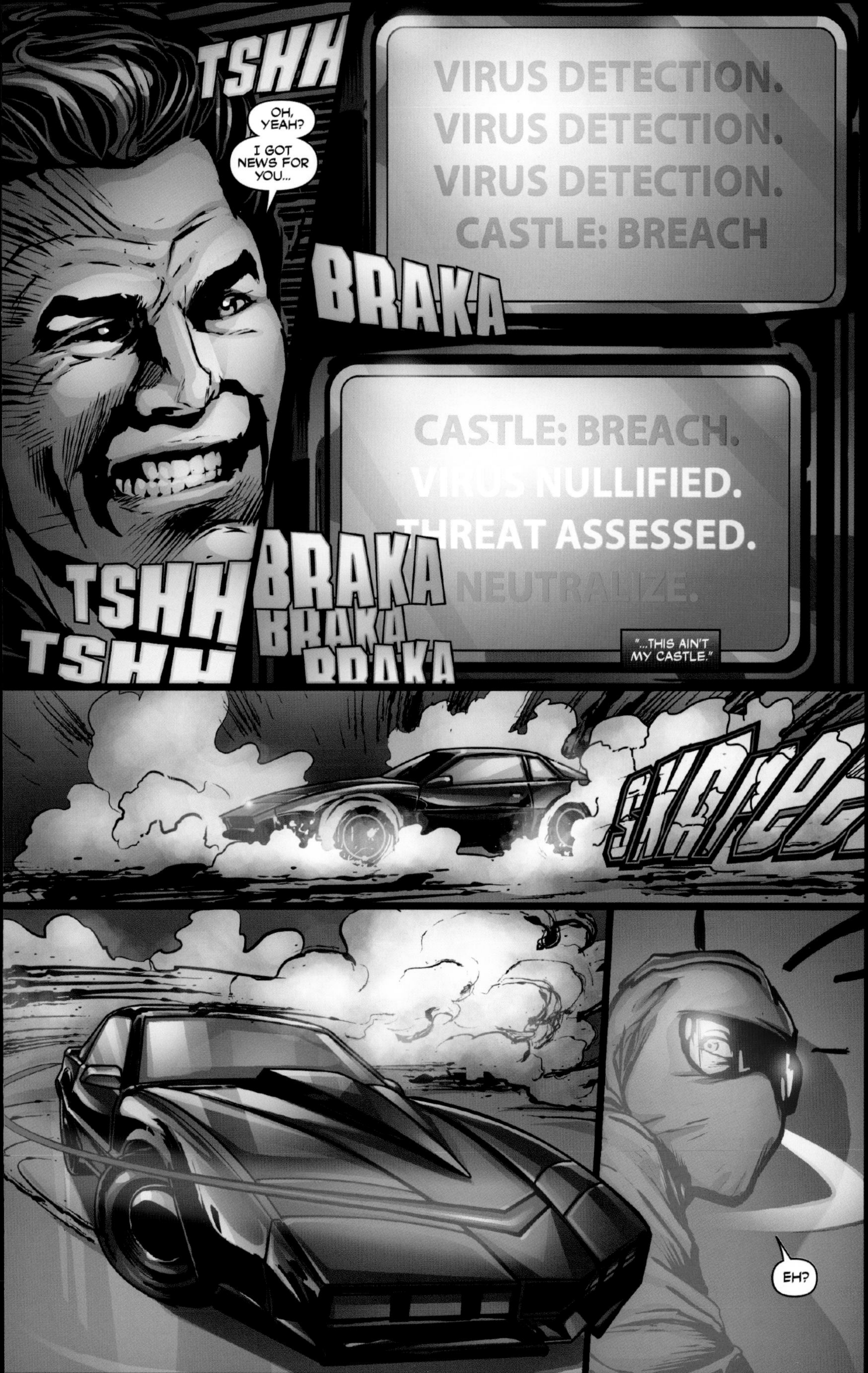
TSHH
OH, YEAH?
I GOT NEWS FOR YOU...
VIRUS DETECTION.
VIRUS DETECTION.
VIRUS DETECTION.
CASTLE: BREACH
BRAKA
CASTLE: BREACH.
VIRUS NULLIFIED.
THREAT ASSESSED.
NEUTRALIZE.
TSHH BRAKA
TSHH BRAKA BRAKA
"...THIS AIN'T MY CASTLE."
EH?

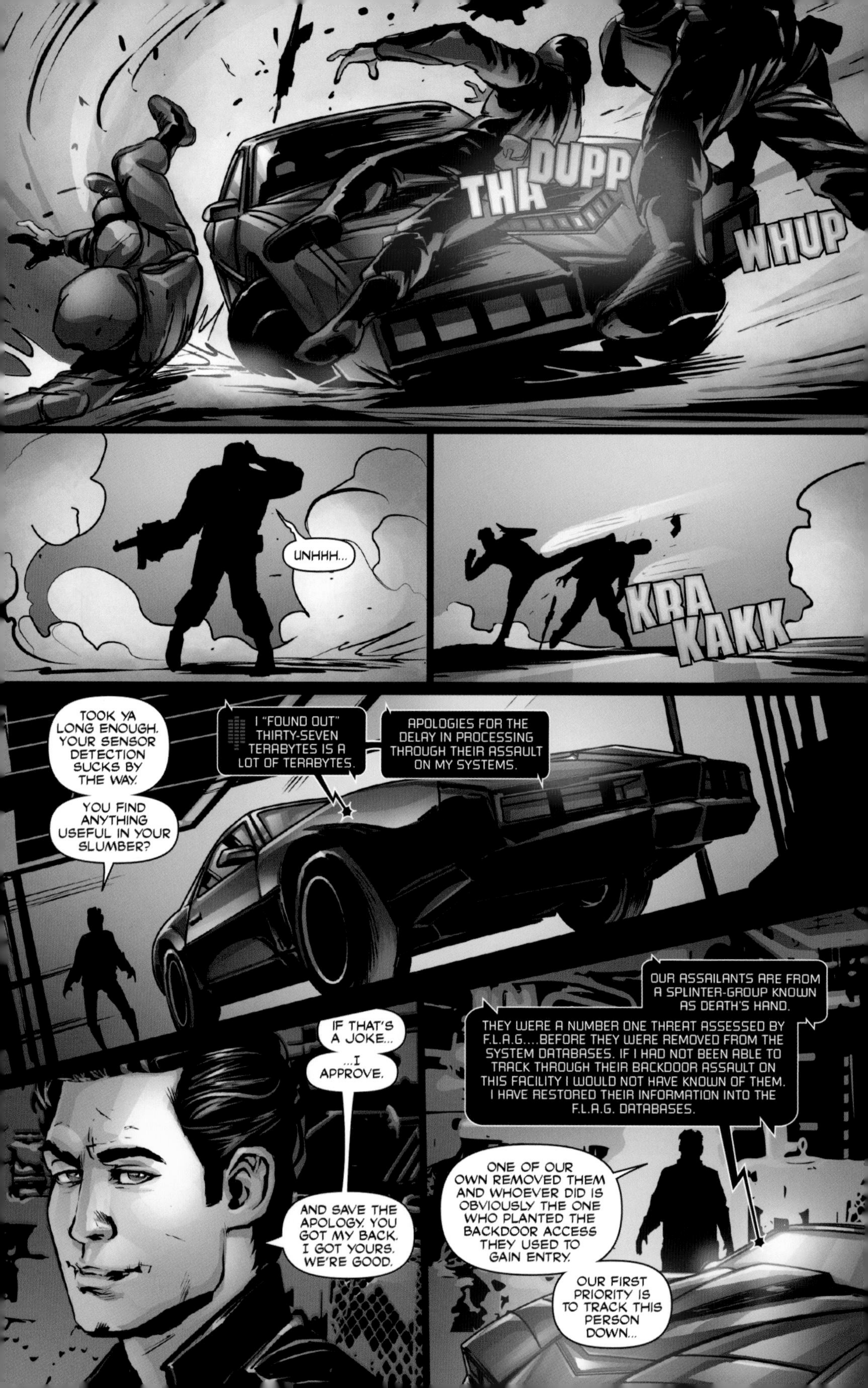
THA DUPP
WHUP
UNHHH...
KRA KAKK
TOOK YA LONG ENOUGH. YOUR SENSOR DETECTION SUCKS BY THE WAY.
YOU FIND ANYTHING USEFUL IN YOUR SLUMBER?
I "FOUND OUT" THIRTY-SEVEN TERABYTES IS A LOT OF TERABYTES.
APOLOGIES FOR THE DELAY IN PROCESSING THROUGH THEIR ASSAULT ON MY SYSTEMS.
IF THAT'S A JOKE...
...I APPROVE.
AND SAVE THE APOLOGY. YOU GOT MY BACK. I GOT YOURS. WE'RE GOOD.
OUR ASSAILANTS ARE FROM A SPLINTER-GROUP KNOWN AS DEATH'S HAND.
THEY WERE A NUMBER ONE THREAT ASSESSED BY F.L.A.G....BEFORE THEY WERE REMOVED FROM THE SYSTEM DATABASES. IF I HAD NOT BEEN ABLE TO TRACK THROUGH THEIR BACKDOOR ASSAULT ON THIS FACILITY I WOULD NOT HAVE KNOWN OF THEM. I HAVE RESTORED THEIR INFORMATION INTO THE F.L.A.G. DATABASES.
ONE OF OUR OWN REMOVED THEM AND WHOEVER DID IS OBVIOUSLY THE ONE WHO PLANTED THE BACKDOOR ACCESS THEY USED TO GAIN ENTRY.
OUR FIRST PRIORITY IS TO TRACK THIS PERSON DOWN...

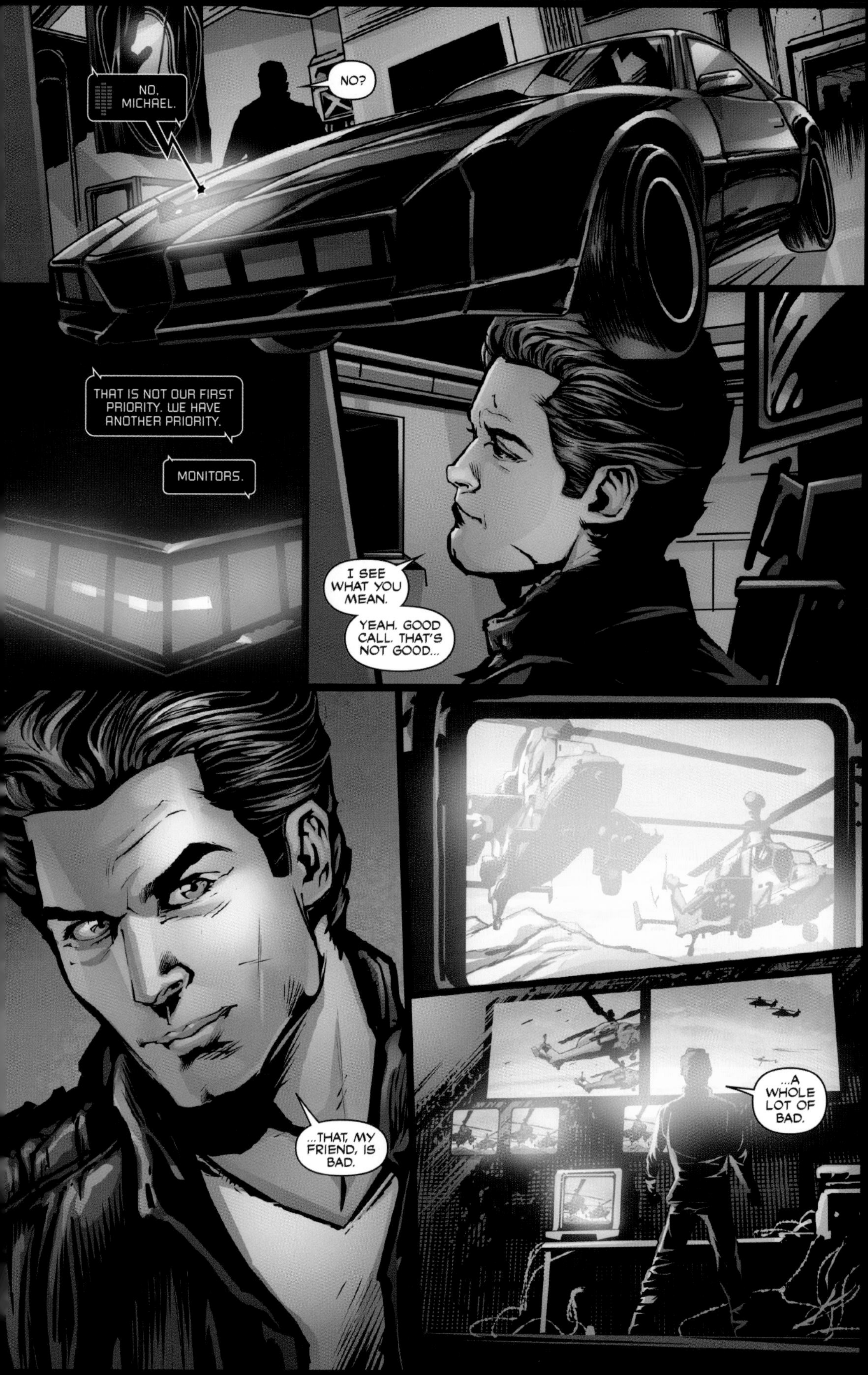
NO, MICHAEL.
NO?
THAT IS NOT OUR FIRST PRIORITY. WE HAVE ANOTHER PRIORITY.
MONITORS.
I SEE WHAT YOU MEAN.
YEAH. GOOD CALL. THAT'S NOT GOOD...
...THAT, MY FRIEND, IS BAD.
...A WHOLE LOT OF BAD.

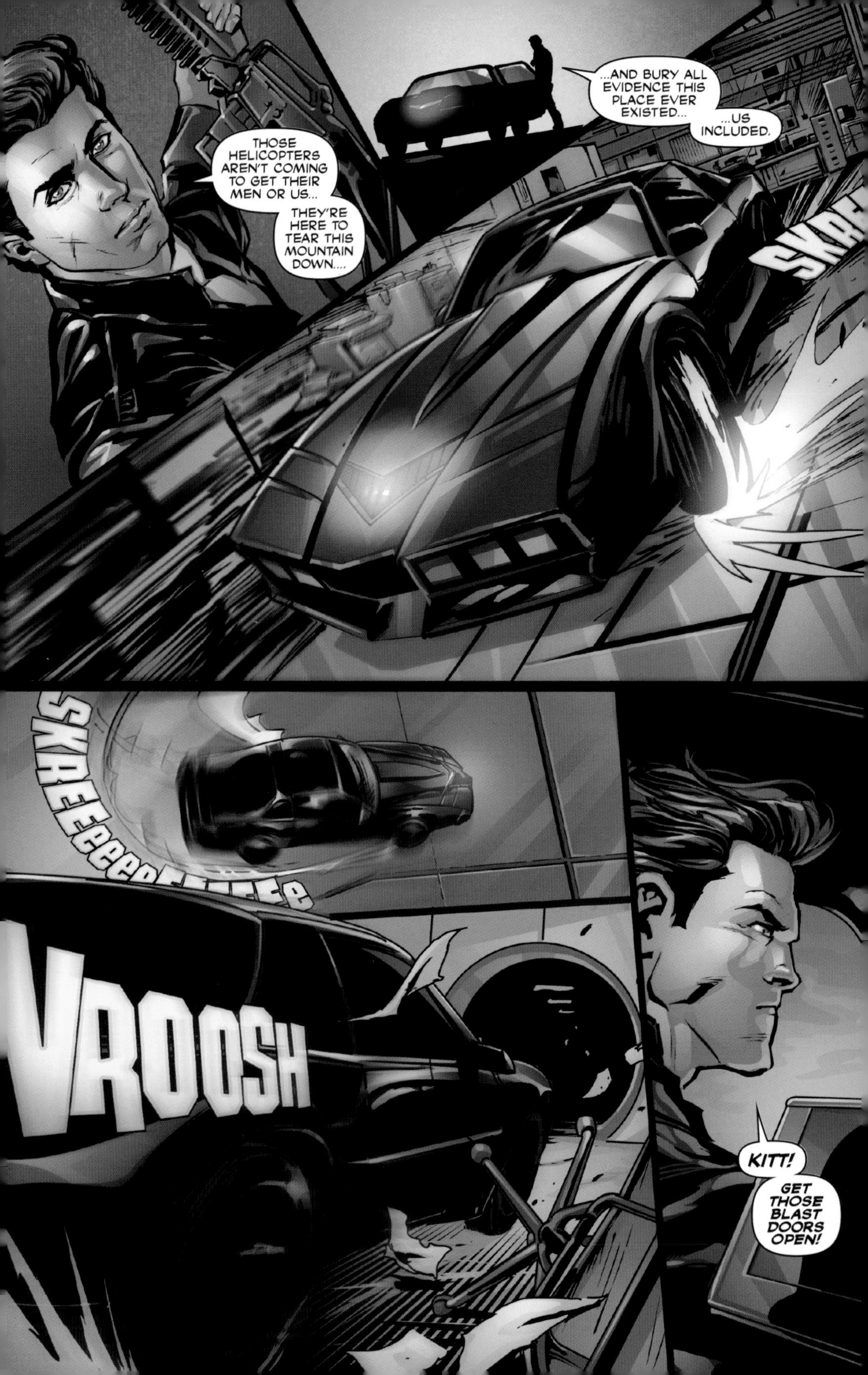
THOSE HELICOPTERS AREN'T COMING TO GET THEIR MEN OR US...
THEY'RE HERE TO TEAR THIS MOUNTAIN DOWN....
...AND BURY ALL EVIDENCE THIS PLACE EVER EXISTED...
...US INCLUDED.
VROOSH
KITT!
GET THOSE BLAST DOORS OPEN!

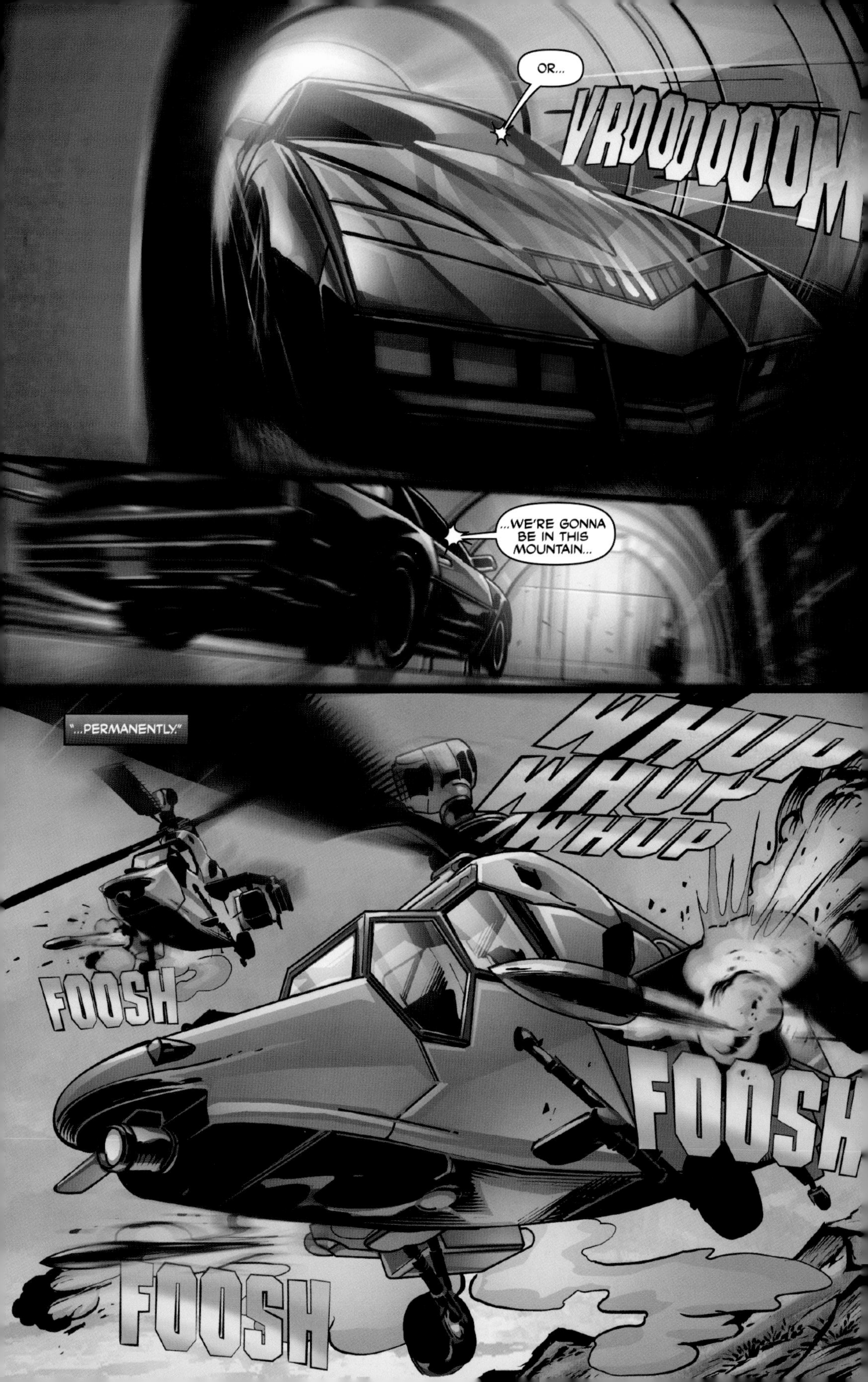
OR...
VROOOOOOM
...WE'RE GONNA BE IN THIS MOUNTAIN...
"...PERMANENTLY."
WHUP
WHUP
WHUP
FOOSH
FOOSH
FOOSH

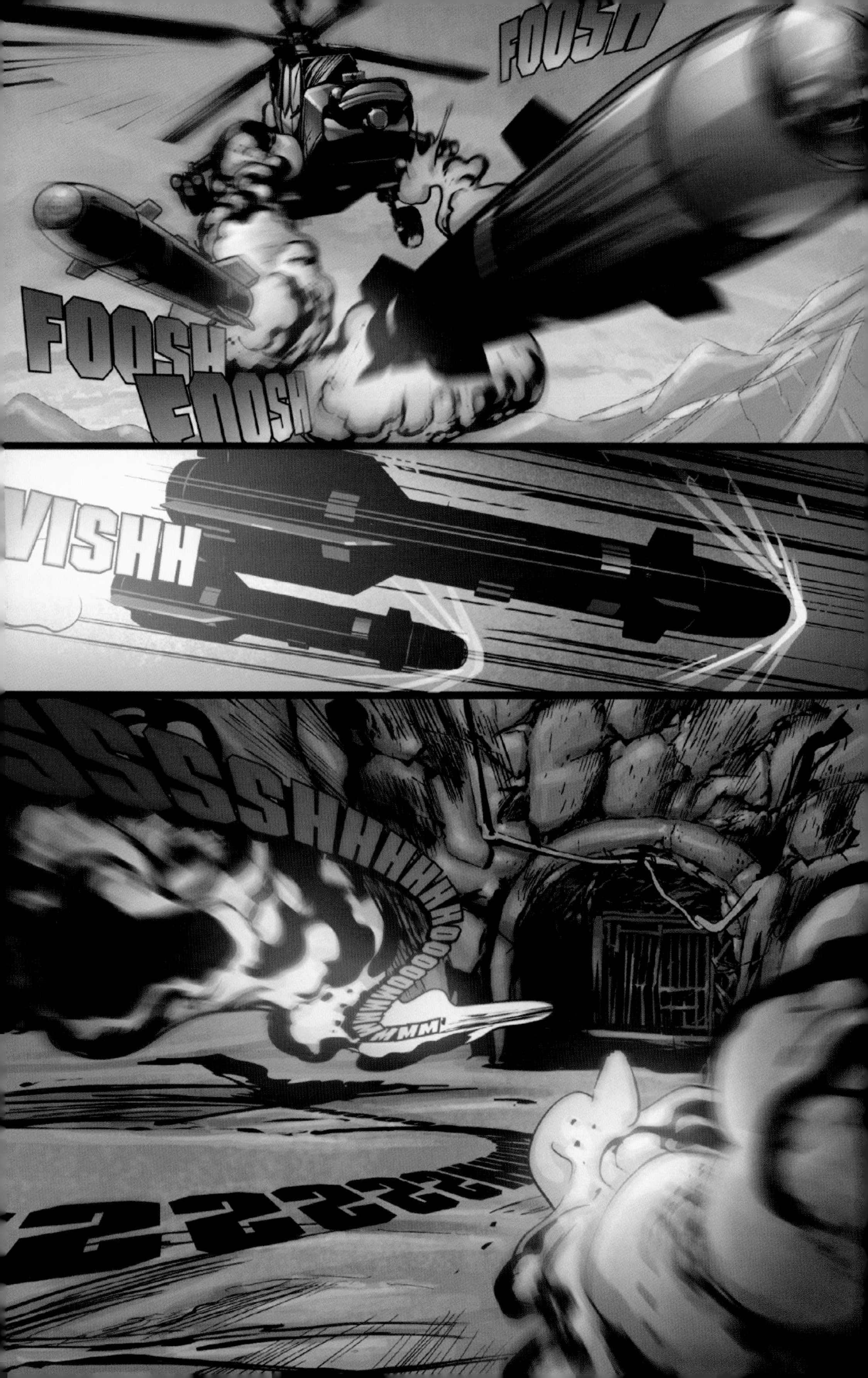
FOOSH
FOOSH
FOOSH
VISHH

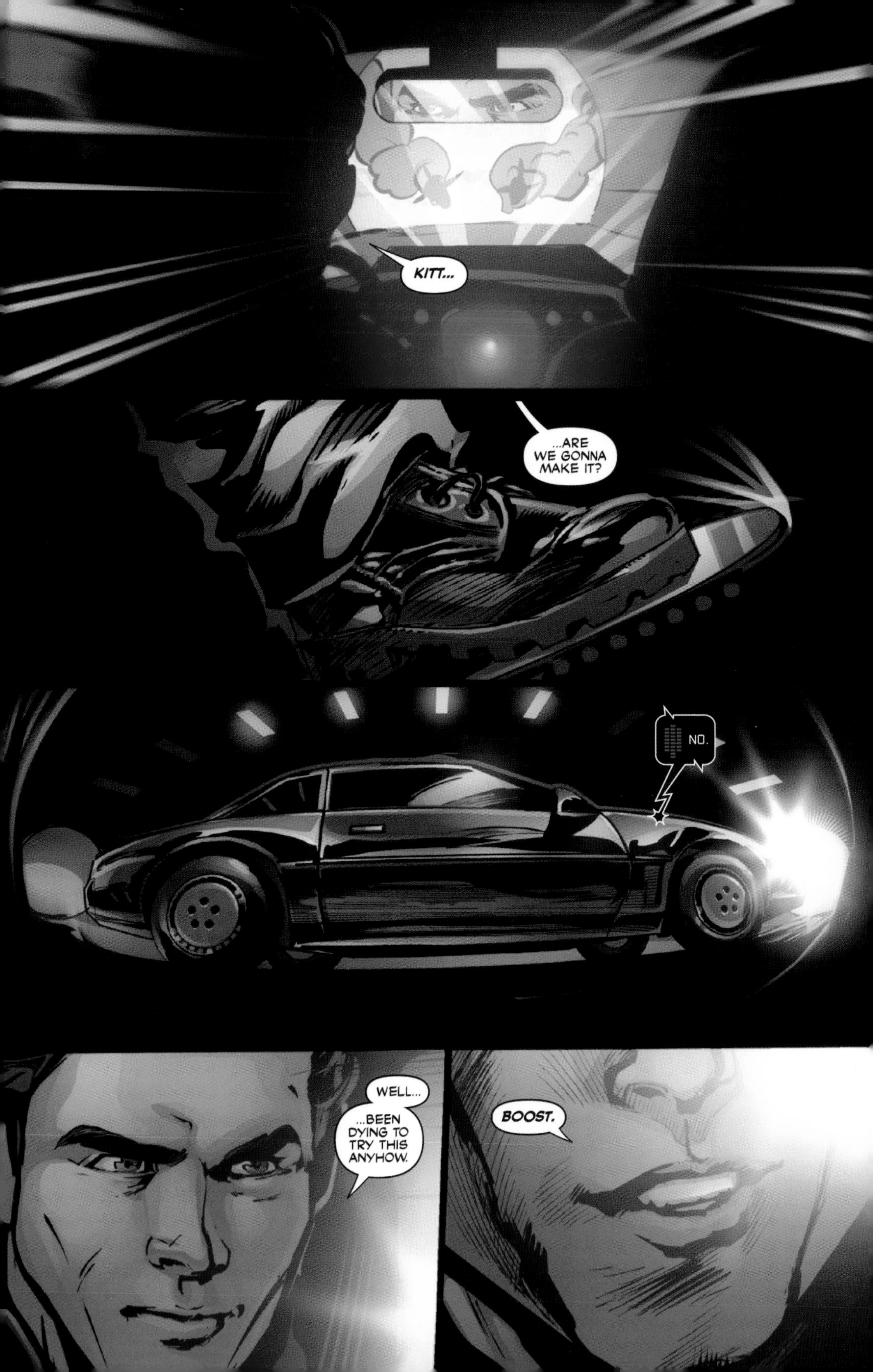
KITT...
...ARE WE GONNA MAKE IT?
NO.
WELL...
...BEEN DYING TO TRY THIS ANYHOW.
BOOST.

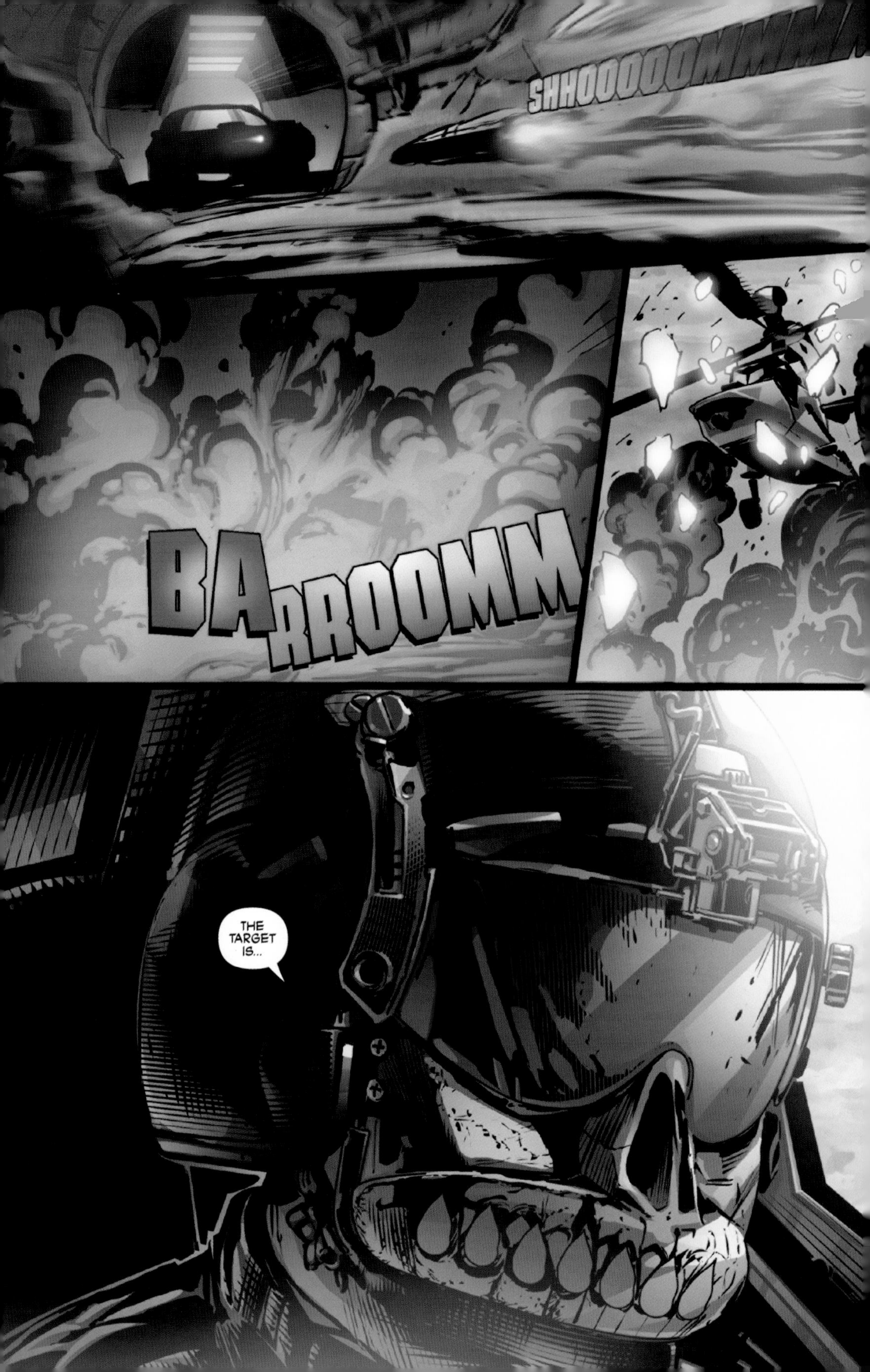
SHHOOOOOMMMMM
BAARROOMM
THE TARGET IS...

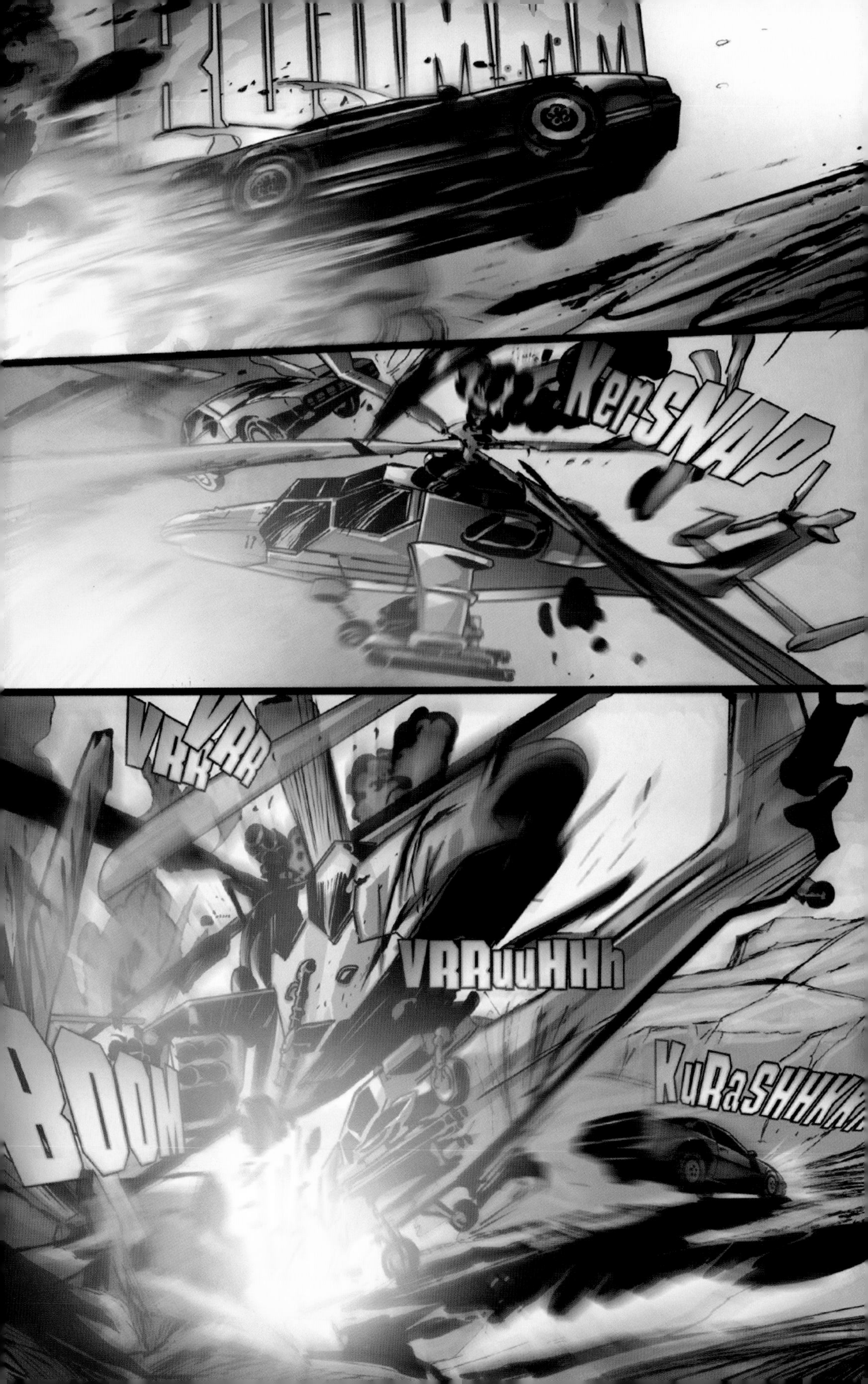
KerSNAP!
VRR
VRR
VRRuuHHh
BOOM
KuRaSHHH

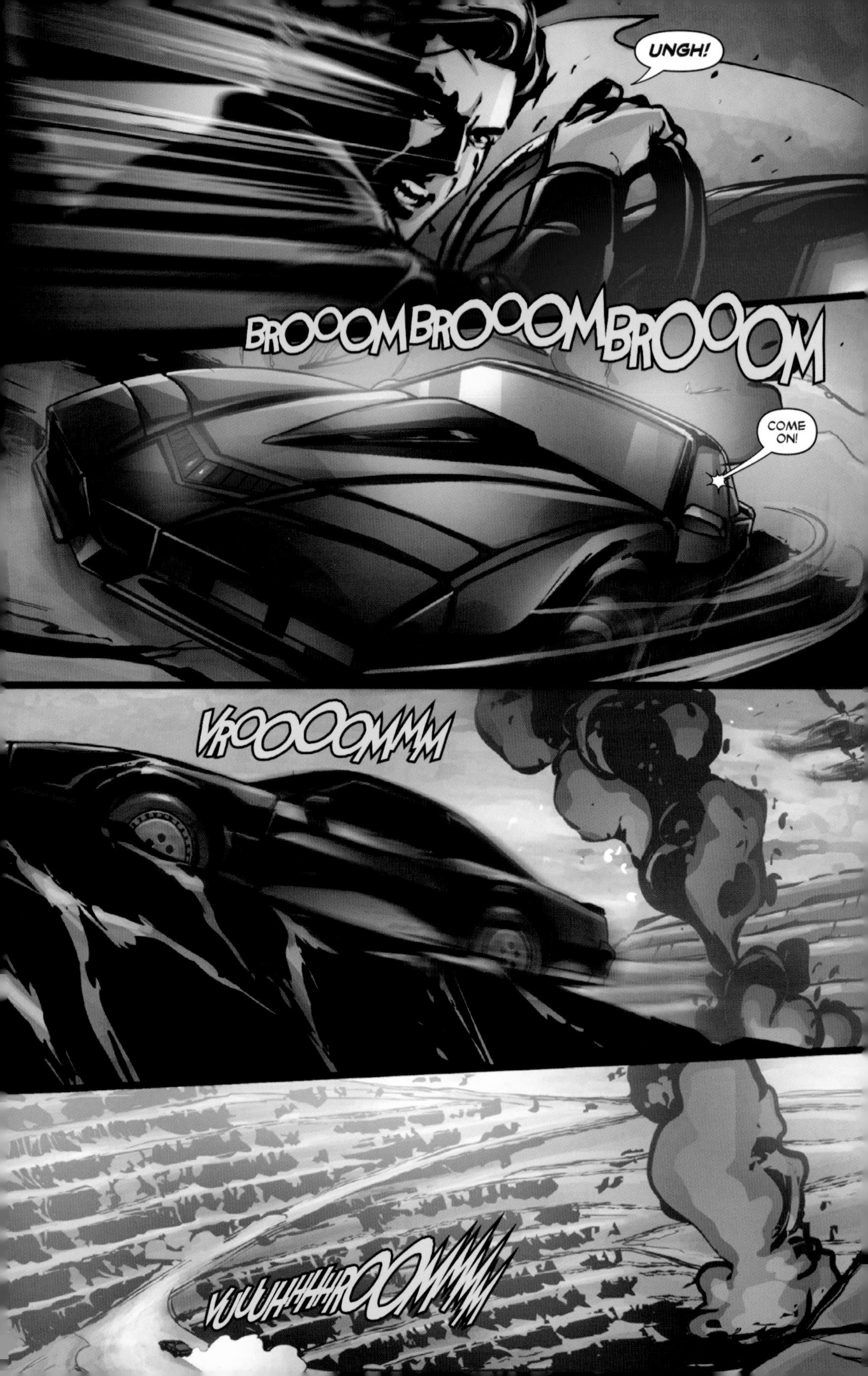
UNGH!
BROOOMBROOOMBROOOM
COME ON!
VROOOOMMM

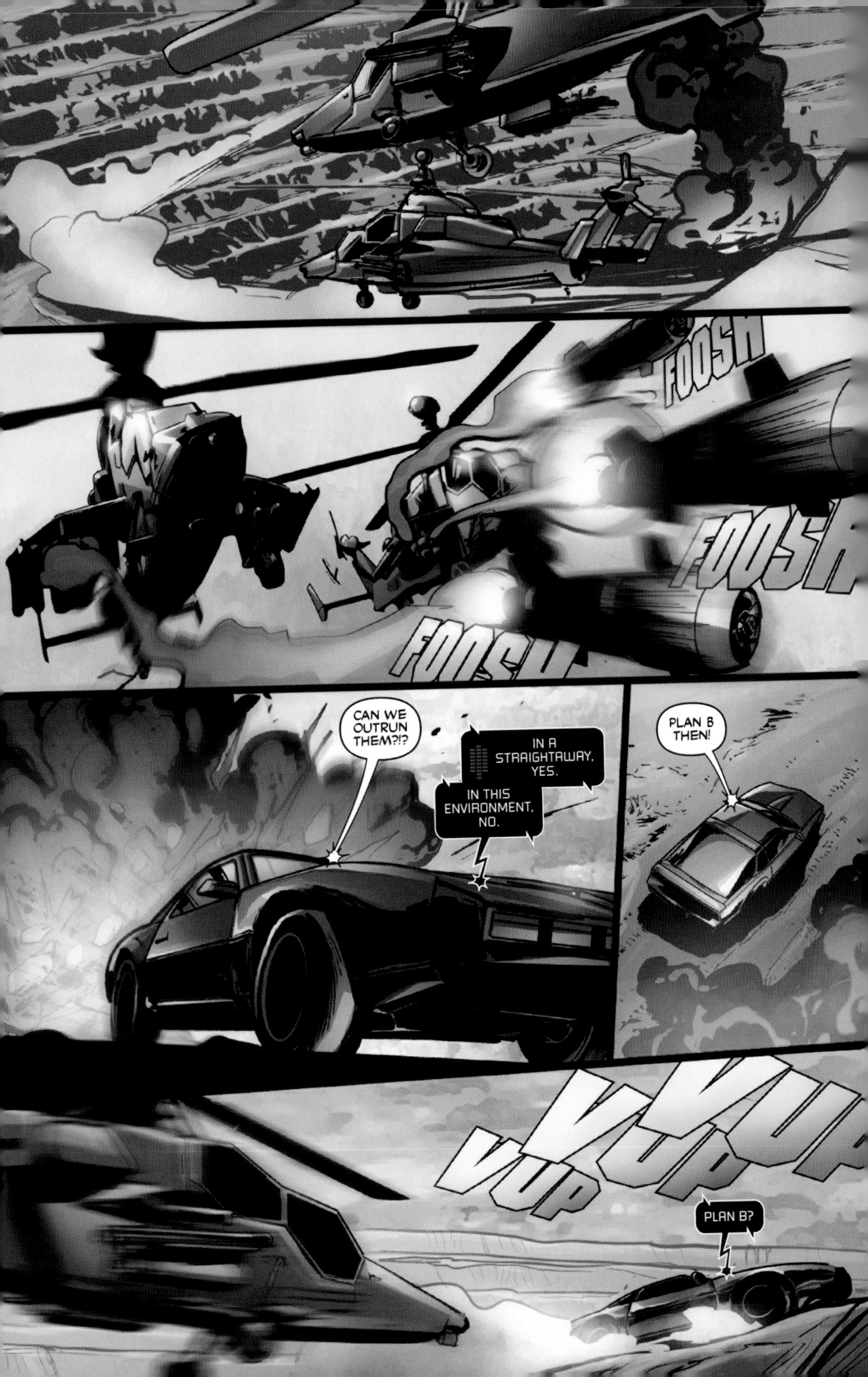
FOOSH
FOOSH
FOOSH
CAN WE OUTRUN THEM?!?
IN A STRAIGHTAWAY, YES.
IN THIS ENVIRONMENT, NO.
PLAN B THEN!
VUP VUP VUP
PLAN B?

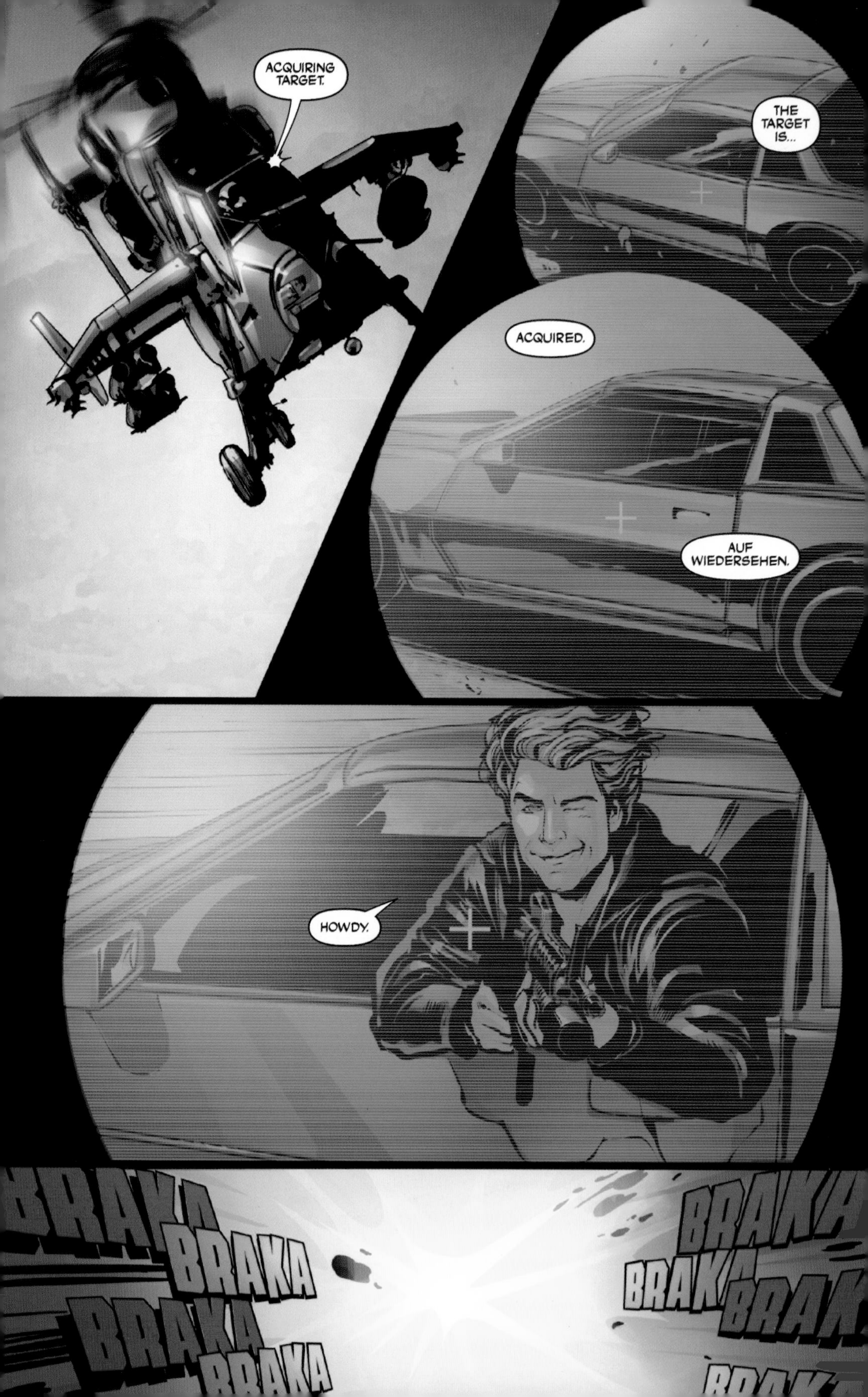
ACQUIRING TARGET.
THE TARGET IS...
ACQUIRED.
AUF WIEDERSEHEN.
HOWDY.
BRAKA
BRAKA
BRAKA
BRAKA
BRAKA
BRAKA
BRAKA

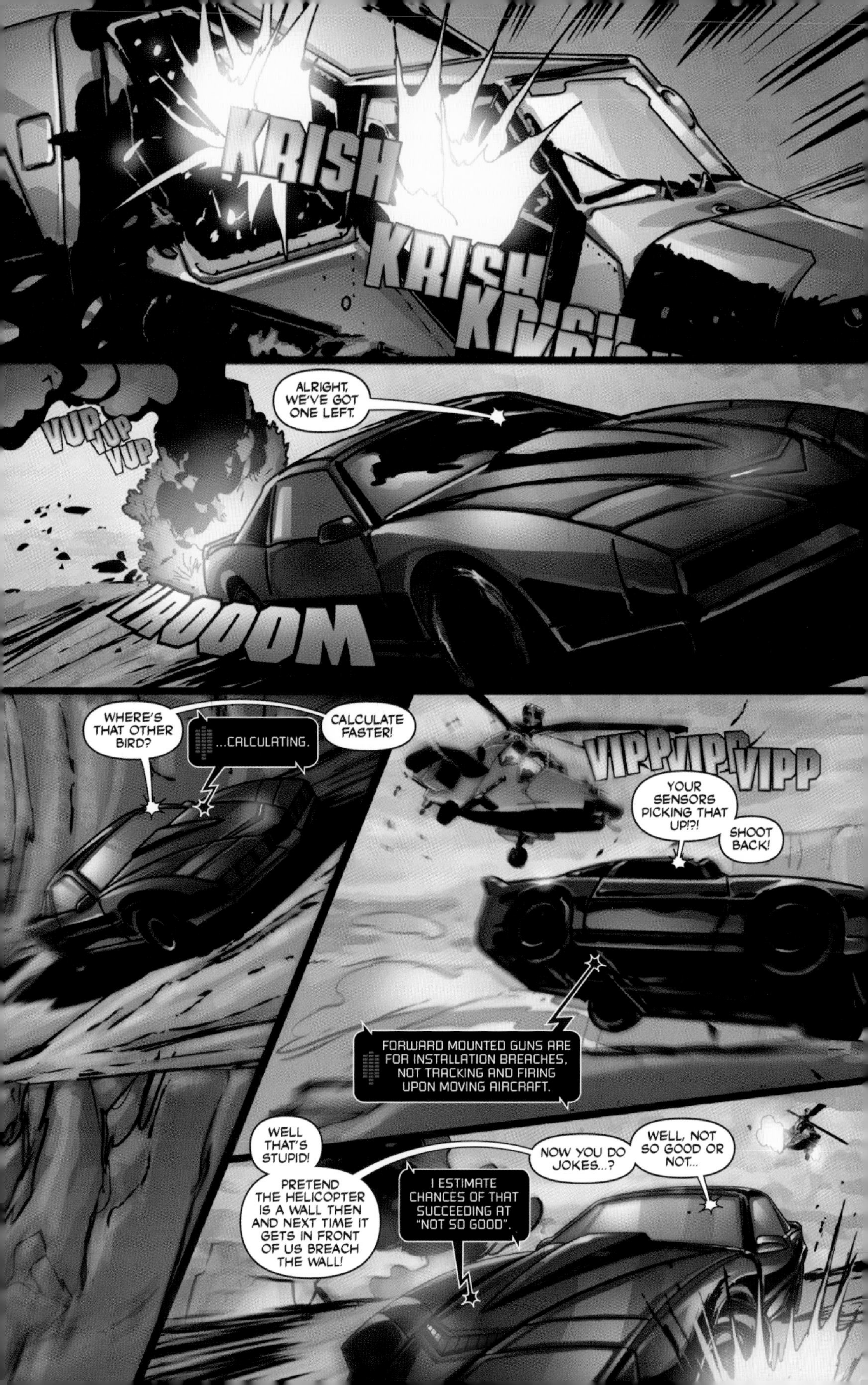
KRISH
KRISH
ALRIGHT, WE'VE GOT ONE LEFT.
VUP VUP VUP
VROOOOM
WHERE'S THAT OTHER BIRD?
...CALCULATING.
CALCULATE FASTER!
VIPP VIPP VIPP
YOUR SENSORS PICKING THAT UP!?!
SHOOT BACK!
FORWARD MOUNTED GUNS ARE FOR INSTALLATION BREACHES, NOT TRACKING AND FIRING UPON MOVING AIRCRAFT.
WELL THAT'S STUPID!
PRETEND THE HELICOPTER IS A WALL THEN AND NEXT TIME IT GETS IN FRONT OF US BREACH THE WALL!
I ESTIMATE CHANCES OF THAT SUCCEEDING AT "NOT SO GOOD".
NOW YOU DO JOKES...?
WELL, NOT SO GOOD OR NOT...

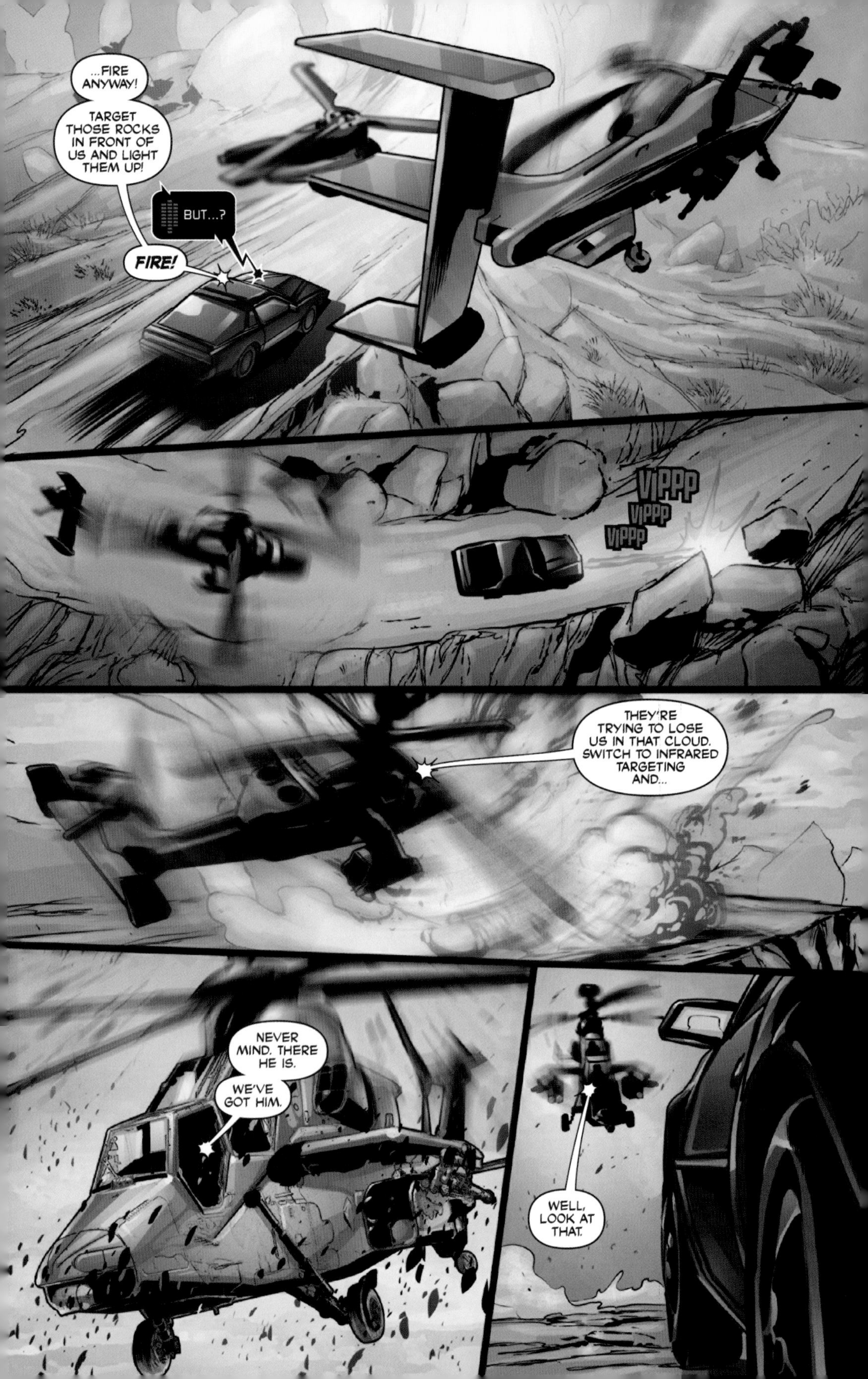

...FIRE ANYWAY!
TARGET THOSE ROCKS IN FRONT OF US AND LIGHT THEM UP!
BUT...?
FIRE!
VIPPP
VIPPP
VIPPP
THEY'RE TRYING TO LOSE US IN THAT CLOUD. SWITCH TO INFRARED TARGETING AND...
NEVER MIND. THERE HE IS.
WE'VE GOT HIM.
WELL, LOOK AT THAT.

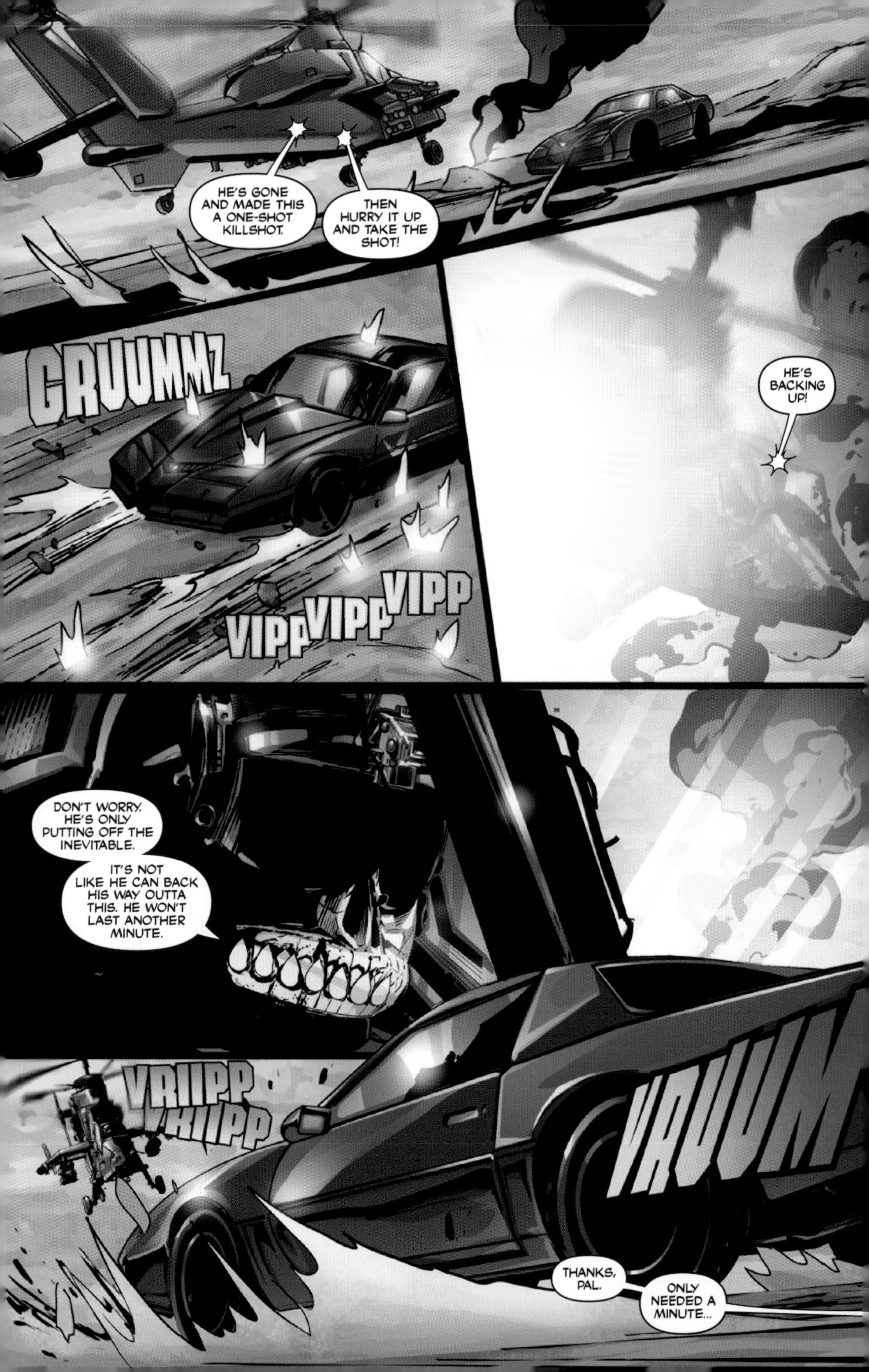
HE'S GONE AND MADE THIS A ONE-SHOT KILLSHOT.
THEN HURRY IT UP AND TAKE THE SHOT!
GRUUMMZ
VIPP VIPP VIPP
HE'S BACKING UP!
DON'T WORRY. HE'S ONLY PUTTING OFF THE INEVITABLE.
IT'S NOT LIKE HE CAN BACK HIS WAY OUTTA THIS. HE WON'T LAST ANOTHER MINUTE.
VRIIPP VRIIPP
VAUUM
THANKS, PAL.
ONLY NEEDED A MINUTE...

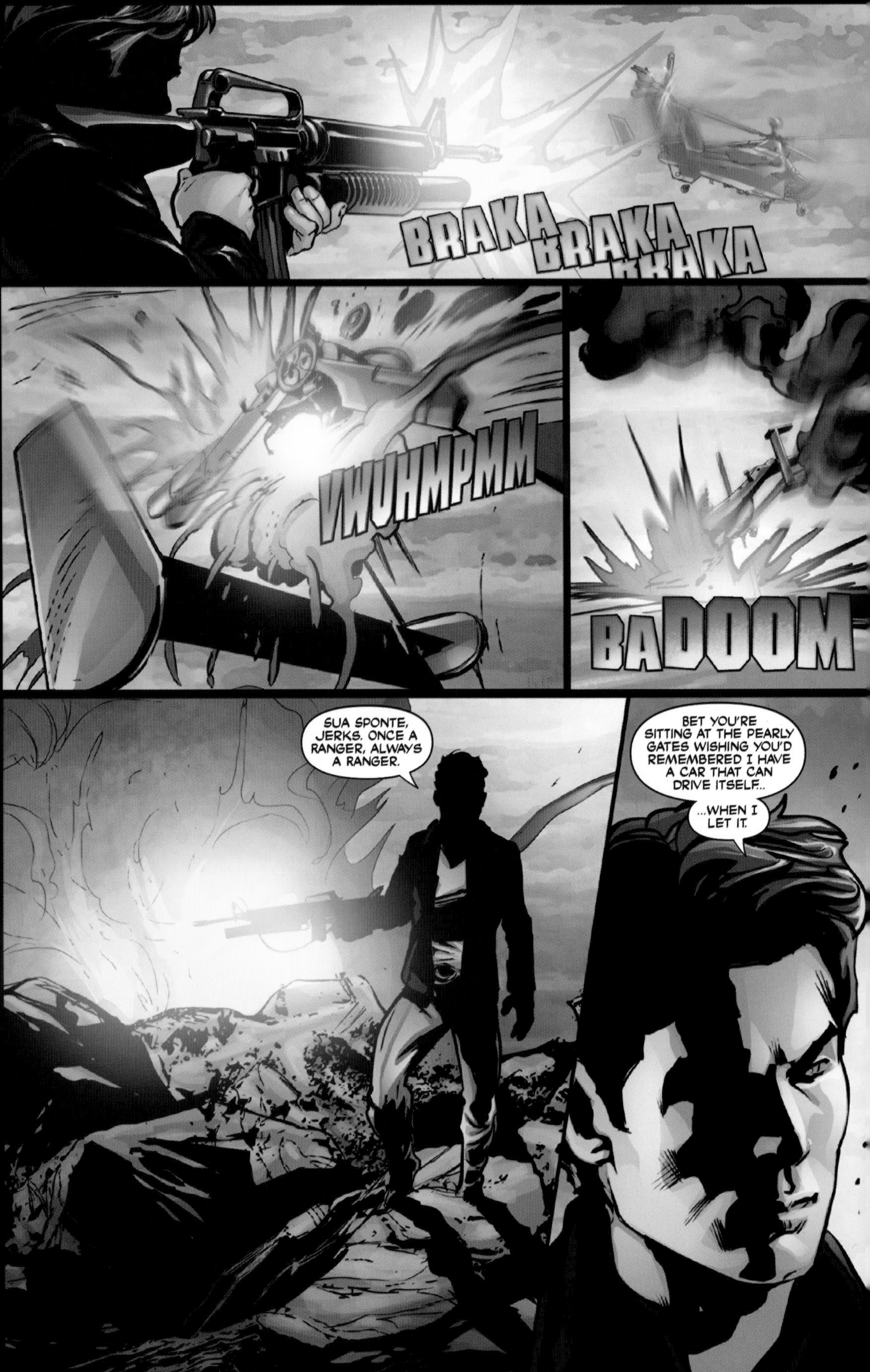
BRAKA BRAKA BRAKA
VWUHMPMM
BADOOM
SUA SPONTE, JERKS. ONCE A RANGER, ALWAYS A RANGER.
BET YOU'RE SITTING AT THE PEARLY GATES WISHING YOU'D REMEMBERED I HAVE A CAR THAT CAN DRIVE ITSELF...
...WHEN I LET IT.

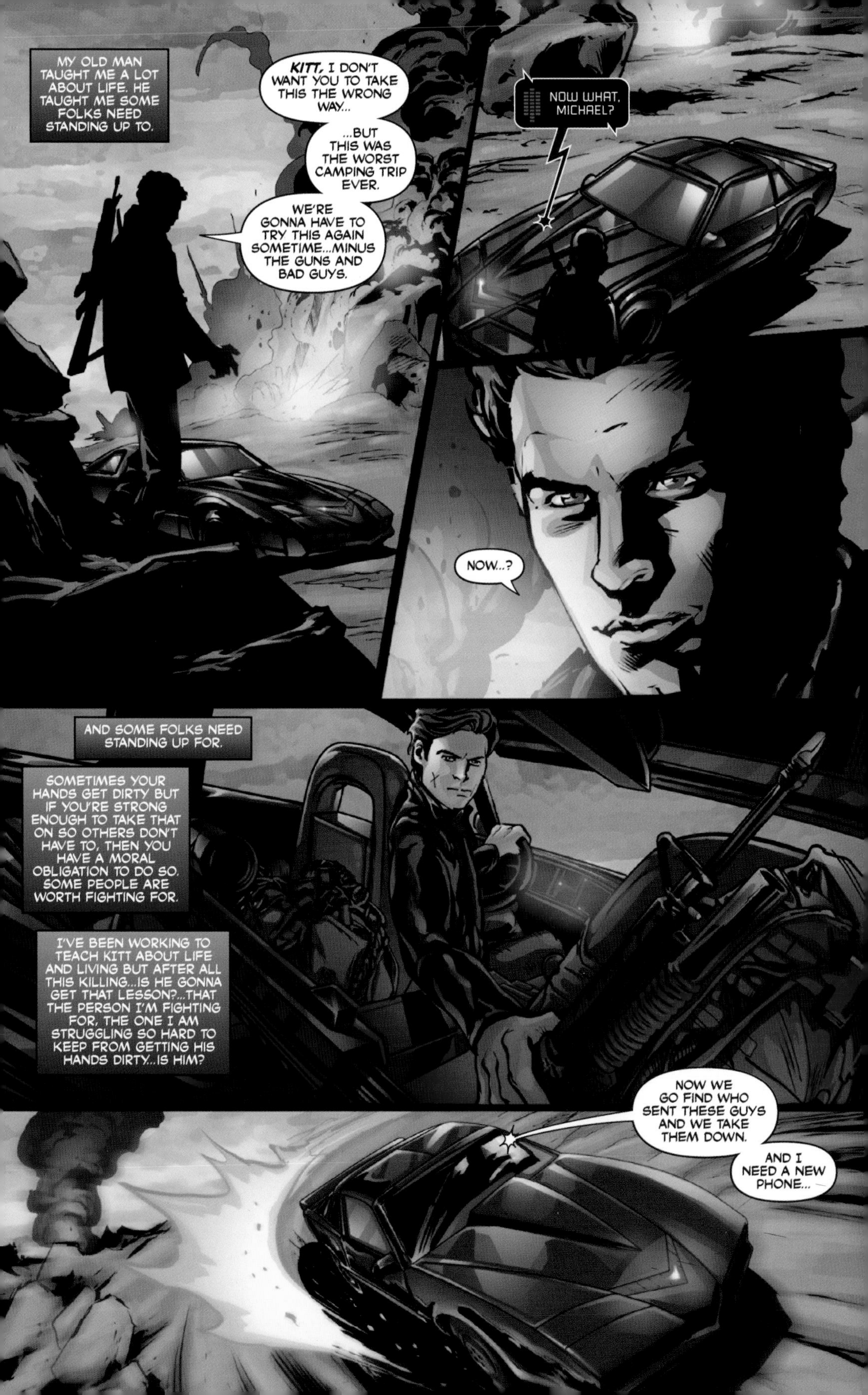
MY OLD MAN TAUGHT ME A LOT ABOUT LIFE. HE TAUGHT ME SOME FOLKS NEED STANDING UP TO.
KITT, I DON'T WANT YOU TO TAKE THIS THE WRONG WAY...
...BUT THIS WAS THE WORST CAMPING TRIP EVER.
WE'RE GONNA HAVE TO TRY THIS AGAIN SOMETIME...MINUS THE GUNS AND BAD GUYS.
NOW WHAT, MICHAEL?
NOW...?
AND SOME FOLKS NEED STANDING UP FOR.
SOMETIMES YOUR HANDS GET DIRTY BUT IF YOU'RE STRONG ENOUGH TO TAKE THAT ON SO OTHERS DON'T HAVE TO, THEN YOU HAVE A MORAL OBLIGATION TO DO SO. SOME PEOPLE ARE WORTH FIGHTING FOR.
I'VE BEEN WORKING TO TEACH KITT ABOUT LIFE AND LIVING BUT AFTER ALL THIS KILLING...IS HE GONNA GET THAT LESSON?...THAT THE PERSON I'M FIGHTING FOR, THE ONE I AM STRUGGLING SO HARD TO KEEP FROM GETTING HIS HANDS DIRTY...IS HIM?
NOW WE GO FIND WHO SENT THESE GUYS AND WE TAKE THEM DOWN.
AND I NEED A NEW PHONE...

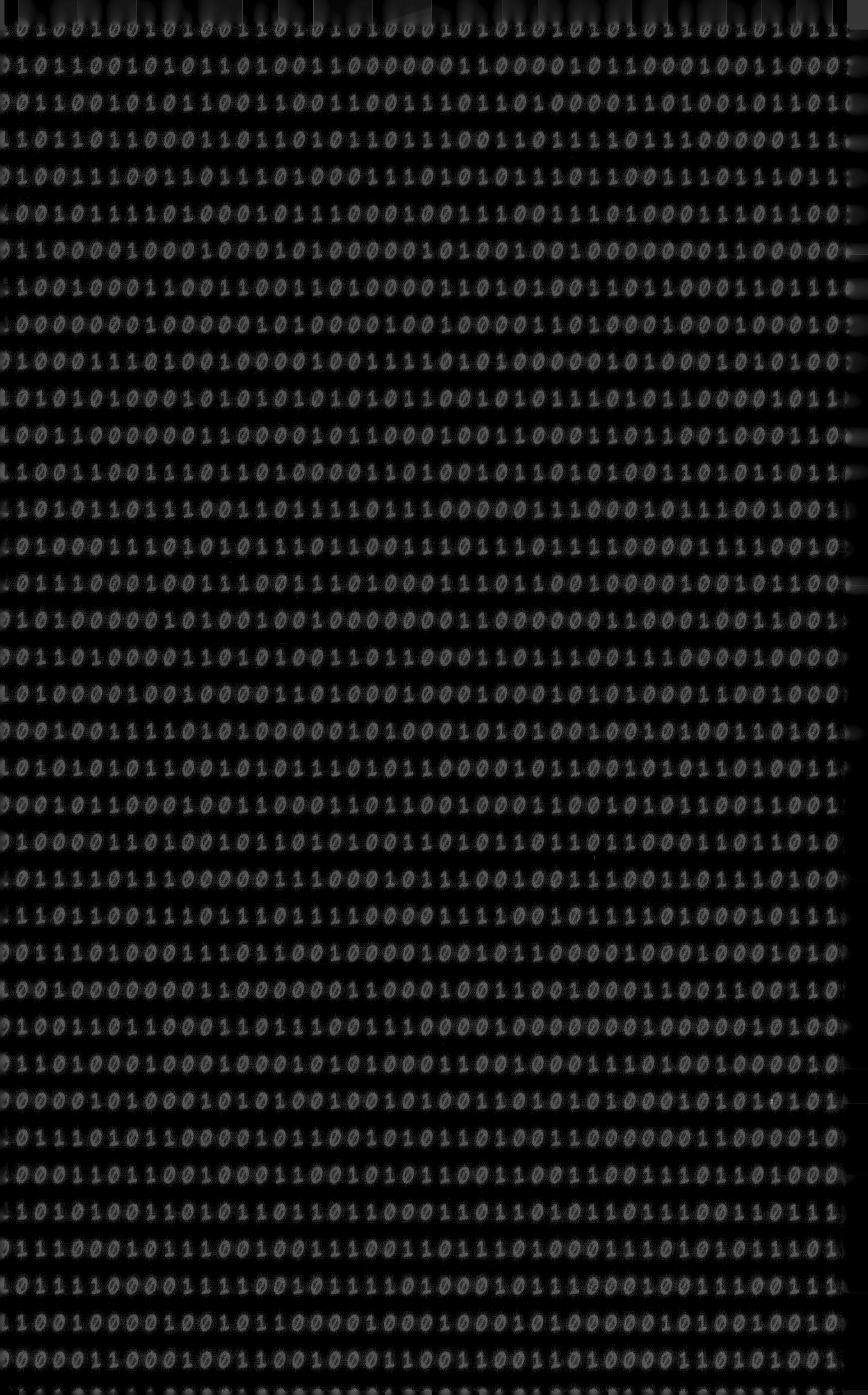

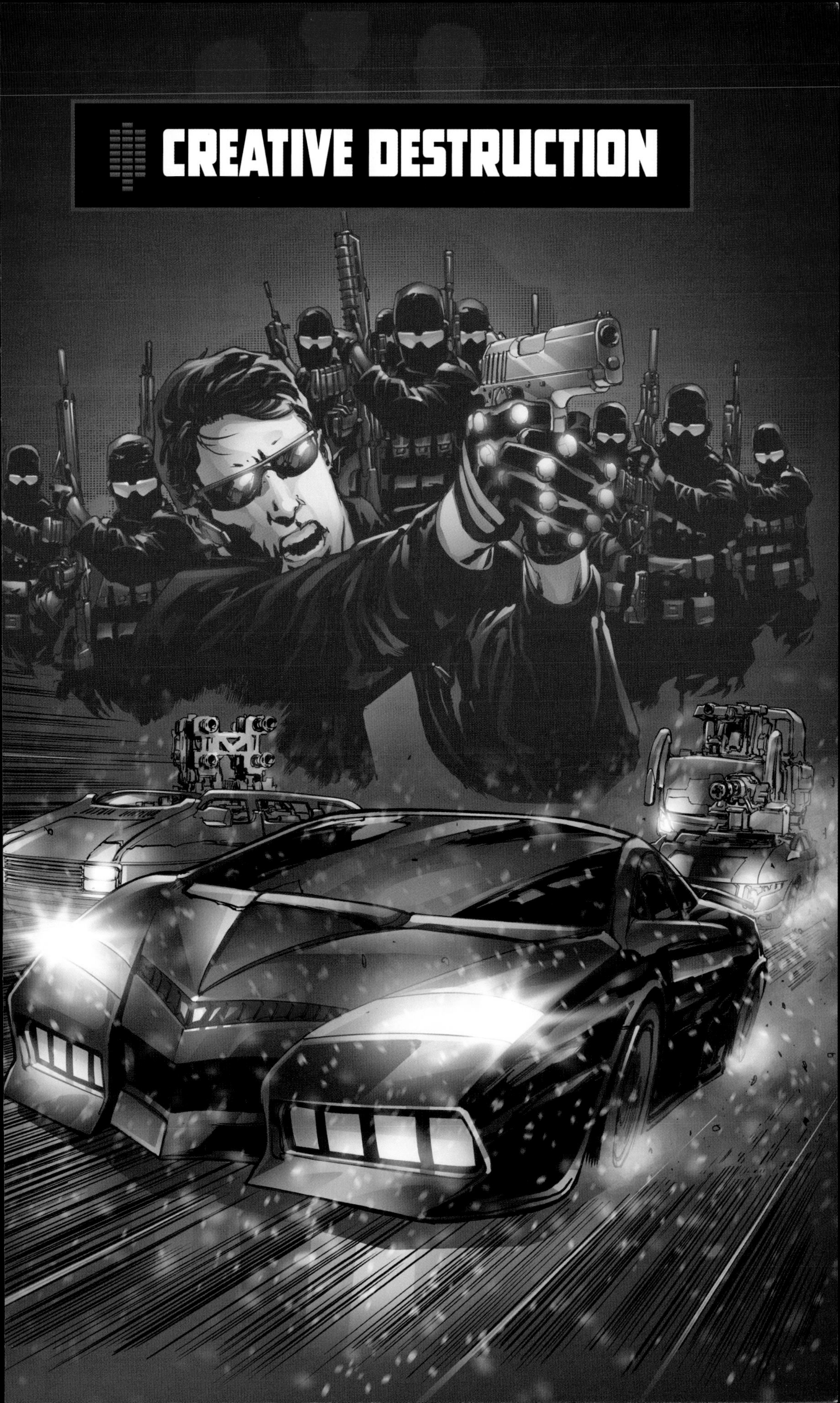
CREATIVE DESTRUCTION

KNIGHT RIDER
KNIGHT STRIKES

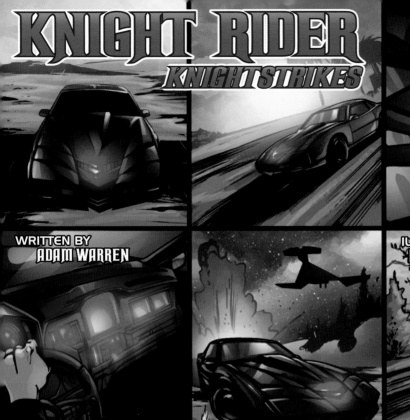

WRITTEN BY
ADAM WARREN

ILLUSTRATED BY
BRIAN DENHAM

COLORED BY
MILEN PARVANOV

LETTERED BY
ERIKA TERRIQUEZ

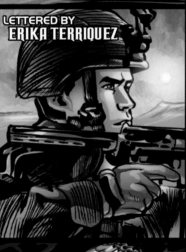

EDITED BY
SHANNON ERIC DENTON

FRONT COVER BY
LENO CARVALHO

KNIGHT RIDER CREATED BY
GLEN A. LARSON

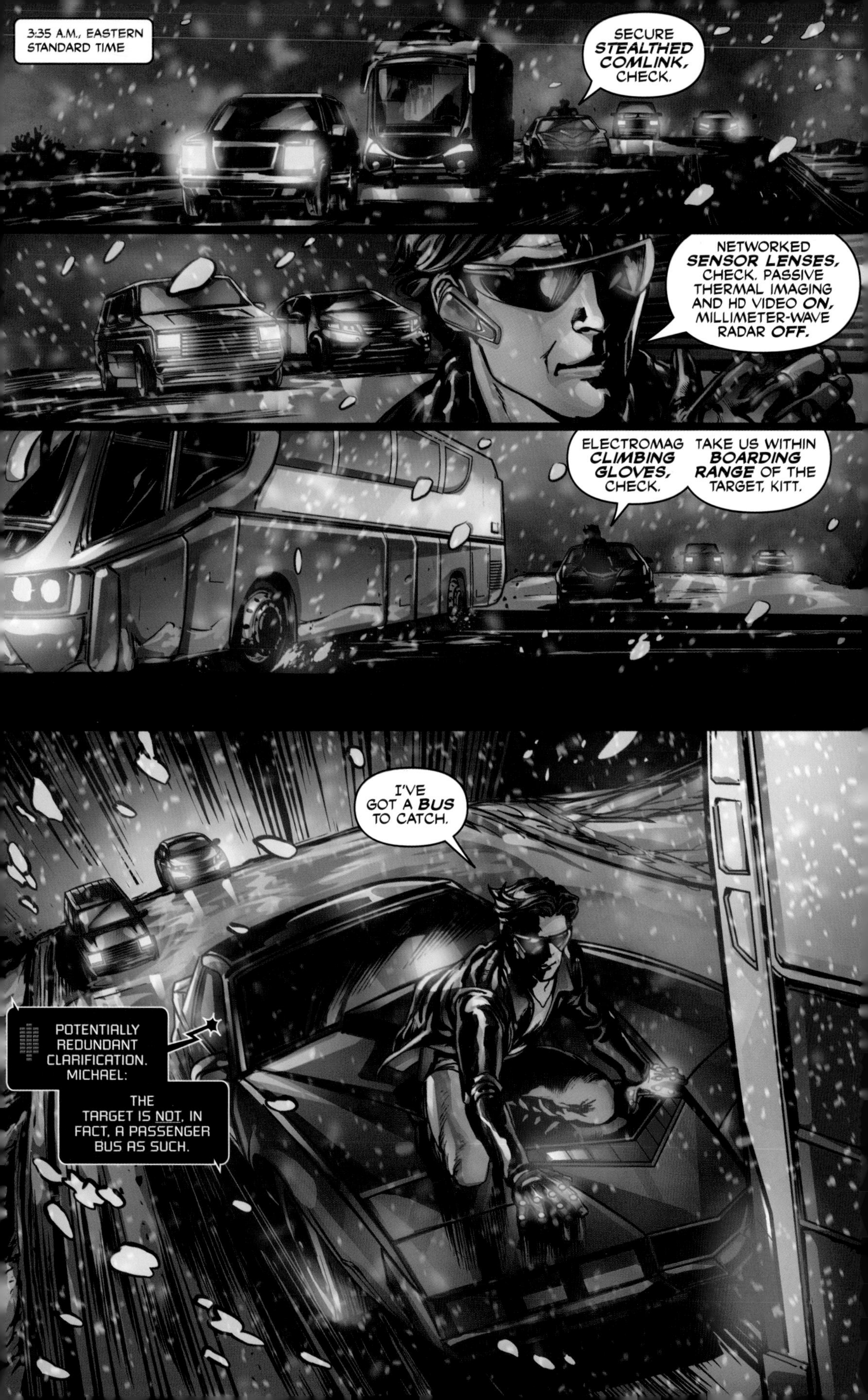
3:35 A.M., EASTERN STANDARD TIME
SECURE STEALTHED COMLINK, CHECK.
NETWORKED SENSOR LENSES, CHECK. PASSIVE THERMAL IMAGING AND HD VIDEO ON, MILLIMETER-WAVE RADAR OFF.
ELECTROMAG CLIMBING GLOVES, CHECK.
TAKE US WITHIN BOARDING RANGE OF THE TARGET, KITT.
I'VE GOT A BUS TO CATCH.
POTENTIALLY REDUNDANT CLARIFICATION. MICHAEL:
THE TARGET IS NOT, IN FACT, A PASSENGER BUS AS SUCH.

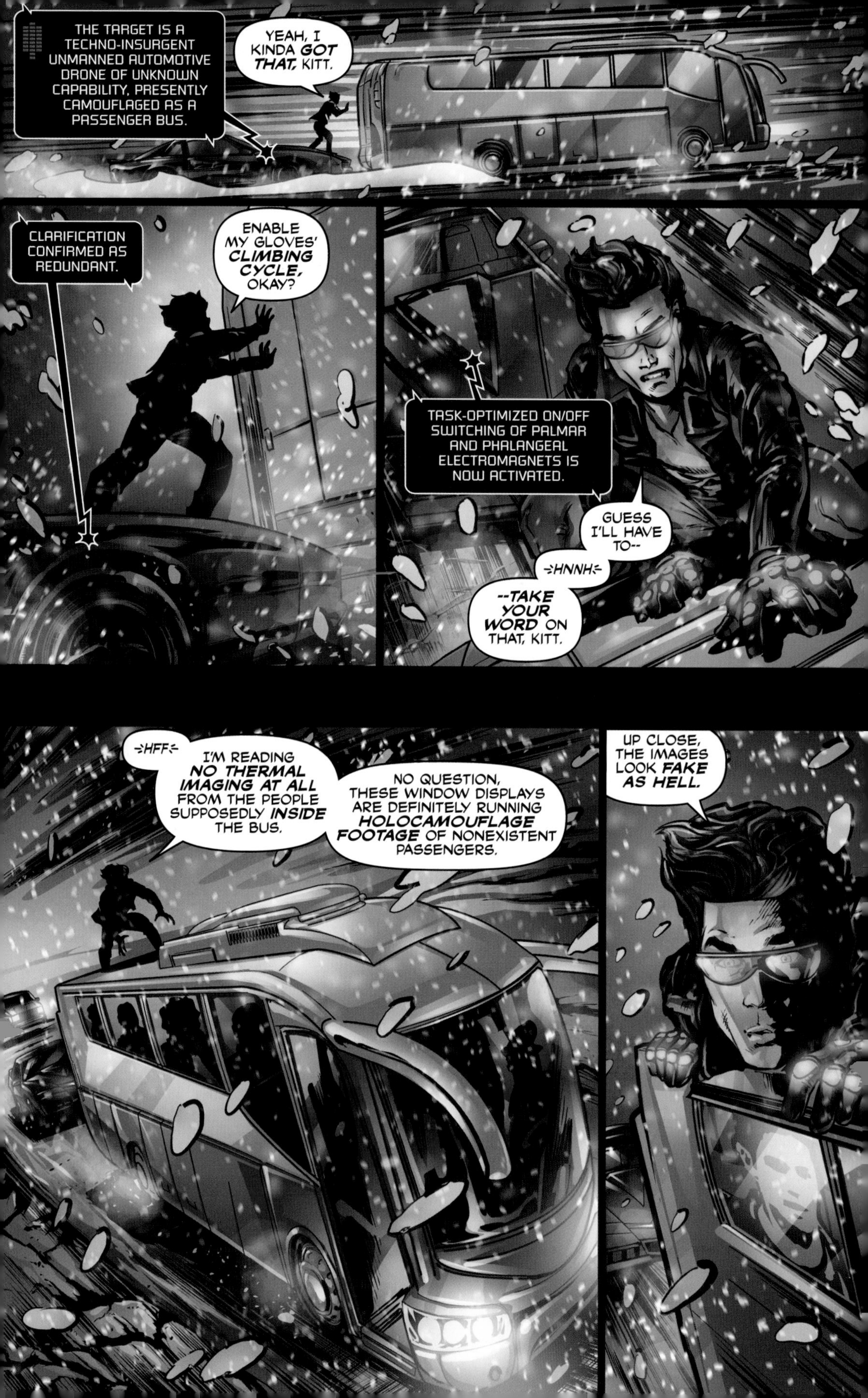
THE TARGET IS A TECHNO-INSURGENT UNMANNED AUTOMOTIVE DRONE OF UNKNOWN CAPABILITY, PRESENTLY CAMOUFLAGED AS A PASSENGER BUS.
YEAH, I KINDA **GOT THAT,** KITT.
CLARIFICATION CONFIRMED AS REDUNDANT.
ENABLE MY GLOVES' **CLIMBING CYCLE,** OKAY?
TASK-OPTIMIZED ON/OFF SWITCHING OF PALMAR AND PHALANGEAL ELECTROMAGNETS IS NOW ACTIVATED.
GUESS I'LL HAVE TO--
HNNH
--TAKE YOUR WORD ON THAT, KITT.
HFF
I'M READING **NO THERMAL IMAGING AT ALL** FROM THE PEOPLE SUPPOSEDLY **INSIDE** THE BUS.
NO QUESTION, THESE WINDOW DISPLAYS ARE DEFINITELY RUNNING **HOLOCAMOUFLAGE FOOTAGE** OF NONEXISTENT PASSENGERS.
UP CLOSE, THE IMAGES LOOK **FAKE AS HELL.**

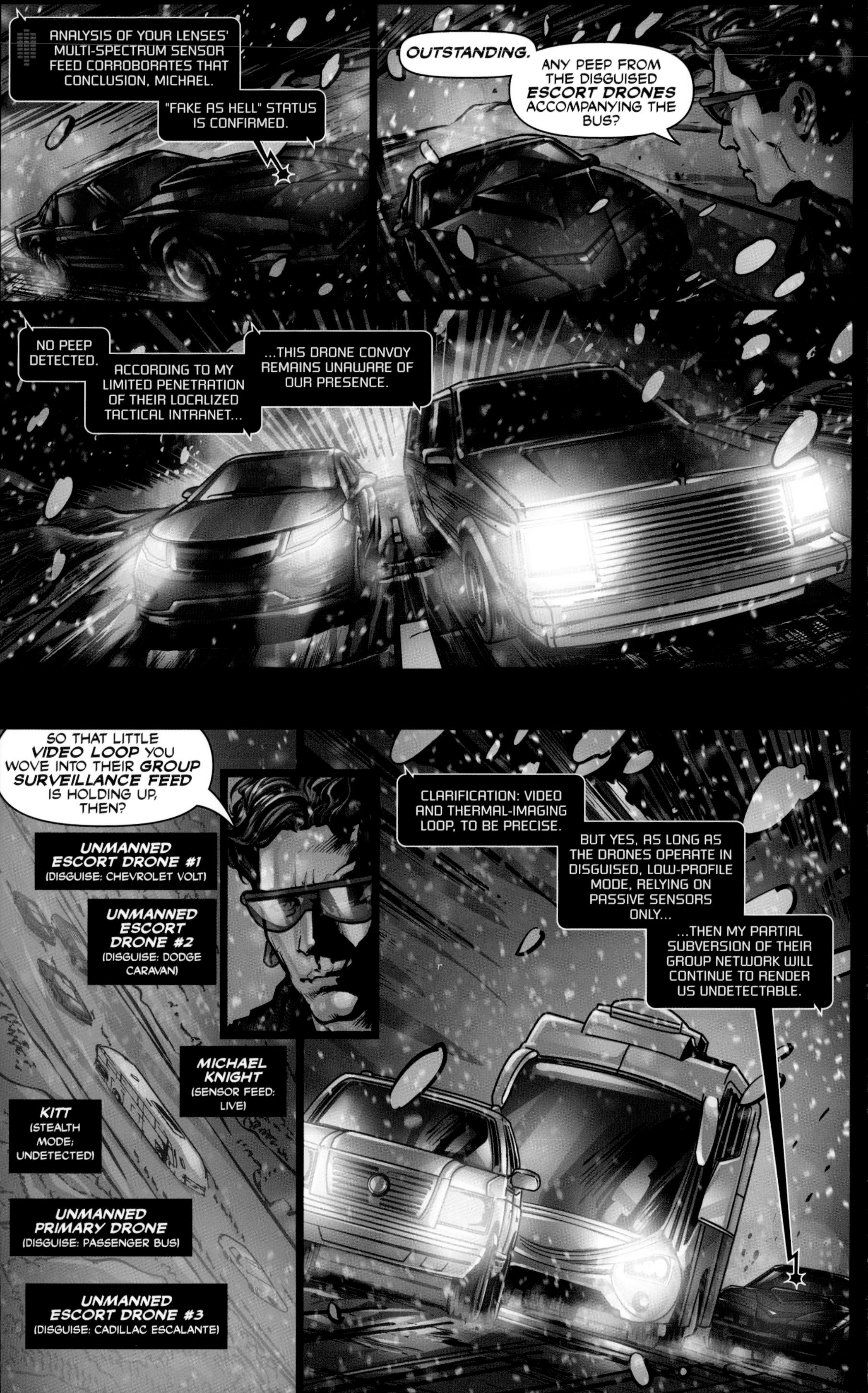

ANALYSIS OF YOUR LENSES' MULTI-SPECTRUM SENSOR FEED CORROBORATES THAT CONCLUSION, MICHAEL.
"FAKE AS HELL" STATUS IS CONFIRMED.
OUTSTANDING.
ANY PEEP FROM THE DISGUISED ESCORT DRONES ACCOMPANYING THE BUS?
NO PEEP DETECTED.
ACCORDING TO MY LIMITED PENETRATION OF THEIR LOCALIZED TACTICAL INTRANET...
...THIS DRONE CONVOY REMAINS UNAWARE OF OUR PRESENCE.
SO THAT LITTLE VIDEO LOOP YOU WOVE INTO THEIR GROUP SURVEILLANCE FEED IS HOLDING UP, THEN?
UNMANNED ESCORT DRONE #1 (DISGUISE: CHEVROLET VOLT)
UNMANNED ESCORT DRONE #2 (DISGUISE: DODGE CARAVAN)
MICHAEL KNIGHT (SENSOR FEED: LIVE)
KITT (STEALTH MODE; UNDETECTED)
UNMANNED PRIMARY DRONE (DISGUISE: PASSENGER BUS)
UNMANNED ESCORT DRONE #3 (DISGUISE: CADILLAC ESCALANTE)
CLARIFICATION: VIDEO AND THERMAL-IMAGING LOOP, TO BE PRECISE.
BUT YES, AS LONG AS THE DRONES OPERATE IN DISGUISED, LOW-PROFILE MODE, RELYING ON PASSIVE SENSORS ONLY...
...THEN MY PARTIAL SUBVERSION OF THEIR GROUP NETWORK WILL CONTINUE TO RENDER US UNDETECTABLE.

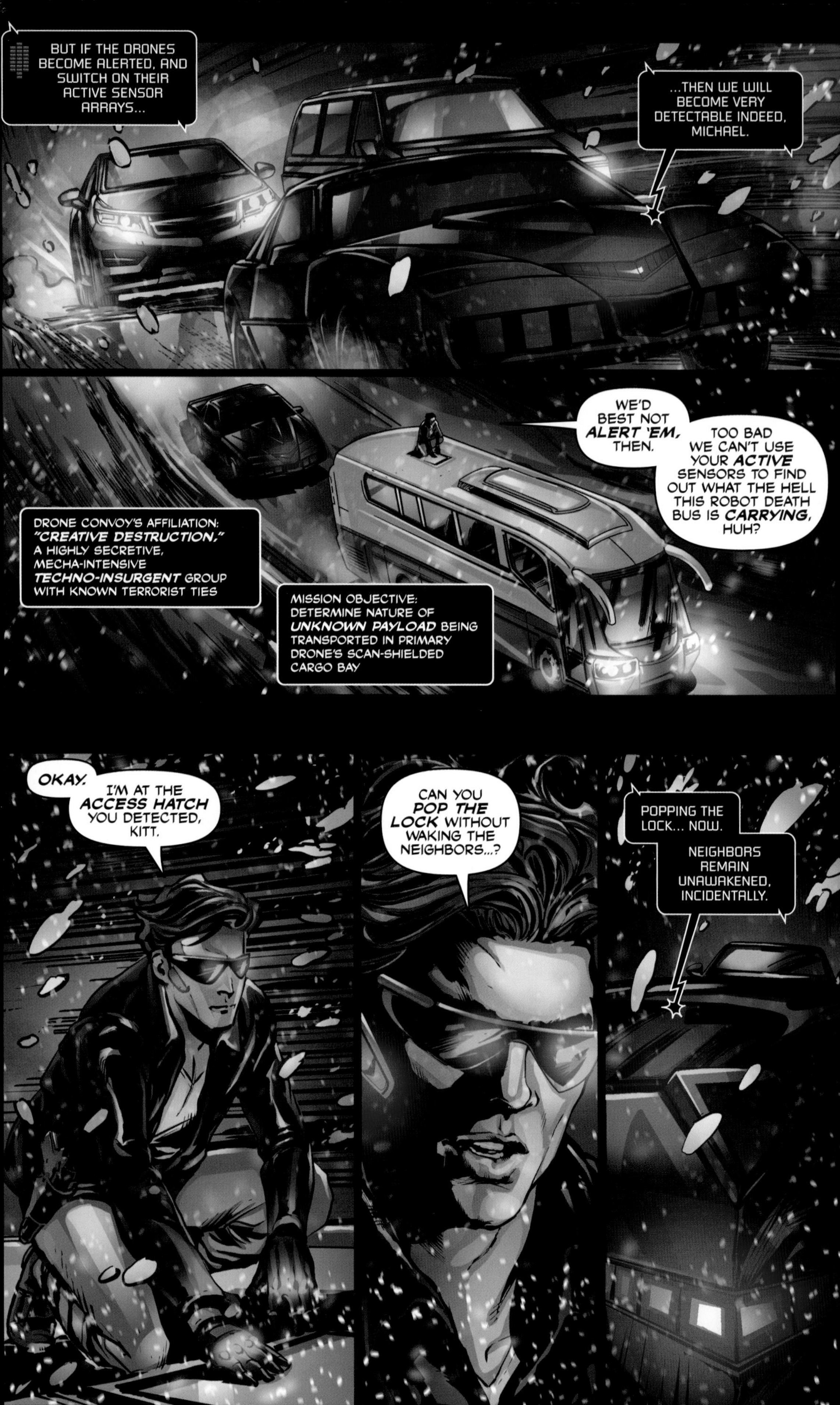
BUT IF THE DRONES BECOME ALERTED, AND SWITCH ON THEIR ACTIVE SENSOR ARRAYS...
...THEN WE WILL BECOME VERY DETECTABLE INDEED, MICHAEL.
WE'D BEST NOT ALERT 'EM, THEN.
TOO BAD WE CAN'T USE YOUR ACTIVE SENSORS TO FIND OUT WHAT THE HELL THIS ROBOT DEATH BUS IS CARRYING, HUH?
DRONE CONVOY'S AFFILIATION: "CREATIVE DESTRUCTION," A HIGHLY SECRETIVE, MECHA-INTENSIVE TECHNO-INSURGENT GROUP WITH KNOWN TERRORIST TIES
MISSION OBJECTIVE: DETERMINE NATURE OF UNKNOWN PAYLOAD BEING TRANSPORTED IN PRIMARY DRONE'S SCAN-SHIELDED CARGO BAY
OKAY. I'M AT THE ACCESS HATCH YOU DETECTED, KITT.
CAN YOU POP THE LOCK WITHOUT WAKING THE NEIGHBORS...?
POPPING THE LOCK... NOW.
NEIGHBORS REMAIN UNAWAKENED, INCIDENTALLY.

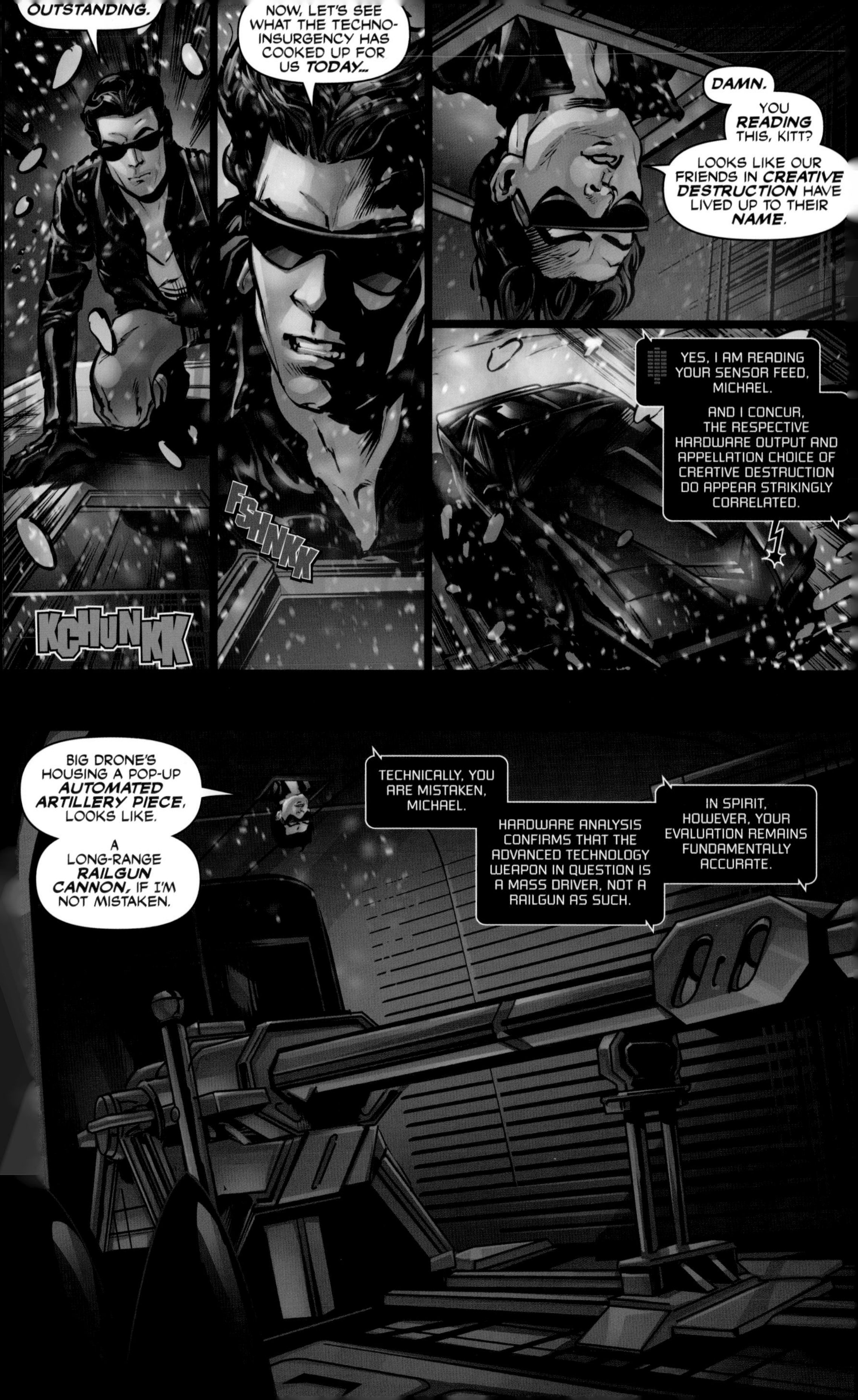
OUTSTANDING.
KCHUNKK
NOW, LET'S SEE WHAT THE TECHNO-INSURGENCY HAS COOKED UP FOR US TODAY...
FSHNKK
DAMN.
YOU READING THIS, KITT?
LOOKS LIKE OUR FRIENDS IN CREATIVE DESTRUCTION HAVE LIVED UP TO THEIR NAME.
YES, I AM READING YOUR SENSOR FEED, MICHAEL.
AND I CONCUR, THE RESPECTIVE HARDWARE OUTPUT AND APPELLATION CHOICE OF CREATIVE DESTRUCTION DO APPEAR STRIKINGLY CORRELATED.
BIG DRONE'S HOUSING A POP-UP AUTOMATED ARTILLERY PIECE, LOOKS LIKE.
A LONG-RANGE RAILGUN CANNON, IF I'M NOT MISTAKEN.
TECHNICALLY, YOU ARE MISTAKEN, MICHAEL.
HARDWARE ANALYSIS CONFIRMS THAT THE ADVANCED TECHNOLOGY WEAPON IN QUESTION IS A MASS DRIVER, NOT A RAILGUN AS SUCH.
IN SPIRIT, HOWEVER, YOUR EVALUATION REMAINS FUNDAMENTALLY ACCURATE.

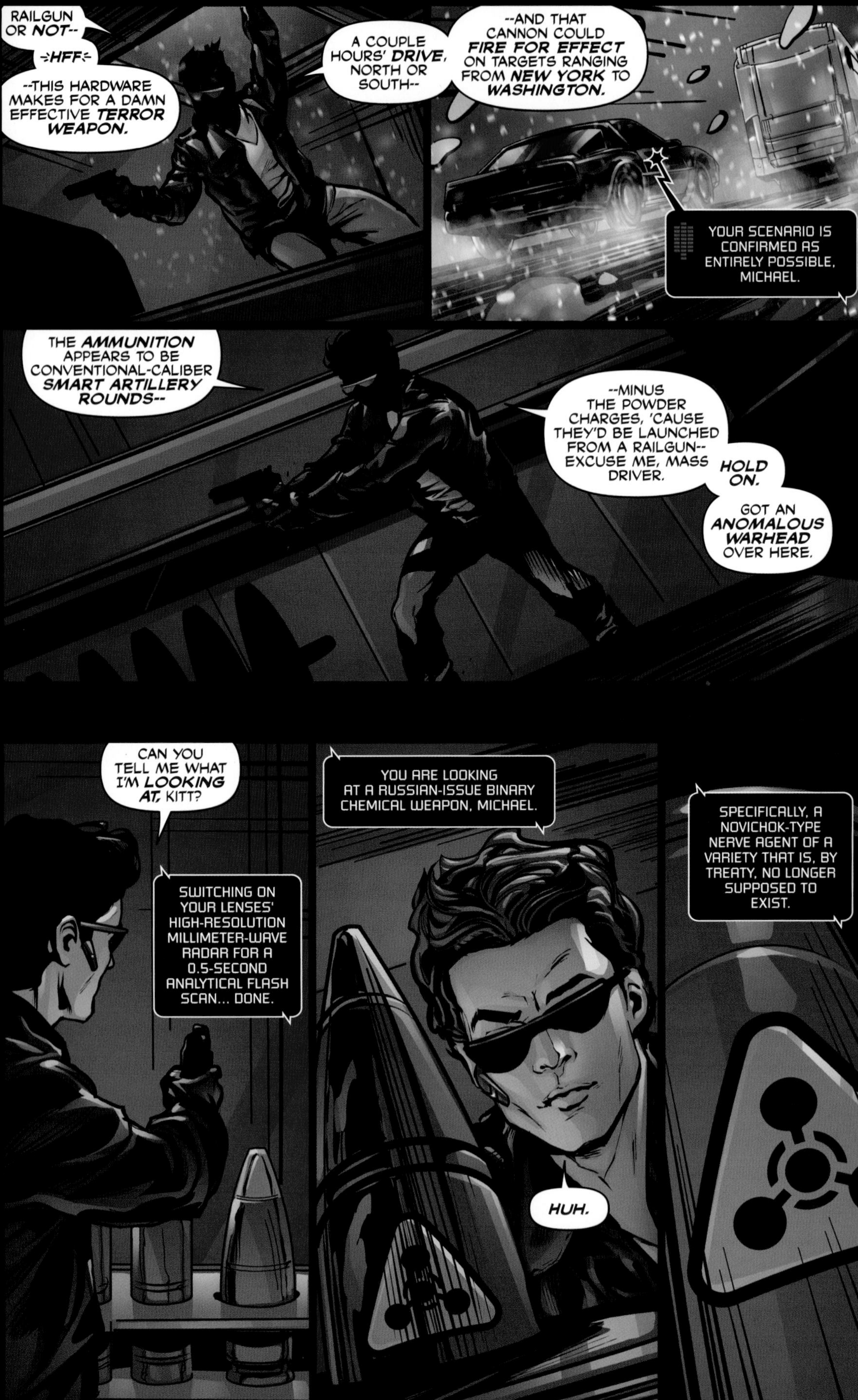
RAILGUN OR NOT--
HFF
--THIS HARDWARE MAKES FOR A DAMN EFFECTIVE TERROR WEAPON.
A COUPLE HOURS' DRIVE, NORTH OR SOUTH--
--AND THAT CANNON COULD FIRE FOR EFFECT ON TARGETS RANGING FROM NEW YORK TO WASHINGTON.
YOUR SCENARIO IS CONFIRMED AS ENTIRELY POSSIBLE, MICHAEL.
THE AMMUNITION APPEARS TO BE CONVENTIONAL-CALIBER SMART ARTILLERY ROUNDS--
--MINUS THE POWDER CHARGES, 'CAUSE THEY'D BE LAUNCHED FROM A RAILGUN-- EXCUSE ME, MASS DRIVER.
HOLD ON.
GOT AN ANOMALOUS WARHEAD OVER HERE.
CAN YOU TELL ME WHAT I'M LOOKING AT, KITT?
SWITCHING ON YOUR LENSES' HIGH-RESOLUTION MILLIMETER-WAVE RADAR FOR A 0.5-SECOND ANALYTICAL FLASH SCAN... DONE.
YOU ARE LOOKING AT A RUSSIAN-ISSUE BINARY CHEMICAL WEAPON, MICHAEL.
HUH.
SPECIFICALLY, A NOVICHOK-TYPE NERVE AGENT OF A VARIETY THAT IS, BY TREATY, NO LONGER SUPPOSED TO EXIST.

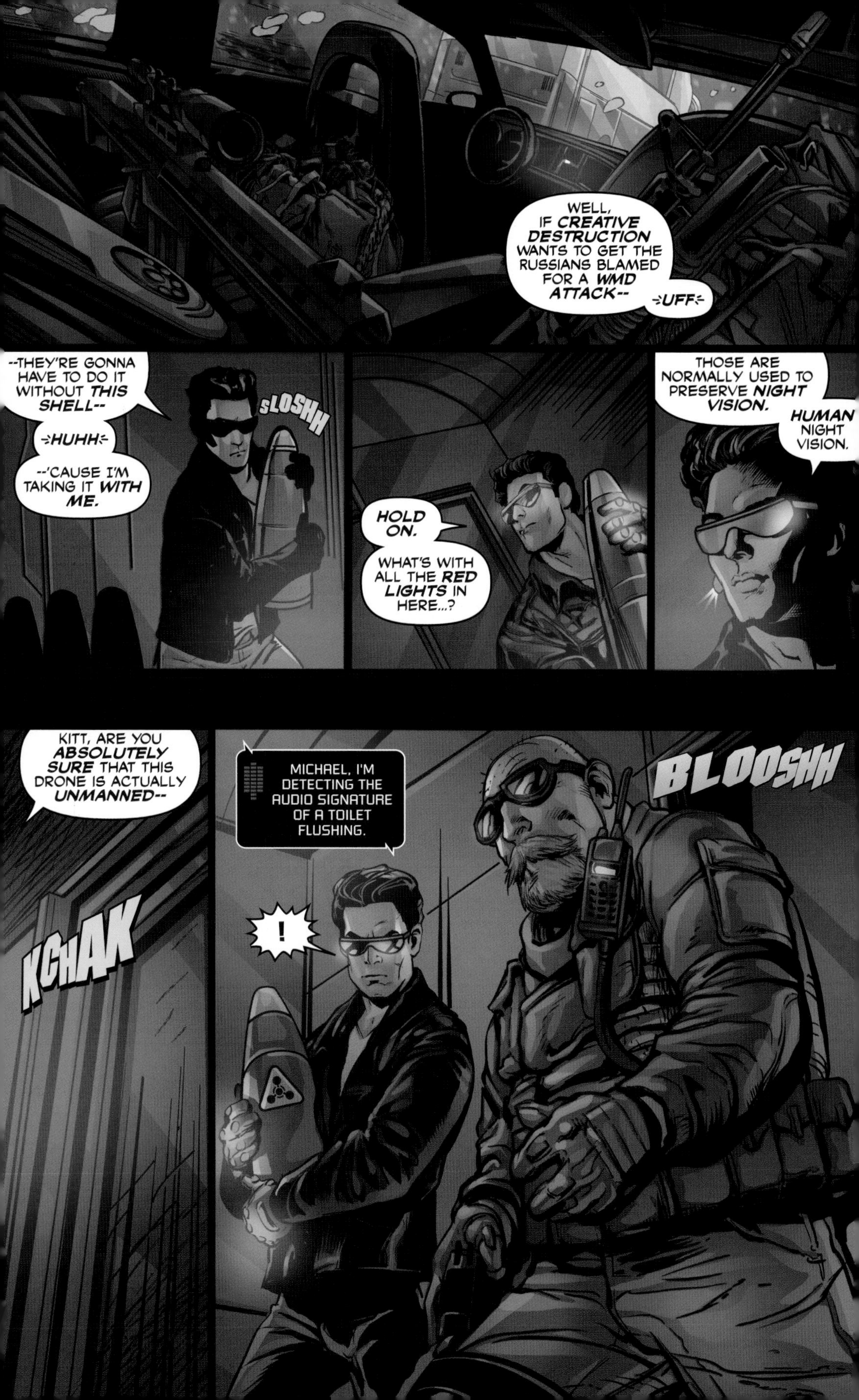
WELL, IF CREATIVE DESTRUCTION WANTS TO GET THE RUSSIANS BLAMED FOR A WMD ATTACK--
UFF
--THEY'RE GONNA HAVE TO DO IT WITHOUT THIS SHELL--
HUHH
--'CAUSE I'M TAKING IT WITH ME.
SLOSHH
HOLD ON.
WHAT'S WITH ALL THE RED LIGHTS IN HERE...?
THOSE ARE NORMALLY USED TO PRESERVE NIGHT VISION.
HUMAN NIGHT VISION.
KITT, ARE YOU ABSOLUTELY SURE THAT THIS DRONE IS ACTUALLY UNMANNED--
MICHAEL, I'M DETECTING THE AUDIO SIGNATURE OF A TOILET FLUSHING.
BLOOSHH
KCHAK
!

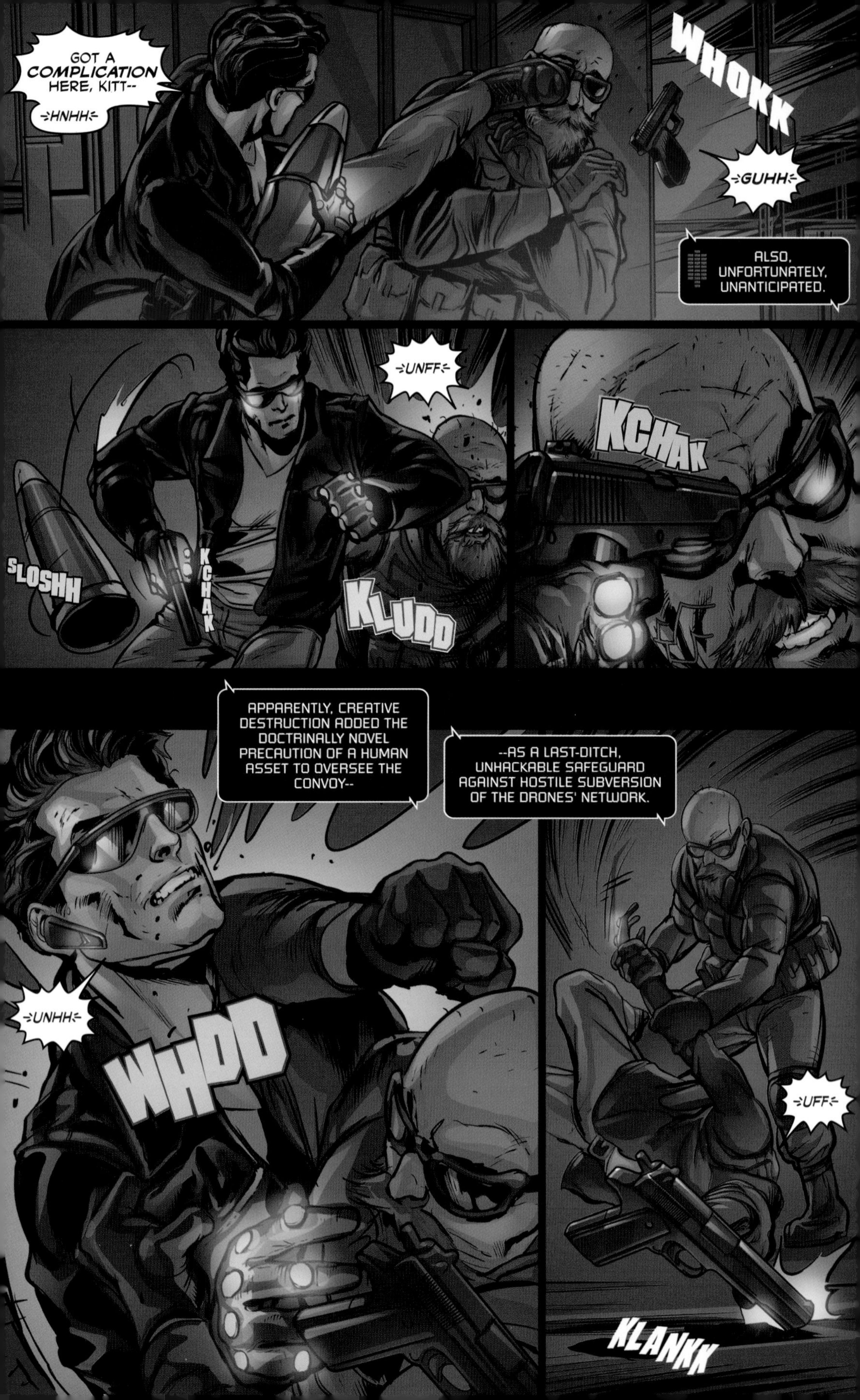
GOT A COMPLICATION HERE, KITT--
-HNHH-
WHOKK
-GUHH-
ALSO, UNFORTUNATELY, UNANTICIPATED.
-UNFF-
SLOSHH
KCHAK
KLUDD
KCHAK
APPARENTLY, CREATIVE DESTRUCTION ADDED THE DOCTRINALLY NOVEL PRECAUTION OF A HUMAN ASSET TO OVERSEE THE CONVOY--
--AS A LAST-DITCH, UNHACKABLE SAFEGUARD AGAINST HOSTILE SUBVERSION OF THE DRONES' NETWORK.
-UNHH-
WHDD
-UFF-
KLANKK

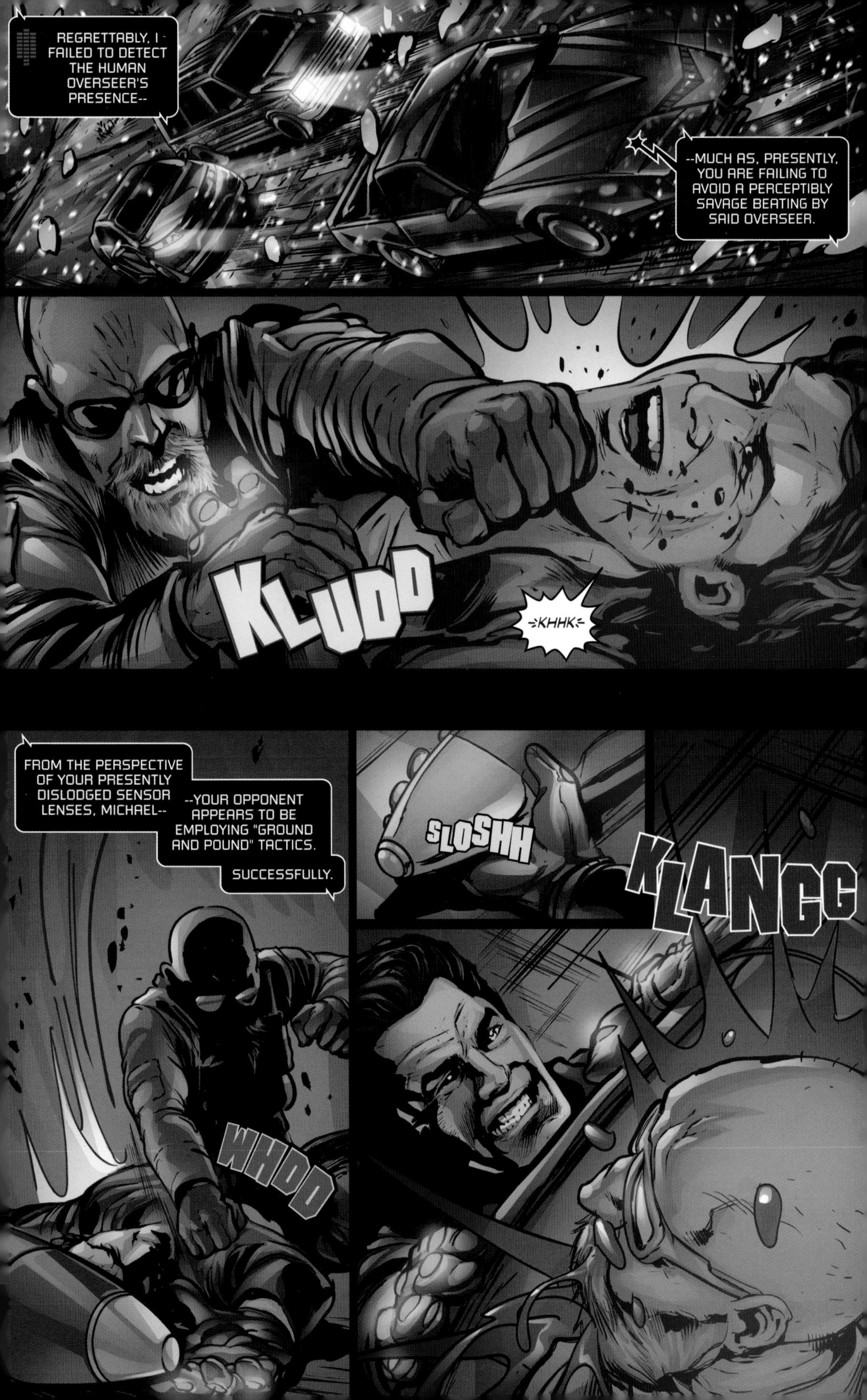
REGRETTABLY, I FAILED TO DETECT THE HUMAN OVERSEER'S PRESENCE--
--MUCH AS, PRESENTLY, YOU ARE FAILING TO AVOID A PERCEPTIBLY SAVAGE BEATING BY SAID OVERSEER.
KLUDD
KHHK
FROM THE PERSPECTIVE OF YOUR PRESENTLY DISLODGED SENSOR LENSES, MICHAEL--
--YOUR OPPONENT APPEARS TO BE EMPLOYING "GROUND AND POUND" TACTICS.
SUCCESSFULLY.
WHDD
SLOSHH
KLANGG

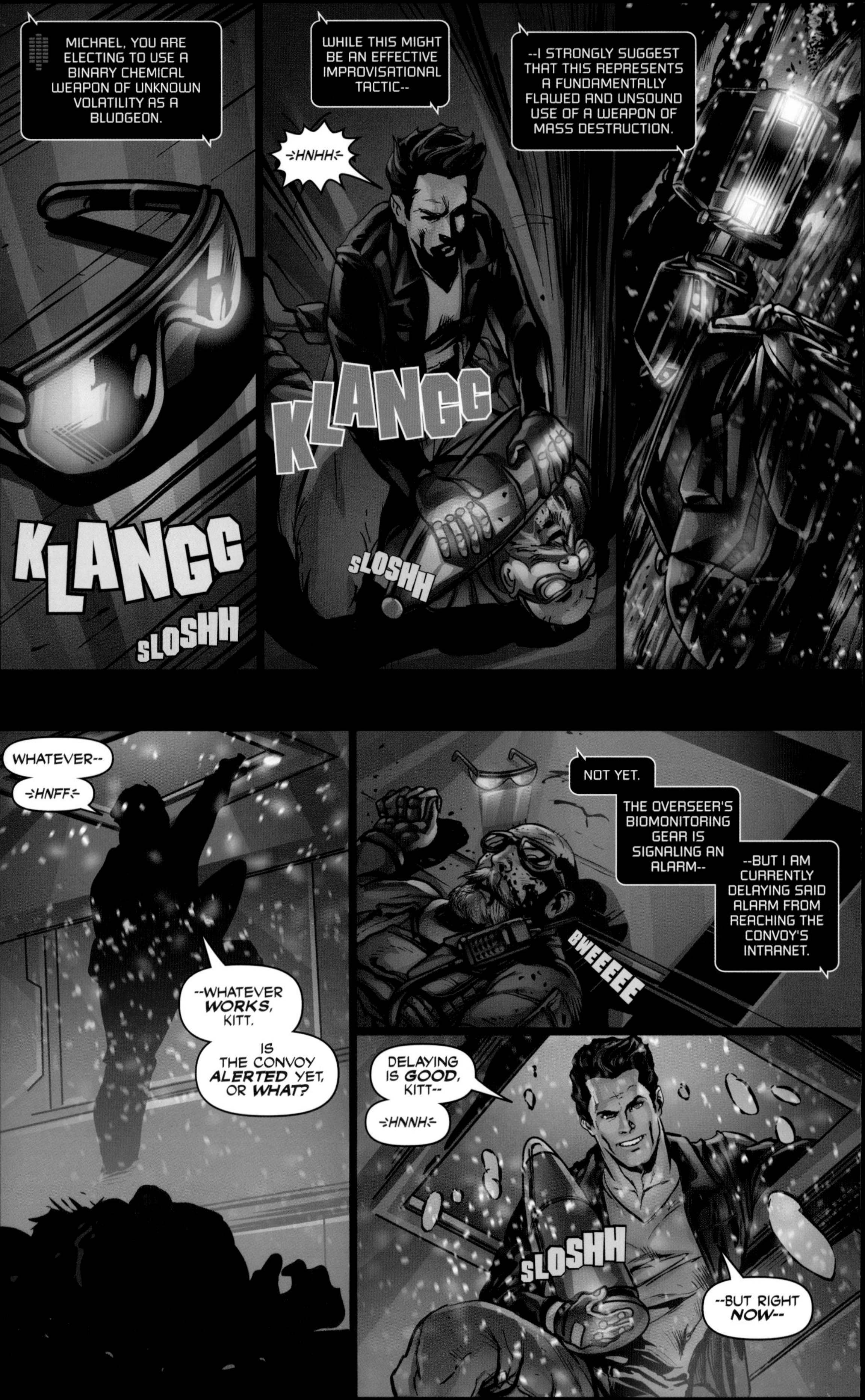
MICHAEL, YOU ARE ELECTING TO USE A BINARY CHEMICAL WEAPON OF UNKNOWN VOLATILITY AS A BLUDGEON.
KLANGG
SLOSHH
WHILE THIS MIGHT BE AN EFFECTIVE IMPROVISATIONAL TACTIC--
HNHH
KLANGG
SLOSHH
--I STRONGLY SUGGEST THAT THIS REPRESENTS A FUNDAMENTALLY FLAWED AND UNSOUND USE OF A WEAPON OF MASS DESTRUCTION.
WHATEVER--
HNFF
--WHATEVER *WORKS*, KITT.
IS THE CONVOY *ALERTED* YET, OR *WHAT?*
NOT YET.
THE OVERSEER'S BIOMONITORING GEAR IS SIGNALING AN ALARM--
--BUT I AM CURRENTLY DELAYING SAID ALARM FROM REACHING THE CONVOY'S INTRANET.
BWEEEEE
DELAYING IS *GOOD*, KITT--
HNNH
SLOSHH
--BUT RIGHT *NOW*--

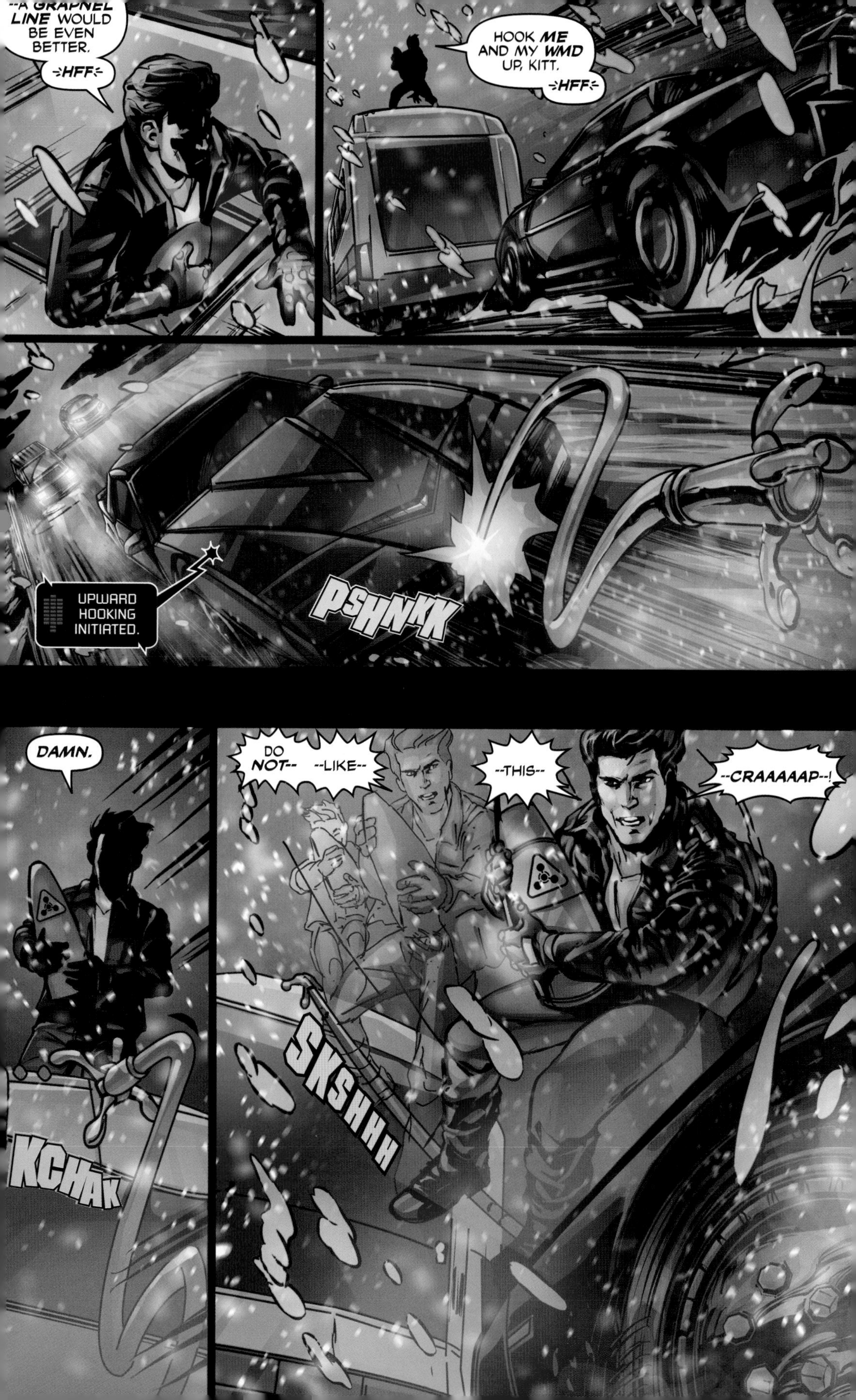
--A GRAPNEL LINE WOULD BE EVEN BETTER.
-HFF-
HOOK ME AND MY WMD UP, KITT.
-HFF-
UPWARD HOOKING INITIATED.
PSHNKK
DAMN.
KCHAK
DO NOT--
--LIKE--
--THIS--
--CRAAAAAP--!
SKSHHH

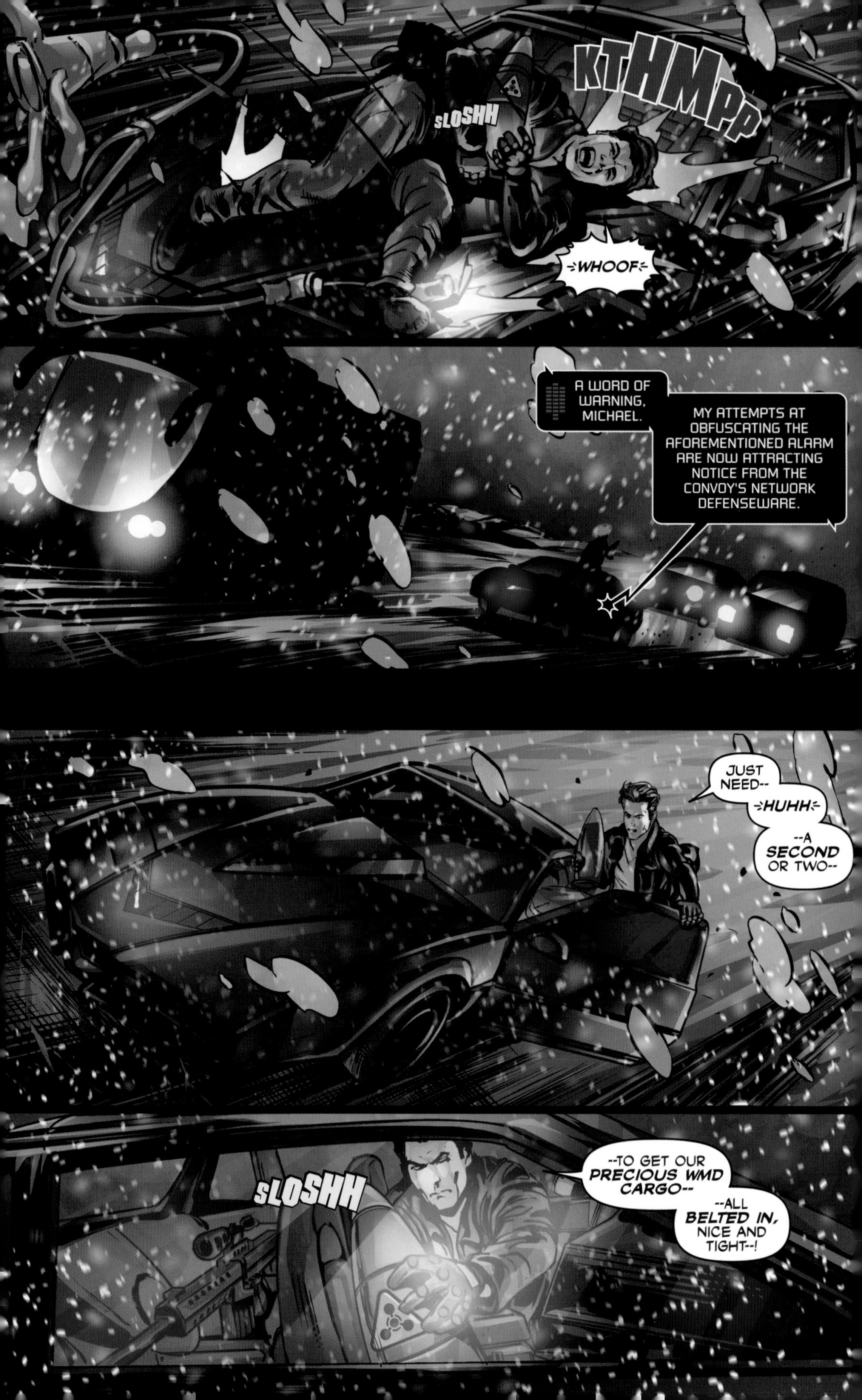
SLOSHH
KTHMPP
WHOOF
A WORD OF WARNING, MICHAEL.
MY ATTEMPTS AT OBFUSCATING THE AFOREMENTIONED ALARM ARE NOW ATTRACTING NOTICE FROM THE CONVOY'S NETWORK DEFENSEWARE.
JUST NEED--
HUHH
--A SECOND OR TWO--
SLOSHH
--TO GET OUR PRECIOUS WMD CARGO--
--ALL BELTED IN, NICE AND TIGHT--!

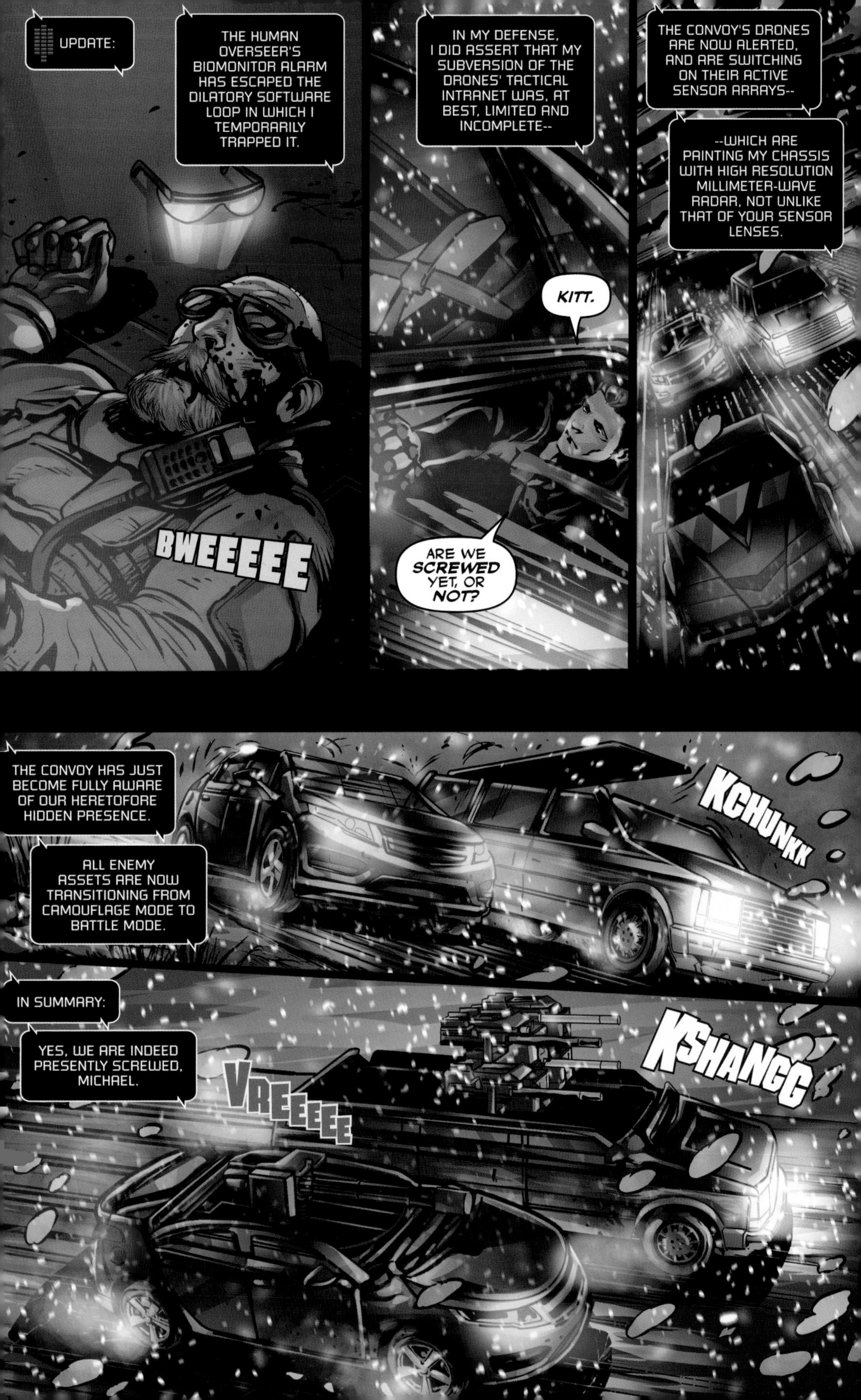
UPDATE:
THE HUMAN OVERSEER'S BIOMONITOR ALARM HAS ESCAPED THE DILATORY SOFTWARE LOOP IN WHICH I TEMPORARILY TRAPPED IT.
BWEEEEE
IN MY DEFENSE, I DID ASSERT THAT MY SUBVERSION OF THE DRONES' TACTICAL INTRANET WAS, AT BEST, LIMITED AND INCOMPLETE--
KITT.
ARE WE SCREWED YET, OR NOT?
THE CONVOY'S DRONES ARE NOW ALERTED, AND ARE SWITCHING ON THEIR ACTIVE SENSOR ARRAYS--
--WHICH ARE PAINTING MY CHASSIS WITH HIGH RESOLUTION MILLIMETER-WAVE RADAR, NOT UNLIKE THAT OF YOUR SENSOR LENSES.
THE CONVOY HAS JUST BECOME FULLY AWARE OF OUR HERETOFORE HIDDEN PRESENCE.
ALL ENEMY ASSETS ARE NOW TRANSITIONING FROM CAMOUFLAGE MODE TO BATTLE MODE.
KCHUNKK
IN SUMMARY:
YES, WE ARE INDEED PRESENTLY SCREWED, MICHAEL.
VREEEEEE
KSHANGG

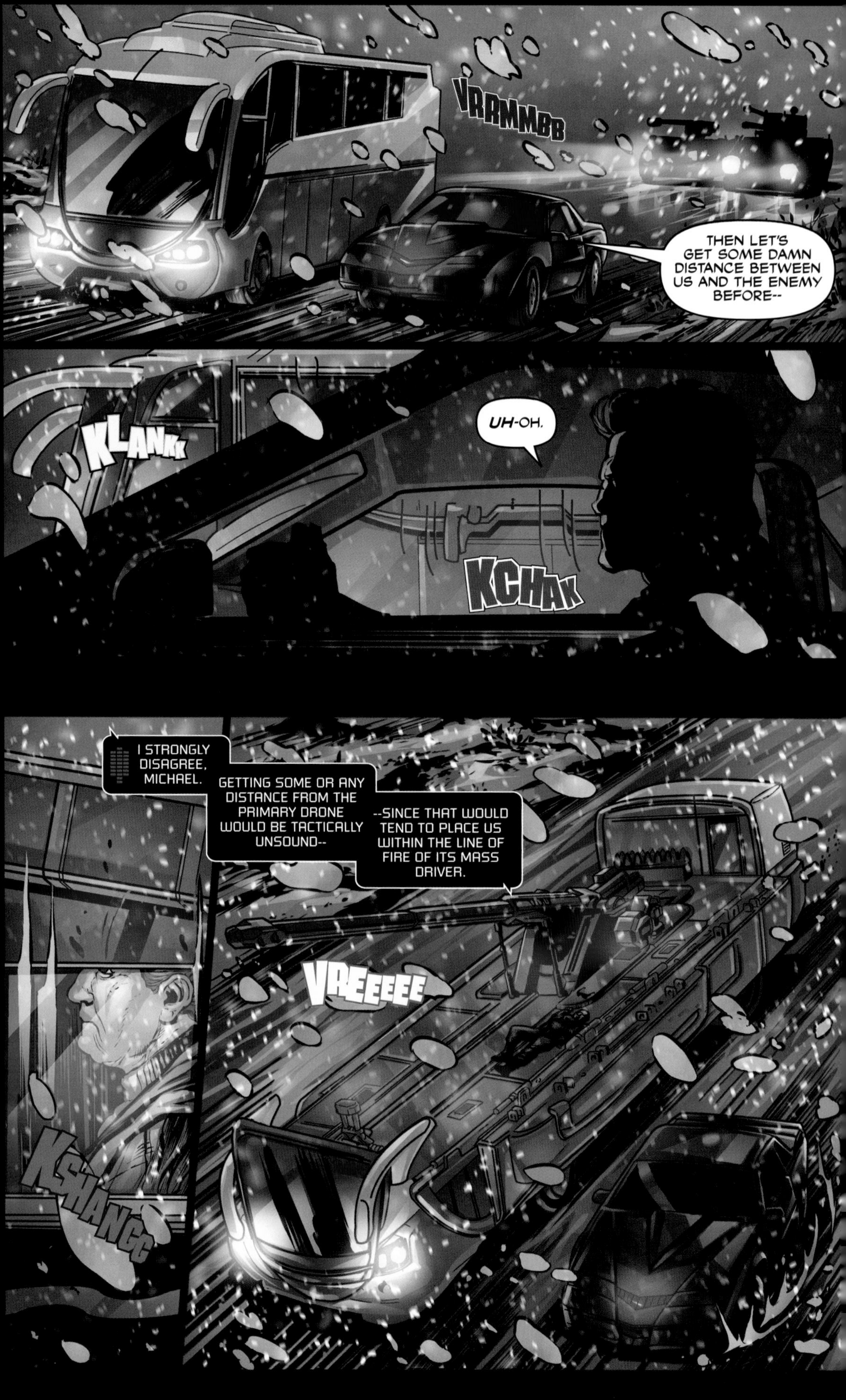
VRRMMBB
THEN LET'S GET SOME DAMN DISTANCE BETWEEN US AND THE ENEMY BEFORE--
KLANKK
UH-OH.
KCHAK
I STRONGLY DISAGREE, MICHAEL.
GETTING SOME OR ANY DISTANCE FROM THE PRIMARY DRONE WOULD BE TACTICALLY UNSOUND--
--SINCE THAT WOULD TEND TO PLACE US WITHIN THE LINE OF FIRE OF ITS MASS DRIVER.
VREEEEE
KSHANGG

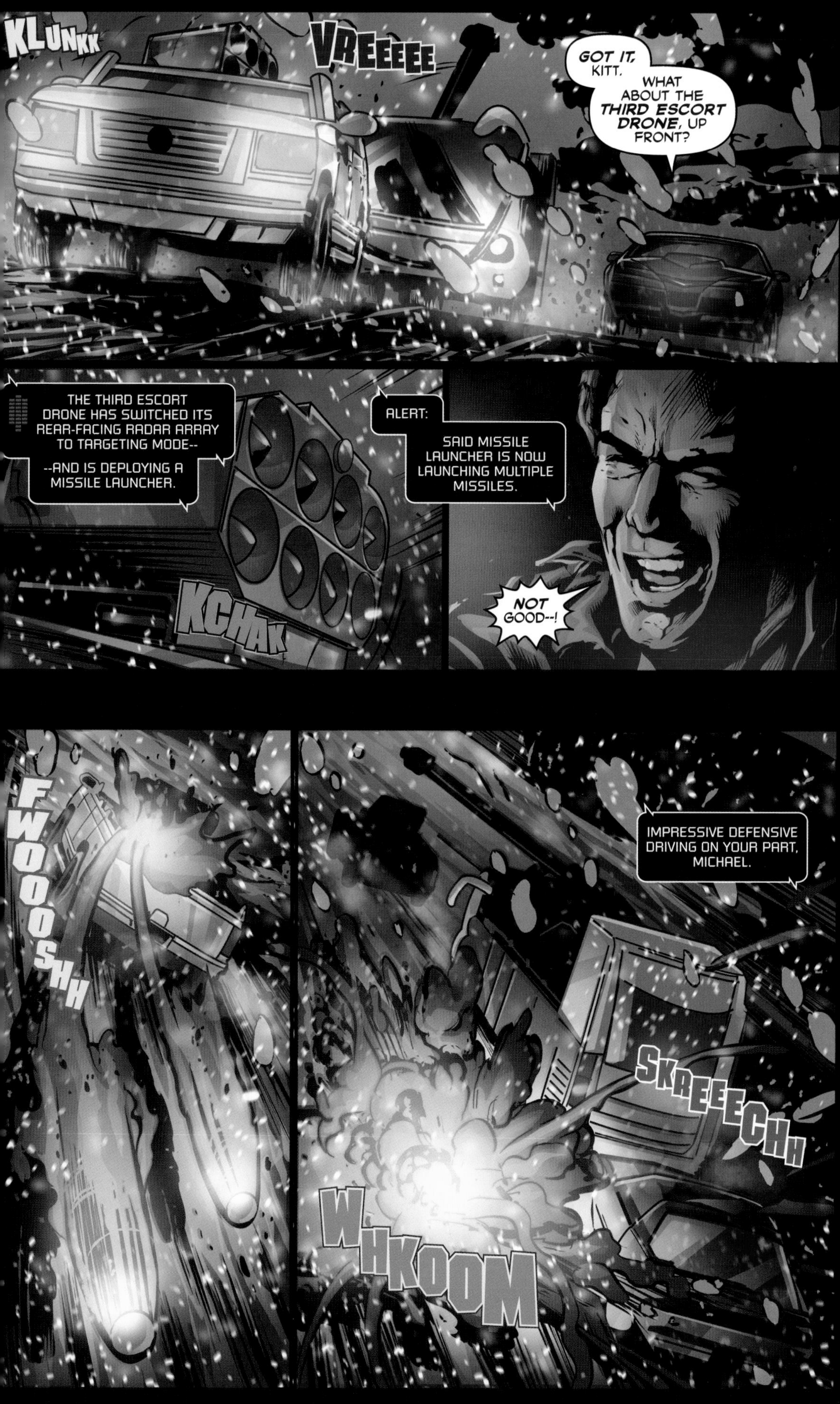
KLUNKK
VREEEEE
GOT IT, KITT. WHAT ABOUT THE THIRD ESCORT DRONE, UP FRONT?
THE THIRD ESCORT DRONE HAS SWITCHED ITS REAR-FACING RADAR ARRAY TO TARGETING MODE--
--AND IS DEPLOYING A MISSILE LAUNCHER.
KCHAK
ALERT:
SAID MISSILE LAUNCHER IS NOW LAUNCHING MULTIPLE MISSILES.
NOT GOOD--!
FWOOOSHH
IMPRESSIVE DEFENSIVE DRIVING ON YOUR PART, MICHAEL.
SKREEEECHH
WHKOOM

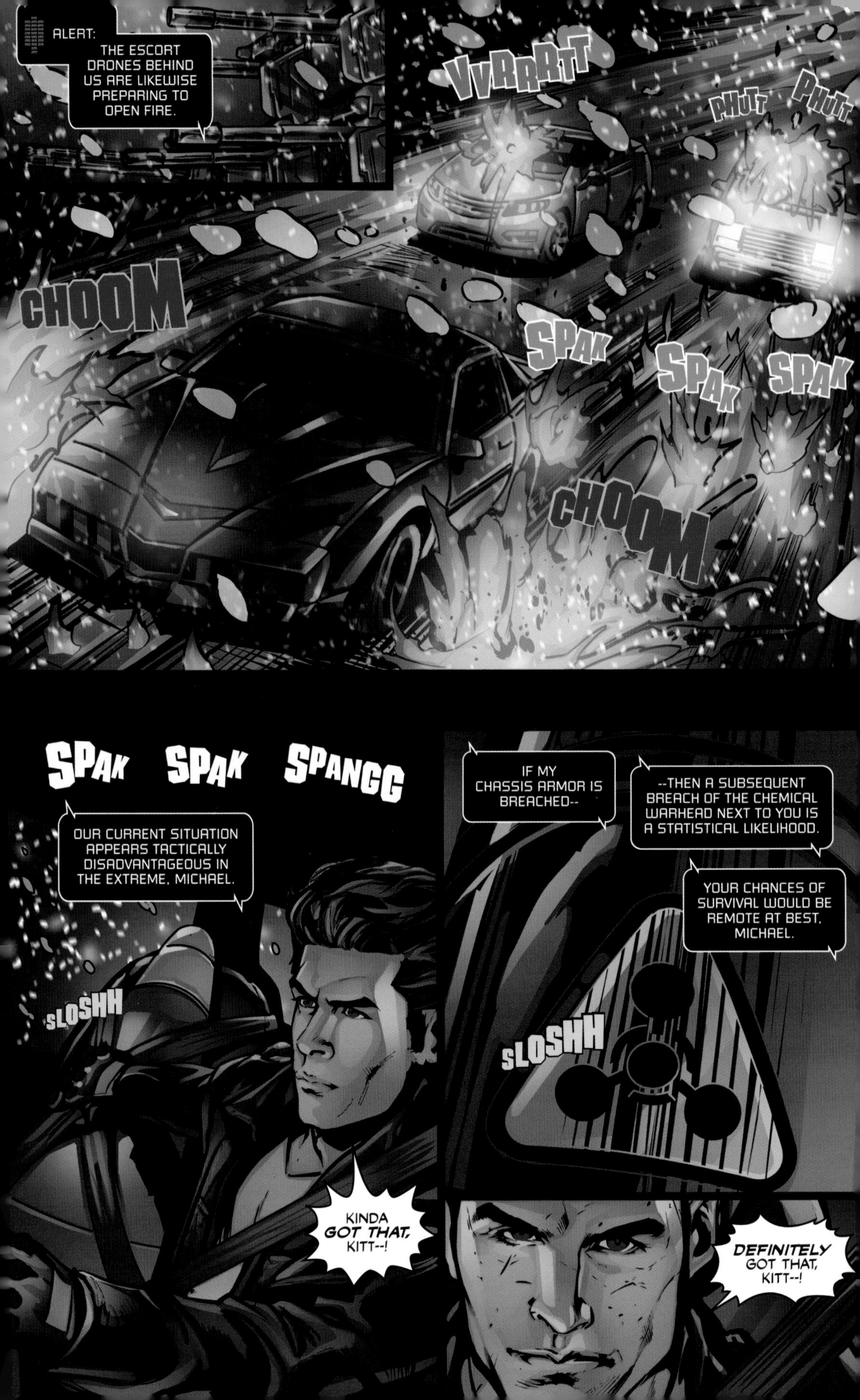

ALERT:
THE ESCORT DRONES BEHIND US ARE LIKEWISE PREPARING TO OPEN FIRE.
VVRRRTT
PHUTT
PHUTT
CHOOM
SPAK
SPAK
SPAK
CHOOM
SPAK SPAK SPANGG
OUR CURRENT SITUATION APPEARS TACTICALLY DISADVANTAGEOUS IN THE EXTREME, MICHAEL.
SLOSHH
KINDA *GOT THAT,* KITT--!
IF MY CHASSIS ARMOR IS BREACHED--
--THEN A SUBSEQUENT BREACH OF THE CHEMICAL WARHEAD NEXT TO YOU IS A STATISTICAL LIKELIHOOD.
YOUR CHANCES OF SURVIVAL WOULD BE REMOTE AT BEST, MICHAEL.
SLOSHH
DEFINITELY GOT THAT, KITT--!

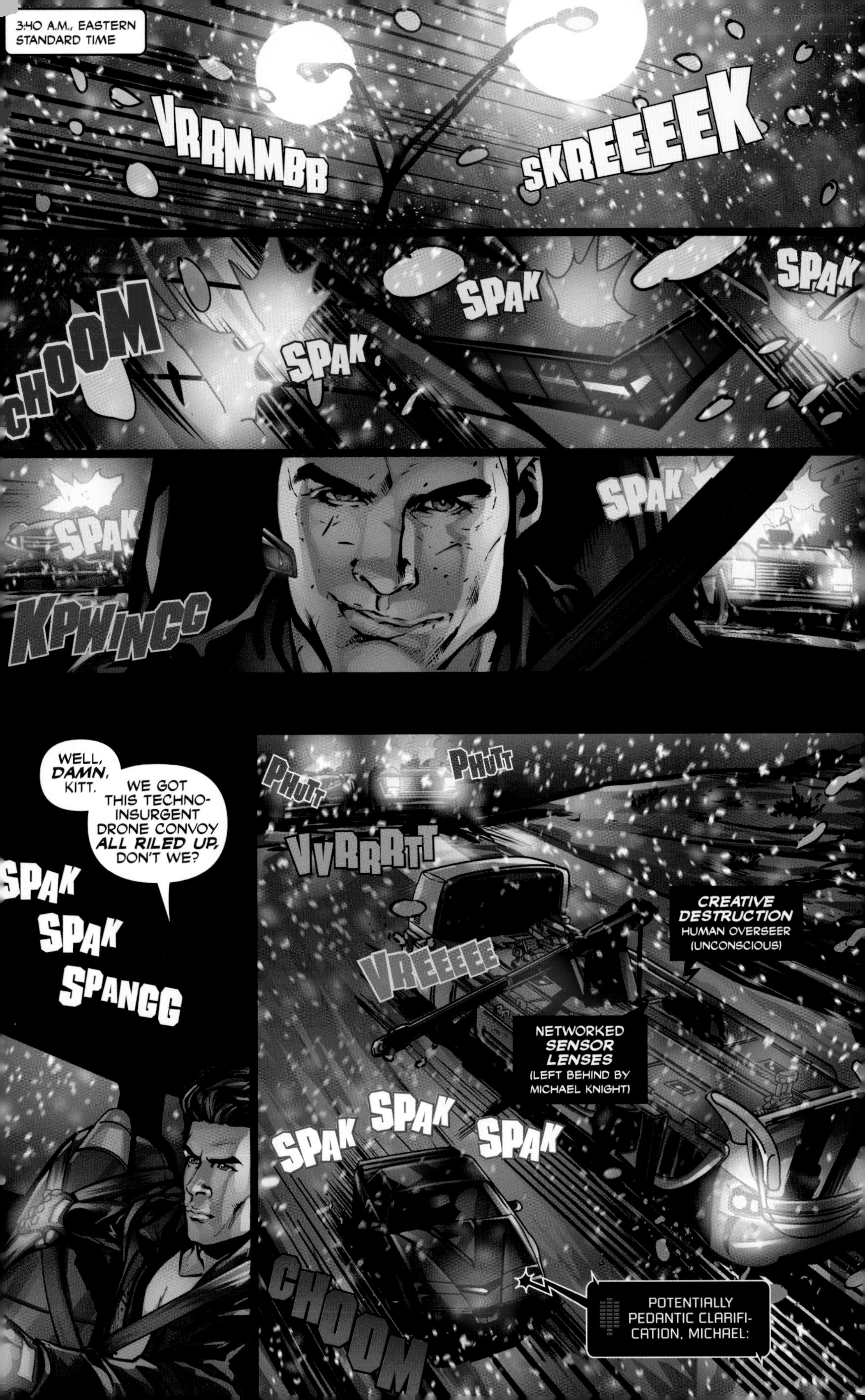
3:40 A.M., EASTERN STANDARD TIME
VRRMMBB
SKREEEEK
CHOOM
SPAK
SPAK
SPAK
SPAK
SPAK
KPWINGG
WELL, DAMN, KITT.
WE GOT THIS TECHNO-INSURGENT DRONE CONVOY ALL RILED UP, DON'T WE?
SPAK
SPAK
SPANGG
PHUTT
PHUTT
VVRRRTT
CREATIVE DESTRUCTION HUMAN OVERSEER (UNCONSCIOUS)
VREEEEE
NETWORKED SENSOR LENSES (LEFT BEHIND BY MICHAEL KNIGHT)
SPAK SPAK SPAK
CHOOM
POTENTIALLY PEDANTIC CLARIFI-CATION, MICHAEL:

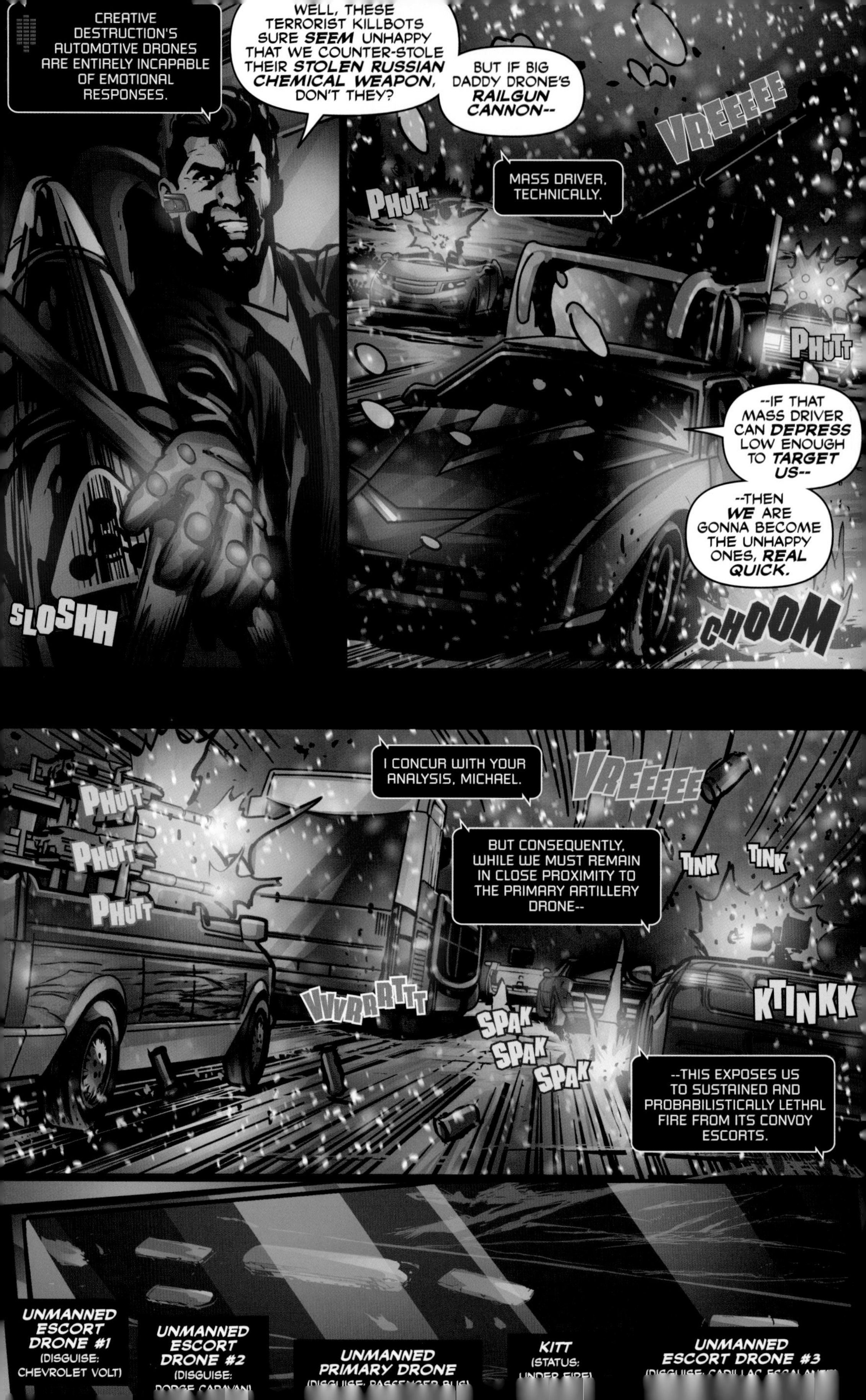
CREATIVE DESTRUCTION'S AUTOMOTIVE DRONES ARE ENTIRELY INCAPABLE OF EMOTIONAL RESPONSES.
WELL, THESE TERRORIST KILLBOTS SURE SEEM UNHAPPY THAT WE COUNTER-STOLE THEIR STOLEN RUSSIAN CHEMICAL WEAPON, DON'T THEY?
BUT IF BIG DADDY DRONE'S RAILGUN CANNON--
VREEEEE
MASS DRIVER, TECHNICALLY.
PHUTT
PHUTT
--IF THAT MASS DRIVER CAN DEPRESS LOW ENOUGH TO TARGET US--
--THEN WE ARE GONNA BECOME THE UNHAPPY ONES, REAL QUICK.
SLOSHH
CHOOM
I CONCUR WITH YOUR ANALYSIS, MICHAEL.
VREEEEE
PHUTT
PHUTT
PHUTT
BUT CONSEQUENTLY, WHILE WE MUST REMAIN IN CLOSE PROXIMITY TO THE PRIMARY ARTILLERY DRONE--
TINK
TINK
VVVRRRTTT
SPAK
SPAK
SPAK
KTINKK
--THIS EXPOSES US TO SUSTAINED AND PROBABILISTICALLY LETHAL FIRE FROM ITS CONVOY ESCORTS.
UNMANNED ESCORT DRONE #1 (DISGUISE: CHEVROLET VOLT)
UNMANNED ESCORT DRONE #2 (DISGUISE:
UNMANNED PRIMARY DRONE
KITT (STATUS:
UNMANNED ESCORT DRONE #3

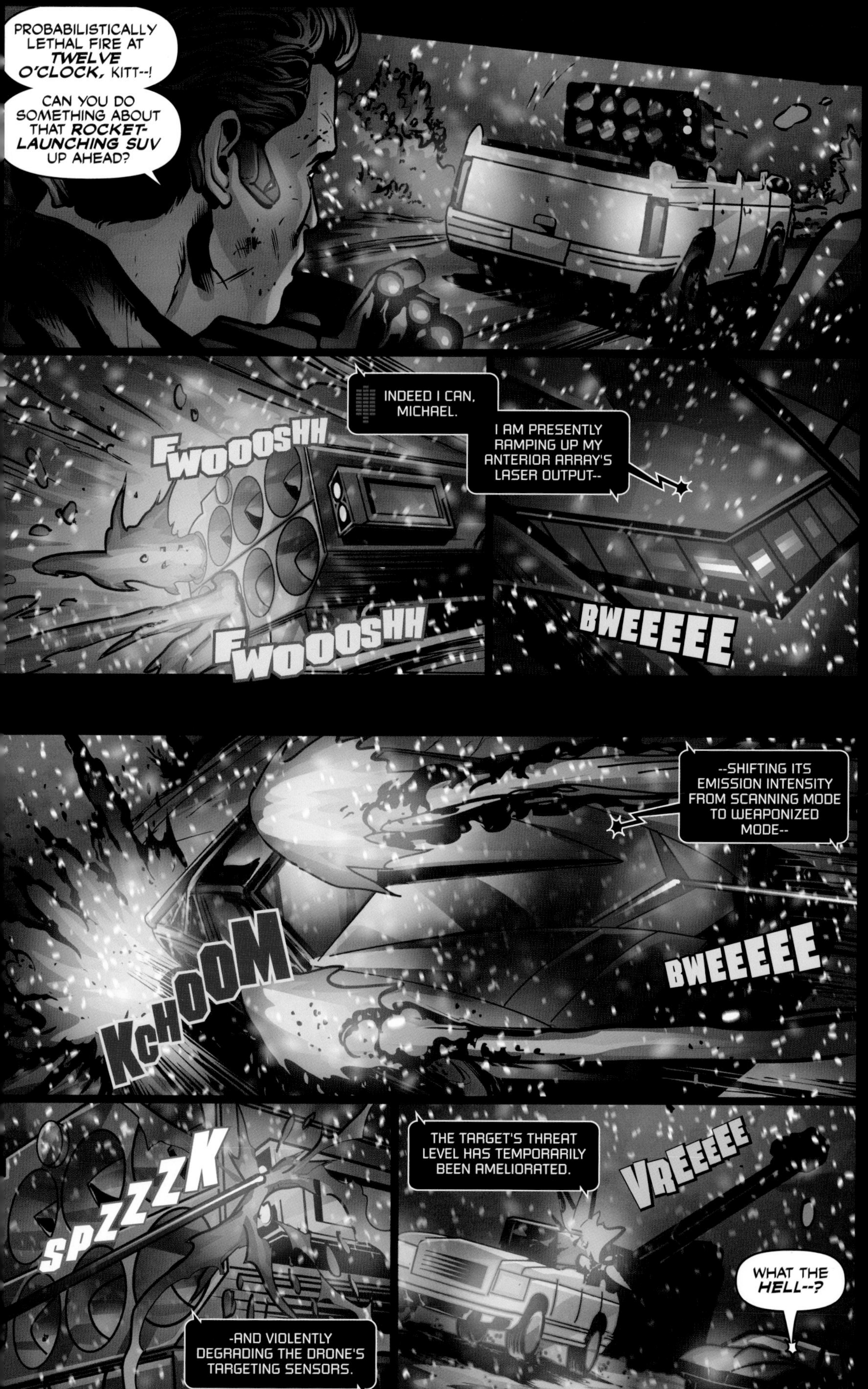
PROBABILISTICALLY LETHAL FIRE AT TWELVE O'CLOCK, KITT--!
CAN YOU DO SOMETHING ABOUT THAT ROCKET-LAUNCHING SUV UP AHEAD?
FWOOOSHH
FWOOOSHH
INDEED I CAN, MICHAEL.
I AM PRESENTLY RAMPING UP MY ANTERIOR ARRAY'S LASER OUTPUT--
BWEEEEE
--SHIFTING ITS EMISSION INTENSITY FROM SCANNING MODE TO WEAPONIZED MODE--
KCHOOM
BWEEEEE
SPZZZZK
-AND VIOLENTLY DEGRADING THE DRONE'S TARGETING SENSORS.
THE TARGET'S THREAT LEVEL HAS TEMPORARILY BEEN AMELIORATED.
VREEEEE
WHAT THE HELL--?

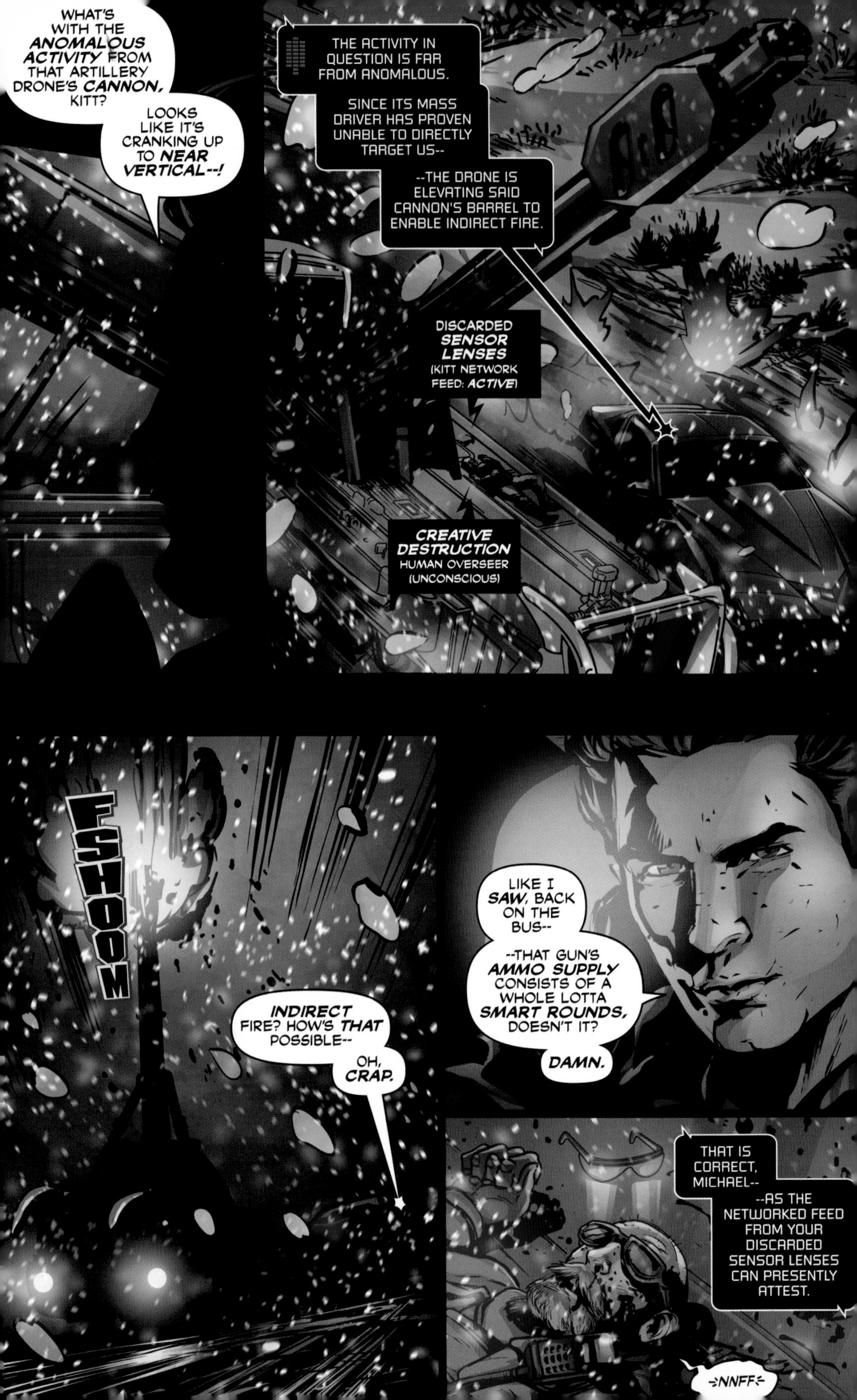

WHAT'S WITH THE ANOMALOUS ACTIVITY FROM THAT ARTILLERY DRONE'S CANNON, KITT?
LOOKS LIKE IT'S CRANKING UP TO NEAR VERTICAL--!
THE ACTIVITY IN QUESTION IS FAR FROM ANOMALOUS.
SINCE ITS MASS DRIVER HAS PROVEN UNABLE TO DIRECTLY TARGET US--
--THE DRONE IS ELEVATING SAID CANNON'S BARREL TO ENABLE INDIRECT FIRE.
DISCARDED SENSOR LENSES (KITT NETWORK FEED: ACTIVE)
CREATIVE DESTRUCTION HUMAN OVERSEER (UNCONSCIOUS)
FSHOOM
INDIRECT FIRE? HOW'S THAT POSSIBLE--
OH, CRAP.
LIKE I SAW, BACK ON THE BUS--
--THAT GUN'S AMMO SUPPLY CONSISTS OF A WHOLE LOTTA SMART ROUNDS, DOESN'T IT?
DAMN.
THAT IS CORRECT, MICHAEL--
--AS THE NETWORKED FEED FROM YOUR DISCARDED SENSOR LENSES CAN PRESENTLY ATTEST.
NNFF

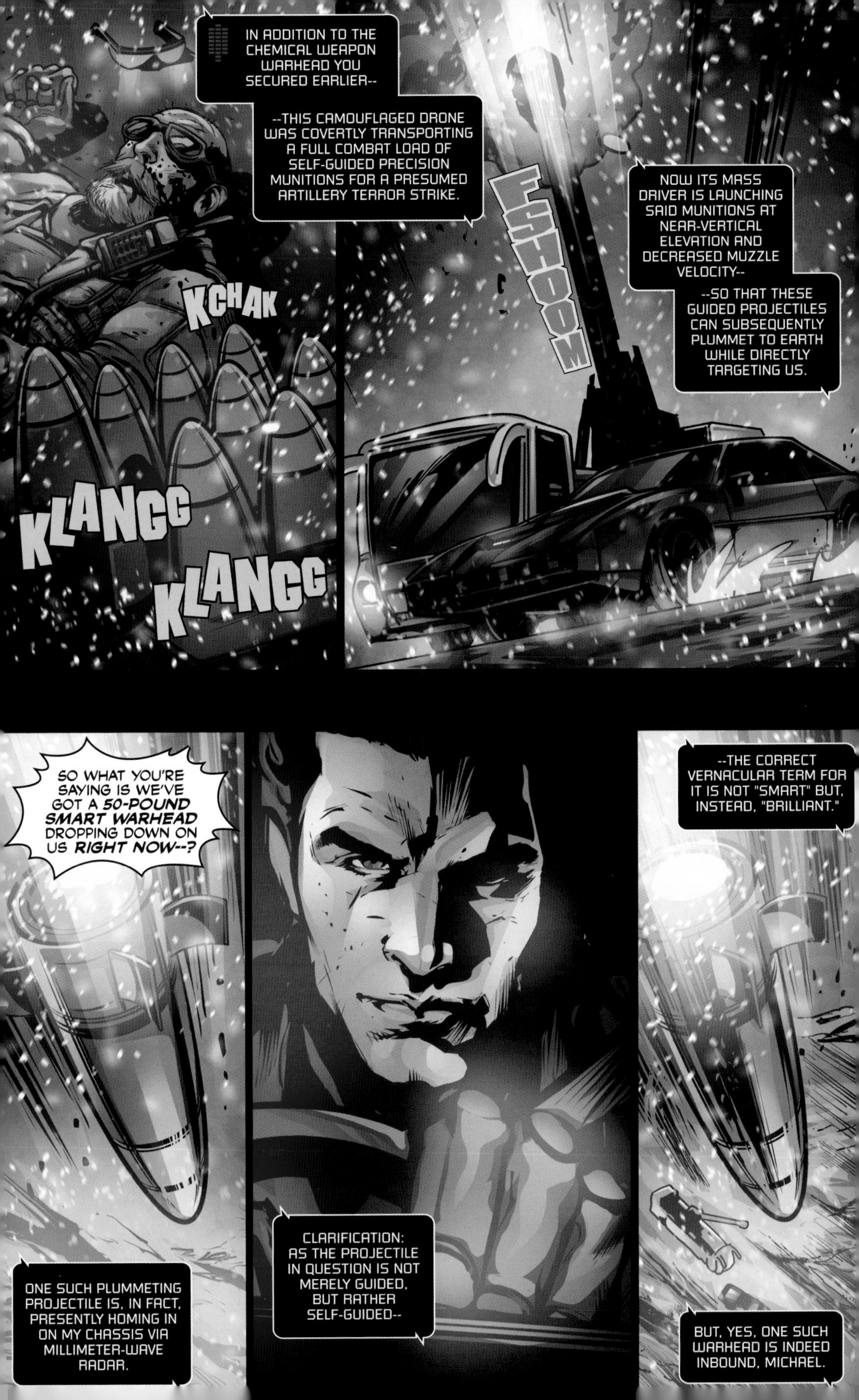
IN ADDITION TO THE CHEMICAL WEAPON WARHEAD YOU SECURED EARLIER--
--THIS CAMOUFLAGED DRONE WAS COVERTLY TRANSPORTING A FULL COMBAT LOAD OF SELF-GUIDED PRECISION MUNITIONS FOR A PRESUMED ARTILLERY TERROR STRIKE.
KCHAK
KLANGG
KLANGG
FSHOOM
NOW ITS MASS DRIVER IS LAUNCHING SAID MUNITIONS AT NEAR-VERTICAL ELEVATION AND DECREASED MUZZLE VELOCITY--
--SO THAT THESE GUIDED PROJECTILES CAN SUBSEQUENTLY PLUMMET TO EARTH WHILE DIRECTLY TARGETING US.
SO WHAT YOU'RE SAYING IS WE'VE GOT A ***50-POUND SMART WARHEAD*** DROPPING DOWN ON US ***RIGHT NOW--?***
ONE SUCH PLUMMETING PROJECTILE IS, IN FACT, PRESENTLY HOMING IN ON MY CHASSIS VIA MILLIMETER-WAVE RADAR.
CLARIFICATION: AS THE PROJECTILE IN QUESTION IS NOT MERELY GUIDED, BUT RATHER SELF-GUIDED--
--THE CORRECT VERNACULAR TERM FOR IT IS NOT "SMART" BUT, INSTEAD, "BRILLIANT."
BUT, YES, ONE SUCH WARHEAD IS INDEED INBOUND, MICHAEL.

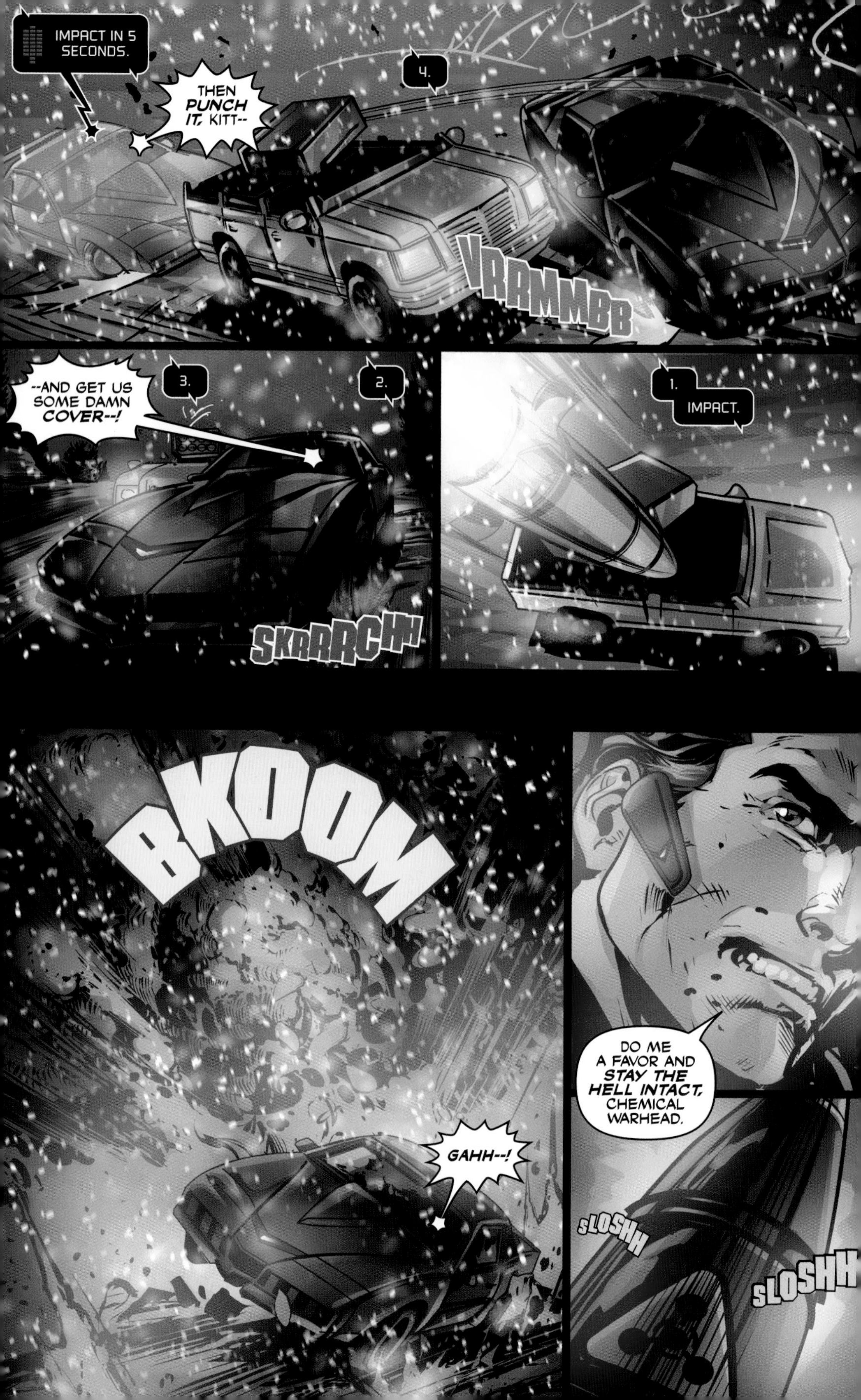

IMPACT IN 5 SECONDS.
THEN PUNCH IT, KITT--
4.
VRRMMBB
--AND GET US SOME DAMN COVER--!
3.
2.
SKRRRCHH
1.
IMPACT.
BKOOM
GAHH--!
DO ME A FAVOR AND STAY THE HELL INTACT, CHEMICAL WARHEAD.
SLOSHH
SLOSHH

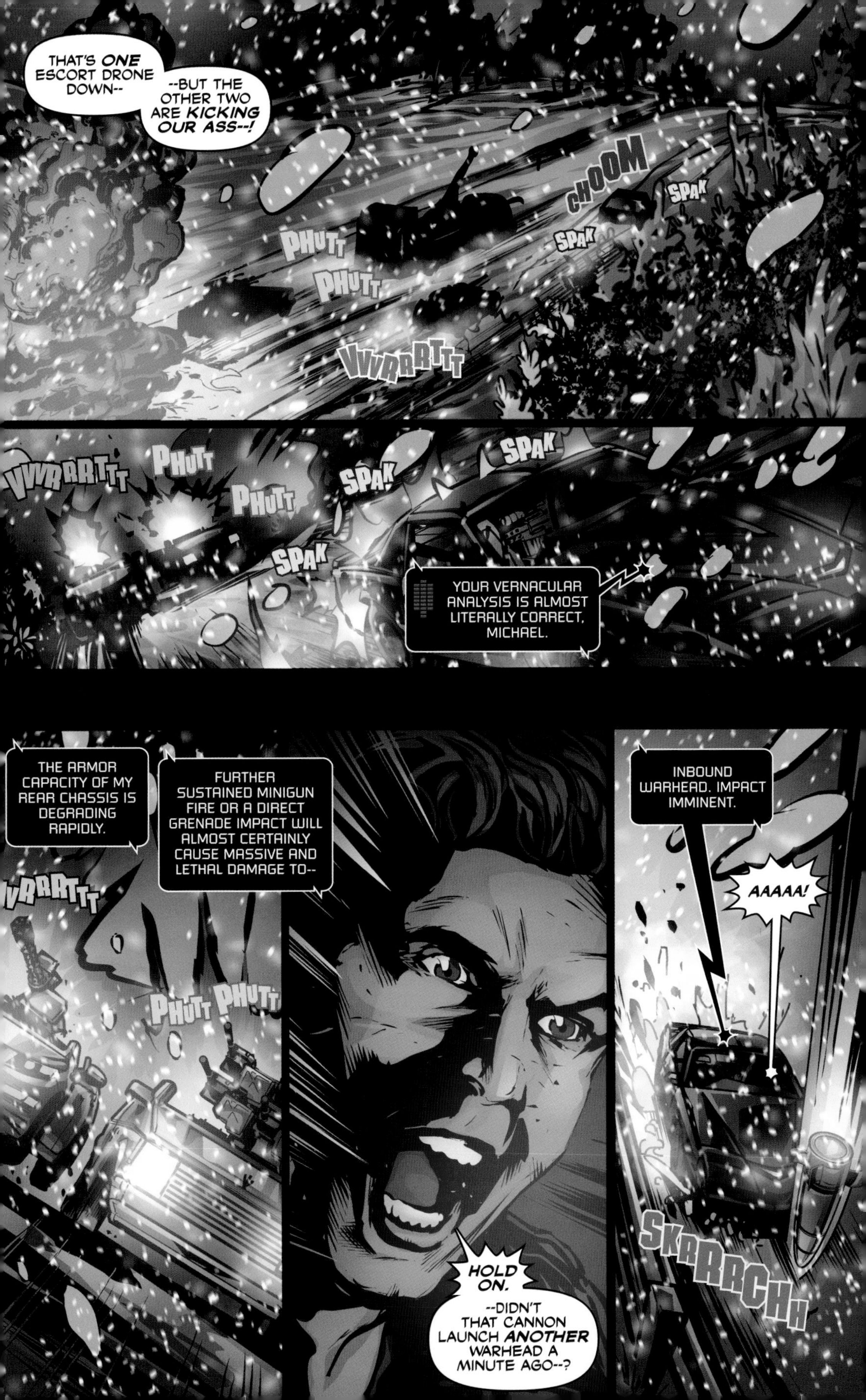
THAT'S ONE ESCORT DRONE DOWN--
--BUT THE OTHER TWO ARE KICKING OUR ASS--!
CHOOM
SPAK
SPAK
PHUTT
PHUTT
VVVRRRTTT
VVVRRRTTT
PHUTT
PHUTT
SPAK
SPAK
SPAK
YOUR VERNACULAR ANALYSIS IS ALMOST LITERALLY CORRECT, MICHAEL.
THE ARMOR CAPACITY OF MY REAR CHASSIS IS DEGRADING RAPIDLY.
FURTHER SUSTAINED MINIGUN FIRE OR A DIRECT GRENADE IMPACT WILL ALMOST CERTAINLY CAUSE MASSIVE AND LETHAL DAMAGE TO--
VRRRTTT
PHUTT PHUTT
HOLD ON.
--DIDN'T THAT CANNON LAUNCH ANOTHER WARHEAD A MINUTE AGO--?
INBOUND WARHEAD. IMPACT IMMINENT.
AAAAA!
SKRRRCHH

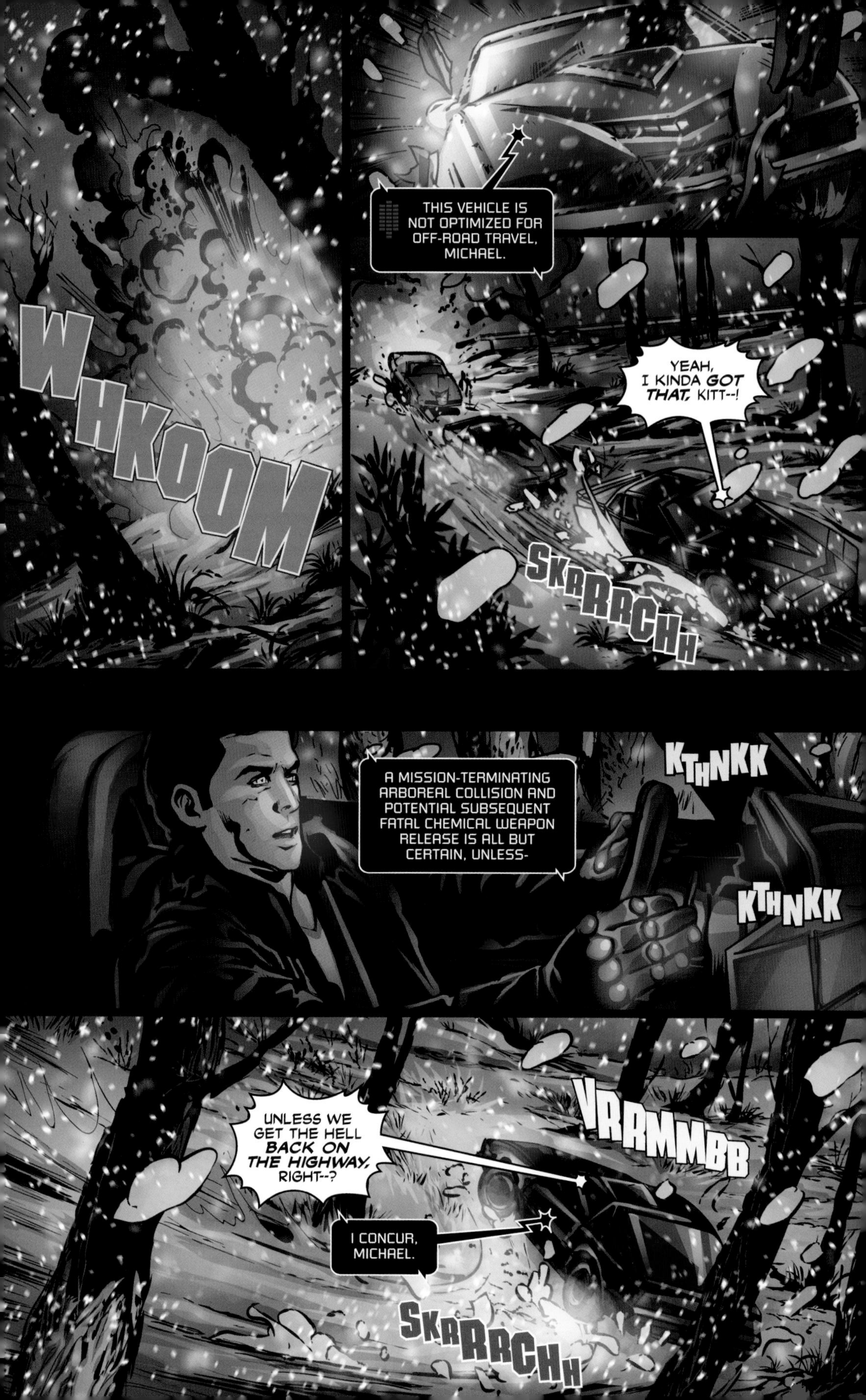
WHKOOM
THIS VEHICLE IS NOT OPTIMIZED FOR OFF-ROAD TRAVEL, MICHAEL.
YEAH, I KINDA GOT THAT, KITT--!
SKRRRCHH
A MISSION-TERMINATING ARBOREAL COLLISION AND POTENTIAL SUBSEQUENT FATAL CHEMICAL WEAPON RELEASE IS ALL BUT CERTAIN, UNLESS-
KTHNKK
KTHNKK
UNLESS WE GET THE HELL BACK ON THE HIGHWAY, RIGHT--?
VRRMMBB
I CONCUR, MICHAEL.
SKRRRCHH

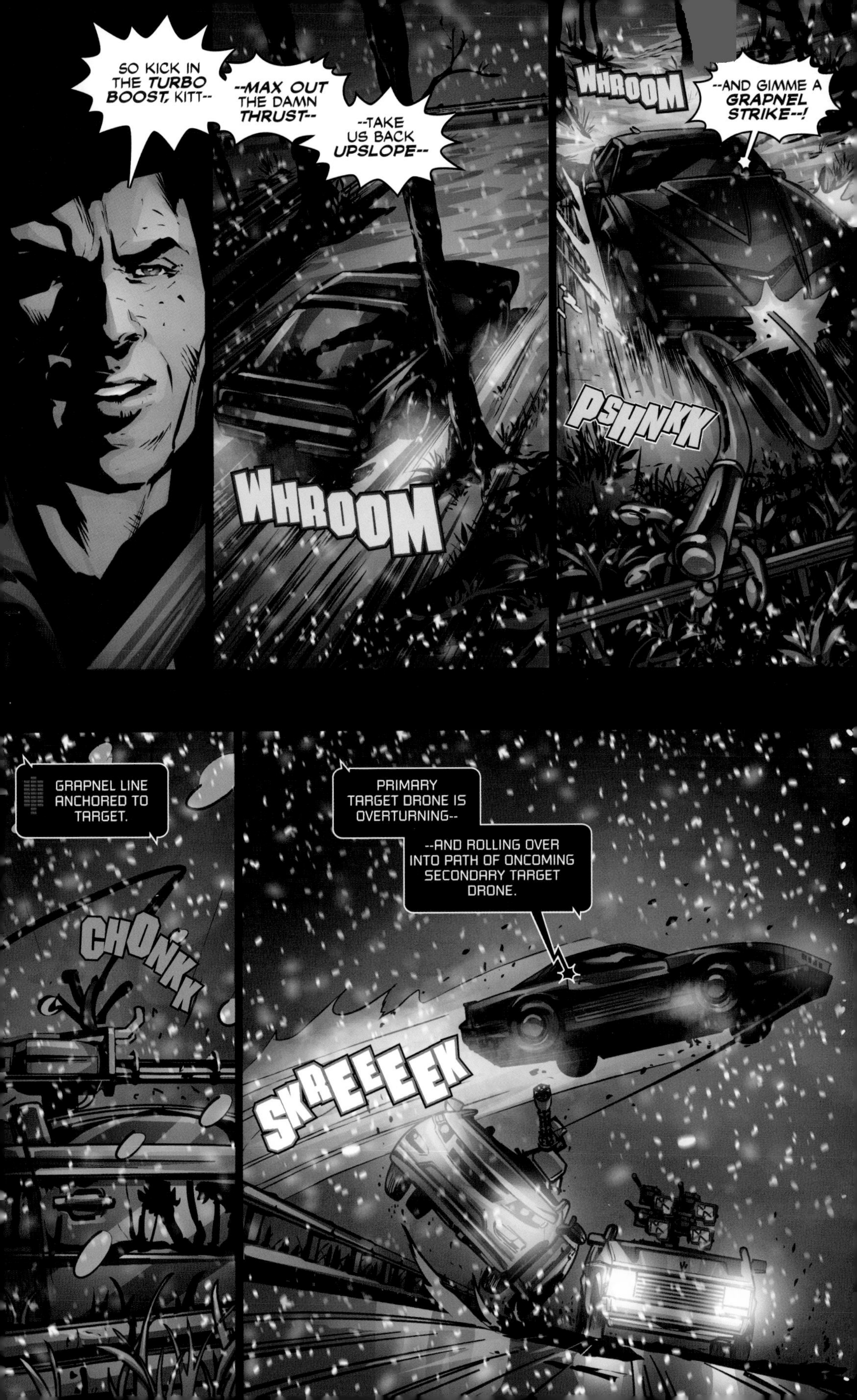
SO KICK IN THE TURBO BOOST, KITT--
--MAX OUT THE DAMN THRUST--
--TAKE US BACK UPSLOPE--
WHROOM
WHROOM
--AND GIMME A GRAPNEL STRIKE--!
PSHNKK
GRAPNEL LINE ANCHORED TO TARGET.
CHONKK
PRIMARY TARGET DRONE IS OVERTURNING--
--AND ROLLING OVER INTO PATH OF ONCOMING SECONDARY TARGET DRONE.
SKREEEEEK

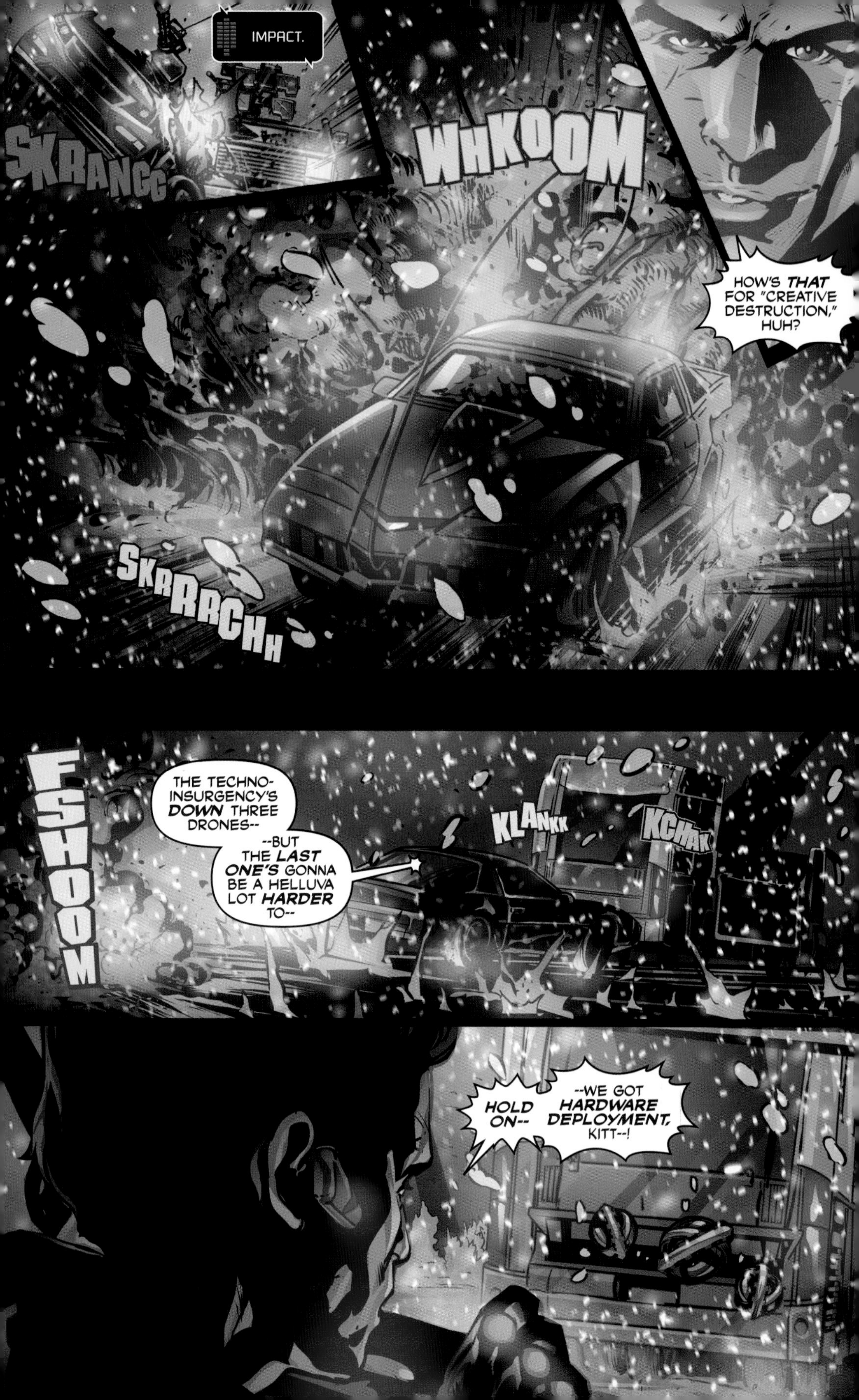
IMPACT.
SKRANGG
WHKOOM
HOW'S THAT FOR "CREATIVE DESTRUCTION," HUH?
SKRRRCHH
FSHOOM
THE TECHNO-INSURGENCY'S DOWN THREE DRONES--
--BUT THE LAST ONE'S GONNA BE A HELLUVA LOT HARDER TO--
KLANKK
KCHAK
HOLD ON--
--WE GOT HARDWARE DEPLOYMENT, KITT--!

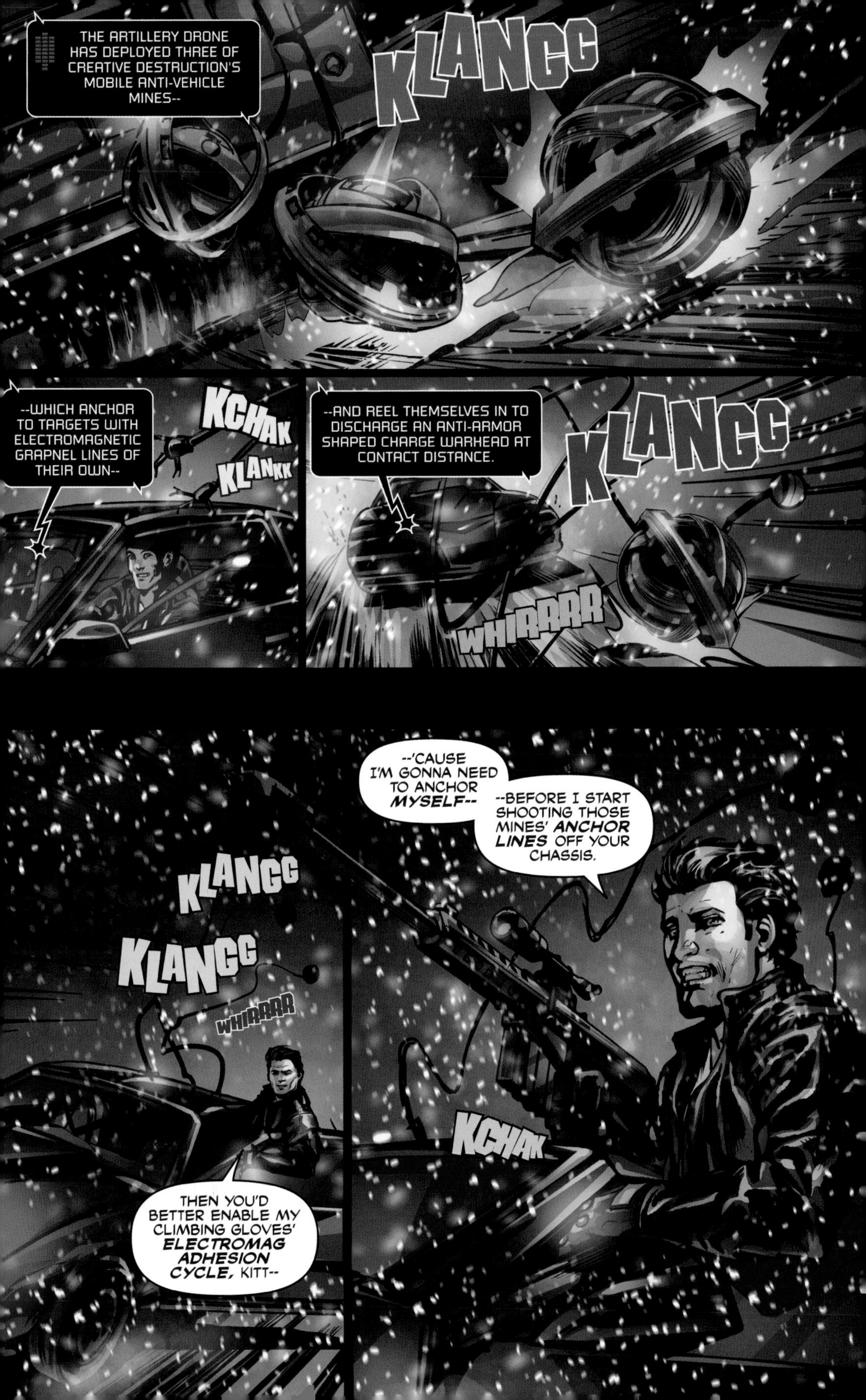
THE ARTILLERY DRONE HAS DEPLOYED THREE OF CREATIVE DESTRUCTION'S MOBILE ANTI-VEHICLE MINES--
KLANGG
--WHICH ANCHOR TO TARGETS WITH ELECTROMAGNETIC GRAPNEL LINES OF THEIR OWN--
KCHAK
KLANKK
--AND REEL THEMSELVES IN TO DISCHARGE AN ANTI-ARMOR SHAPED CHARGE WARHEAD AT CONTACT DISTANCE.
KLANGG
WHIRRRR
KLANGG
KLANGG
WHIRRRR
THEN YOU'D BETTER ENABLE MY CLIMBING GLOVES' ELECTROMAG ADHESION CYCLE, KITT--
--'CAUSE I'M GONNA NEED TO ANCHOR MYSELF--
--BEFORE I START SHOOTING THOSE MINES' ANCHOR LINES OFF YOUR CHASSIS.
KCHAK

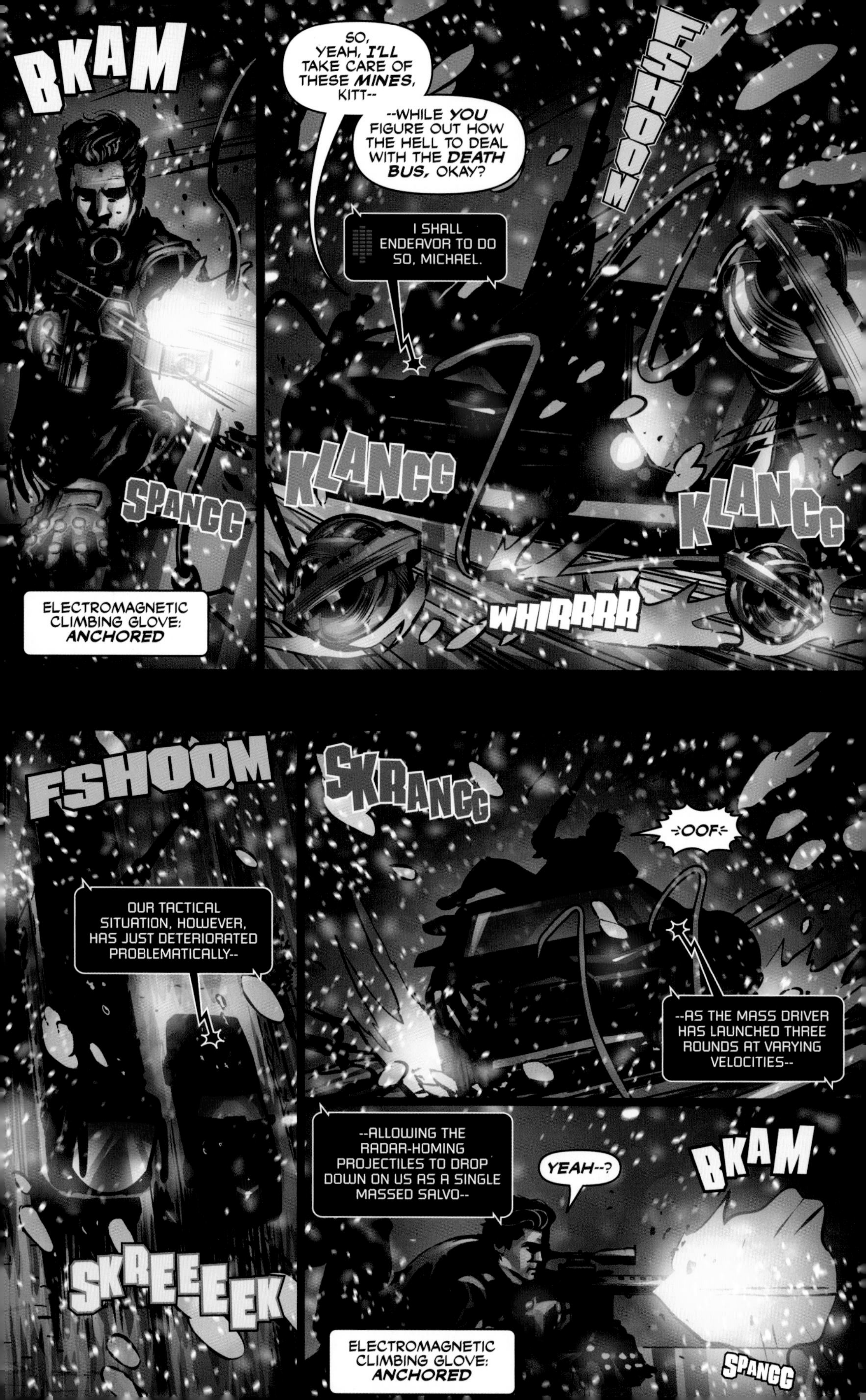
BKAM
SPANGG
ELECTROMAGNETIC CLIMBING GLOVE: ANCHORED
SO, YEAH, I'LL TAKE CARE OF THESE MINES, KITT--
--WHILE YOU FIGURE OUT HOW THE HELL TO DEAL WITH THE DEATH BUS, OKAY?
I SHALL ENDEAVOR TO DO SO, MICHAEL.
FSHOOM
KLANGG
KLANGG
WHIRRRR
FSHOOM
OUR TACTICAL SITUATION, HOWEVER, HAS JUST DETERIORATED PROBLEMATICALLY--
SKREEEEEK
SKRANGG
OOF
--AS THE MASS DRIVER HAS LAUNCHED THREE ROUNDS AT VARYING VELOCITIES--
--ALLOWING THE RADAR-HOMING PROJECTILES TO DROP DOWN ON US AS A SINGLE MASSED SALVO--
YEAH--?
BKAM
ELECTROMAGNETIC CLIMBING GLOVE: ANCHORED
SPANGG

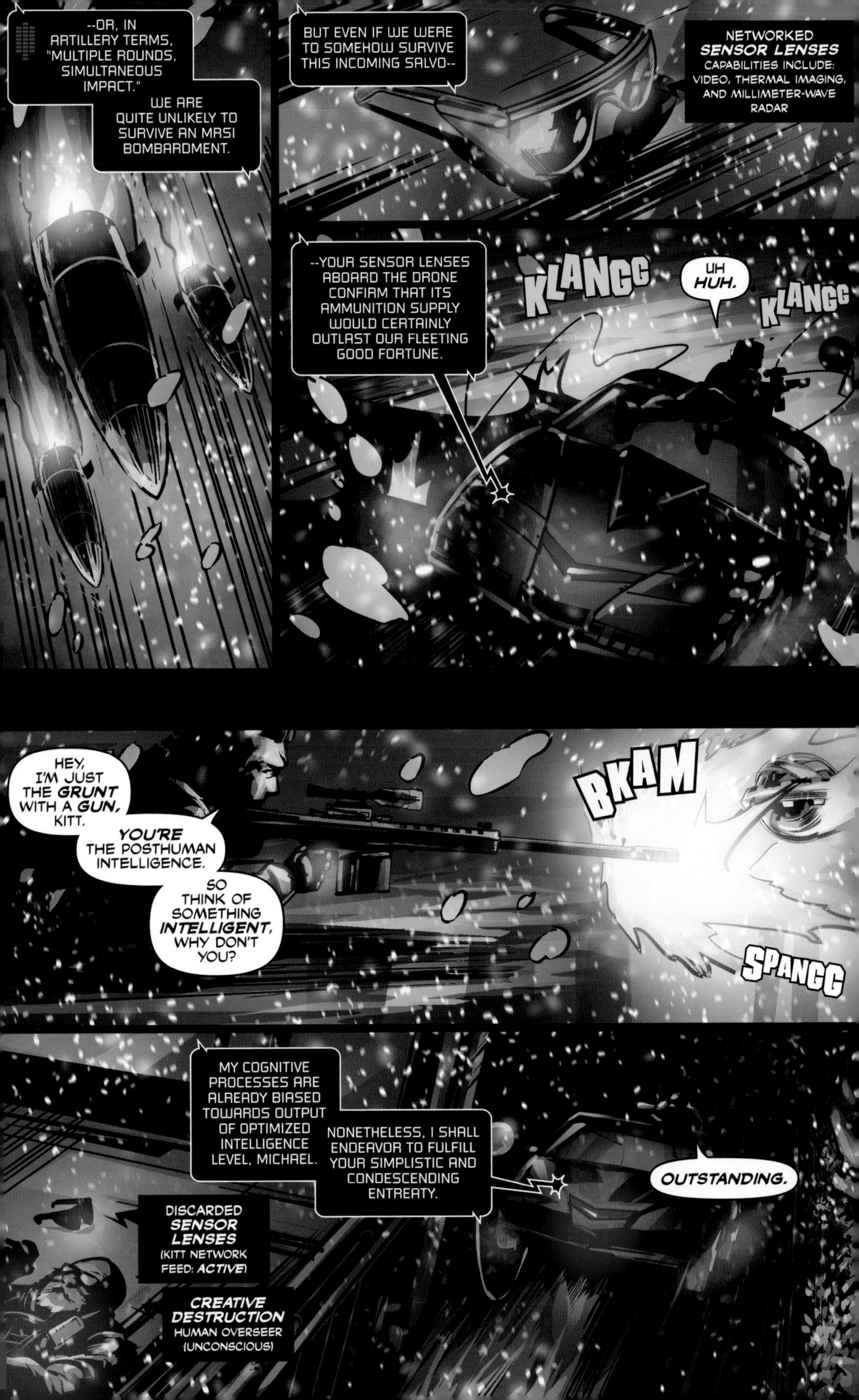
--OR, IN ARTILLERY TERMS, "MULTIPLE ROUNDS, SIMULTANEOUS IMPACT."
WE ARE QUITE UNLIKELY TO SURVIVE AN MRSI BOMBARDMENT.
BUT EVEN IF WE WERE TO SOMEHOW SURVIVE THIS INCOMING SALVO--
NETWORKED SENSOR LENSES CAPABILITIES INCLUDE: VIDEO, THERMAL IMAGING, AND MILLIMETER-WAVE RADAR
--YOUR SENSOR LENSES ABOARD THE DRONE CONFIRM THAT ITS AMMUNITION SUPPLY WOULD CERTAINLY OUTLAST OUR FLEETING GOOD FORTUNE.
KLANGG
UH HUH.
KLANGG
HEY, I'M JUST THE GRUNT WITH A GUN, KITT.
YOU'RE THE POSTHUMAN INTELLIGENCE.
SO THINK OF SOMETHING INTELLIGENT, WHY DON'T YOU?
BKAM
SPANGG
MY COGNITIVE PROCESSES ARE ALREADY BIASED TOWARDS OUTPUT OF OPTIMIZED INTELLIGENCE LEVEL, MICHAEL.
NONETHELESS, I SHALL ENDEAVOR TO FULFILL YOUR SIMPLISTIC AND CONDESCENDING ENTREATY.
OUTSTANDING.
DISCARDED SENSOR LENSES (KITT NETWORK FEED: ACTIVE)
CREATIVE DESTRUCTION HUMAN OVERSEER (UNCONSCIOUS)

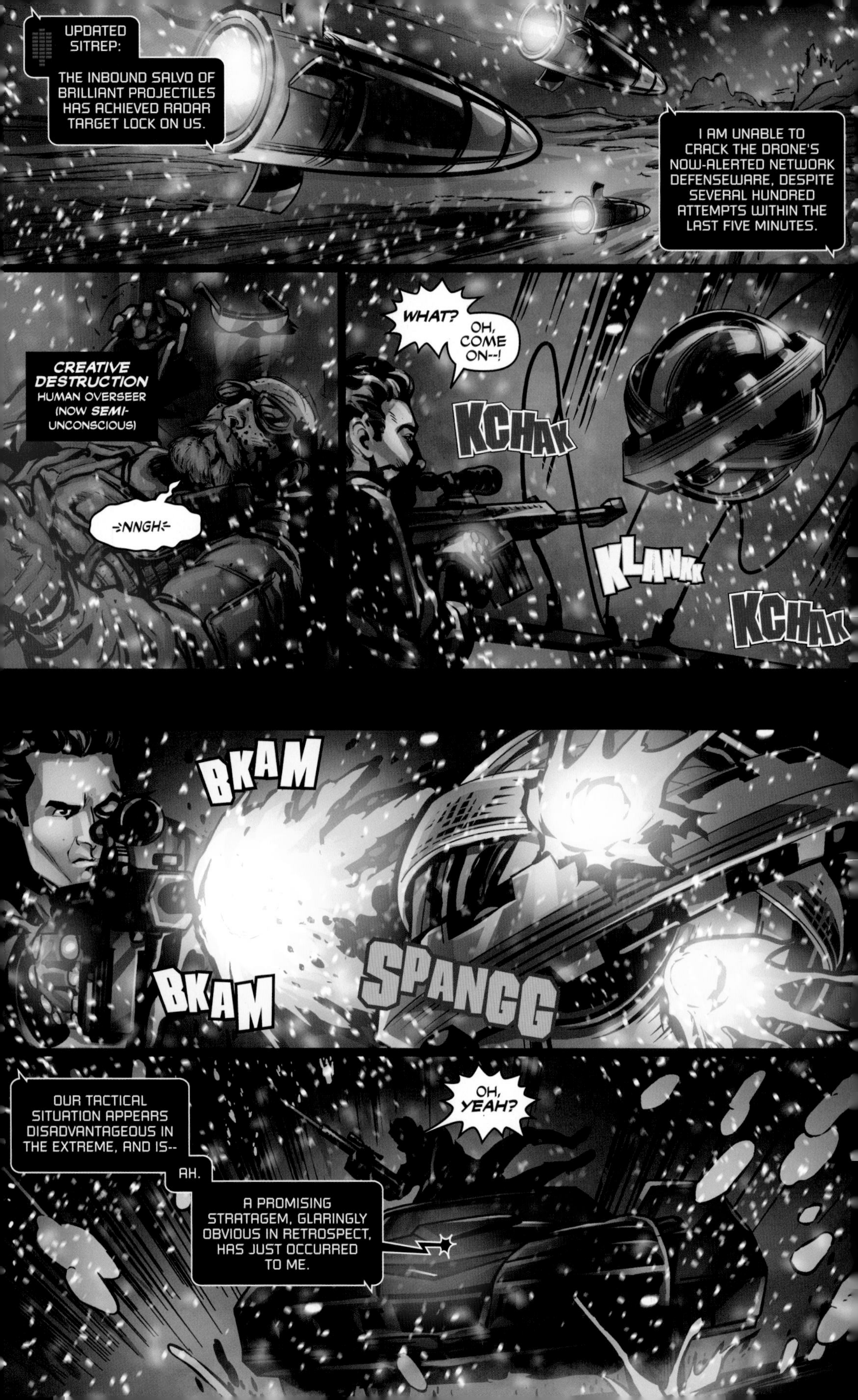
UPDATED SITREP:
THE INBOUND SALVO OF BRILLIANT PROJECTILES HAS ACHIEVED RADAR TARGET LOCK ON US.
I AM UNABLE TO CRACK THE DRONE'S NOW-ALERTED NETWORK DEFENSEWARE, DESPITE SEVERAL HUNDRED ATTEMPTS WITHIN THE LAST FIVE MINUTES.
CREATIVE DESTRUCTION HUMAN OVERSEER (NOW SEMI-UNCONSCIOUS)
=NNGH=
WHAT?
OH, COME ON--!
KCHAK
KLANKK
KCHAK
BKAM
BKAM
SPANGG
OUR TACTICAL SITUATION APPEARS DISADVANTAGEOUS IN THE EXTREME, AND IS--
AH.
OH, YEAH?
A PROMISING STRATAGEM, GLARINGLY OBVIOUS IN RETROSPECT, HAS JUST OCCURRED TO ME.

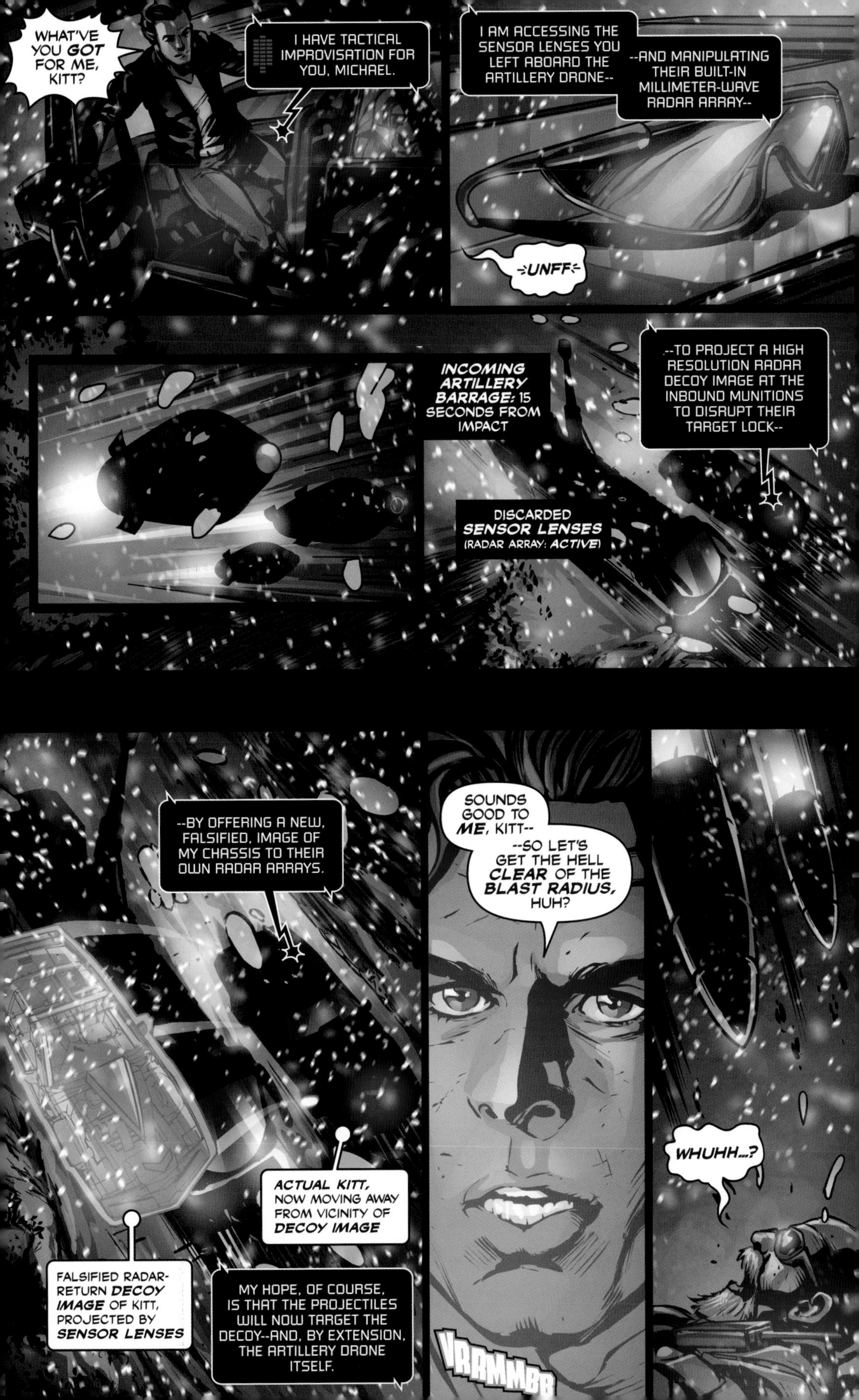
WHAT'VE YOU GOT FOR ME, KITT?
I HAVE TACTICAL IMPROVISATION FOR YOU, MICHAEL.
I AM ACCESSING THE SENSOR LENSES YOU LEFT ABOARD THE ARTILLERY DRONE--
--AND MANIPULATING THEIR BUILT-IN MILLIMETER-WAVE RADAR ARRAY--
UNFF
INCOMING ARTILLERY BARRAGE: 15 SECONDS FROM IMPACT
--TO PROJECT A HIGH RESOLUTION RADAR DECOY IMAGE AT THE INBOUND MUNITIONS TO DISRUPT THEIR TARGET LOCK--
DISCARDED SENSOR LENSES (RADAR ARRAY: ACTIVE)
--BY OFFERING A NEW, FALSIFIED, IMAGE OF MY CHASSIS TO THEIR OWN RADAR ARRAYS.
SOUNDS GOOD TO ME, KITT--
--SO LET'S GET THE HELL CLEAR OF THE BLAST RADIUS, HUH?
WHUHH...?
ACTUAL KITT, NOW MOVING AWAY FROM VICINITY OF DECOY IMAGE
FALSIFIED RADAR-RETURN DECOY IMAGE OF KITT, PROJECTED BY SENSOR LENSES
MY HOPE, OF COURSE, IS THAT THE PROJECTILES WILL NOW TARGET THE DECOY--AND, BY EXTENSION, THE ARTILLERY DRONE ITSELF.
VRRMMBB

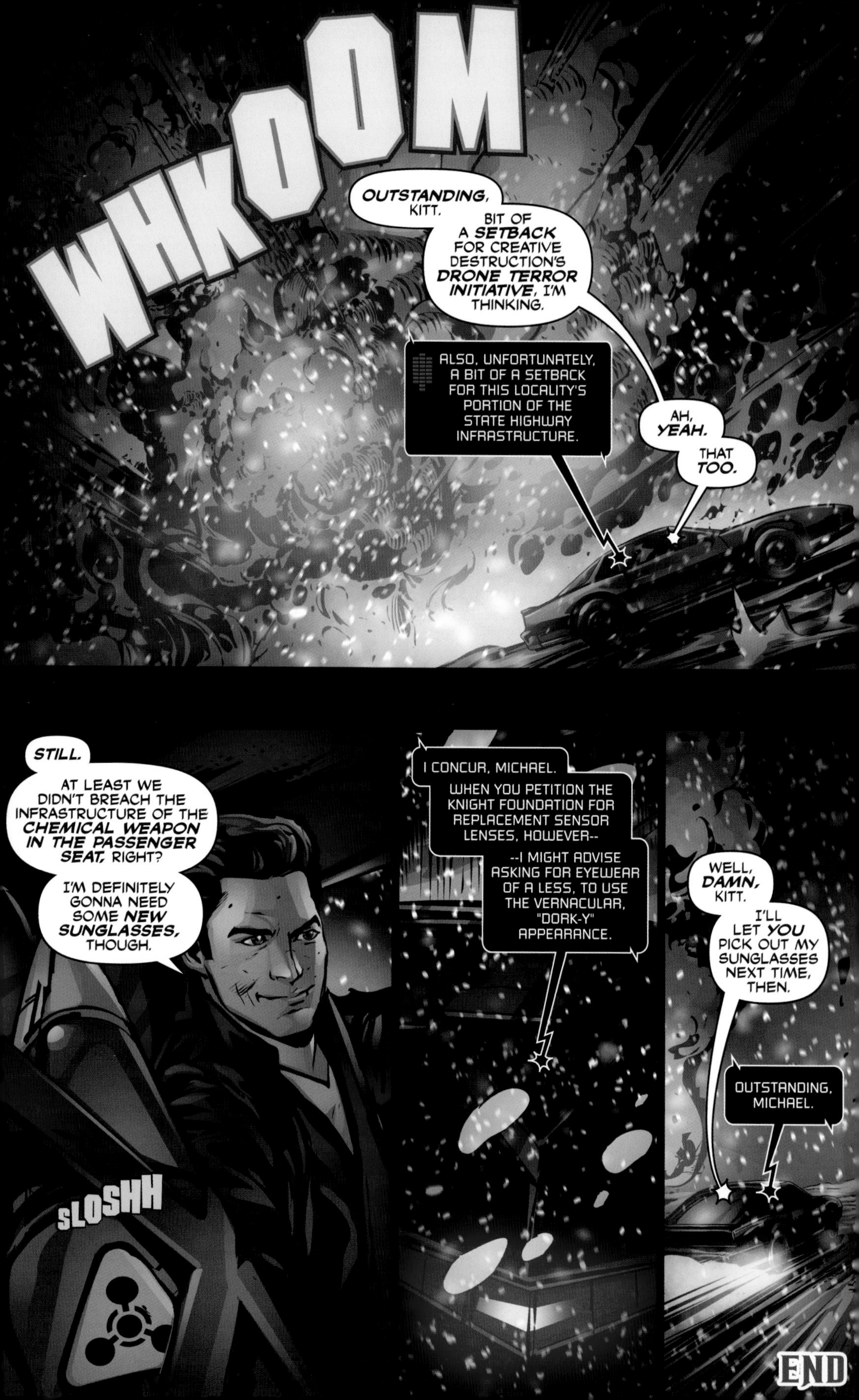
WHKOOM
OUTSTANDING, KITT.
BIT OF A SETBACK FOR CREATIVE DESTRUCTION'S DRONE TERROR INITIATIVE, I'M THINKING.
ALSO, UNFORTUNATELY, A BIT OF A SETBACK FOR THIS LOCALITY'S PORTION OF THE STATE HIGHWAY INFRASTRUCTURE.
AH, YEAH.
THAT TOO.
STILL.
AT LEAST WE DIDN'T BREACH THE INFRASTRUCTURE OF THE CHEMICAL WEAPON IN THE PASSENGER SEAT, RIGHT?
I'M DEFINITELY GONNA NEED SOME NEW SUNGLASSES, THOUGH.
SLOSHH
I CONCUR, MICHAEL.
WHEN YOU PETITION THE KNIGHT FOUNDATION FOR REPLACEMENT SENSOR LENSES, HOWEVER--
--I MIGHT ADVISE ASKING FOR EYEWEAR OF A LESS, TO USE THE VERNACULAR, "DORK-Y" APPEARANCE.
WELL, DAMN, KITT.
I'LL LET YOU PICK OUT MY SUNGLASSES NEXT TIME, THEN.
OUTSTANDING, MICHAEL.
END

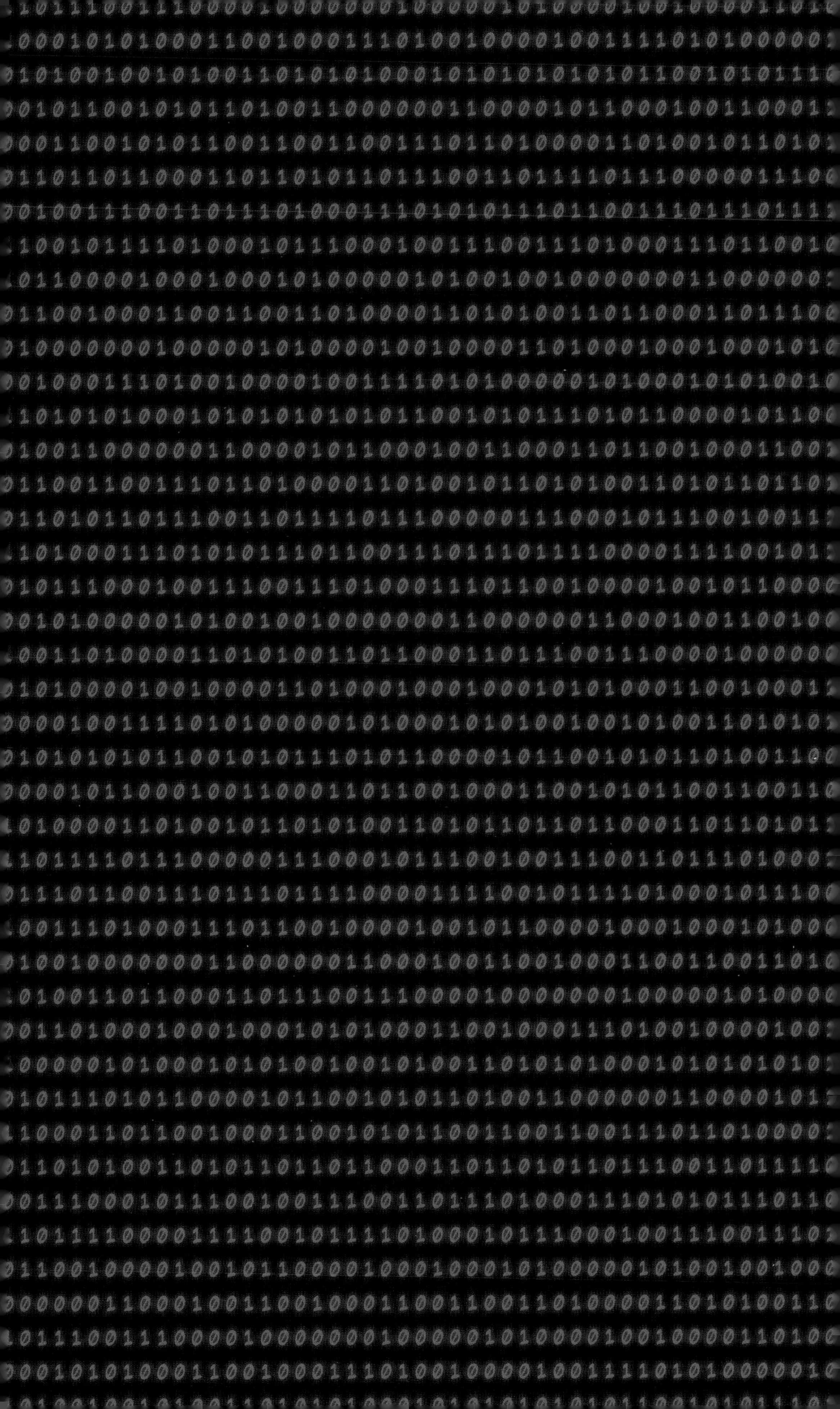

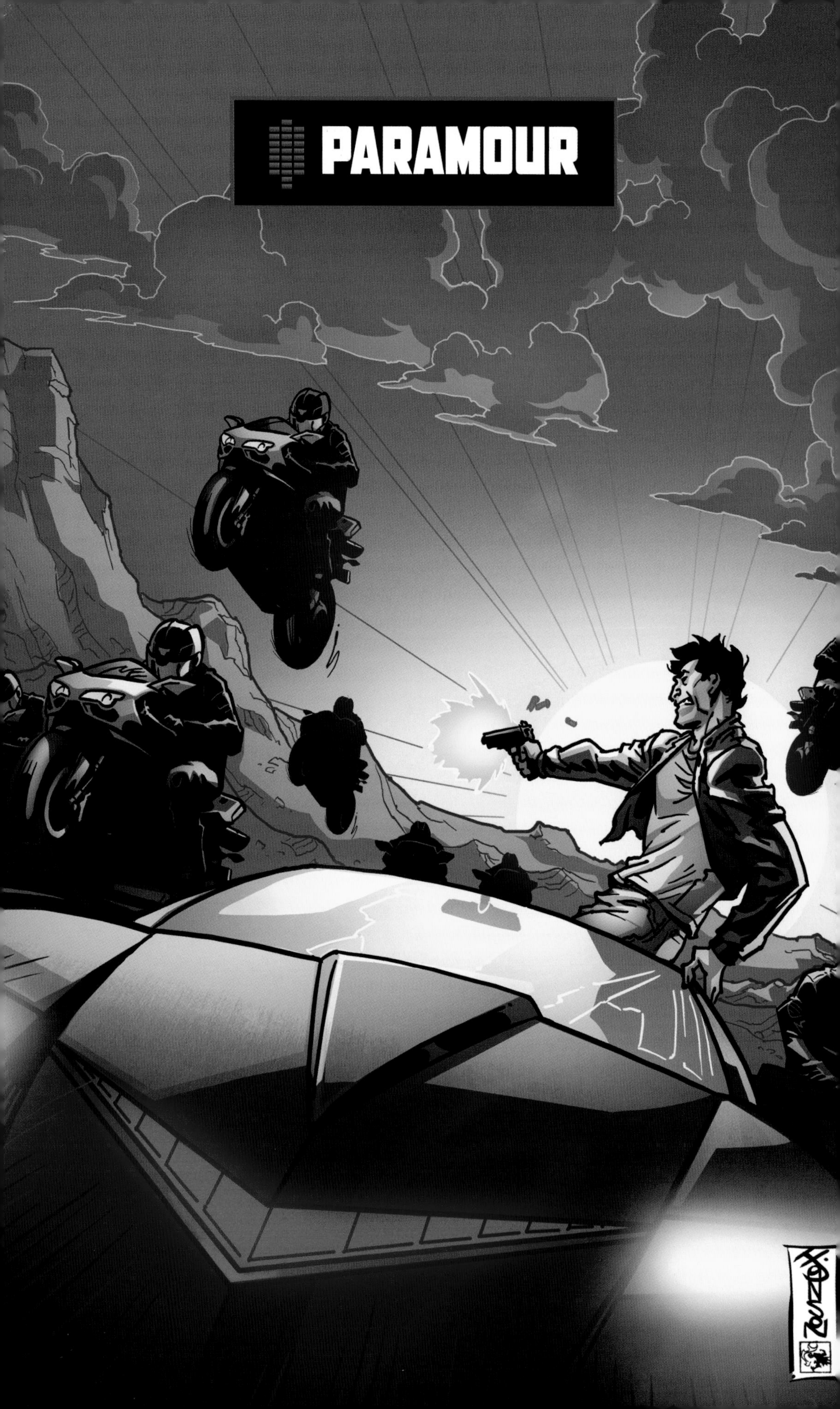
PARAMOUR

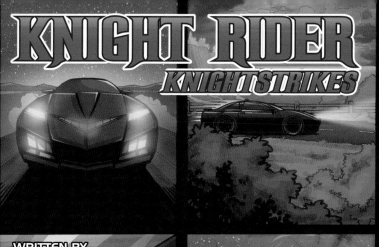

KNIGHT RIDER
KNIGHT STRIKES

WRITTEN BY
CHUCK DIXON

ILLUSTRATED BY
JASON JOHNSON

COLORED BY
SAI STUDIO

LETTERED BY
ERIKA TERRIQUEZ

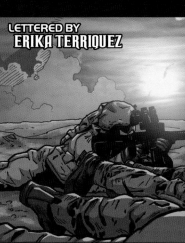

EDITED BY
SHANNON ERIC DENTON

FRONT COVER BY
JASON JOHNSON

KNIGHT RIDER CREATED BY
GLEN A. LARSON

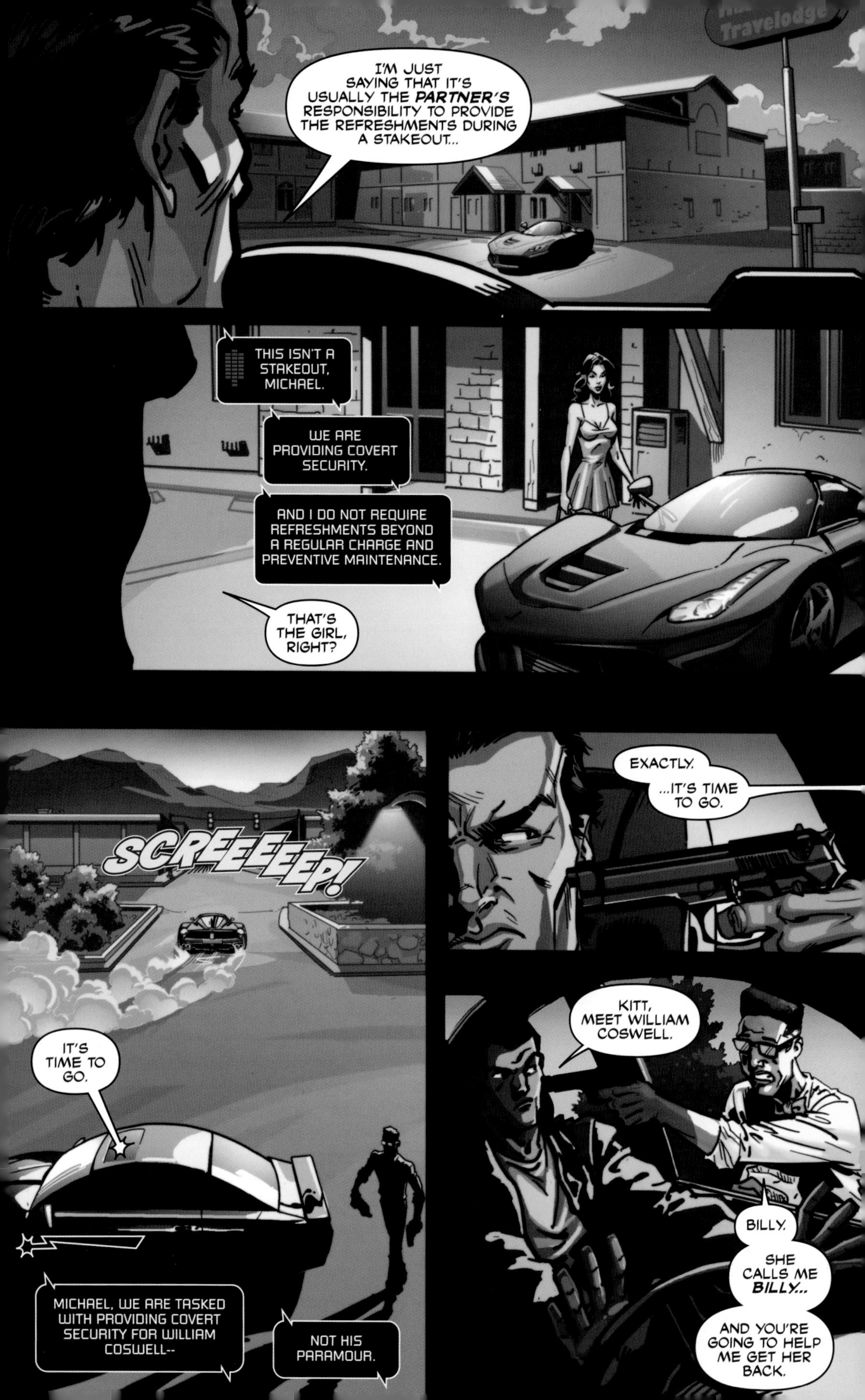

Travelodge
I'M JUST SAYING THAT IT'S USUALLY THE PARTNER'S RESPONSIBILITY TO PROVIDE THE REFRESHMENTS DURING A STAKEOUT...
THIS ISN'T A STAKEOUT, MICHAEL.
WE ARE PROVIDING COVERT SECURITY.
AND I DO NOT REQUIRE REFRESHMENTS BEYOND A REGULAR CHARGE AND PREVENTIVE MAINTENANCE.
THAT'S THE GIRL, RIGHT?
SCREEEEEP!
IT'S TIME TO GO.
MICHAEL, WE ARE TASKED WITH PROVIDING COVERT SECURITY FOR WILLIAM COSWELL--
NOT HIS PARAMOUR.
EXACTLY.
...IT'S TIME TO GO.
KITT, MEET WILLIAM COSWELL.
BILLY.
SHE CALLS ME BILLY...
AND YOU'RE GOING TO HELP ME GET HER BACK.

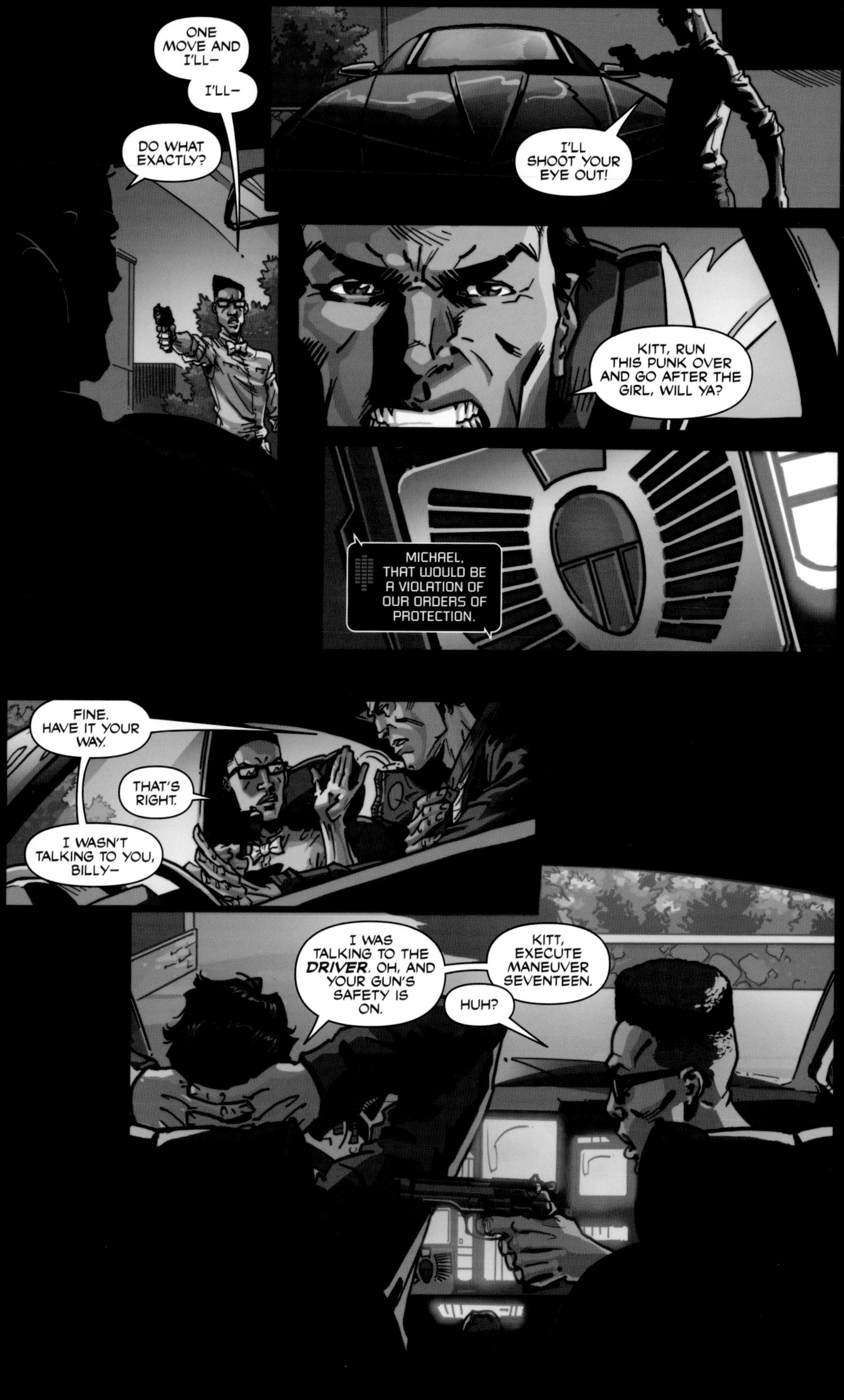

ONE MOVE AND I'LL–
I'LL–
DO WHAT EXACTLY?
I'LL SHOOT YOUR EYE OUT!
KITT, RUN THIS PUNK OVER AND GO AFTER THE GIRL, WILL YA?
MICHAEL, THAT WOULD BE A VIOLATION OF OUR ORDERS OF PROTECTION.
FINE. HAVE IT YOUR WAY.
THAT'S RIGHT.
I WASN'T TALKING TO YOU, BILLY–
I WAS TALKING TO THE **DRIVER**. OH, AND YOUR GUN'S SAFETY IS ON.
HUH?
KITT, EXECUTE MANEUVER SEVENTEEN.

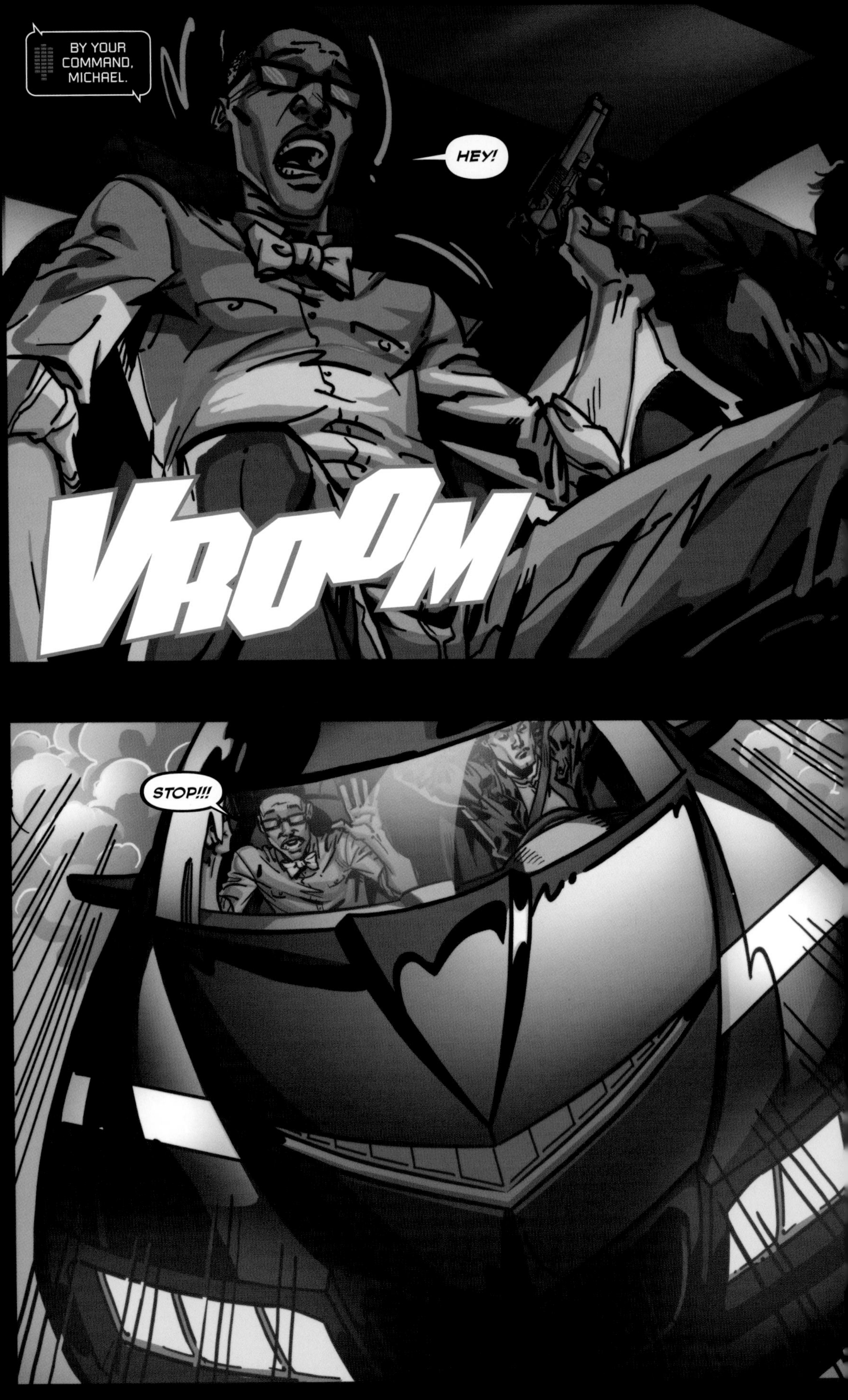

BY YOUR COMMAND, MICHAEL.
HEY!
VROOOM
STOP!!!

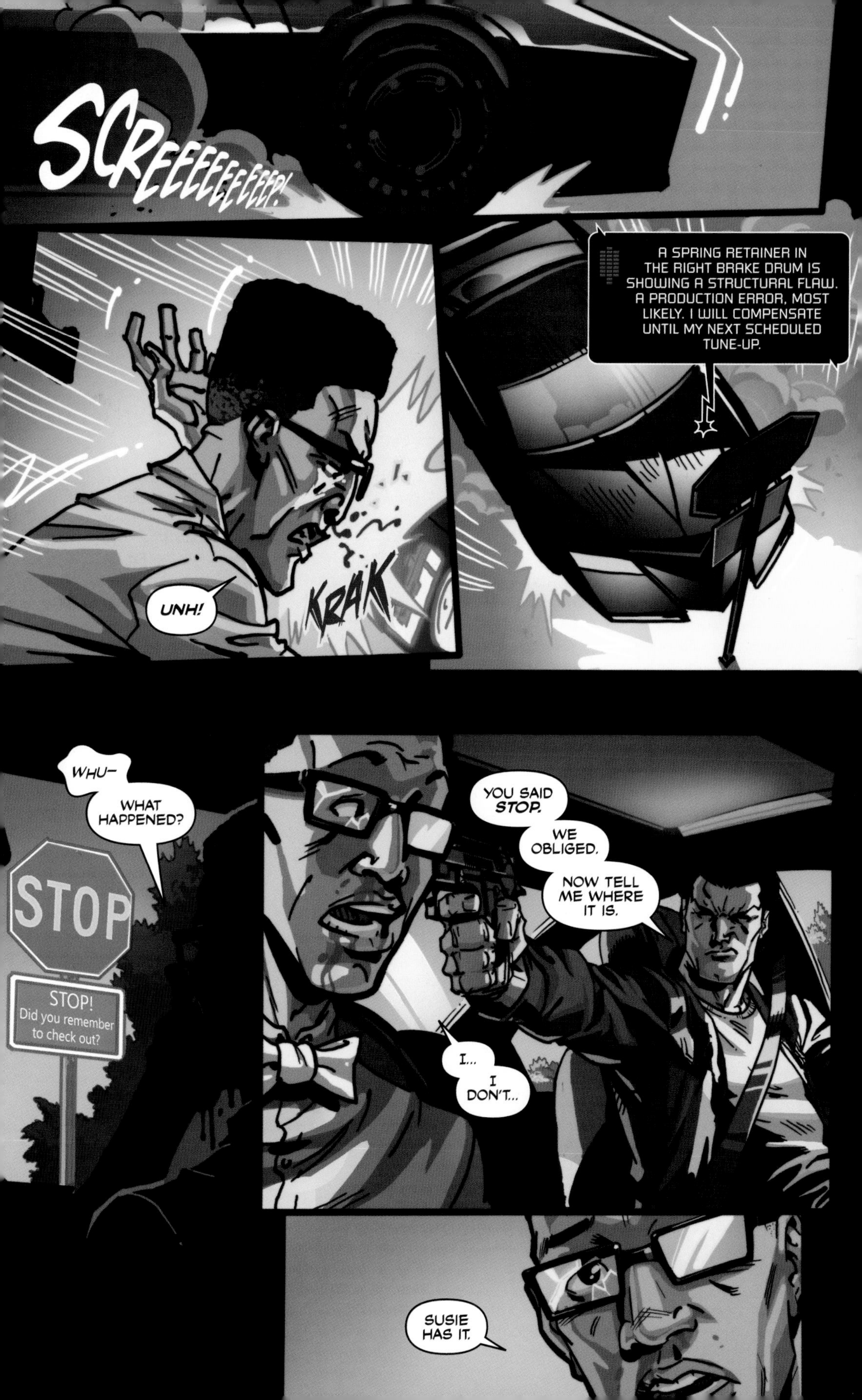
SCREEEEEEEEEEP!
UNH!
KRAK
A SPRING RETAINER IN THE RIGHT BRAKE DRUM IS SHOWING A STRUCTURAL FLAW. A PRODUCTION ERROR, MOST LIKELY. I WILL COMPENSATE UNTIL MY NEXT SCHEDULED TUNE-UP.
WHU–
WHAT HAPPENED?
STOP
STOP! Did you remember to check out?
YOU SAID STOP.
WE OBLIGED.
NOW TELL ME WHERE IT IS.
I...
I DON'T...
SUSIE HAS IT.

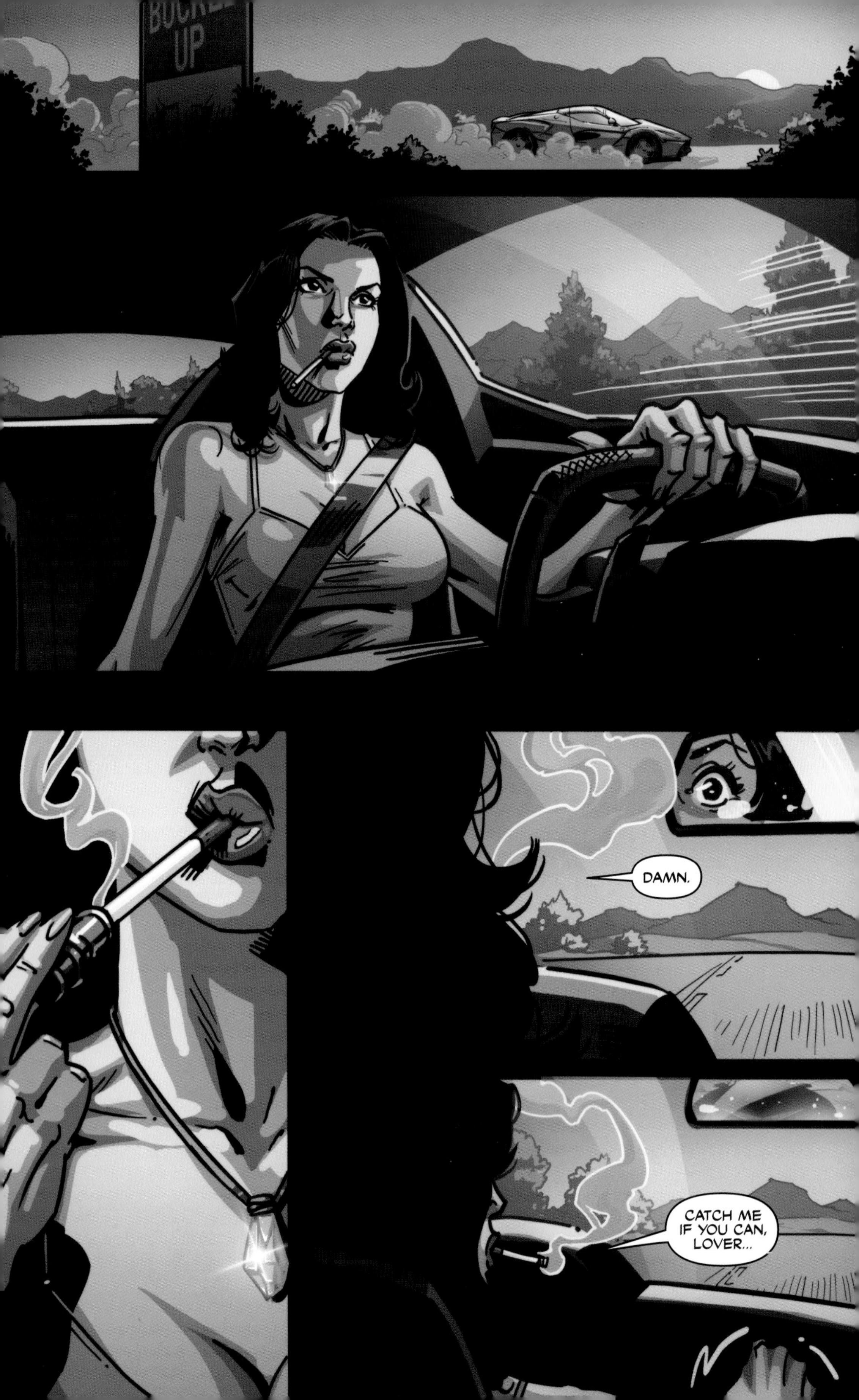
BUCKLE UP
DAMN.
CATCH ME IF YOU CAN, LOVER...

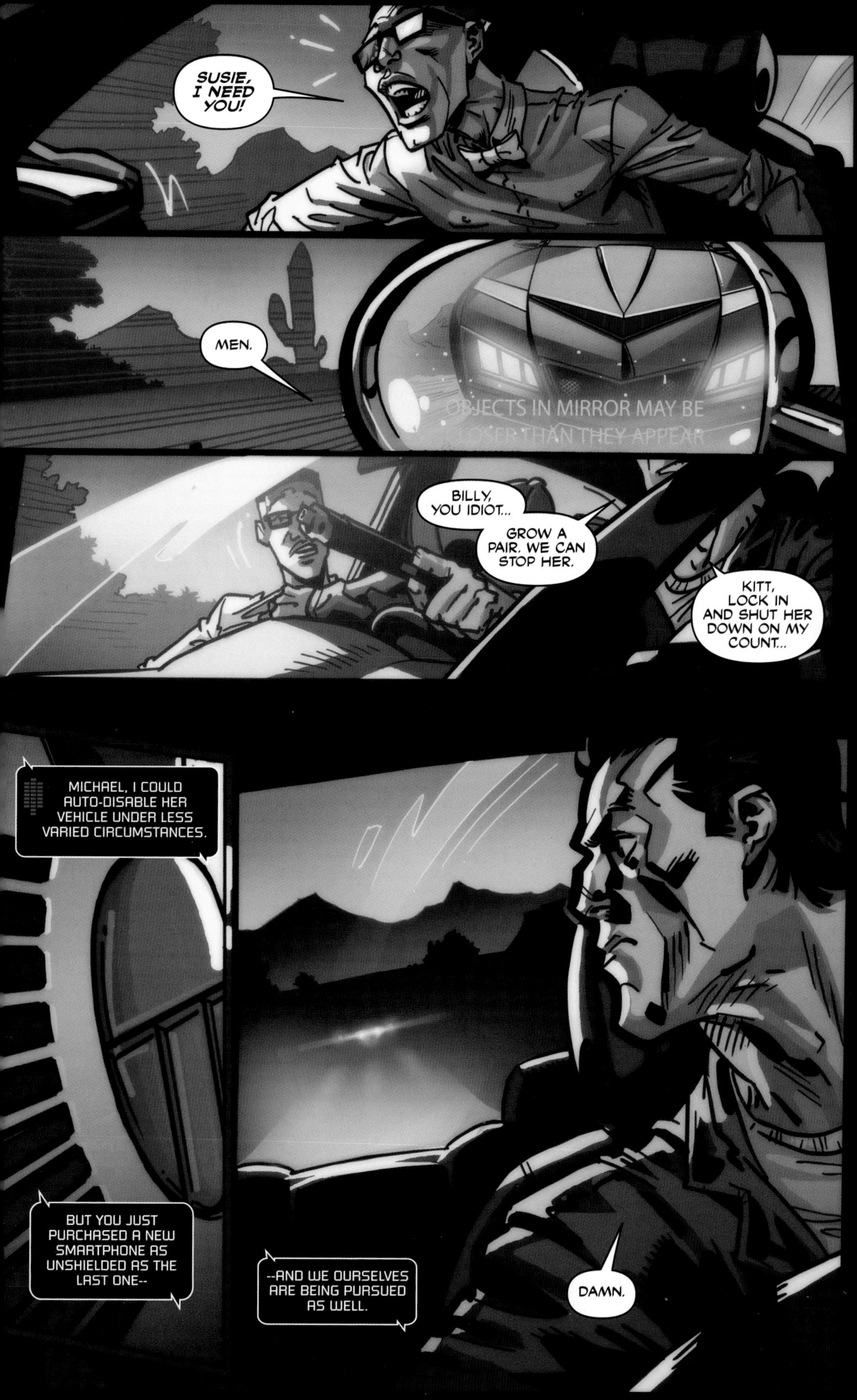
SUSIE, I NEED YOU!
MEN.
OBJECTS IN MIRROR MAY BE CLOSER THAN THEY APPEAR
BILLY, YOU IDIOT...
GROW A PAIR. WE CAN STOP HER.
KITT, LOCK IN AND SHUT HER DOWN ON MY COUNT...
MICHAEL, I COULD AUTO-DISABLE HER VEHICLE UNDER LESS VARIED CIRCUMSTANCES.
BUT YOU JUST PURCHASED A NEW SMARTPHONE AS UNSHIELDED AS THE LAST ONE--
--AND WE OURSELVES ARE BEING PURSUED AS WELL.
DAMN.

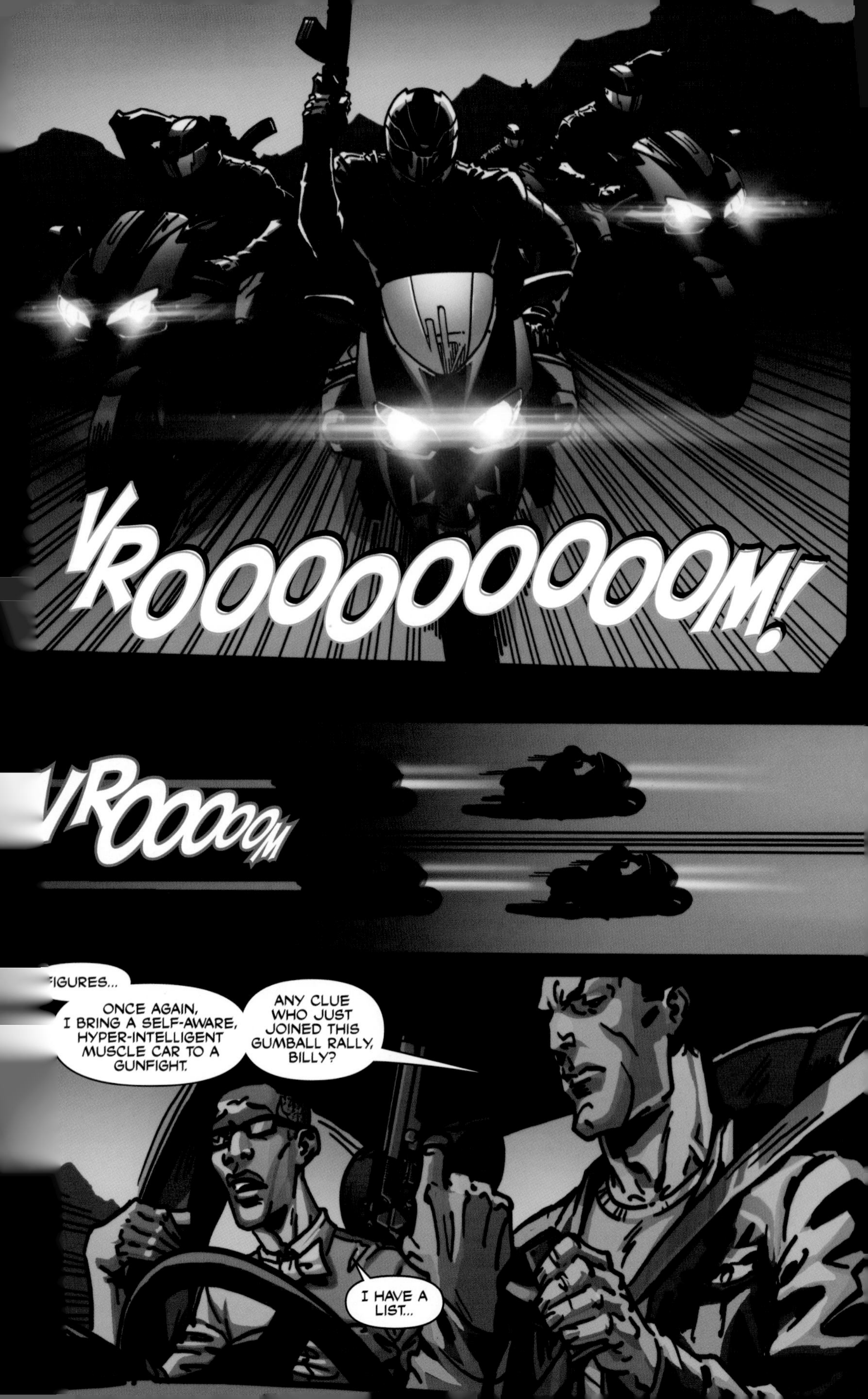
VROOOOOOOOOOM!
VROOOOOM
FIGURES...
ONCE AGAIN, I BRING A SELF-AWARE, HYPER-INTELLIGENT MUSCLE CAR TO A GUNFIGHT.
ANY CLUE WHO JUST JOINED THIS GUMBALL RALLY, BILLY?
I HAVE A LIST...

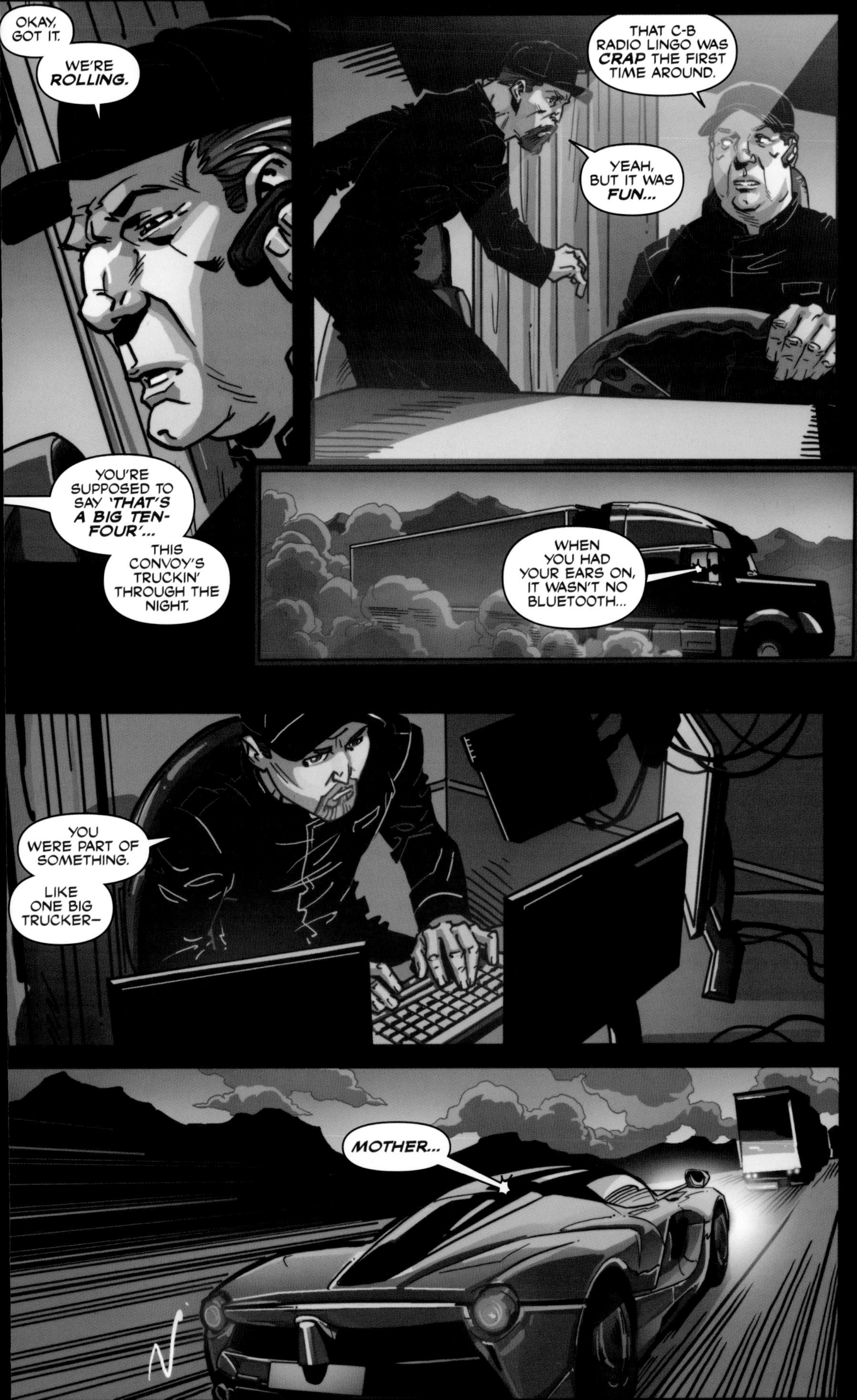
OKAY, GOT IT.
WE'RE ROLLING.
THAT C-B RADIO LINGO WAS CRAP THE FIRST TIME AROUND.
YEAH, BUT IT WAS FUN...
YOU'RE SUPPOSED TO SAY 'THAT'S A BIG TEN-FOUR'...
THIS CONVOY'S TRUCKIN' THROUGH THE NIGHT.
WHEN YOU HAD YOUR EARS ON, IT WASN'T NO BLUETOOTH...
YOU WERE PART OF SOMETHING.
LIKE ONE BIG TRUCKER—
MOTHER...

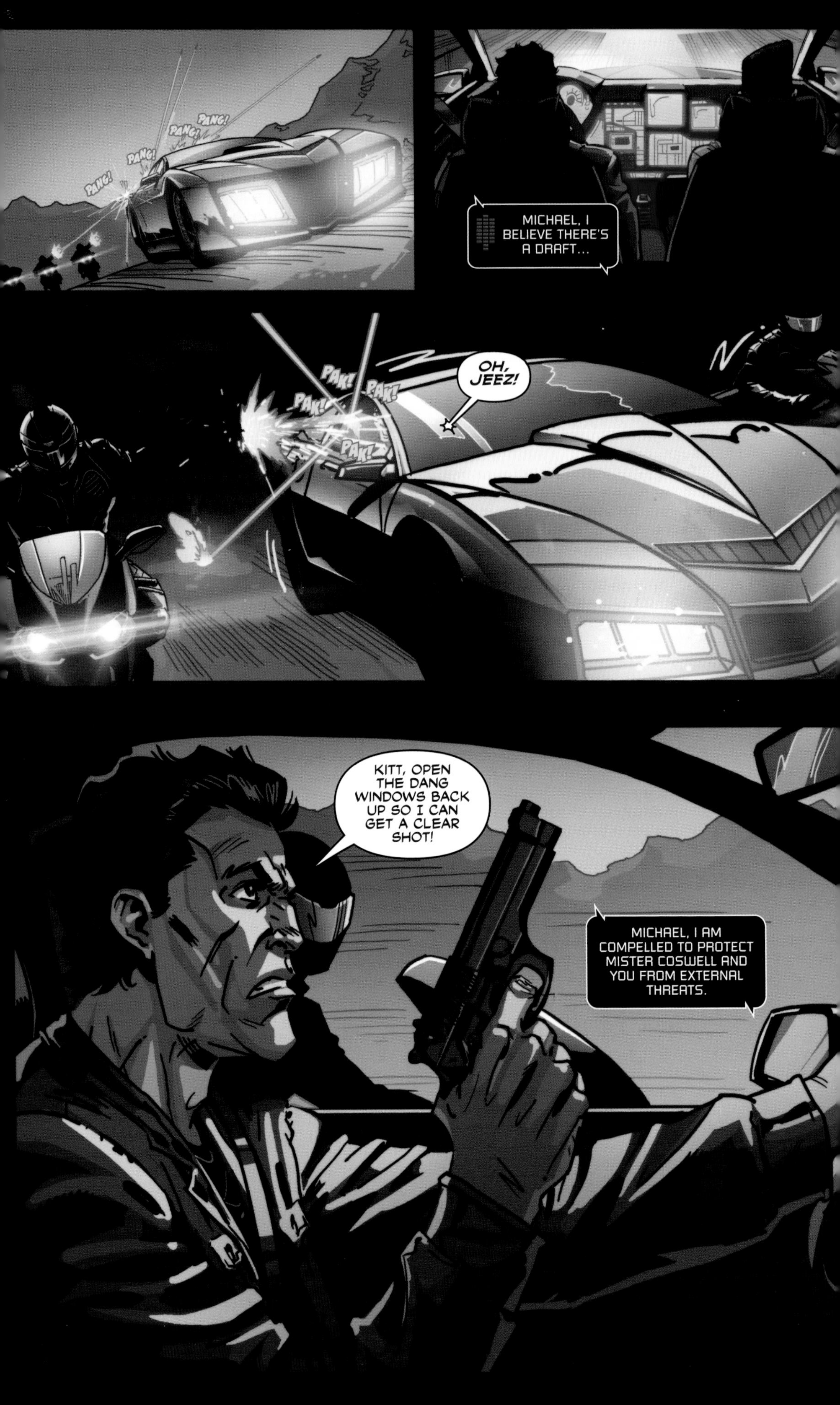
PANG!
PANG!
PANG!
PANG!
MICHAEL, I BELIEVE THERE'S A DRAFT...
PAK!
PAK!
PAK!
PAK!
OH, JEEZ!
KITT, OPEN THE DANG WINDOWS BACK UP SO I CAN GET A CLEAR SHOT!
MICHAEL, I AM COMPELLED TO PROTECT MISTER COSWELL AND YOU FROM EXTERNAL THREATS.

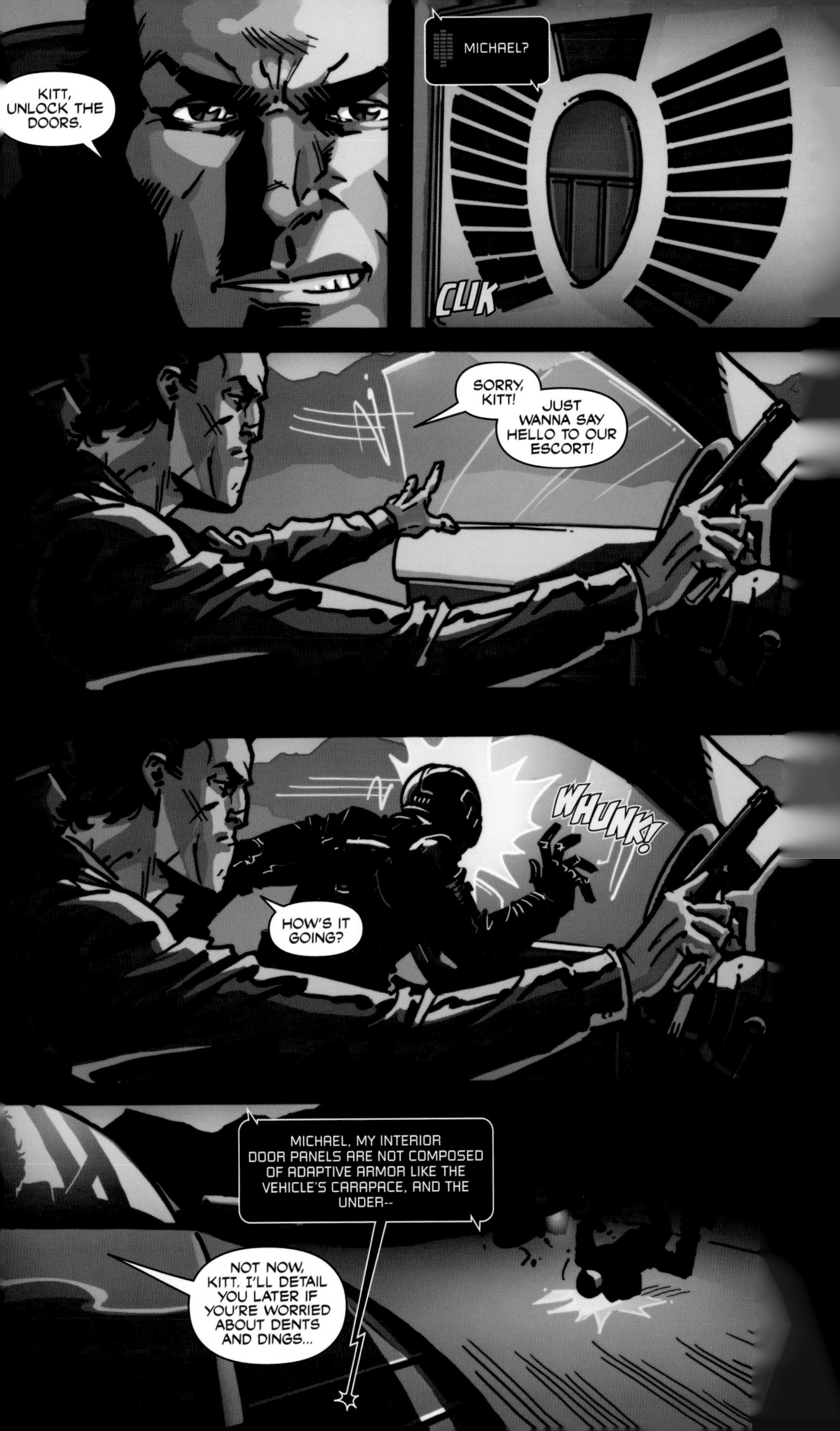

KITT, UNLOCK THE DOORS.
MICHAEL?
CLIK
SORRY, KITT!
JUST WANNA SAY HELLO TO OUR ESCORT!
WHUNK!
HOW'S IT GOING?
MICHAEL, MY INTERIOR DOOR PANELS ARE NOT COMPOSED OF ADAPTIVE ARMOR LIKE THE VEHICLE'S CARAPACE, AND THE UNDER--
NOT NOW, KITT. I'LL DETAIL YOU LATER IF YOU'RE WORRIED ABOUT DENTS AND DINGS...

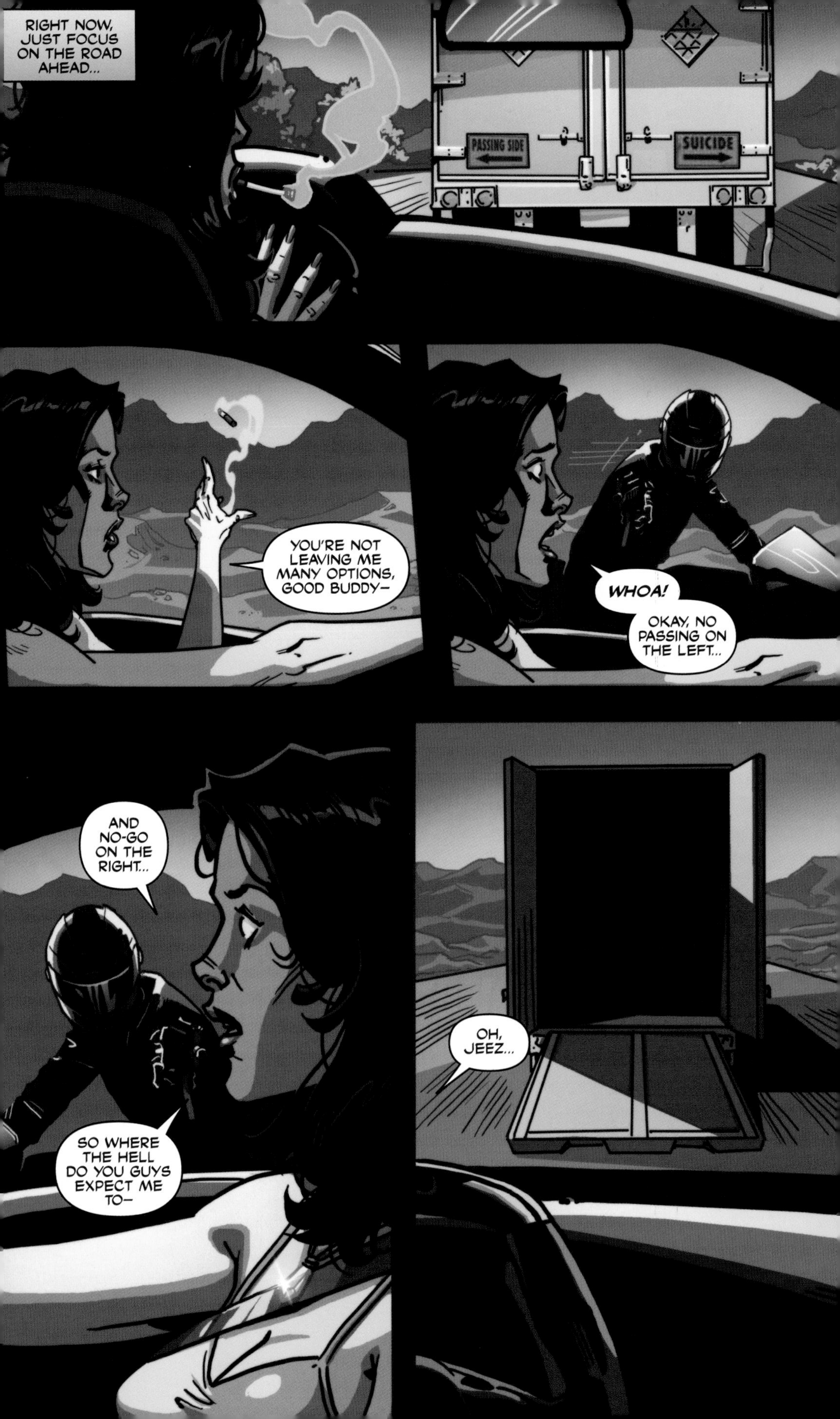
RIGHT NOW, JUST FOCUS ON THE ROAD AHEAD...
PASSING SIDE
SUICIDE
YOU'RE NOT LEAVING ME MANY OPTIONS, GOOD BUDDY–
WHOA!
OKAY, NO PASSING ON THE LEFT...
AND NO-GO ON THE RIGHT...
SO WHERE THE HELL DO YOU GUYS EXPECT ME TO–
OH, JEEZ...

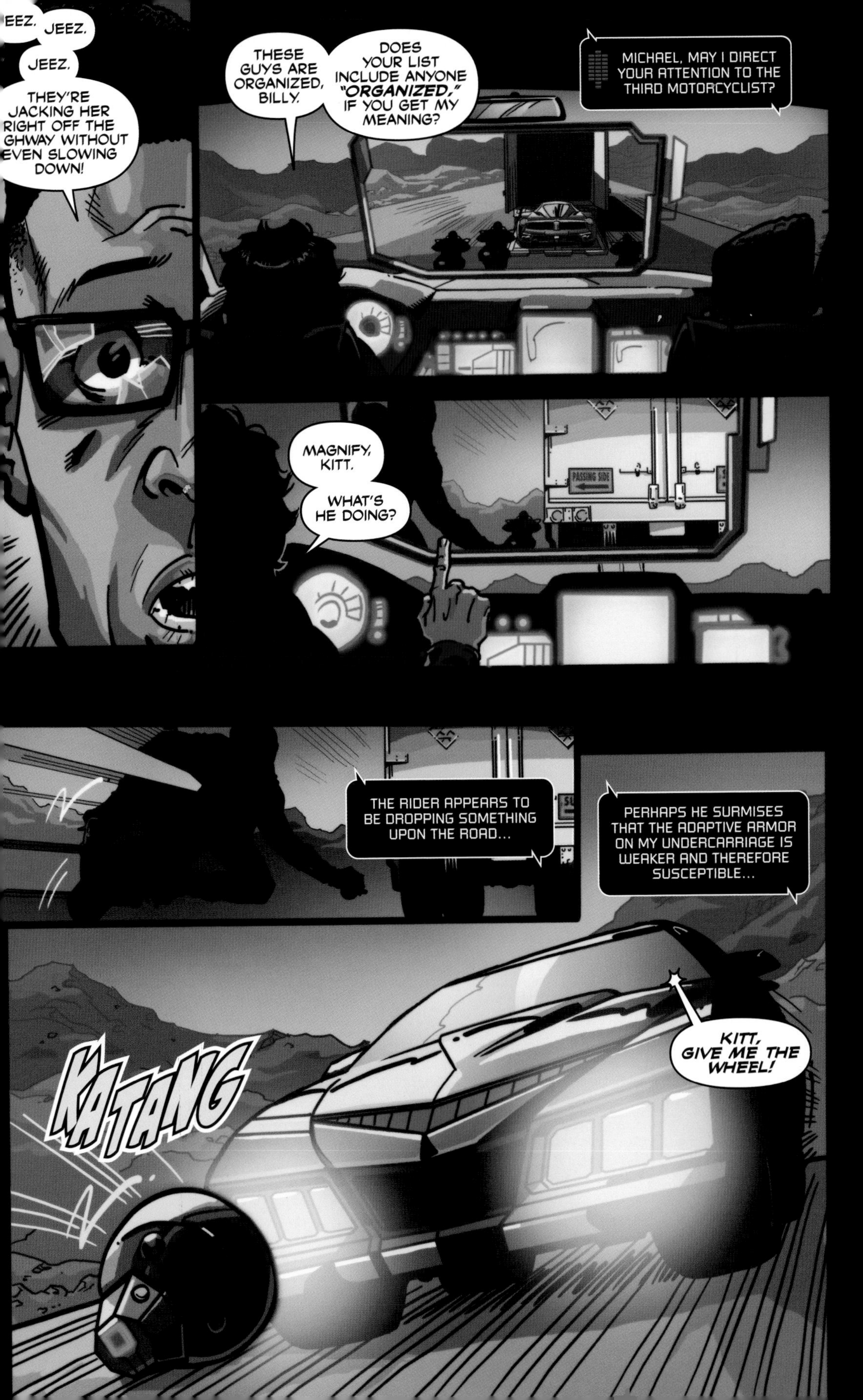
EEZ.
JEEZ.
JEEZ.
THEY'RE JACKING HER RIGHT OFF THE GHWAY WITHOUT EVEN SLOWING DOWN!
THESE GUYS ARE ORGANIZED, BILLY.
DOES YOUR LIST INCLUDE ANYONE "ORGANIZED," IF YOU GET MY MEANING?
MICHAEL, MAY I DIRECT YOUR ATTENTION TO THE THIRD MOTORCYCLIST?
MAGNIFY, KITT.
WHAT'S HE DOING?
PASSING SIDE
THE RIDER APPEARS TO BE DROPPING SOMETHING UPON THE ROAD...
PERHAPS HE SURMISES THAT THE ADAPTIVE ARMOR ON MY UNDERCARRIAGE IS WEAKER AND THEREFORE SUSCEPTIBLE...
KATANG
KITT, GIVE ME THE WHEEL!

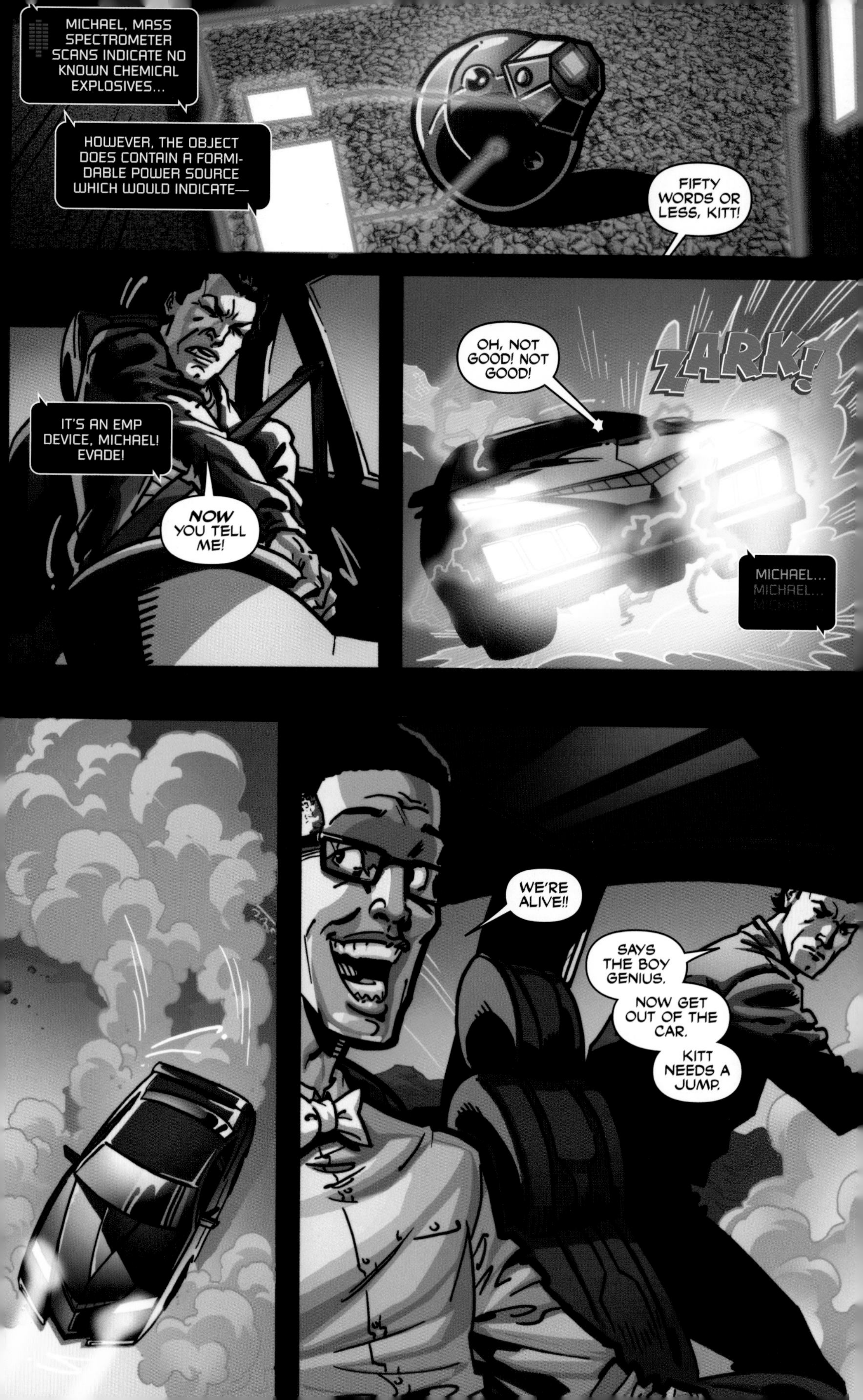
MICHAEL, MASS SPECTROMETER SCANS INDICATE NO KNOWN CHEMICAL EXPLOSIVES...
HOWEVER, THE OBJECT DOES CONTAIN A FORMIDABLE POWER SOURCE WHICH WOULD INDICATE—
FIFTY WORDS OR LESS, KITT!
IT'S AN EMP DEVICE, MICHAEL! EVADE!
NOW YOU TELL ME!
OH, NOT GOOD! NOT GOOD!
ZARK!
MICHAEL...
MICHAEL...
WE'RE ALIVE!!
SAYS THE BOY GENIUS.
NOW GET OUT OF THE CAR.
KITT NEEDS A JUMP.

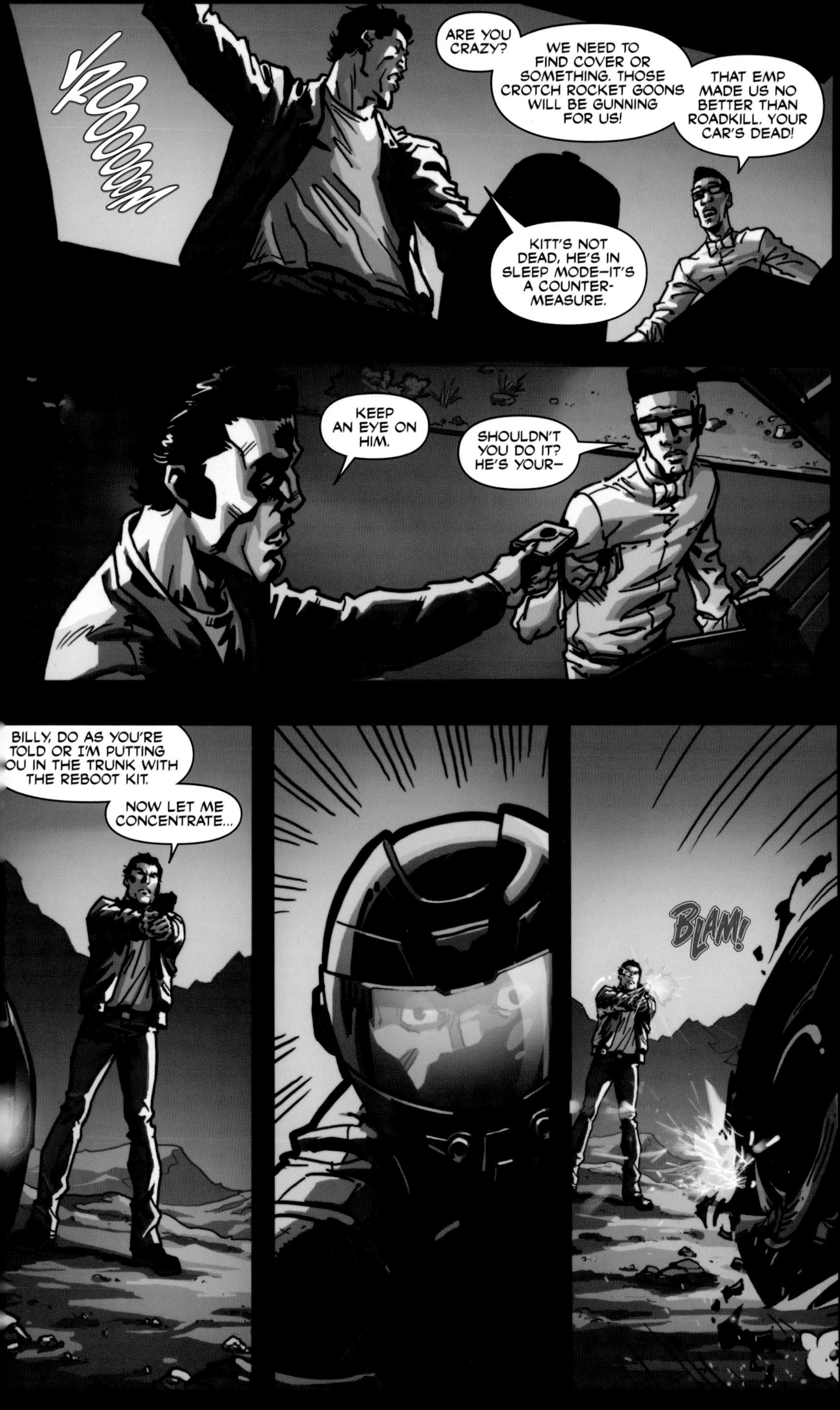

VROOOOOOM
ARE YOU CRAZY?
WE NEED TO FIND COVER OR SOMETHING. THOSE CROTCH ROCKET GOONS WILL BE GUNNING FOR US!
THAT EMP MADE US NO BETTER THAN ROADKILL. YOUR CAR'S DEAD!
KITT'S NOT DEAD, HE'S IN SLEEP MODE—IT'S A COUNTER-MEASURE.
KEEP AN EYE ON HIM.
SHOULDN'T YOU DO IT? HE'S YOUR—
BILLY, DO AS YOU'RE TOLD OR I'M PUTTING OU IN THE TRUNK WITH THE REBOOT KIT.
NOW LET ME CONCENTRATE...
BLAM!

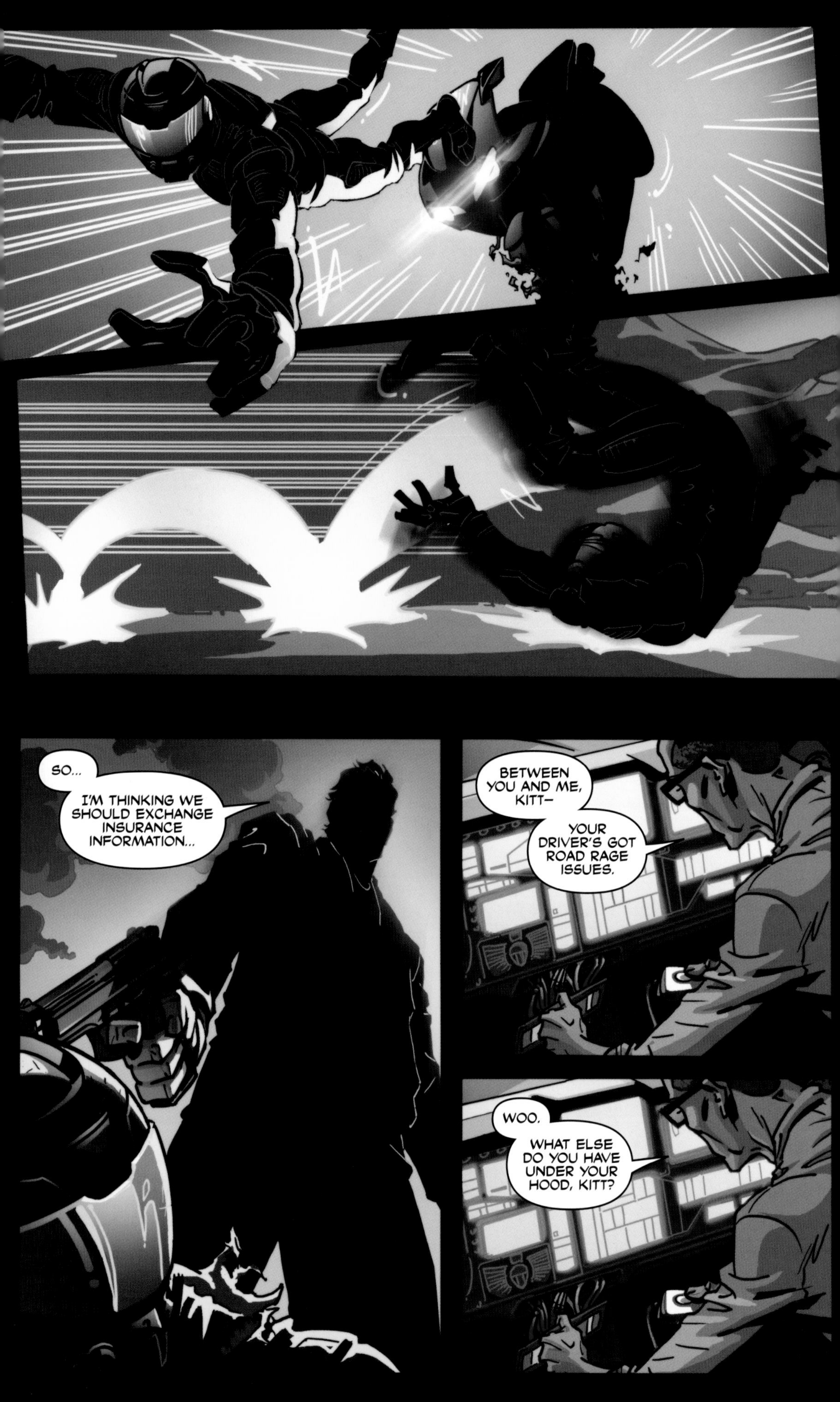
SO...
I'M THINKING WE SHOULD EXCHANGE INSURANCE INFORMATION...
BETWEEN YOU AND ME, KITT–
YOUR DRIVER'S GOT ROAD RAGE ISSUES.
WOO.
WHAT ELSE DO YOU HAVE UNDER YOUR HOOD, KITT?

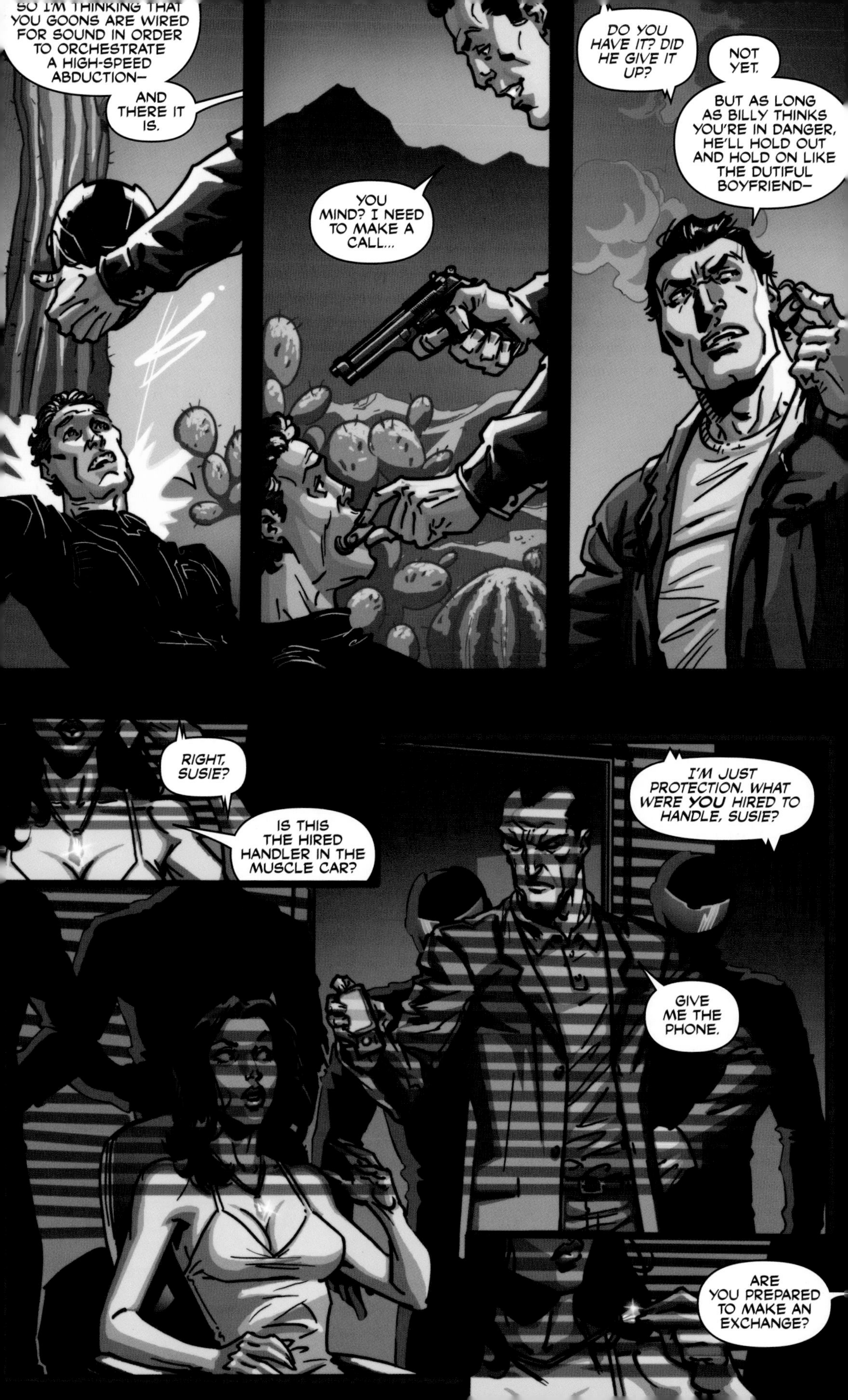
SO I'M THINKING THAT YOU GOONS ARE WIRED FOR SOUND IN ORDER TO ORCHESTRATE A HIGH-SPEED ABDUCTION–
AND THERE IT IS.
YOU MIND? I NEED TO MAKE A CALL...
DO YOU HAVE IT? DID HE GIVE IT UP?
NOT YET.
BUT AS LONG AS BILLY THINKS YOU'RE IN DANGER, HE'LL HOLD OUT AND HOLD ON LIKE THE DUTIFUL BOYFRIEND–
RIGHT, SUSIE?
IS THIS THE HIRED HANDLER IN THE MUSCLE CAR?
I'M JUST PROTECTION. WHAT WERE YOU HIRED TO HANDLE, SUSIE?
GIVE ME THE PHONE.
ARE YOU PREPARED TO MAKE AN EXCHANGE?

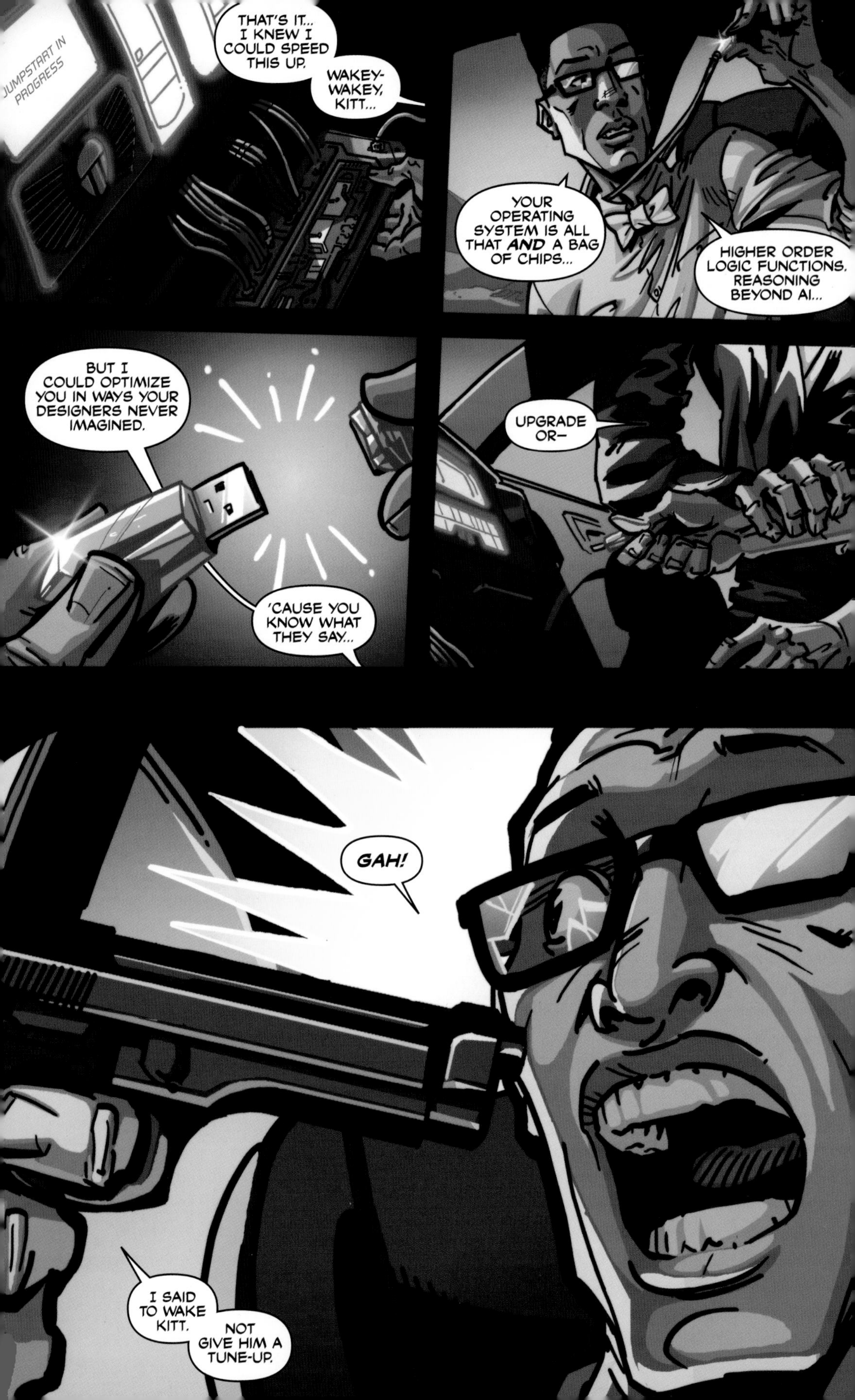
JUMPSTART IN PROGRESS
THAT'S IT... I KNEW I COULD SPEED THIS UP.
WAKEY-WAKEY, KITT...
YOUR OPERATING SYSTEM IS ALL THAT AND A BAG OF CHIPS...
HIGHER ORDER LOGIC FUNCTIONS, REASONING BEYOND AI...
BUT I COULD OPTIMIZE YOU IN WAYS YOUR DESIGNERS NEVER IMAGINED.
'CAUSE YOU KNOW WHAT THEY SAY...
UPGRADE OR–
GAH!
I SAID TO WAKE KITT.
NOT GIVE HIM A TUNE-UP.

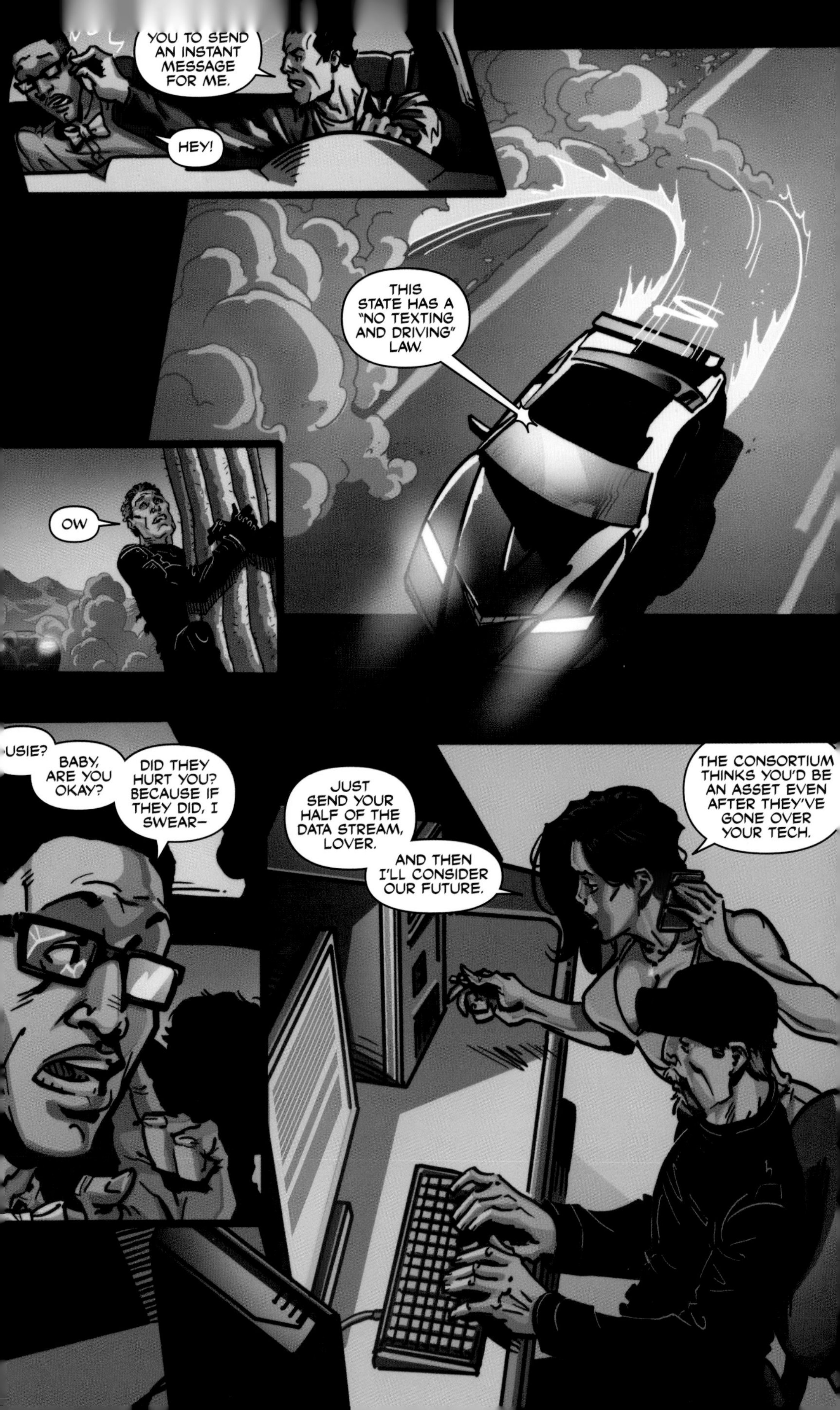

YOU TO SEND AN INSTANT MESSAGE FOR ME.
HEY!
THIS STATE HAS A "NO TEXTING AND DRIVING" LAW.
OW
USIE? BABY, ARE YOU OKAY?
DID THEY HURT YOU? BECAUSE IF THEY DID, I SWEAR–
JUST SEND YOUR HALF OF THE DATA STREAM, LOVER.
AND THEN I'LL CONSIDER OUR FUTURE.
THE CONSORTIUM THINKS YOU'D BE AN ASSET EVEN AFTER THEY'VE GONE OVER YOUR TECH.

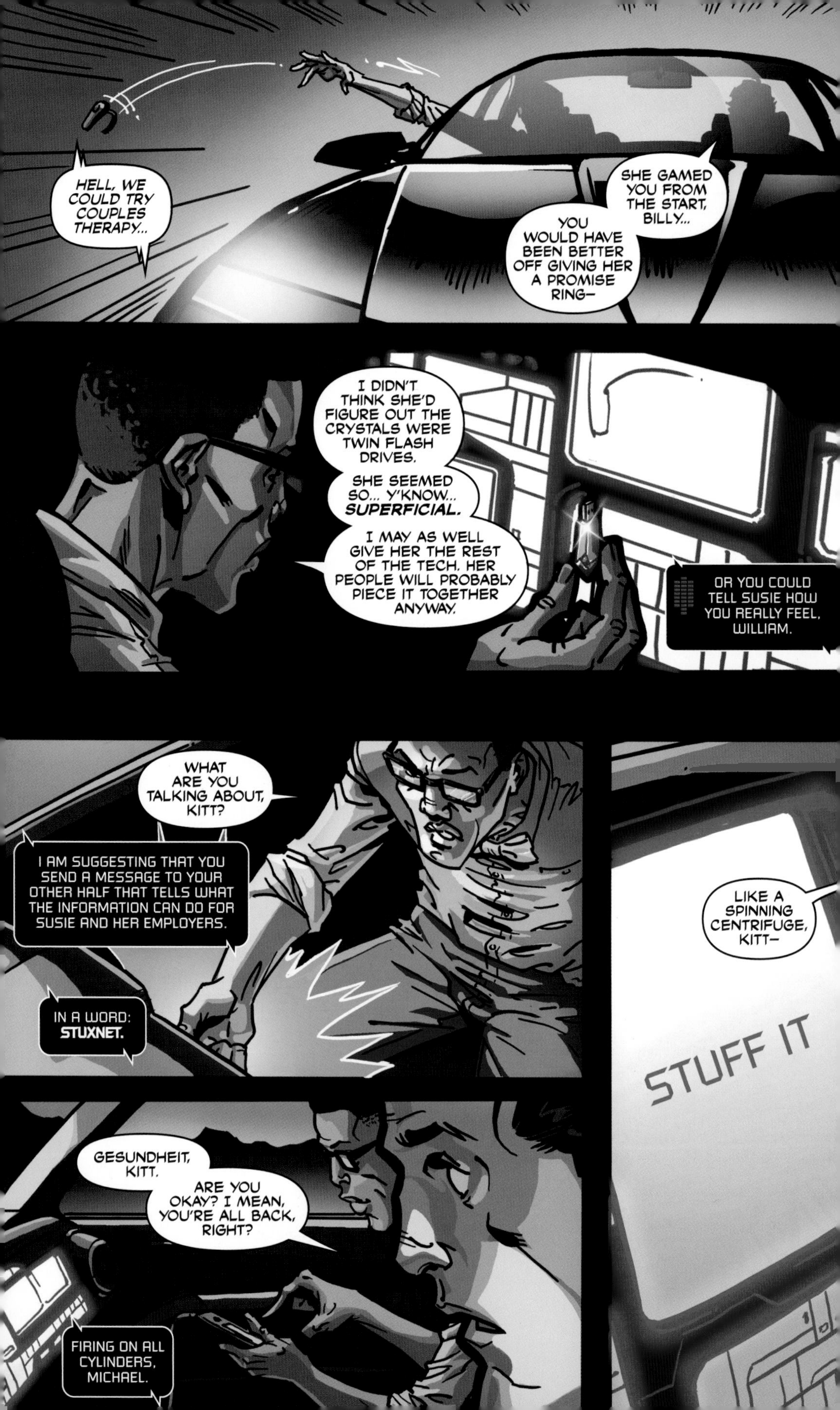
HELL, WE COULD TRY COUPLES THERAPY...
SHE GAMED YOU FROM THE START, BILLY...
YOU WOULD HAVE BEEN BETTER OFF GIVING HER A PROMISE RING—
I DIDN'T THINK SHE'D FIGURE OUT THE CRYSTALS WERE TWIN FLASH DRIVES.
SHE SEEMED SO... Y'KNOW... SUPERFICIAL.
I MAY AS WELL GIVE HER THE REST OF THE TECH. HER PEOPLE WILL PROBABLY PIECE IT TOGETHER ANYWAY.
OR YOU COULD TELL SUSIE HOW YOU REALLY FEEL, WILLIAM.
WHAT ARE YOU TALKING ABOUT, KITT?
I AM SUGGESTING THAT YOU SEND A MESSAGE TO YOUR OTHER HALF THAT TELLS WHAT THE INFORMATION CAN DO FOR SUSIE AND HER EMPLOYERS.
IN A WORD: STUXNET.
LIKE A SPINNING CENTRIFUGE, KITT—
STUFF IT
GESUNDHEIT, KITT.
ARE YOU OKAY? I MEAN, YOU'RE ALL BACK, RIGHT?
FIRING ON ALL CYLINDERS, MICHAEL.

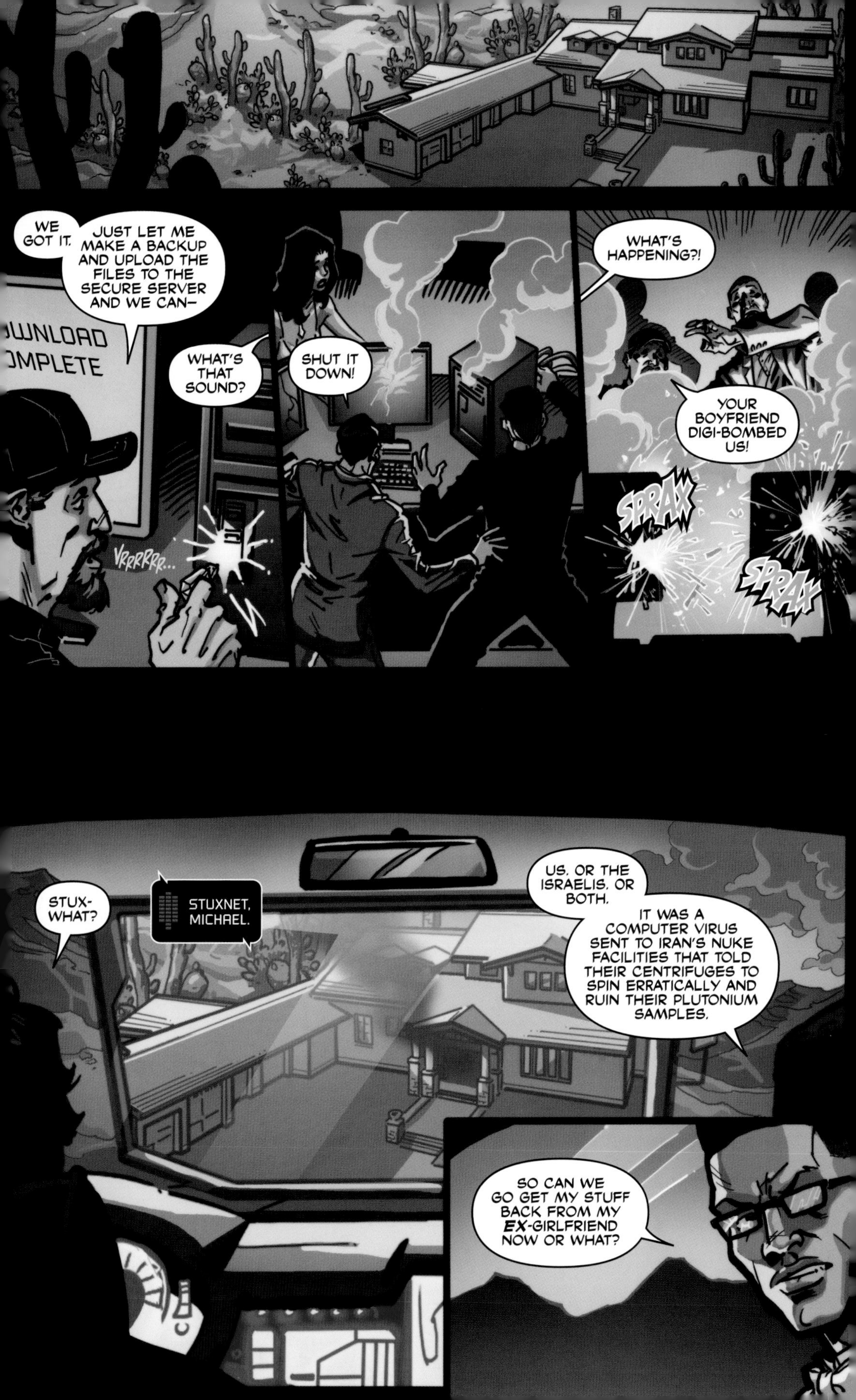

WE GOT IT.
JUST LET ME MAKE A BACKUP AND UPLOAD THE FILES TO THE SECURE SERVER AND WE CAN–
OWNLOAD OMPLETE
VRRRRRR...
WHAT'S THAT SOUND?
SHUT IT DOWN!
WHAT'S HAPPENING?!
YOUR BOYFRIEND DIGI-BOMBED US!
SPRAX
SPRAX
STUX-WHAT?
STUXNET, MICHAEL.
US, OR THE ISRAELIS, OR BOTH.
IT WAS A COMPUTER VIRUS SENT TO IRAN'S NUKE FACILITIES THAT TOLD THEIR CENTRIFUGES TO SPIN ERRATICALLY AND RUIN THEIR PLUTONIUM SAMPLES.
SO CAN WE GO GET MY STUFF BACK FROM MY EX-GIRLFRIEND NOW OR WHAT?

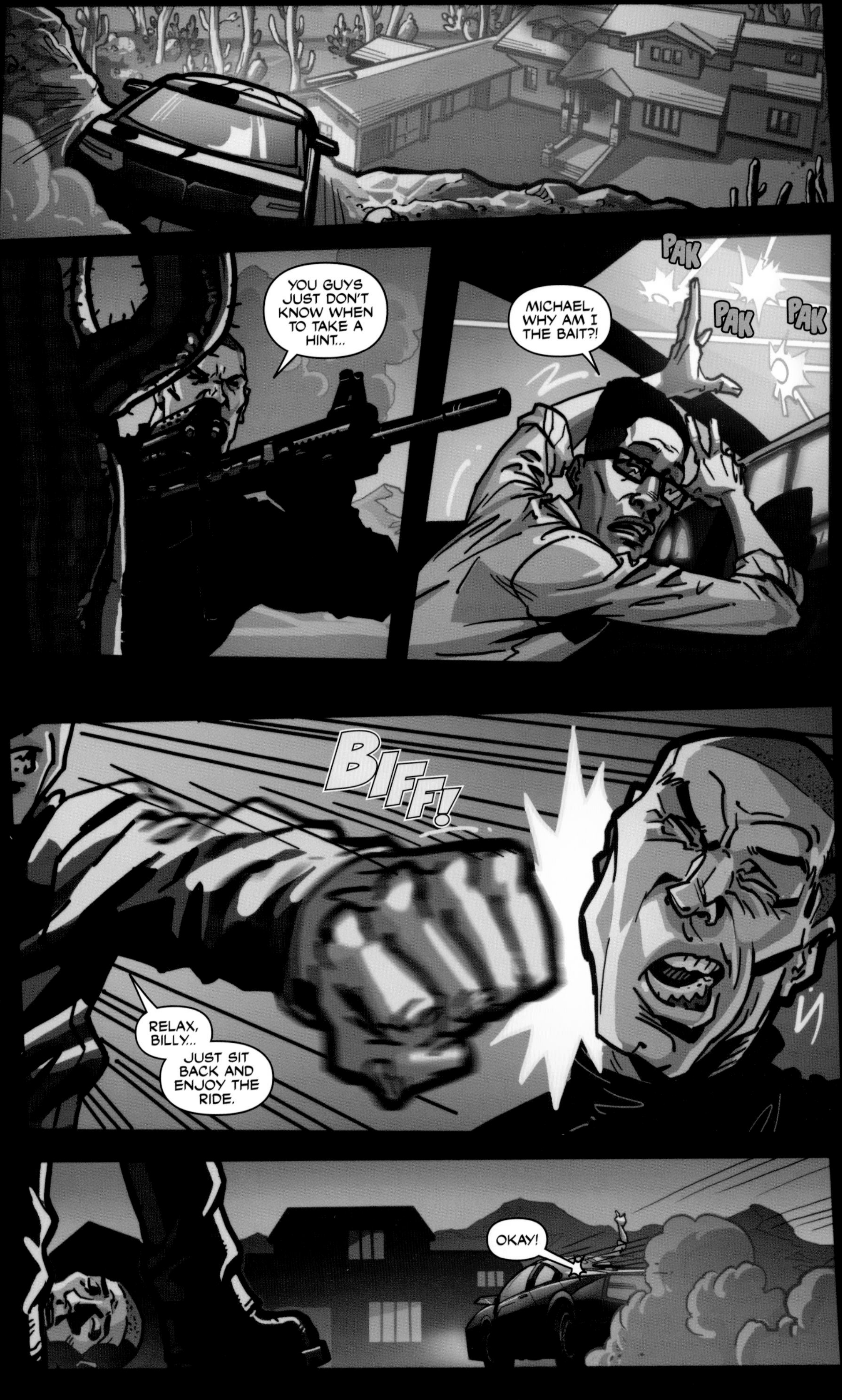
YOU GUYS JUST DON'T KNOW WHEN TO TAKE A HINT...
MICHAEL, WHY AM I THE BAIT?!
PAK
PAK
PAK
BIFF!
RELAX, BILLY...
JUST SIT BACK AND ENJOY THE RIDE.
OKAY!

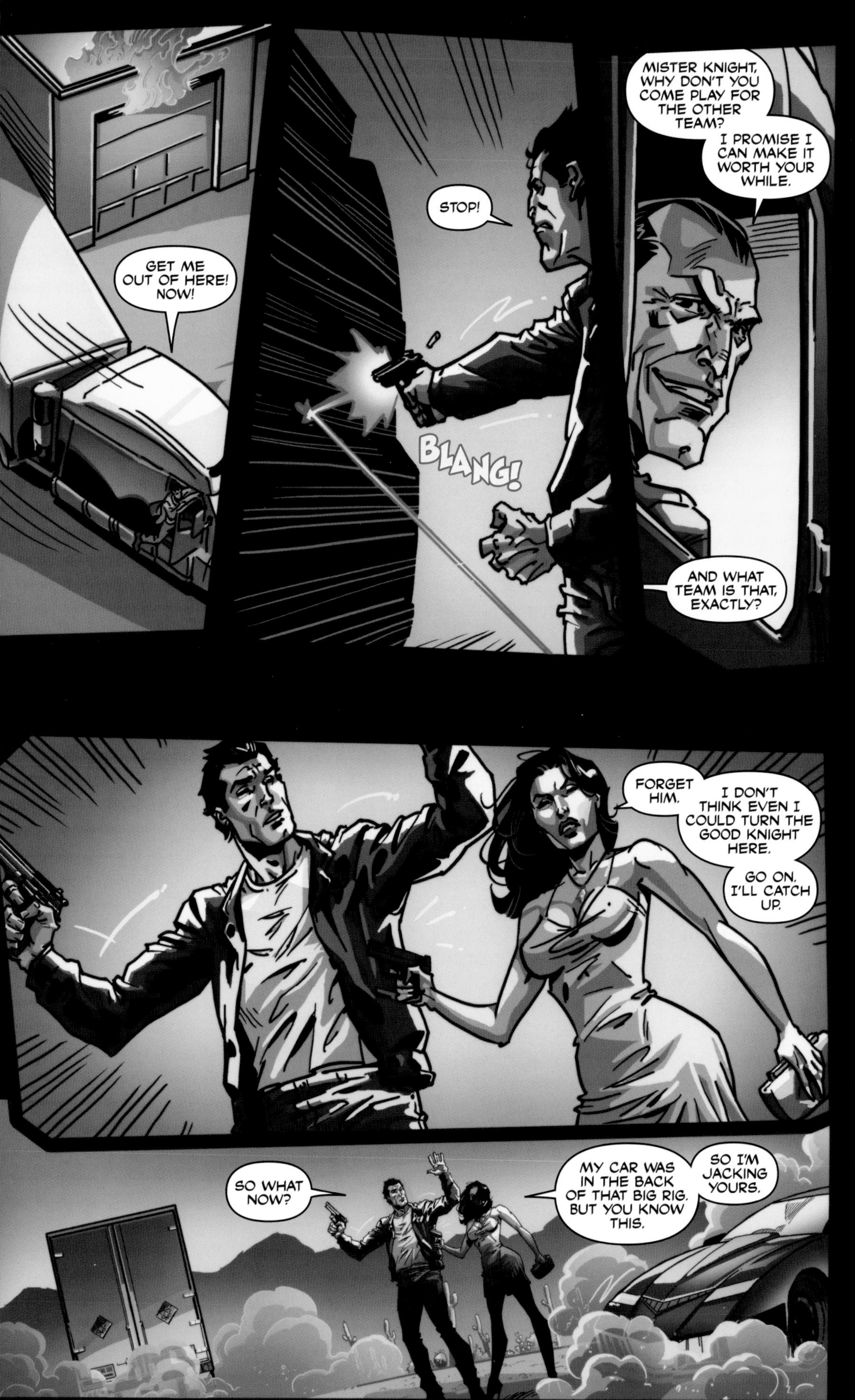
GET ME OUT OF HERE! NOW!
STOP!
BLANG!
MISTER KNIGHT, WHY DON'T YOU COME PLAY FOR THE OTHER TEAM?
I PROMISE I CAN MAKE IT WORTH YOUR WHILE.
AND WHAT TEAM IS THAT, EXACTLY?
FORGET HIM.
I DON'T THINK EVEN I COULD TURN THE GOOD KNIGHT HERE.
GO ON. I'LL CATCH UP.
SO WHAT NOW?
MY CAR WAS IN THE BACK OF THAT BIG RIG. BUT YOU KNOW THIS.
SO I'M JACKING YOURS.

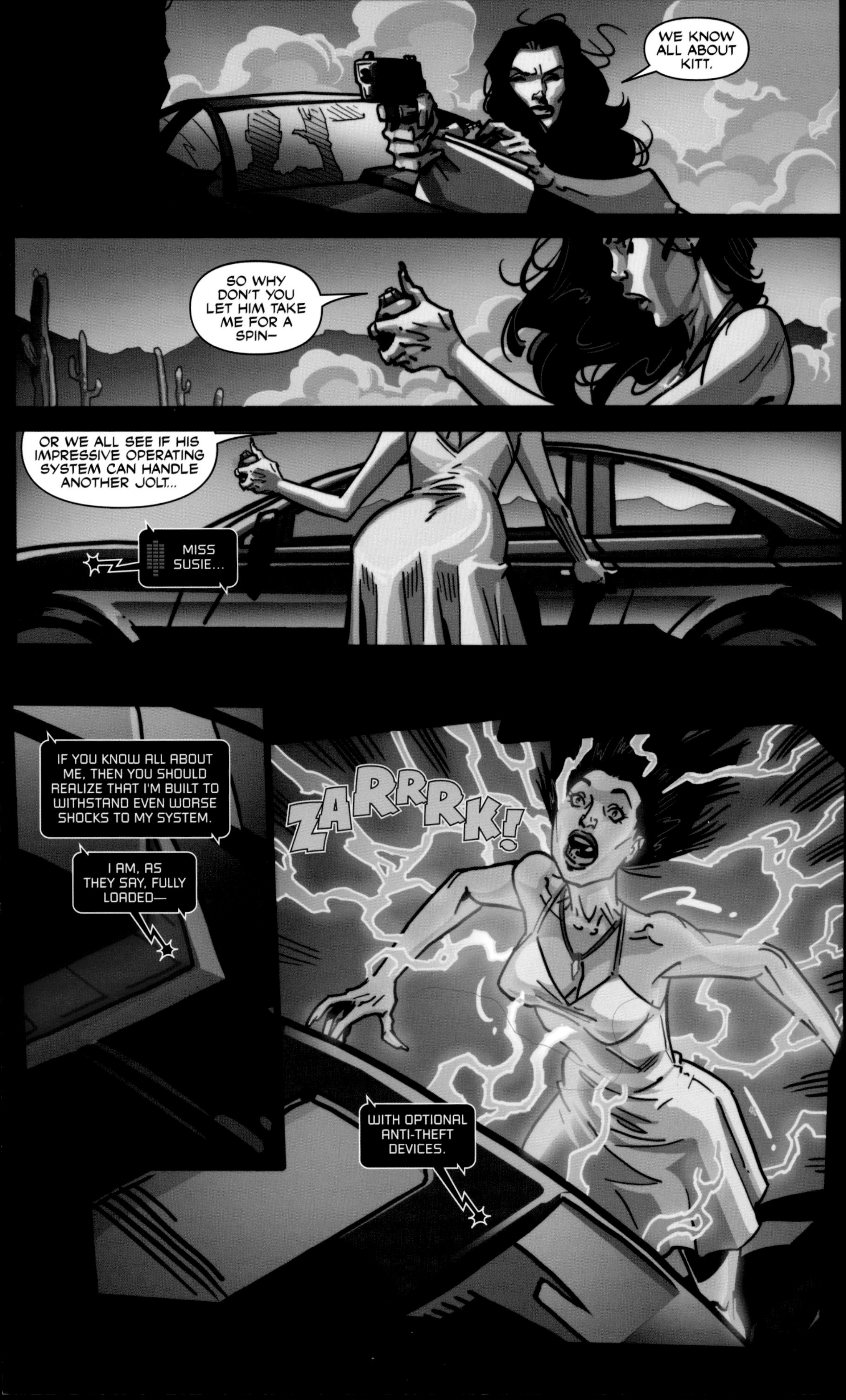
WE KNOW ALL ABOUT KITT.
SO WHY DON'T YOU LET HIM TAKE ME FOR A SPIN–
OR WE ALL SEE IF HIS IMPRESSIVE OPERATING SYSTEM CAN HANDLE ANOTHER JOLT...
MISS SUSIE...
IF YOU KNOW ALL ABOUT ME, THEN YOU SHOULD REALIZE THAT I'M BUILT TO WITHSTAND EVEN WORSE SHOCKS TO MY SYSTEM.
I AM, AS THEY SAY, FULLY LOADED—
ZARRRK!
WITH OPTIONAL ANTI-THEFT DEVICES.

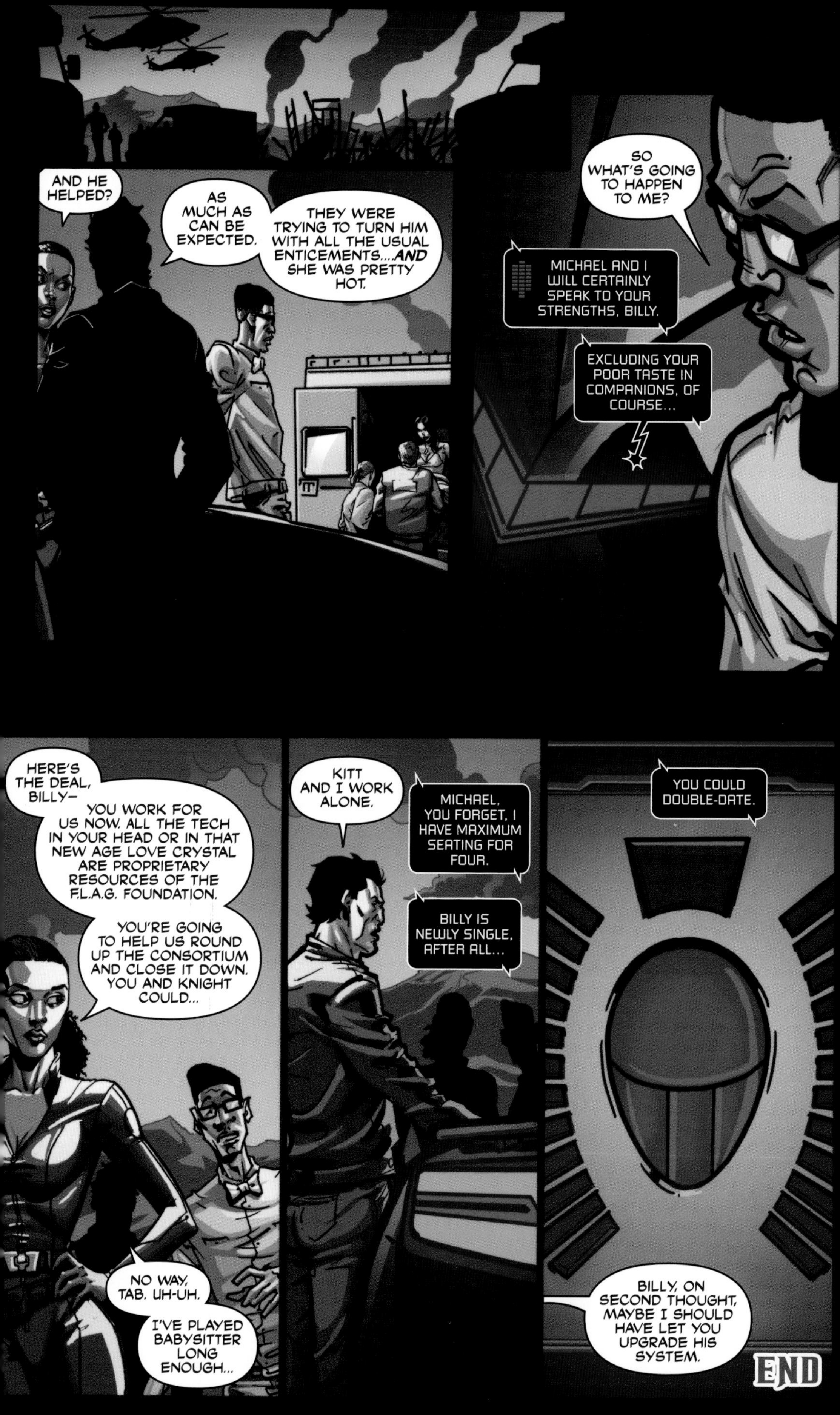
AND HE HELPED?
AS MUCH AS CAN BE EXPECTED.
THEY WERE TRYING TO TURN HIM WITH ALL THE USUAL ENTICEMENTS....AND SHE WAS PRETTY HOT.
SO WHAT'S GOING TO HAPPEN TO ME?
MICHAEL AND I WILL CERTAINLY SPEAK TO YOUR STRENGTHS, BILLY.
EXCLUDING YOUR POOR TASTE IN COMPANIONS, OF COURSE...
HERE'S THE DEAL, BILLY—
YOU WORK FOR US NOW. ALL THE TECH IN YOUR HEAD OR IN THAT NEW AGE LOVE CRYSTAL ARE PROPRIETARY RESOURCES OF THE F.L.A.G. FOUNDATION.
YOU'RE GOING TO HELP US ROUND UP THE CONSORTIUM AND CLOSE IT DOWN. YOU AND KNIGHT COULD...
NO WAY, TAB. UH-UH.
I'VE PLAYED BABYSITTER LONG ENOUGH...
KITT AND I WORK ALONE.
MICHAEL, YOU FORGET, I HAVE MAXIMUM SEATING FOR FOUR.
BILLY IS NEWLY SINGLE, AFTER ALL...
YOU COULD DOUBLE-DATE.
BILLY, ON SECOND THOUGHT, MAYBE I SHOULD HAVE LET YOU UPGRADE HIS SYSTEM.
END

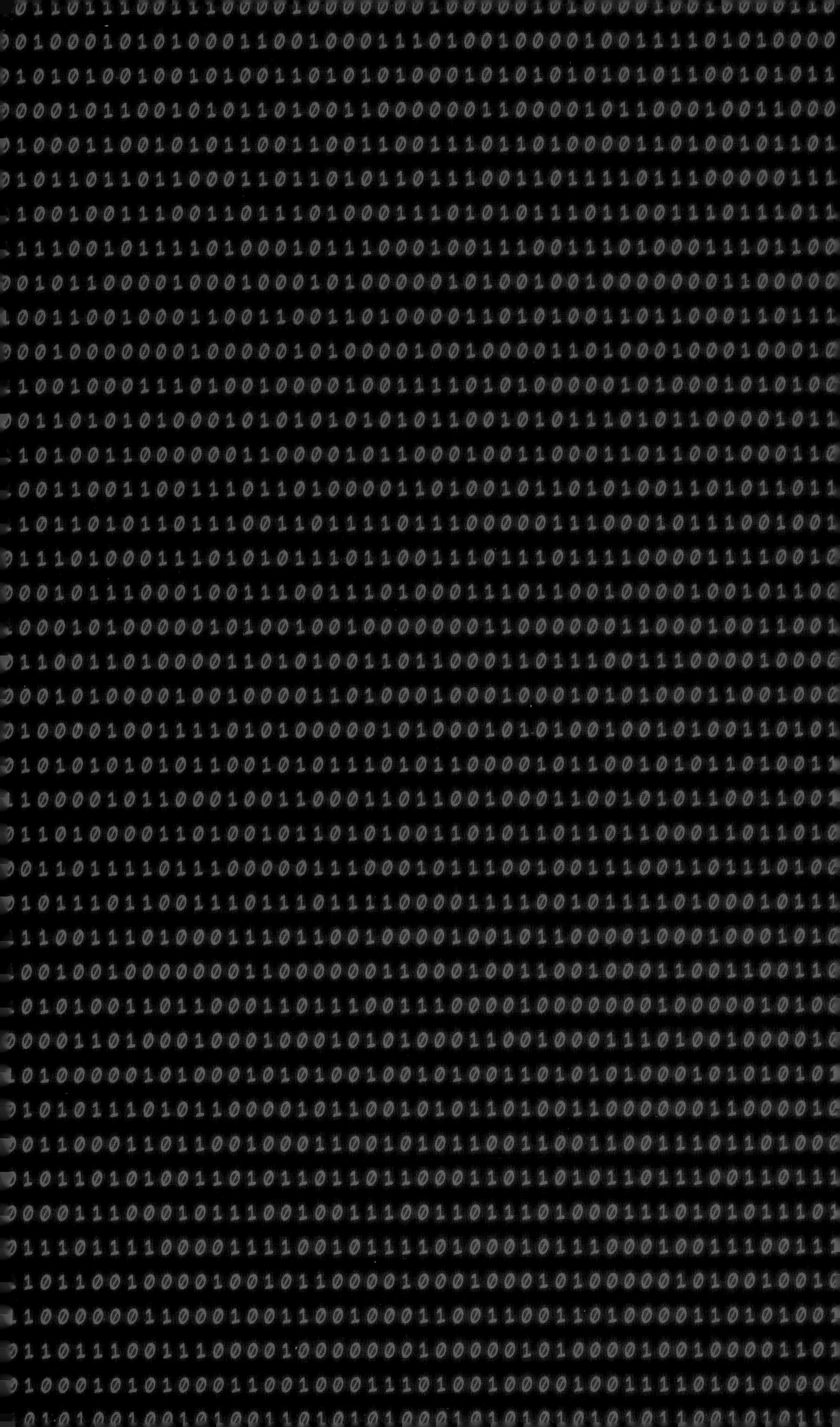

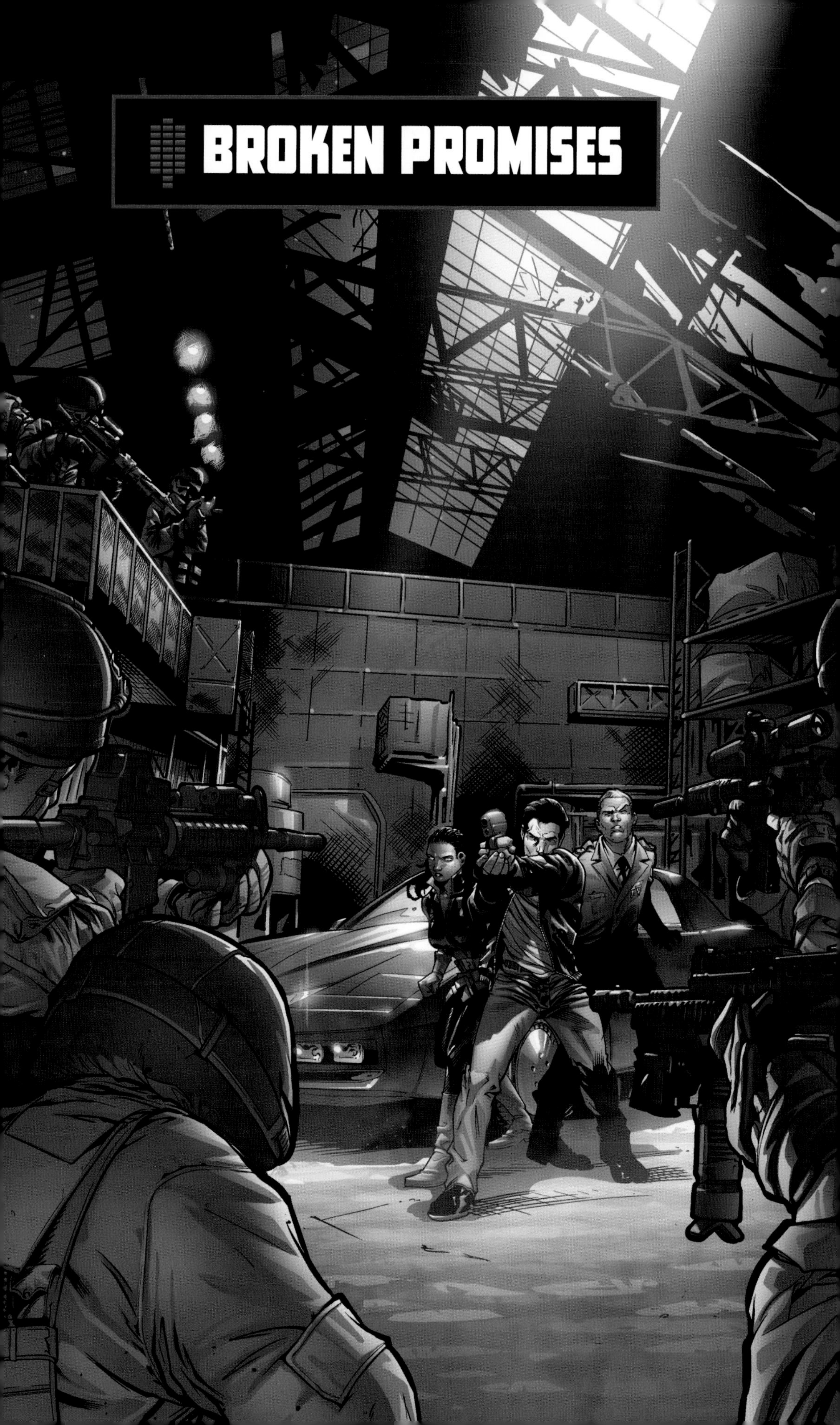
BROKEN PROMISES

KNIGHT RIDER
KNIGHT STRIKES

WRITTEN BY
FRANK HANNAH

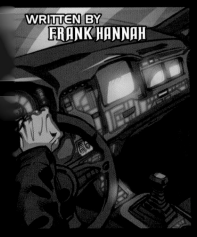

ILLUSTRATED BY
JB BASTOS

COLORED BY
MILEN PARVANOV

LETTERED BY
ERIKA TERRIQUEZ

EDITED BY
SHANNON ERIC DENTON

FRONT COVER BY
FRANCESCO MANNA

KNIGHT RIDER CREATED BY
GLEN A. LARSON

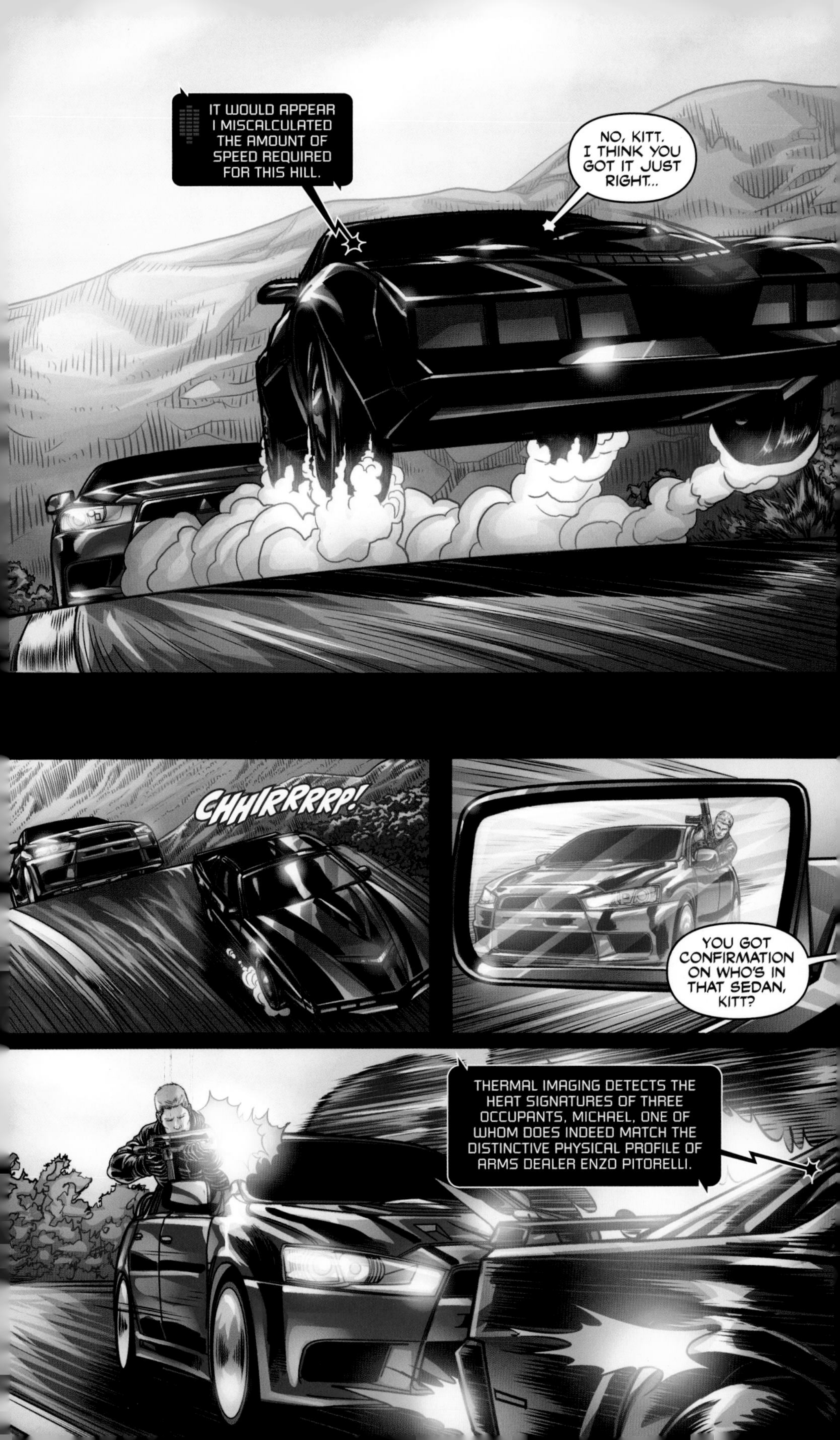
IT WOULD APPEAR I MISCALCULATED THE AMOUNT OF SPEED REQUIRED FOR THIS HILL.
NO, KITT. I THINK YOU GOT IT JUST RIGHT...
CHHIRRRRP!
YOU GOT CONFIRMATION ON WHO'S IN THAT SEDAN, KITT?
THERMAL IMAGING DETECTS THE HEAT SIGNATURES OF THREE OCCUPANTS, MICHAEL, ONE OF WHOM DOES INDEED MATCH THE DISTINCTIVE PHYSICAL PROFILE OF ARMS DEALER ENZO PITORELLI.

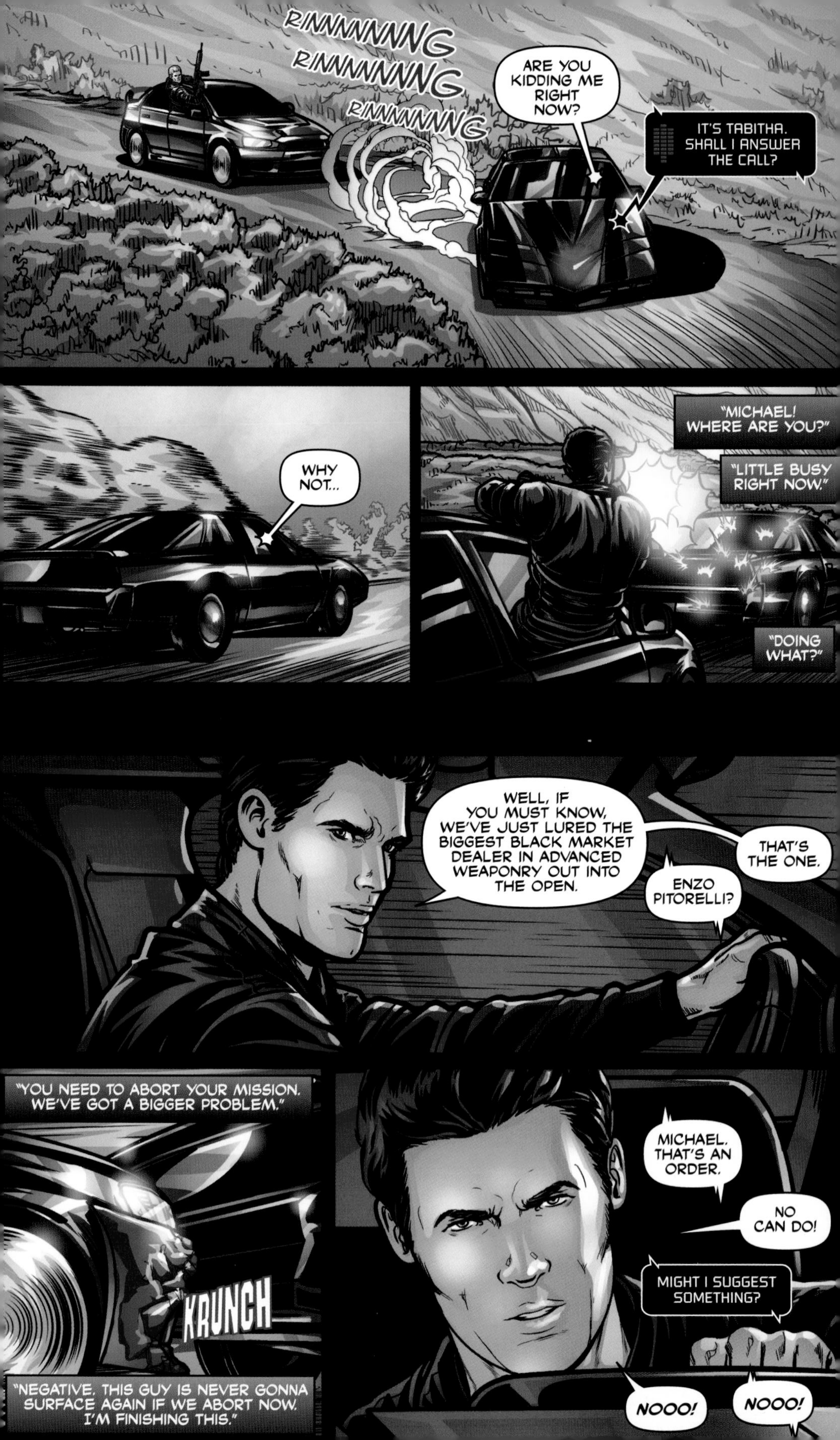
RINNNNNNNG
RINNNNNNNG
RINNNNNNNG
ARE YOU KIDDING ME RIGHT NOW?
IT'S TABITHA. SHALL I ANSWER THE CALL?
WHY NOT...
"MICHAEL! WHERE ARE YOU?"
"LITTLE BUSY RIGHT NOW."
"DOING WHAT?"
WELL, IF YOU MUST KNOW, WE'VE JUST LURED THE BIGGEST BLACK MARKET DEALER IN ADVANCED WEAPONRY OUT INTO THE OPEN.
ENZO PITORELLI?
THAT'S THE ONE.
"YOU NEED TO ABORT YOUR MISSION. WE'VE GOT A BIGGER PROBLEM."
KRUNCH
"NEGATIVE. THIS GUY IS NEVER GONNA SURFACE AGAIN IF WE ABORT NOW. I'M FINISHING THIS."
MICHAEL. THAT'S AN ORDER.
NO CAN DO!
MIGHT I SUGGEST SOMETHING?
NOOO!
NOOO!

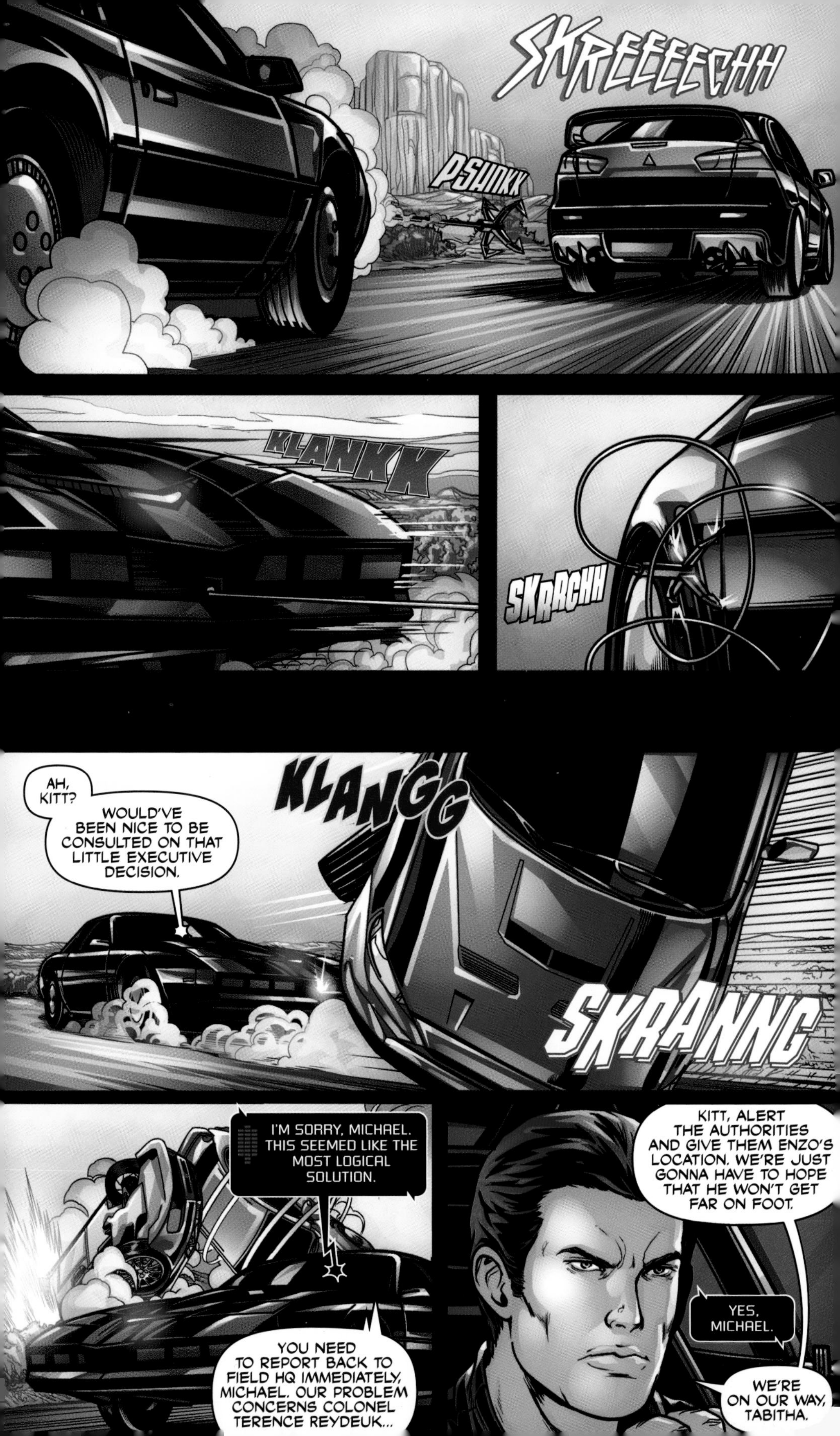
SKREEEECHH
PSHNKK
KLANKK
SKRRCHH
AH, KITT?
WOULD'VE BEEN NICE TO BE CONSULTED ON THAT LITTLE EXECUTIVE DECISION.
KLANGG
SKRANNG
I'M SORRY, MICHAEL. THIS SEEMED LIKE THE MOST LOGICAL SOLUTION.
YOU NEED TO REPORT BACK TO FIELD HQ IMMEDIATELY, MICHAEL. OUR PROBLEM CONCERNS COLONEL TERENCE REYDEUK...
KITT, ALERT THE AUTHORITIES AND GIVE THEM ENZO'S LOCATION. WE'RE JUST GONNA HAVE TO HOPE THAT HE WON'T GET FAR ON FOOT.
YES, MICHAEL.
WE'RE ON OUR WAY, TABITHA.

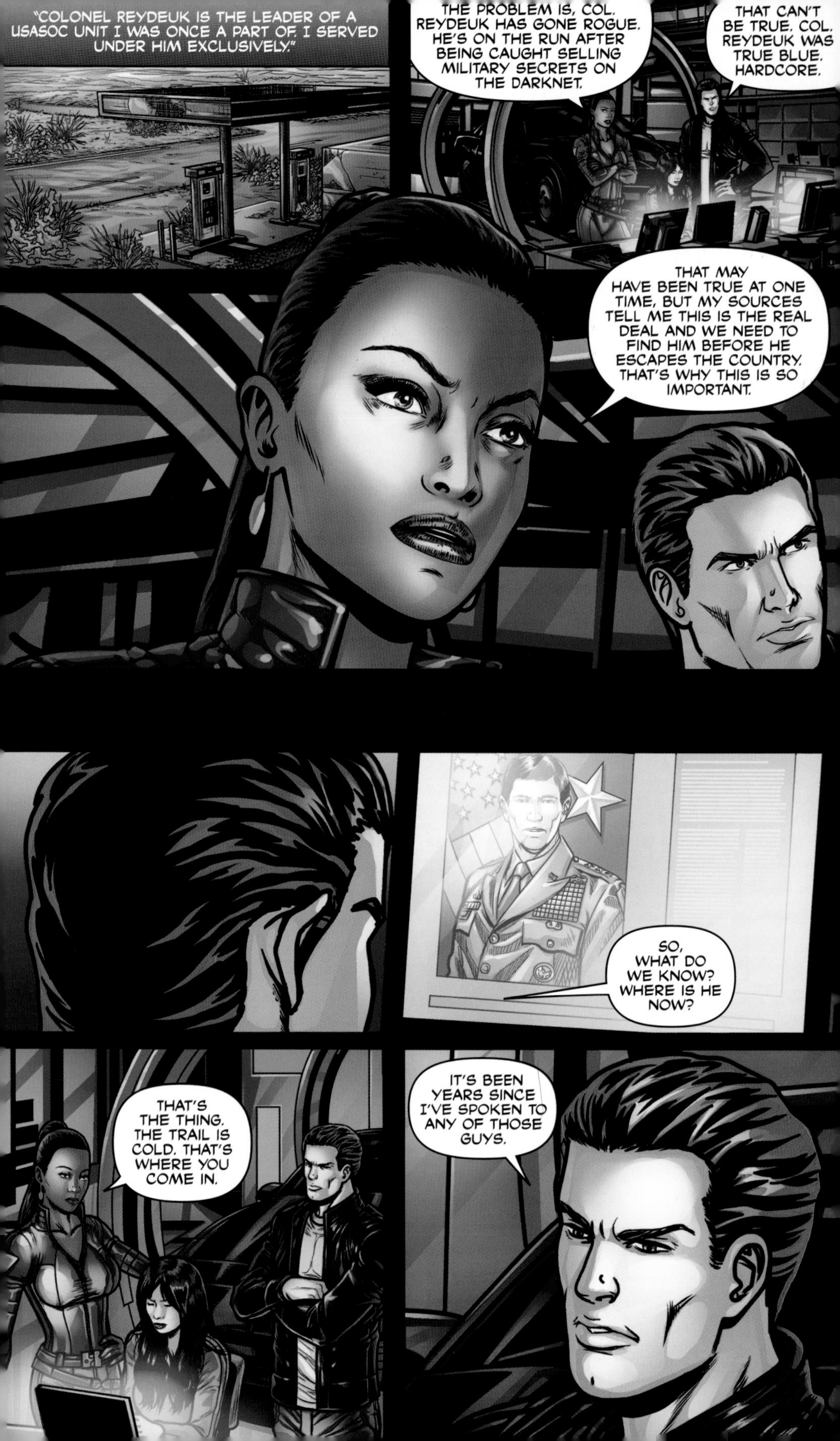
"COLONEL REYDEUK IS THE LEADER OF A USASOC UNIT I WAS ONCE A PART OF. I SERVED UNDER HIM EXCLUSIVELY."
THE PROBLEM IS, COL. REYDEUK HAS GONE ROGUE. HE'S ON THE RUN AFTER BEING CAUGHT SELLING MILITARY SECRETS ON THE DARKNET.
THAT CAN'T BE TRUE. COL. REYDEUK WAS TRUE BLUE. HARDCORE.
THAT MAY HAVE BEEN TRUE AT ONE TIME, BUT MY SOURCES TELL ME THIS IS THE REAL DEAL AND WE NEED TO FIND HIM BEFORE HE ESCAPES THE COUNTRY. THAT'S WHY THIS IS SO IMPORTANT.
SO, WHAT DO WE KNOW? WHERE IS HE NOW?
THAT'S THE THING. THE TRAIL IS COLD. THAT'S WHERE YOU COME IN.
IT'S BEEN YEARS SINCE I'VE SPOKEN TO ANY OF THOSE GUYS.

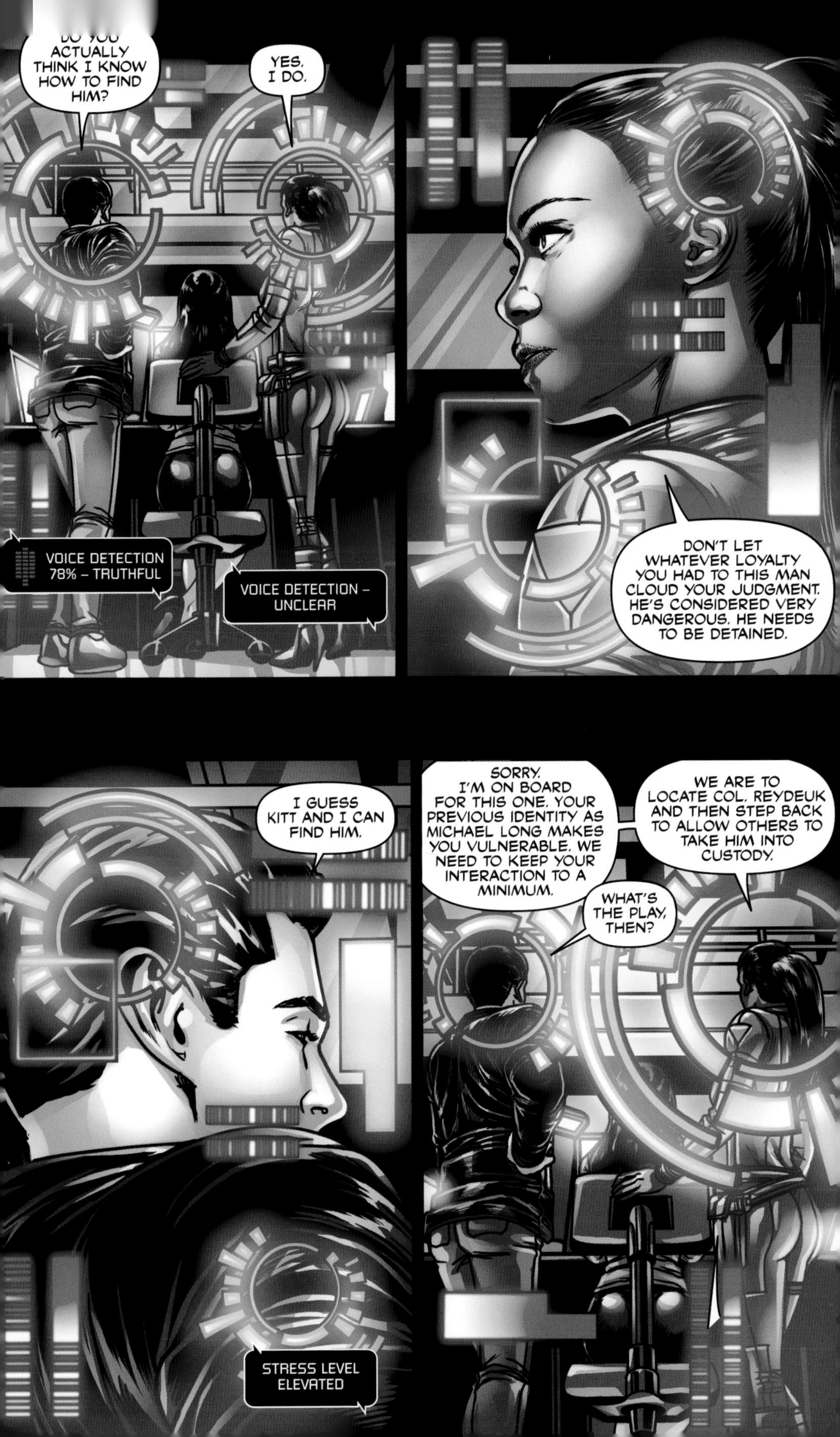
DO YOU ACTUALLY THINK I KNOW HOW TO FIND HIM?
YES, I DO.
VOICE DETECTION 78% – TRUTHFUL
VOICE DETECTION – UNCLEAR
DON'T LET WHATEVER LOYALTY YOU HAD TO THIS MAN CLOUD YOUR JUDGMENT. HE'S CONSIDERED VERY DANGEROUS. HE NEEDS TO BE DETAINED.
I GUESS KITT AND I CAN FIND HIM.
STRESS LEVEL ELEVATED
SORRY. I'M ON BOARD FOR THIS ONE. YOUR PREVIOUS IDENTITY AS MICHAEL LONG MAKES YOU VULNERABLE. WE NEED TO KEEP YOUR INTERACTION TO A MINIMUM.
WHAT'S THE PLAY, THEN?
WE ARE TO LOCATE COL. REYDEUK AND THEN STEP BACK TO ALLOW OTHERS TO TAKE HIM INTO CUSTODY.

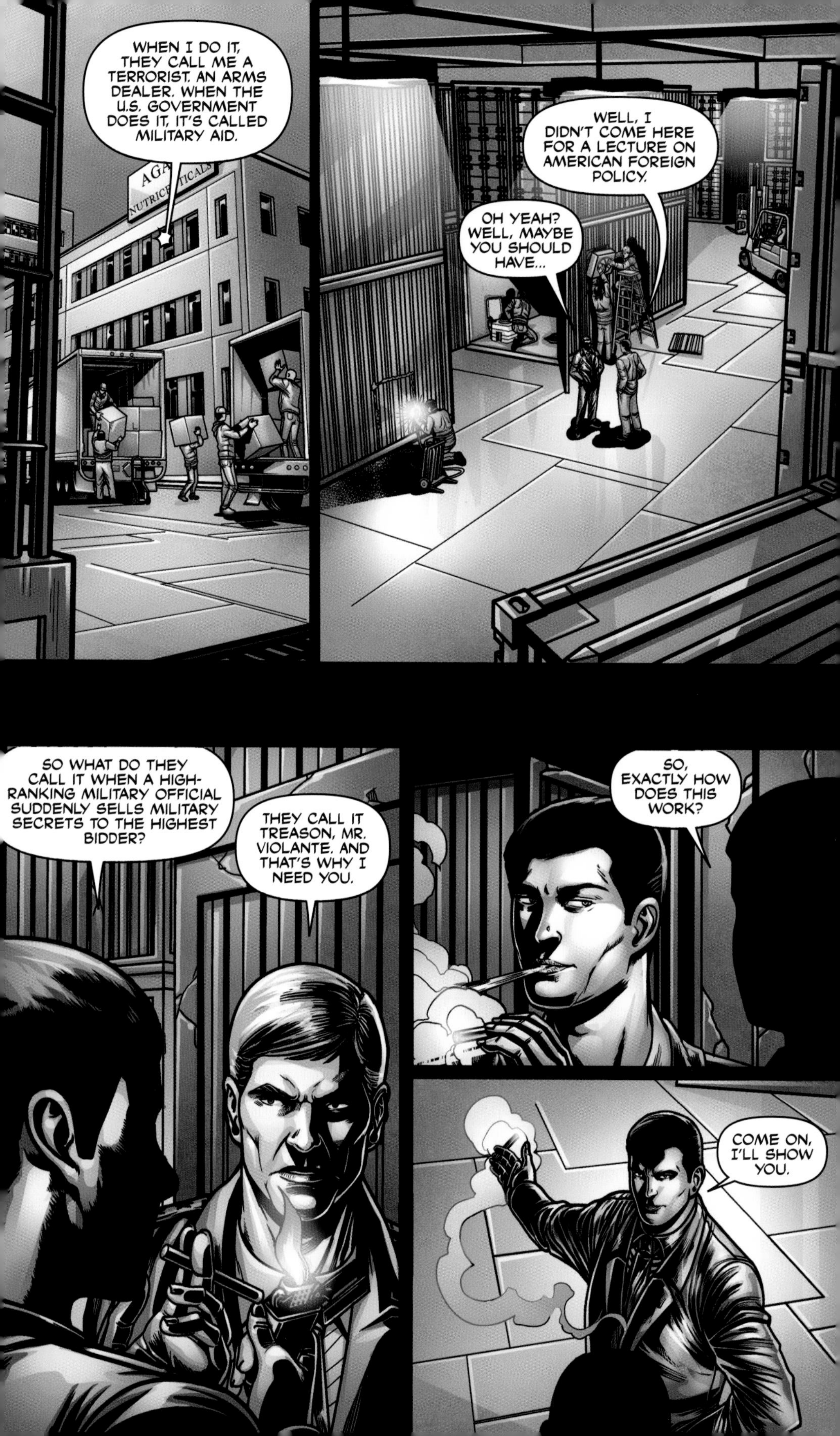
WHEN I DO IT, THEY CALL ME A TERRORIST. AN ARMS DEALER. WHEN THE U.S. GOVERNMENT DOES IT, IT'S CALLED MILITARY AID.
NUTRICEUTICALS
WELL, I DIDN'T COME HERE FOR A LECTURE ON AMERICAN FOREIGN POLICY.
OH YEAH? WELL, MAYBE YOU SHOULD HAVE...
SO WHAT DO THEY CALL IT WHEN A HIGH-RANKING MILITARY OFFICIAL SUDDENLY SELLS MILITARY SECRETS TO THE HIGHEST BIDDER?
THEY CALL IT TREASON, MR. VIOLANTE. AND THAT'S WHY I NEED YOU.
SO, EXACTLY HOW DOES THIS WORK?
COME ON, I'LL SHOW YOU.

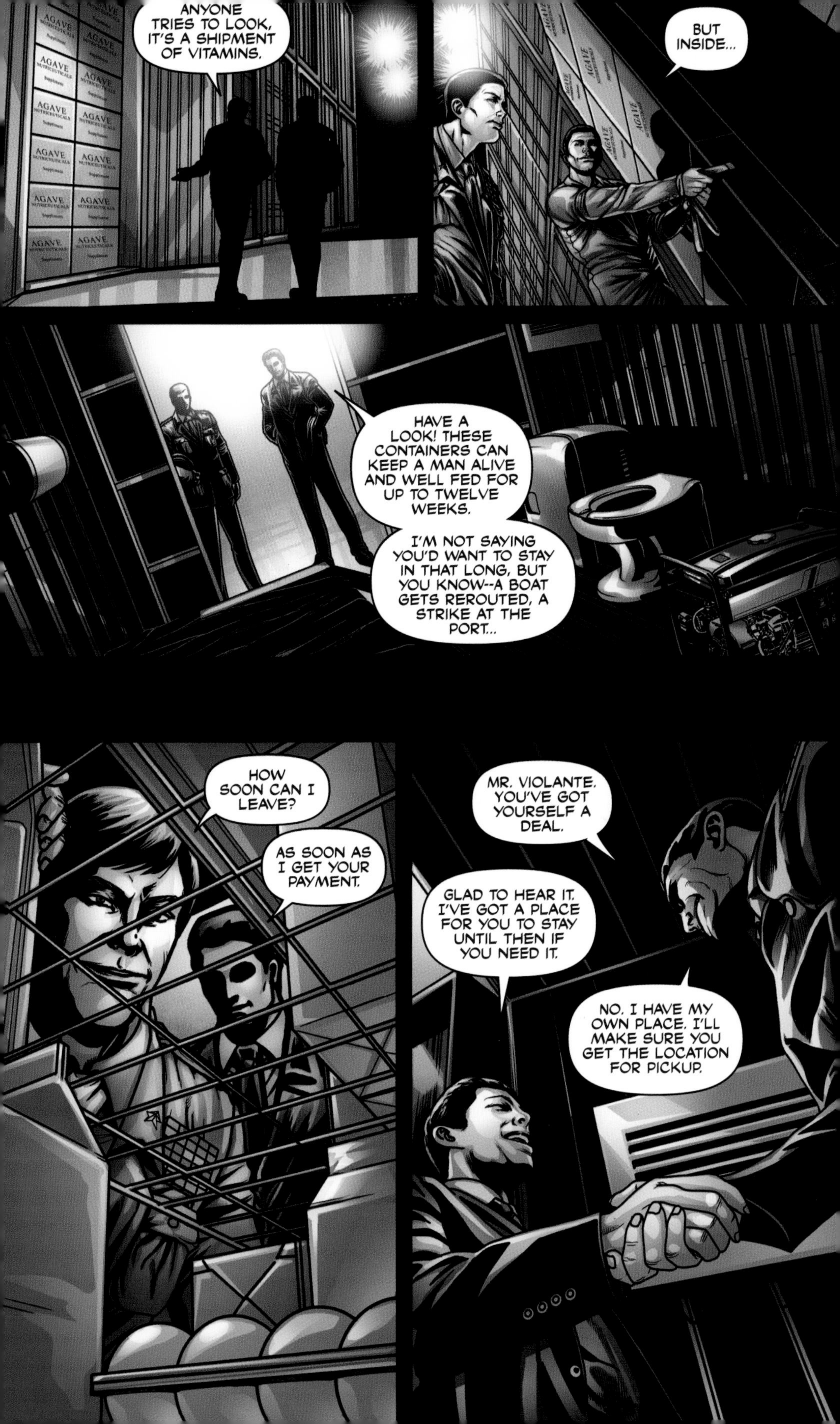
ANYONE TRIES TO LOOK, IT'S A SHIPMENT OF VITAMINS.
BUT INSIDE...
HAVE A LOOK! THESE CONTAINERS CAN KEEP A MAN ALIVE AND WELL FED FOR UP TO TWELVE WEEKS.
I'M NOT SAYING YOU'D WANT TO STAY IN THAT LONG, BUT YOU KNOW--A BOAT GETS REROUTED, A STRIKE AT THE PORT...
HOW SOON CAN I LEAVE?
AS SOON AS I GET YOUR PAYMENT.
MR. VIOLANTE, YOU'VE GOT YOURSELF A DEAL.
GLAD TO HEAR IT. I'VE GOT A PLACE FOR YOU TO STAY UNTIL THEN IF YOU NEED IT.
NO. I HAVE MY OWN PLACE. I'LL MAKE SURE YOU GET THE LOCATION FOR PICKUP.

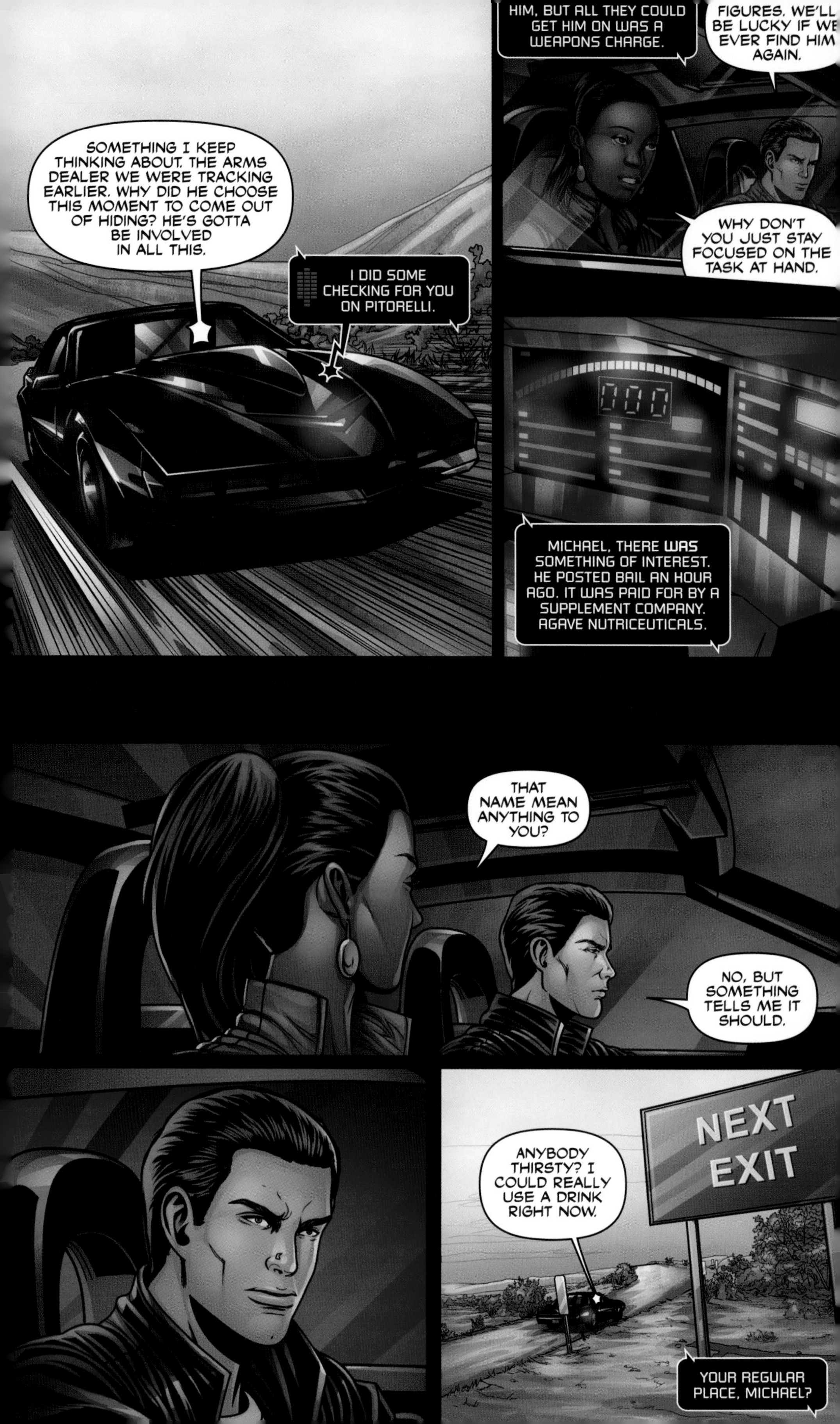
HIM, BUT ALL THEY COULD GET HIM ON WAS A WEAPONS CHARGE.
FIGURES. WE'LL BE LUCKY IF WE EVER FIND HIM AGAIN.
SOMETHING I KEEP THINKING ABOUT. THE ARMS DEALER WE WERE TRACKING EARLIER. WHY DID HE CHOOSE THIS MOMENT TO COME OUT OF HIDING? HE'S GOTTA BE INVOLVED IN ALL THIS.
I DID SOME CHECKING FOR YOU ON PITORELLI.
WHY DON'T YOU JUST STAY FOCUSED ON THE TASK AT HAND.
MICHAEL, THERE WAS SOMETHING OF INTEREST. HE POSTED BAIL AN HOUR AGO. IT WAS PAID FOR BY A SUPPLEMENT COMPANY. AGAVE NUTRICEUTICALS.
THAT NAME MEAN ANYTHING TO YOU?
NO, BUT SOMETHING TELLS ME IT SHOULD.
NEXT EXIT
ANYBODY THIRSTY? I COULD REALLY USE A DRINK RIGHT NOW.
YOUR REGULAR PLACE, MICHAEL?

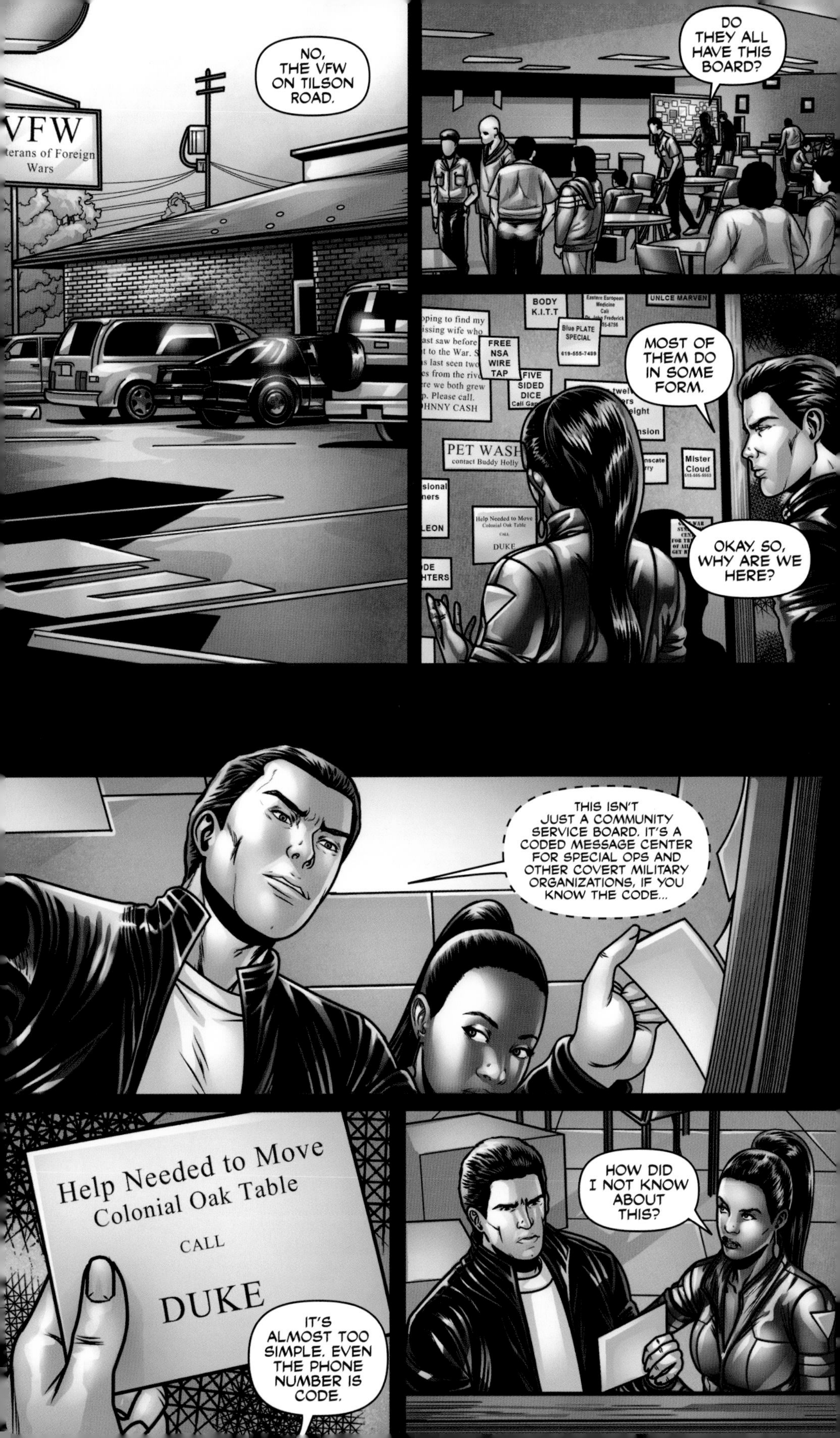
VFW
terans of Foreign
Wars
NO, THE VFW ON TILSON ROAD.
DO THEY ALL HAVE THIS BOARD?
BODY K.I.T.T
UNLCE MARVEN
Blue PLATE SPECIAL
619-555-7489
FREE NSA WIRE TAP
FIVE SIDED DICE
PET WASH contact Buddy Holly
Mister Cloud
Help Needed to Move Colonial Oak Table CALL DUKE
MOST OF THEM DO IN SOME FORM.
OKAY. SO, WHY ARE WE HERE?
THIS ISN'T JUST A COMMUNITY SERVICE BOARD. IT'S A CODED MESSAGE CENTER FOR SPECIAL OPS AND OTHER COVERT MILITARY ORGANIZATIONS, IF YOU KNOW THE CODE...
Help Needed to Move
Colonial Oak Table
CALL
DUKE
IT'S ALMOST TOO SIMPLE. EVEN THE PHONE NUMBER IS CODE.
HOW DID I NOT KNOW ABOUT THIS?

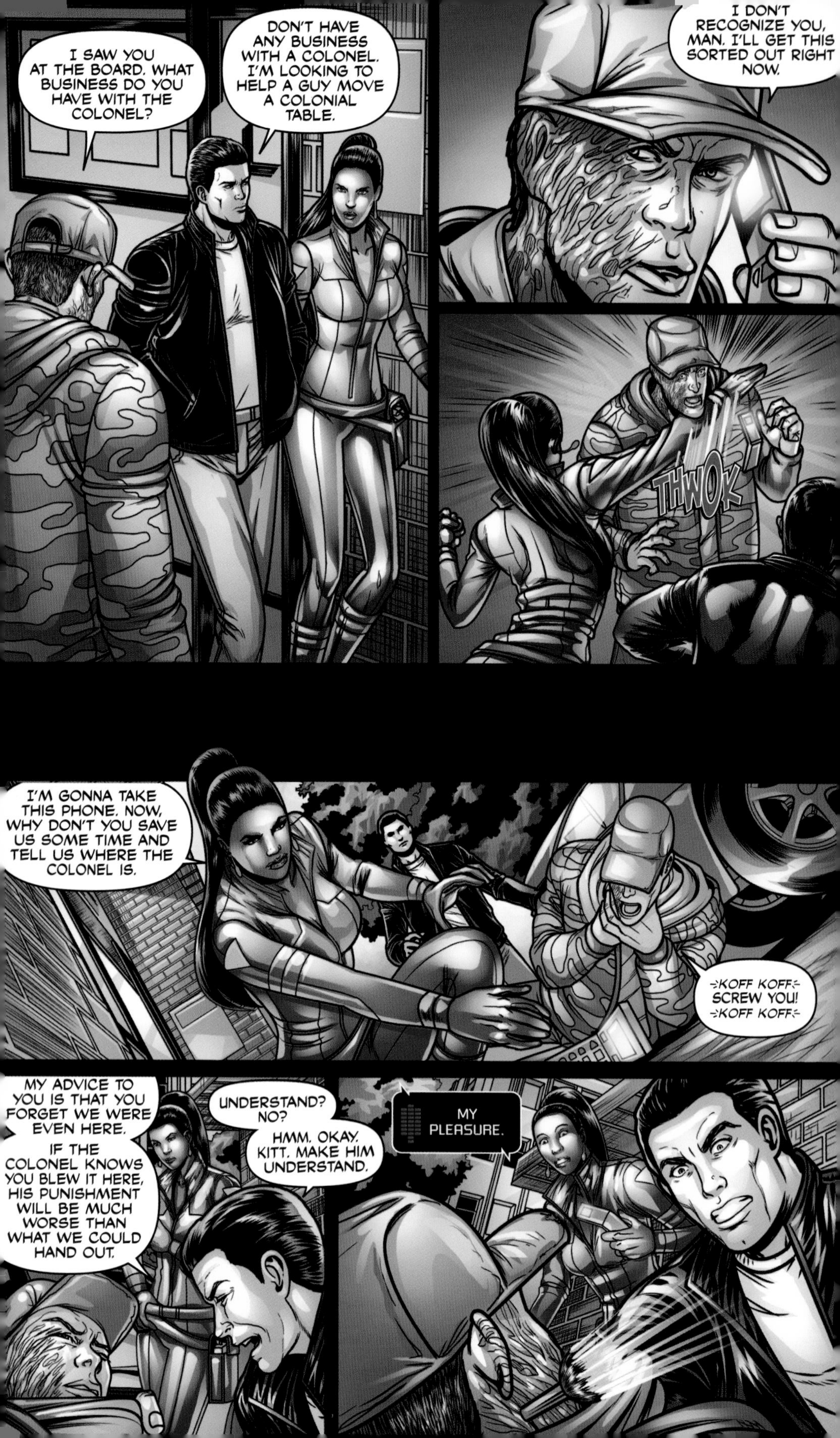
I SAW YOU AT THE BOARD. WHAT BUSINESS DO YOU HAVE WITH THE COLONEL?
DON'T HAVE ANY BUSINESS WITH A COLONEL. I'M LOOKING TO HELP A GUY MOVE A COLONIAL TABLE.
I DON'T RECOGNIZE YOU, MAN. I'LL GET THIS SORTED OUT RIGHT NOW.
THWOK
I'M GONNA TAKE THIS PHONE. NOW, WHY DON'T YOU SAVE US SOME TIME AND TELL US WHERE THE COLONEL IS.
KOFF KOFF
SCREW YOU!
KOFF KOFF
MY ADVICE TO YOU IS THAT YOU FORGET WE WERE EVEN HERE.
IF THE COLONEL KNOWS YOU BLEW IT HERE, HIS PUNISHMENT WILL BE MUCH WORSE THAN WHAT WE COULD HAND OUT.
UNDERSTAND? NO?
HMM. OKAY. KITT, MAKE HIM UNDERSTAND.
MY PLEASURE.

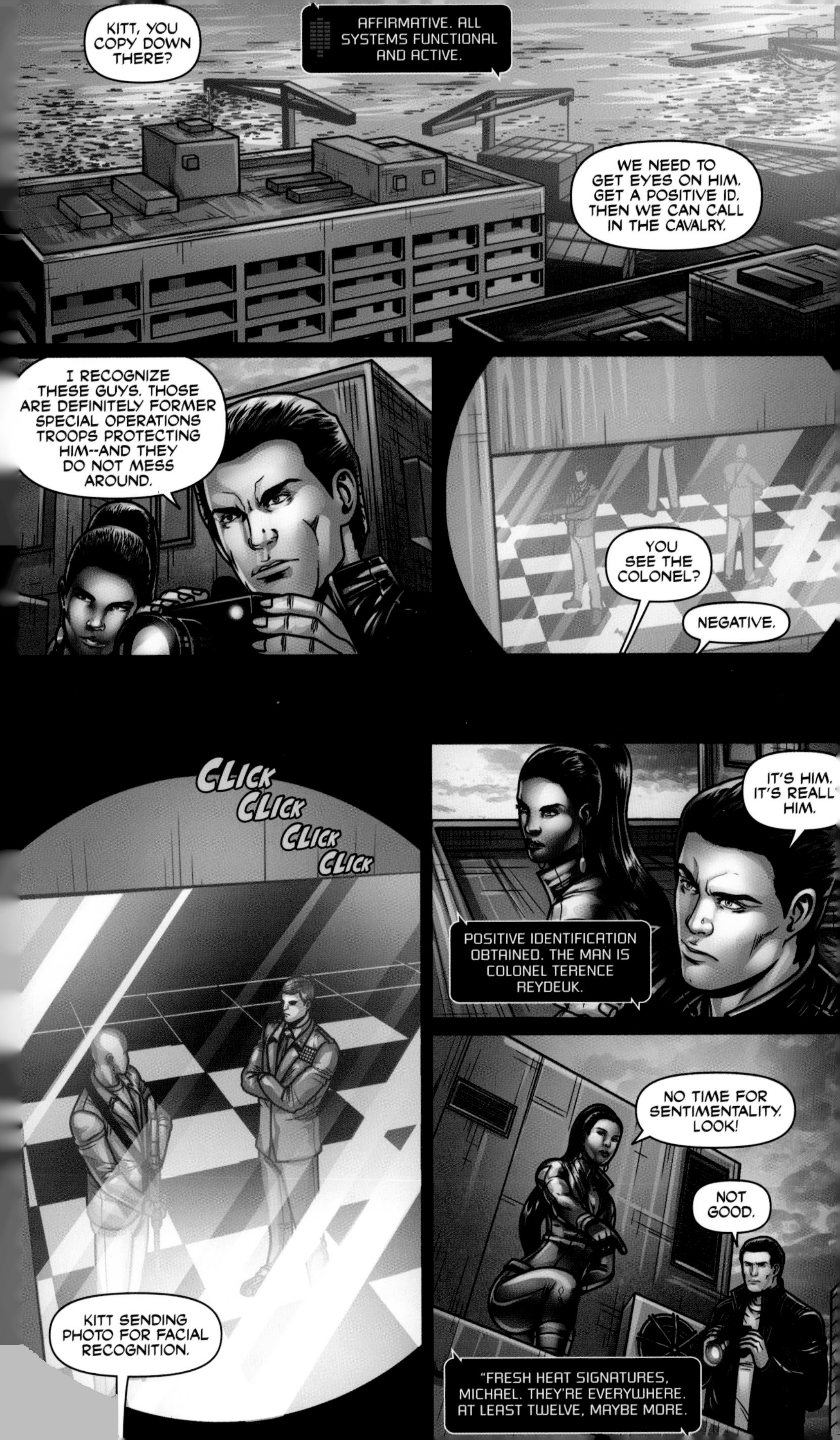
KITT, YOU COPY DOWN THERE?
AFFIRMATIVE. ALL SYSTEMS FUNCTIONAL AND ACTIVE.
WE NEED TO GET EYES ON HIM, GET A POSITIVE ID, THEN WE CAN CALL IN THE CAVALRY.
I RECOGNIZE THESE GUYS. THOSE ARE DEFINITELY FORMER SPECIAL OPERATIONS TROOPS PROTECTING HIM--AND THEY DO NOT MESS AROUND.
YOU SEE THE COLONEL?
NEGATIVE.
CLICK CLICK CLICK CLICK
KITT SENDING PHOTO FOR FACIAL RECOGNITION.
POSITIVE IDENTIFICATION OBTAINED. THE MAN IS COLONEL TERENCE REYDEUK.
IT'S HIM. IT'S REALL HIM.
NO TIME FOR SENTIMENTALITY. LOOK!
NOT GOOD.
"FRESH HEAT SIGNATURES, MICHAEL. THEY'RE EVERYWHERE. AT LEAST TWELVE, MAYBE MORE.

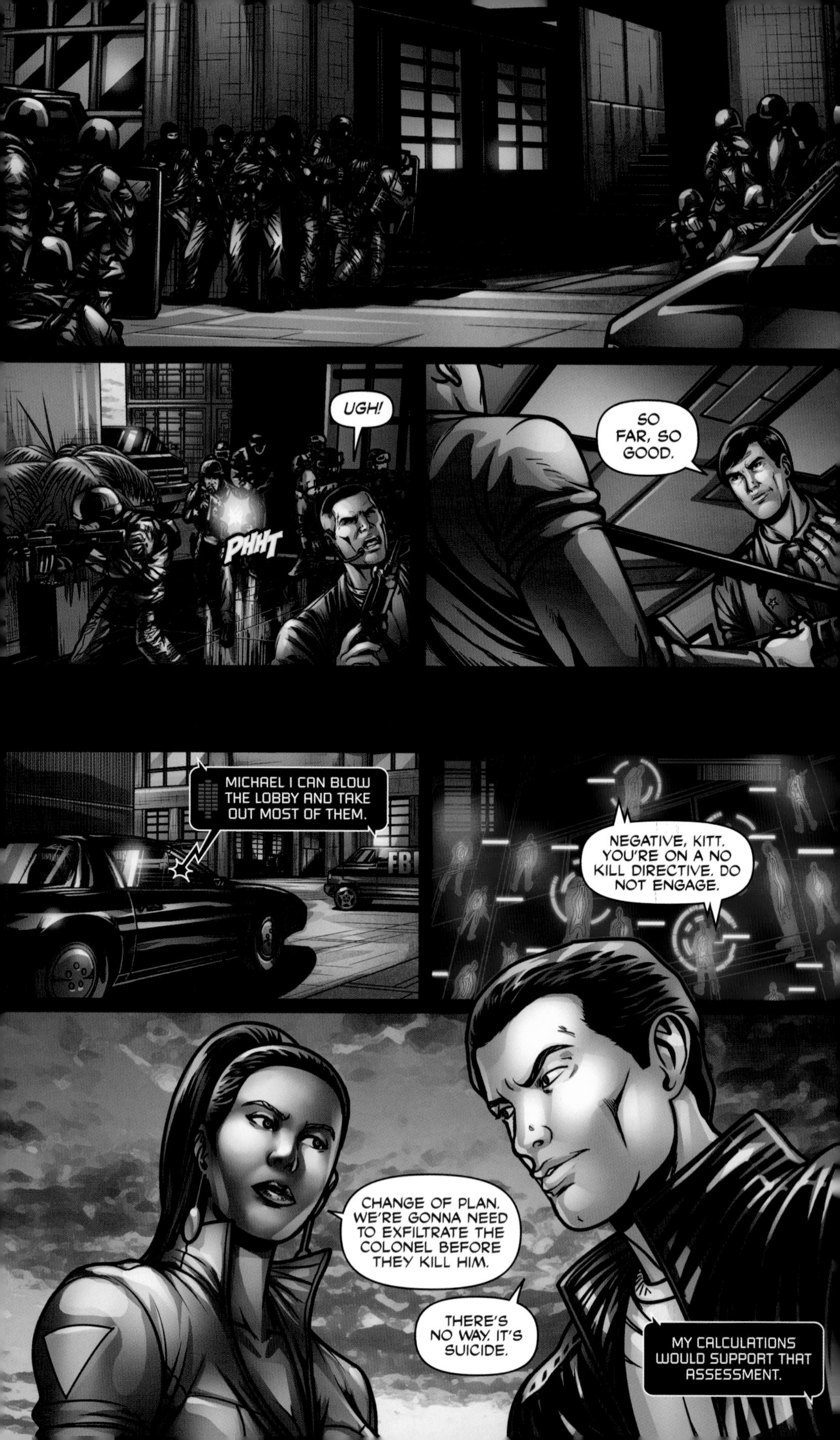
UGH!
PHHT
SO FAR, SO GOOD.
MICHAEL I CAN BLOW THE LOBBY AND TAKE OUT MOST OF THEM.
FBI
NEGATIVE, KITT. YOU'RE ON A NO KILL DIRECTIVE. DO NOT ENGAGE.
CHANGE OF PLAN. WE'RE GONNA NEED TO EXFILTRATE THE COLONEL BEFORE THEY KILL HIM.
THERE'S NO WAY. IT'S SUICIDE.
MY CALCULATIONS WOULD SUPPORT THAT ASSESSMENT.

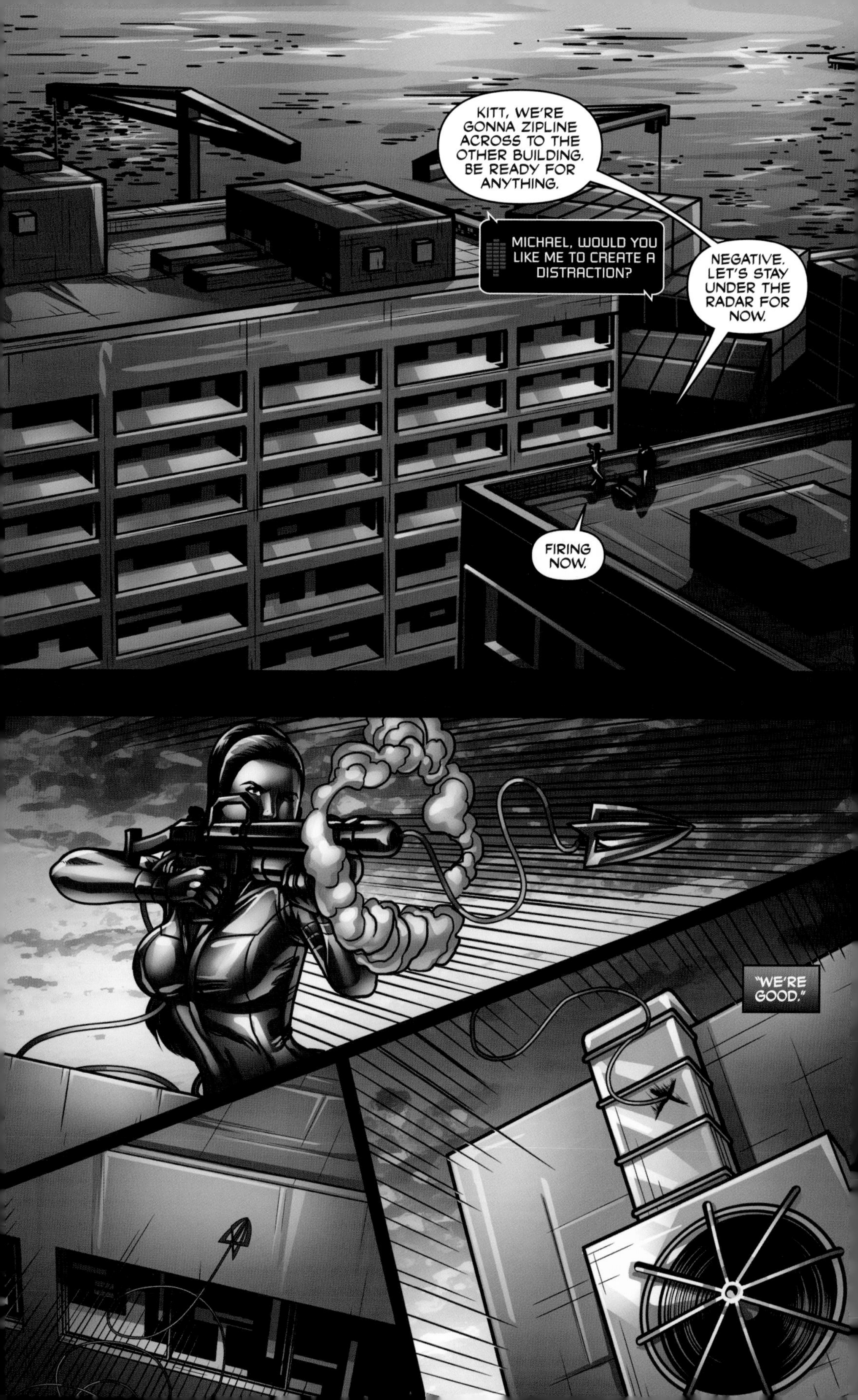
KITT, WE'RE GONNA ZIPLINE ACROSS TO THE OTHER BUILDING. BE READY FOR ANYTHING.
MICHAEL, WOULD YOU LIKE ME TO CREATE A DISTRACTION?
NEGATIVE. LET'S STAY UNDER THE RADAR FOR NOW.
FIRING NOW.
"WE'RE GOOD."

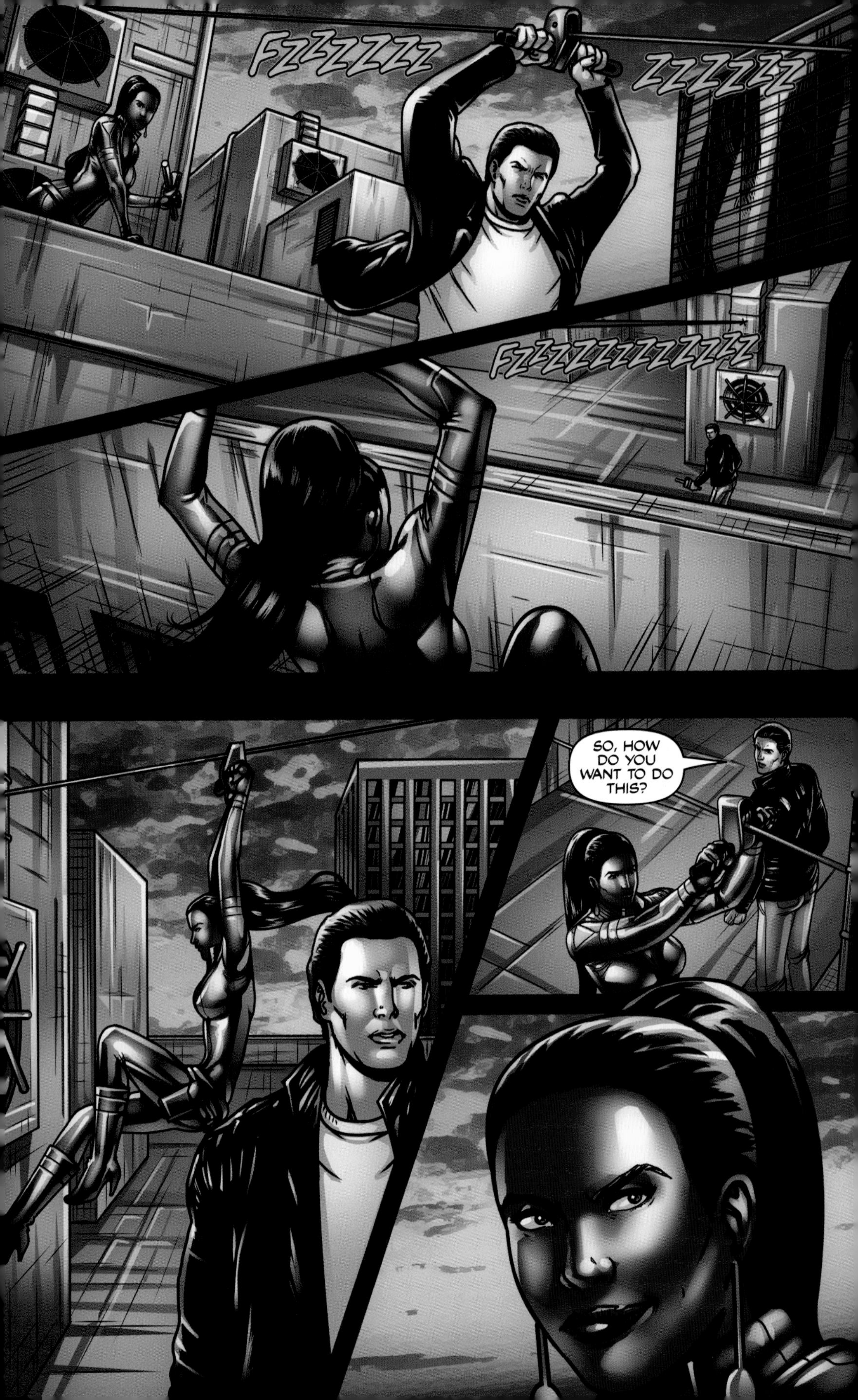
FZZZZZZZ
ZZZZZZ
FZZZZZZZZZZZZZ
SO, HOW DO YOU WANT TO DO THIS?

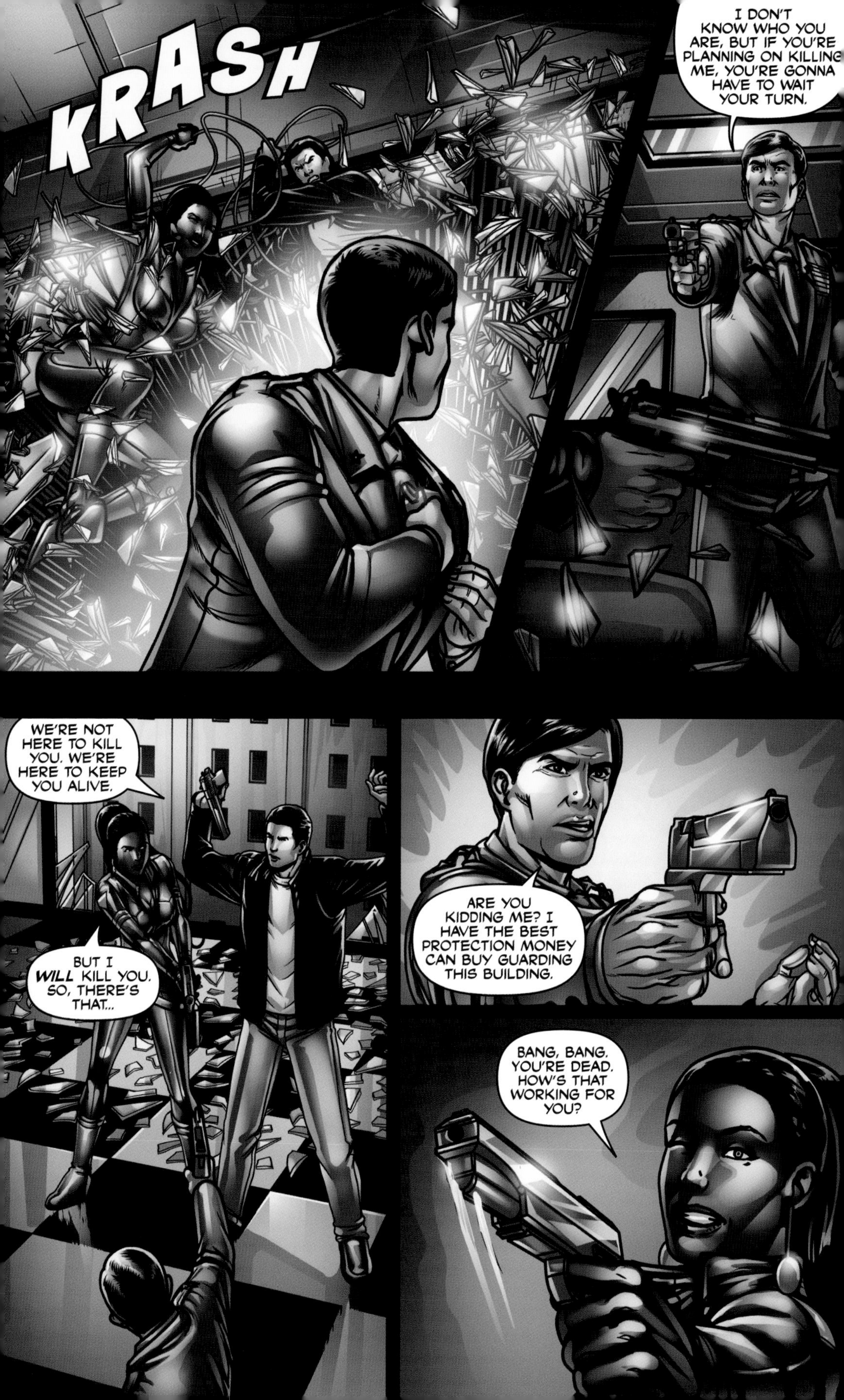
KRASH
I DON'T KNOW WHO YOU ARE, BUT IF YOU'RE PLANNING ON KILLING ME, YOU'RE GONNA HAVE TO WAIT YOUR TURN.
WE'RE NOT HERE TO KILL YOU. WE'RE HERE TO KEEP YOU ALIVE.
BUT I *WILL* KILL YOU. SO, THERE'S THAT...
ARE YOU KIDDING ME? I HAVE THE BEST PROTECTION MONEY CAN BUY GUARDING THIS BUILDING.
BANG, BANG. YOU'RE DEAD. HOW'S THAT WORKING FOR YOU?

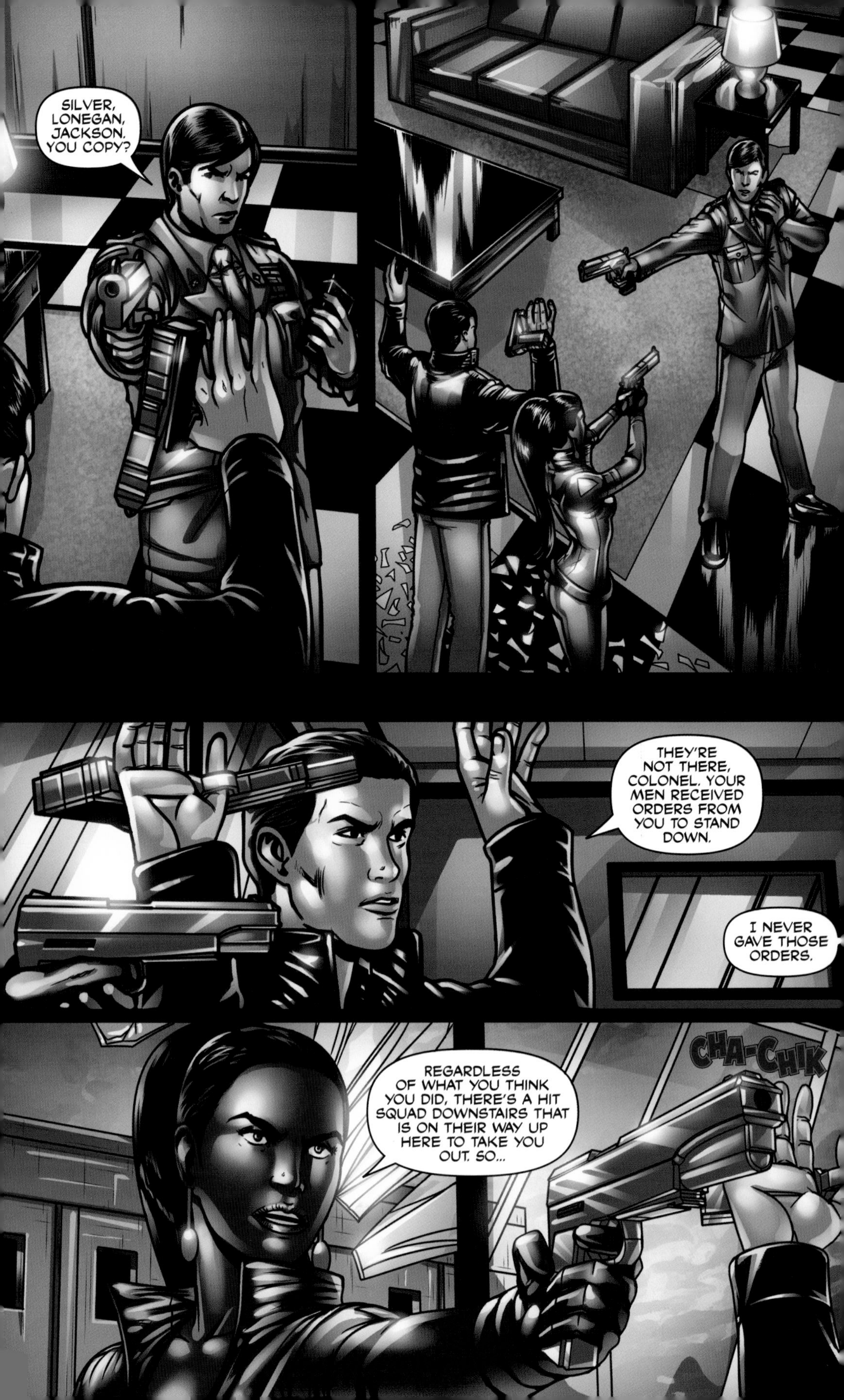
SILVER, LONEGAN, JACKSON. YOU COPY?
THEY'RE NOT THERE, COLONEL. YOUR MEN RECEIVED ORDERS FROM YOU TO STAND DOWN.
I NEVER GAVE THOSE ORDERS.
CHA-CHIK
REGARDLESS OF WHAT YOU THINK YOU DID, THERE'S A HIT SQUAD DOWNSTAIRS THAT IS ON THEIR WAY UP HERE TO TAKE YOU OUT. SO...

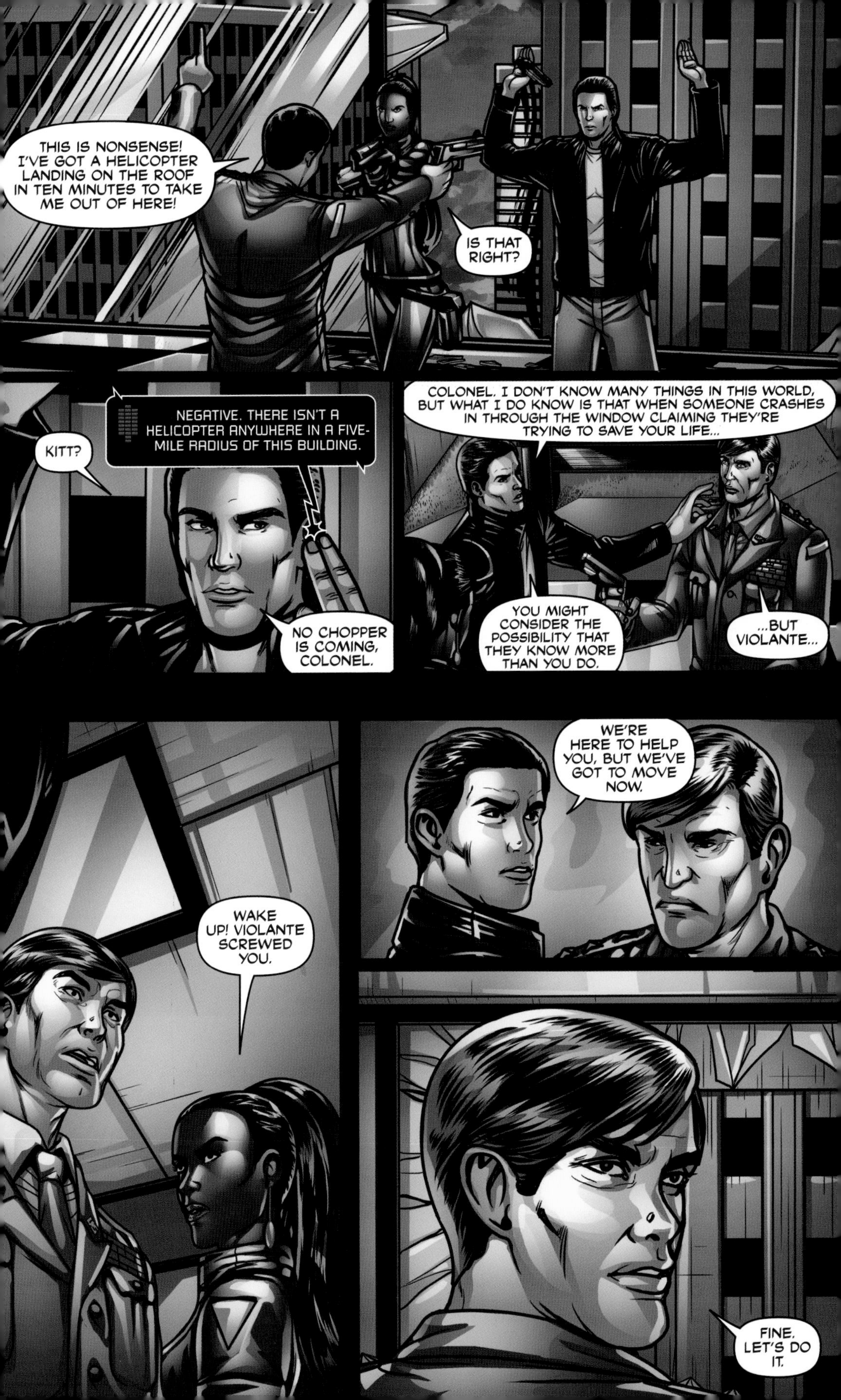
THIS IS NONSENSE! I'VE GOT A HELICOPTER LANDING ON THE ROOF IN TEN MINUTES TO TAKE ME OUT OF HERE!
IS THAT RIGHT?
KITT?
NEGATIVE. THERE ISN'T A HELICOPTER ANYWHERE IN A FIVE-MILE RADIUS OF THIS BUILDING.
NO CHOPPER IS COMING, COLONEL.
COLONEL, I DON'T KNOW MANY THINGS IN THIS WORLD, BUT WHAT I DO KNOW IS THAT WHEN SOMEONE CRASHES IN THROUGH THE WINDOW CLAIMING THEY'RE TRYING TO SAVE YOUR LIFE...
YOU MIGHT CONSIDER THE POSSIBILITY THAT THEY KNOW MORE THAN YOU DO.
...BUT VIOLANTE...
WAKE UP! VIOLANTE SCREWED YOU.
WE'RE HERE TO HELP YOU, BUT WE'VE GOT TO MOVE NOW.
FINE. LET'S DO IT.

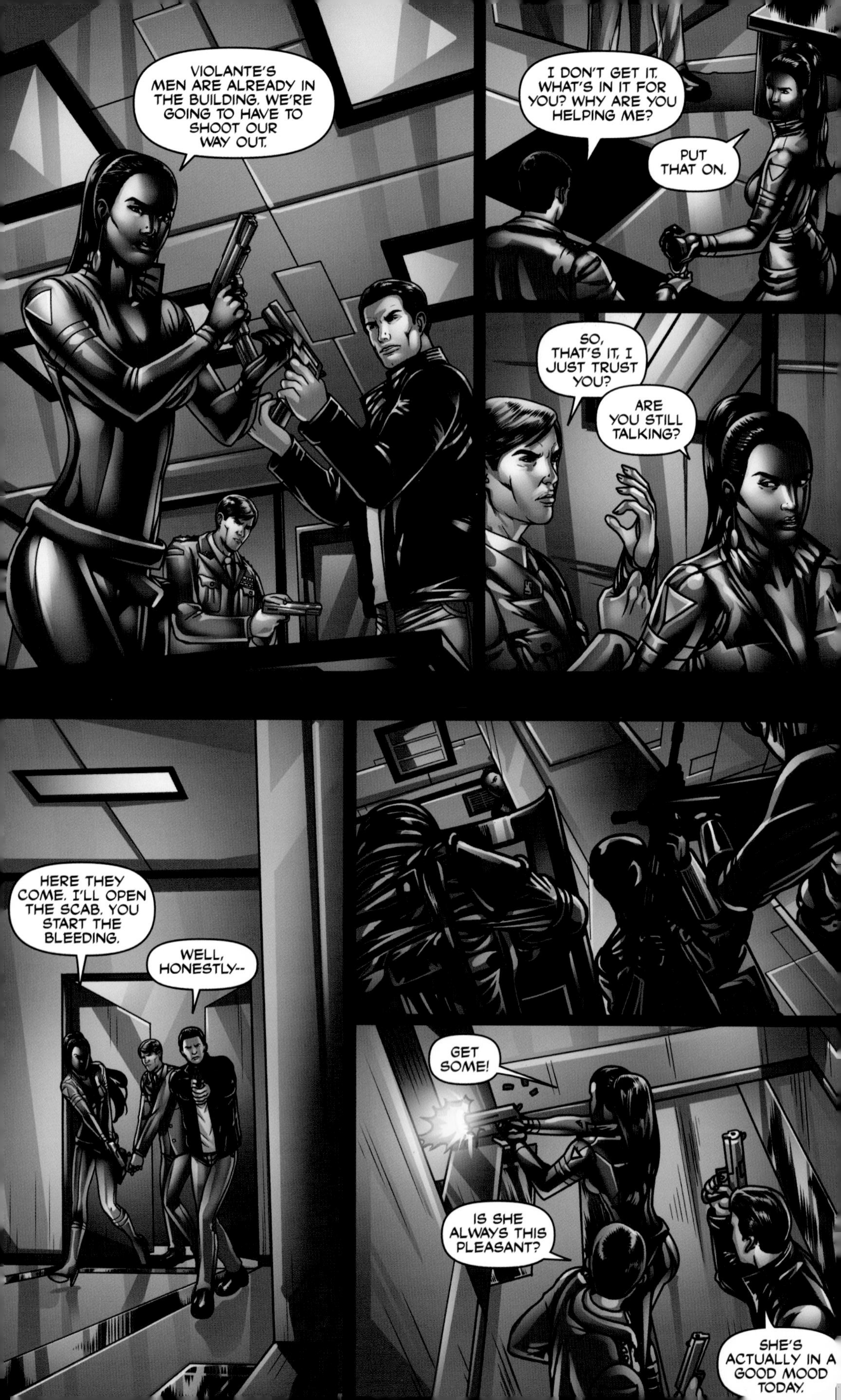
VIOLANTE'S MEN ARE ALREADY IN THE BUILDING. WE'RE GOING TO HAVE TO SHOOT OUR WAY OUT.
I DON'T GET IT. WHAT'S IN IT FOR YOU? WHY ARE YOU HELPING ME?
PUT THAT ON.
SO, THAT'S IT, I JUST TRUST YOU?
ARE YOU STILL TALKING?
HERE THEY COME. I'LL OPEN THE SCAB. YOU START THE BLEEDING.
WELL, HONESTLY--
GET SOME!
IS SHE ALWAYS THIS PLEASANT?
SHE'S ACTUALLY IN A GOOD MOOD TODAY.

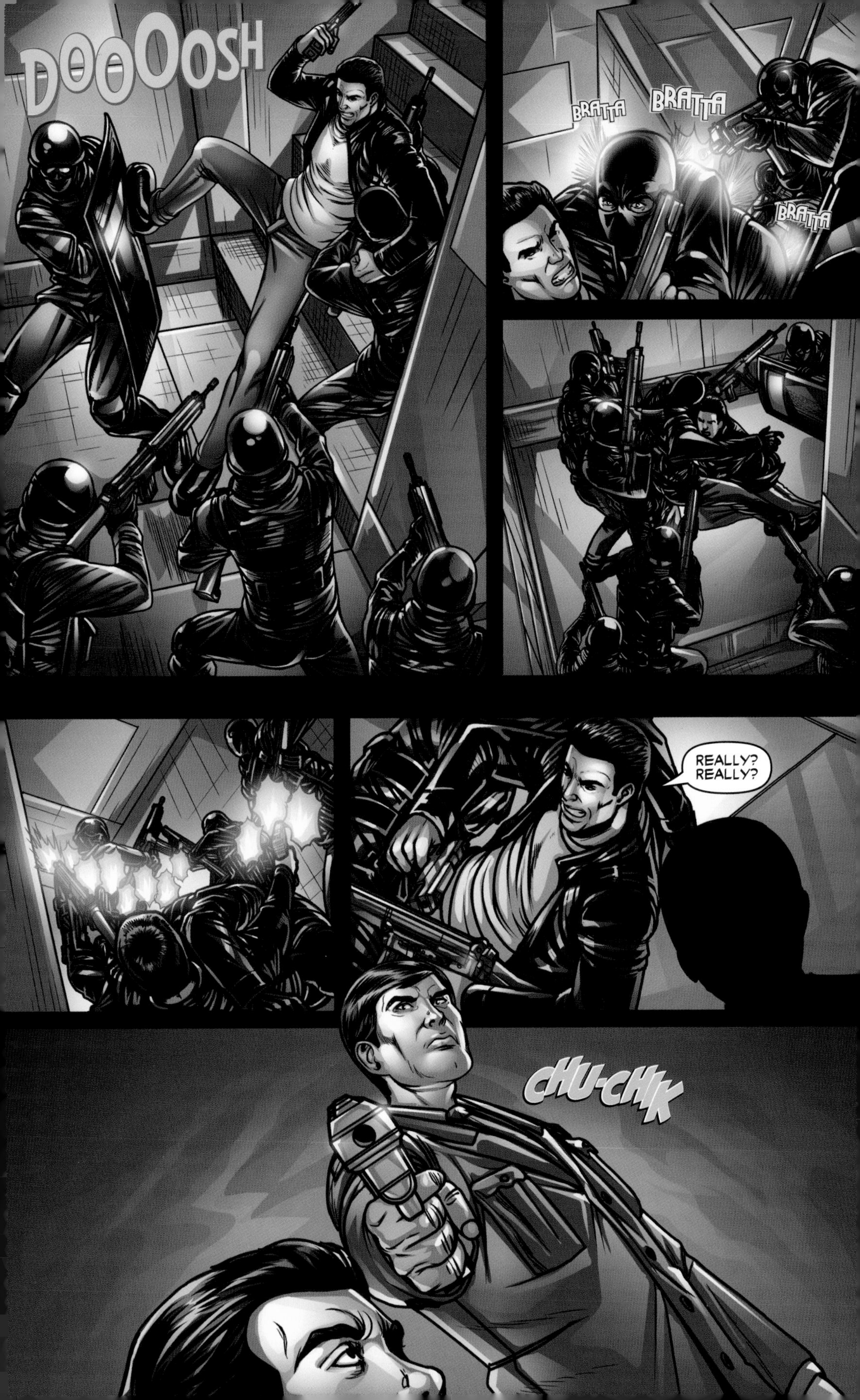
DOOOOSH
BRATTA
BRATTA
BRATTA
REALLY? REALLY?
CHU-CHIK

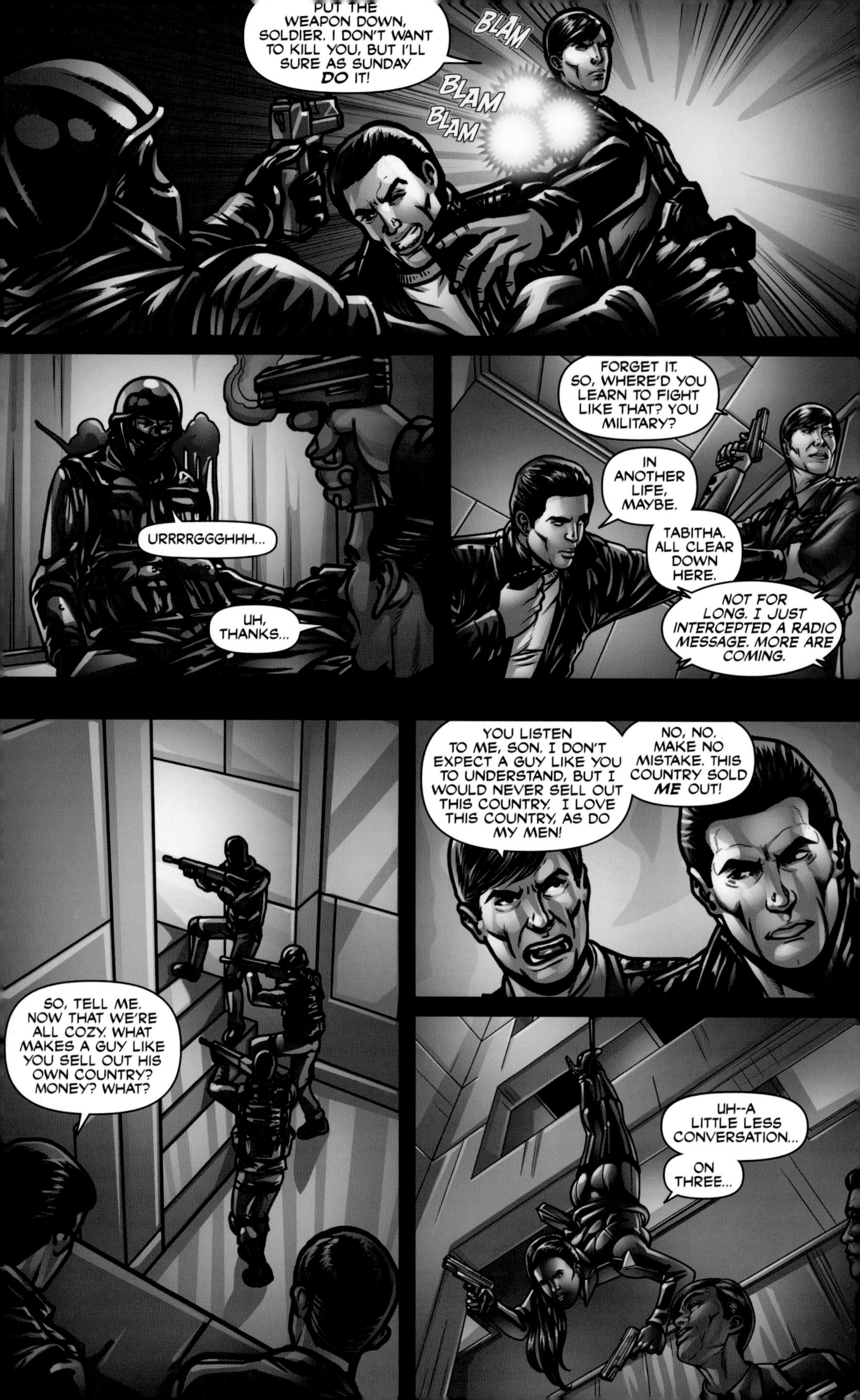
PUT THE WEAPON DOWN, SOLDIER. I DON'T WANT TO KILL YOU, BUT I'LL SURE AS SUNDAY DO IT!
BLAM
BLAM
BLAM
URRRRGGGHHH...
UH, THANKS...
FORGET IT. SO, WHERE'D YOU LEARN TO FIGHT LIKE THAT? YOU MILITARY?
IN ANOTHER LIFE, MAYBE.
TABITHA. ALL CLEAR DOWN HERE.
NOT FOR LONG. I JUST INTERCEPTED A RADIO MESSAGE. MORE ARE COMING.
SO, TELL ME. NOW THAT WE'RE ALL COZY. WHAT MAKES A GUY LIKE YOU SELL OUT HIS OWN COUNTRY? MONEY? WHAT?
YOU LISTEN TO ME, SON. I DON'T EXPECT A GUY LIKE YOU TO UNDERSTAND, BUT I WOULD NEVER SELL OUT THIS COUNTRY. I LOVE THIS COUNTRY, AS DO MY MEN!
NO, NO. MAKE NO MISTAKE. THIS COUNTRY SOLD ME OUT!
UH--A LITTLE LESS CONVERSATION...
ON THREE...

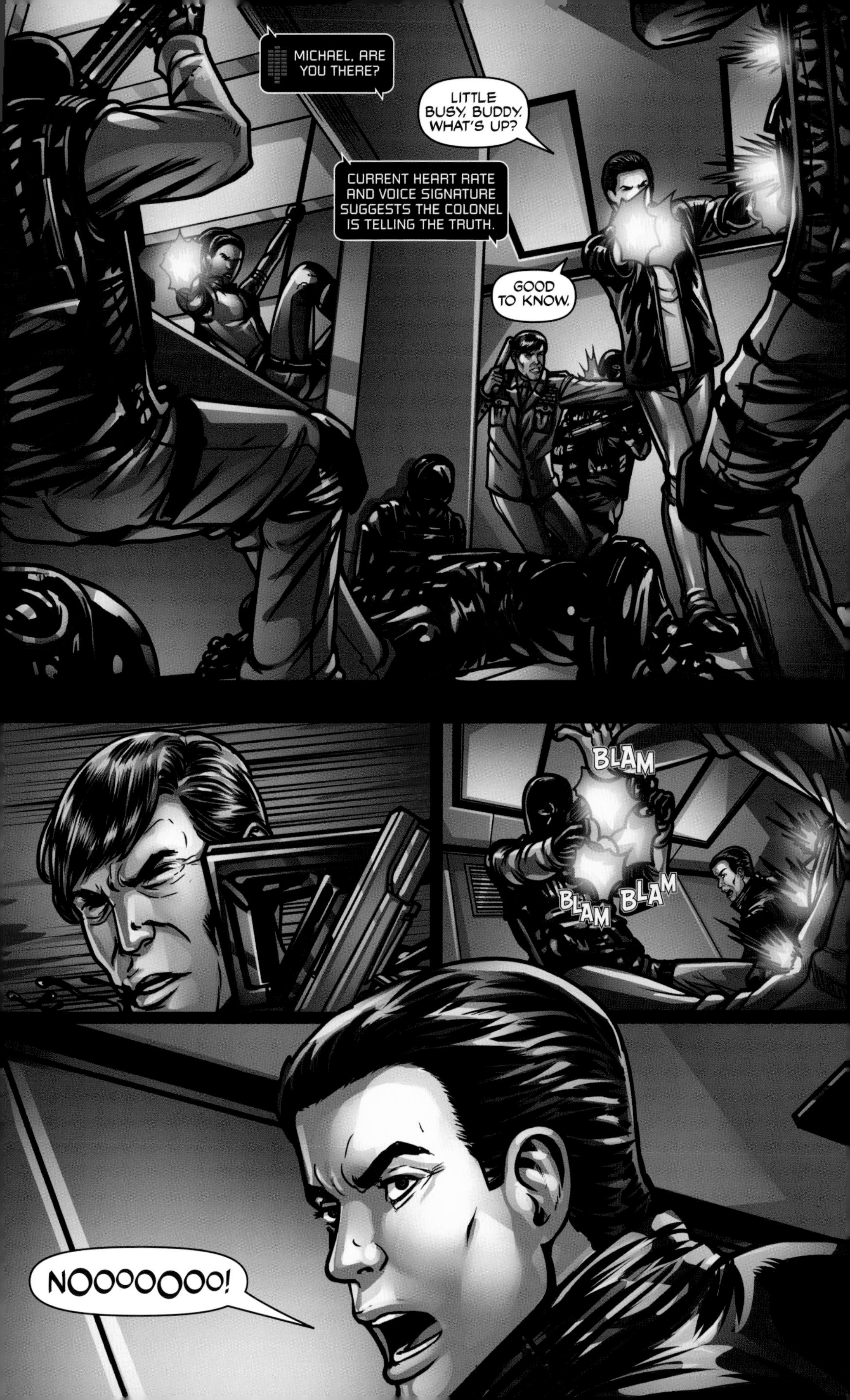
MICHAEL, ARE YOU THERE?
LITTLE BUSY, BUDDY. WHAT'S UP?
CURRENT HEART RATE AND VOICE SIGNATURE SUGGESTS THE COLONEL IS TELLING THE TRUTH.
GOOD TO KNOW.
BLAM
BLAM
BLAM
NOOOOOOO!

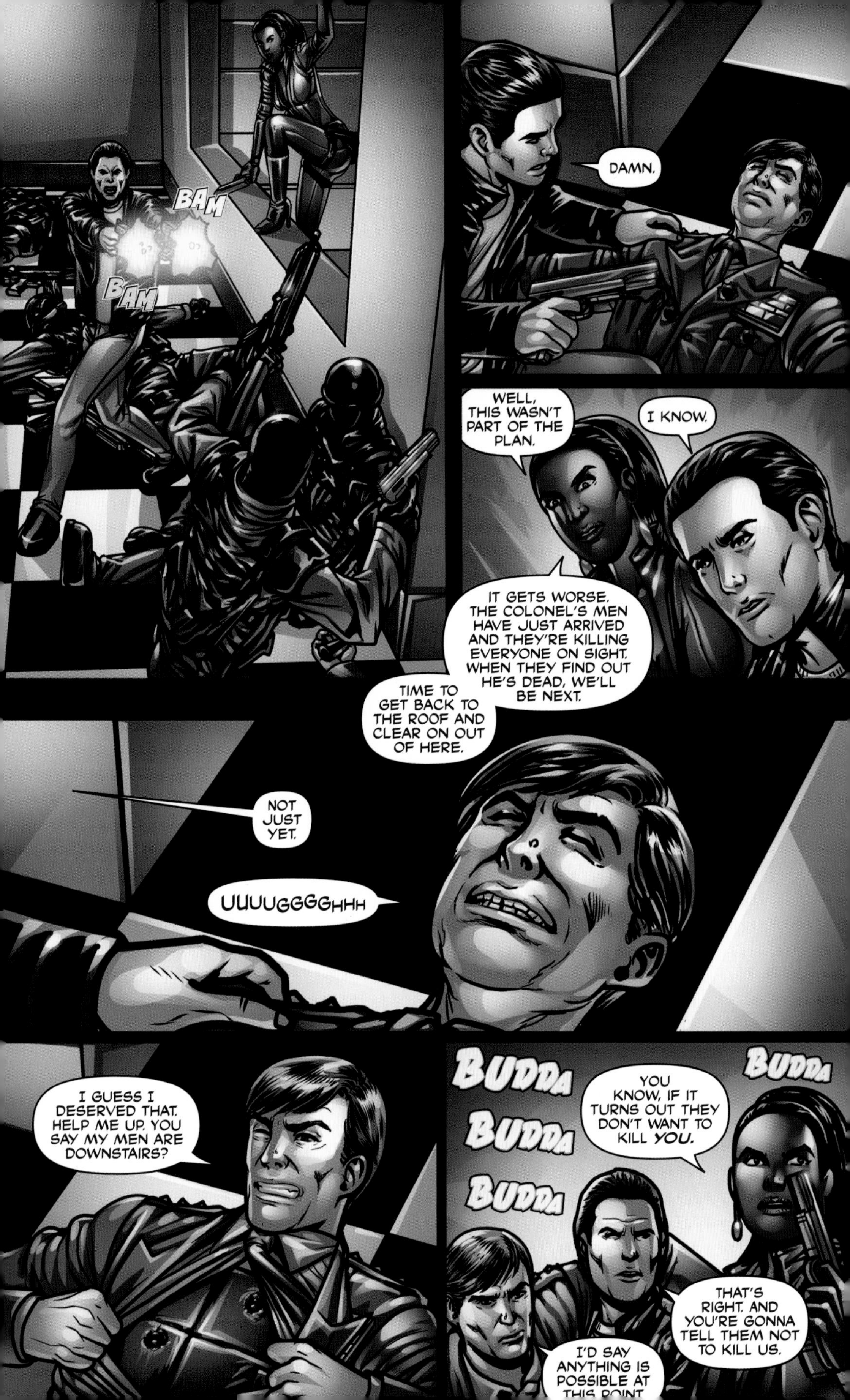
BAM
BAM
DAMN.
WELL, THIS WASN'T PART OF THE PLAN.
I KNOW.
IT GETS WORSE. THE COLONEL'S MEN HAVE JUST ARRIVED AND THEY'RE KILLING EVERYONE ON SIGHT. WHEN THEY FIND OUT HE'S DEAD, WE'LL BE NEXT.
TIME TO GET BACK TO THE ROOF AND CLEAR ON OUT OF HERE.
NOT JUST YET.
UUUUGGGGHHH
I GUESS I DESERVED THAT. HELP ME UP. YOU SAY MY MEN ARE DOWNSTAIRS?
BUDDA
BUDDA
BUDDA
BUDDA
YOU KNOW, IF IT TURNS OUT THEY DON'T WANT TO KILL *YOU.*
THAT'S RIGHT. AND YOU'RE GONNA TELL THEM NOT TO KILL US.
I'D SAY ANYTHING IS POSSIBLE AT THIS POINT

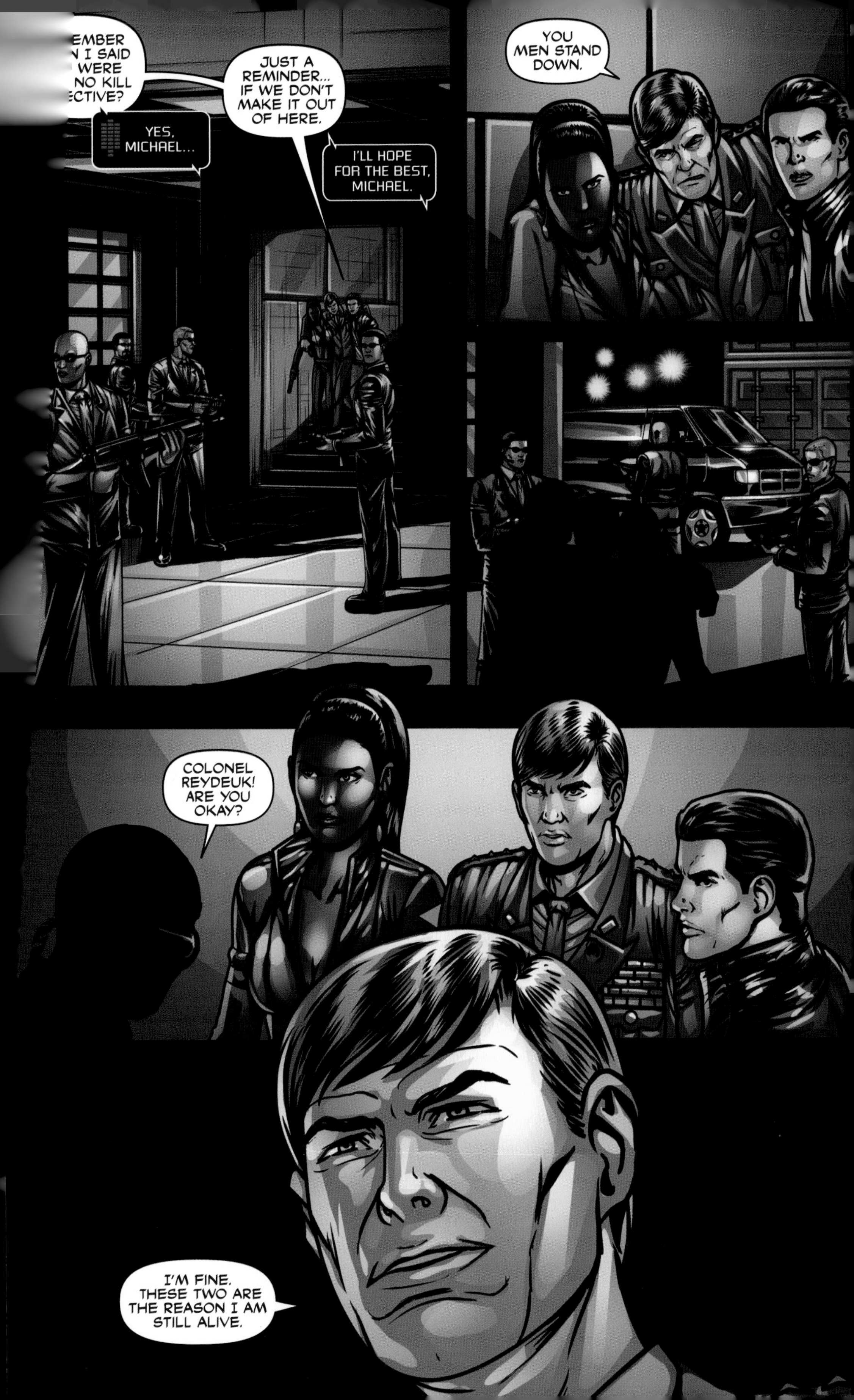
EMBER I SAID WERE NO KILL ECTIVE?
YES, MICHAEL...
JUST A REMINDER... IF WE DON'T MAKE IT OUT OF HERE.
I'LL HOPE FOR THE BEST, MICHAEL.
YOU MEN STAND DOWN.
COLONEL REYDEUK! ARE YOU OKAY?
I'M FINE. THESE TWO ARE THE REASON I AM STILL ALIVE.

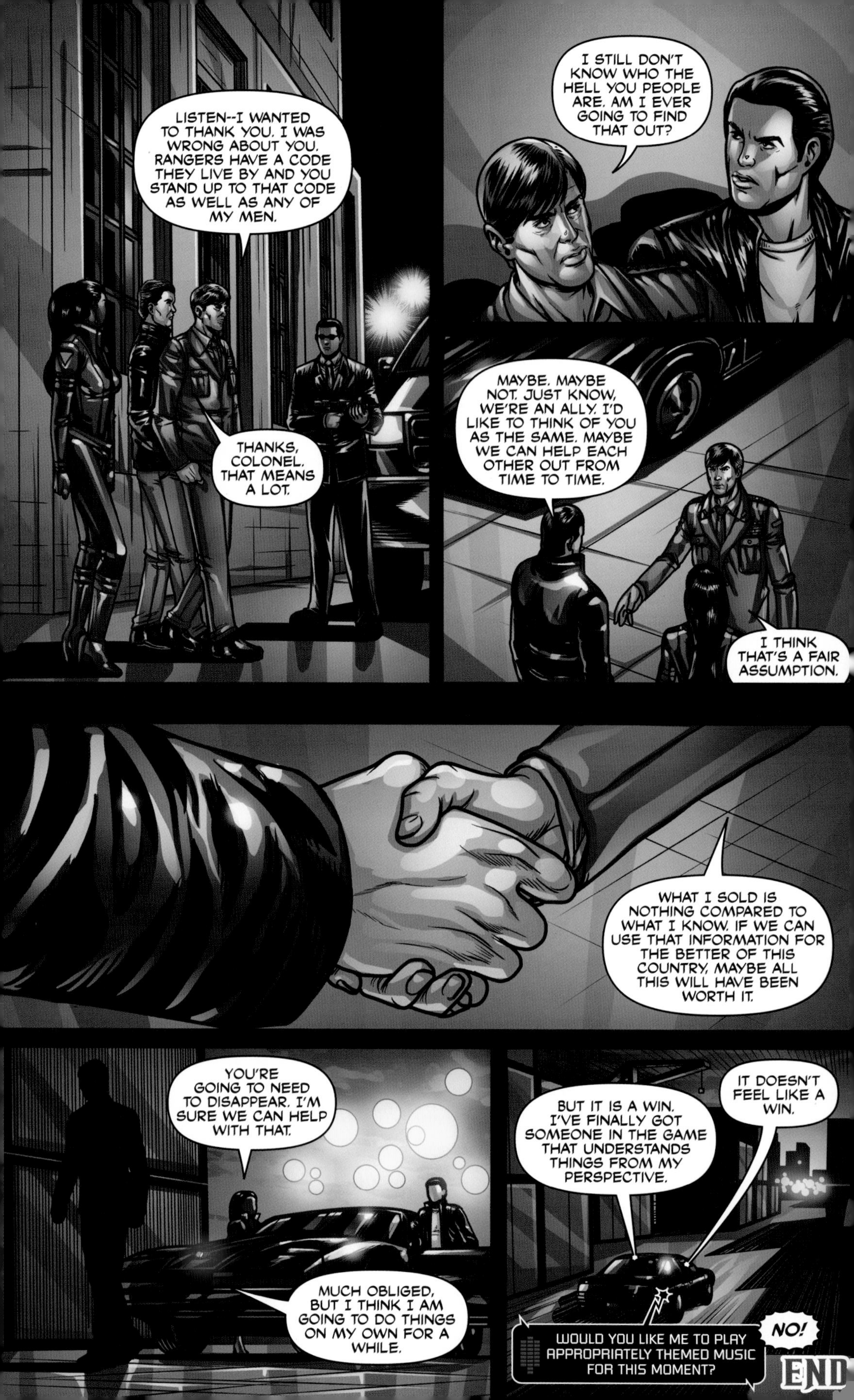
LISTEN--I WANTED TO THANK YOU. I WAS WRONG ABOUT YOU. RANGERS HAVE A CODE THEY LIVE BY AND YOU STAND UP TO THAT CODE AS WELL AS ANY OF MY MEN.
THANKS, COLONEL. THAT MEANS A LOT.
I STILL DON'T KNOW WHO THE HELL YOU PEOPLE ARE. AM I EVER GOING TO FIND THAT OUT?
MAYBE. MAYBE NOT. JUST KNOW, WE'RE AN ALLY. I'D LIKE TO THINK OF YOU AS THE SAME. MAYBE WE CAN HELP EACH OTHER OUT FROM TIME TO TIME.
I THINK THAT'S A FAIR ASSUMPTION.
WHAT I SOLD IS NOTHING COMPARED TO WHAT I KNOW. IF WE CAN USE THAT INFORMATION FOR THE BETTER OF THIS COUNTRY, MAYBE ALL THIS WILL HAVE BEEN WORTH IT.
YOU'RE GOING TO NEED TO DISAPPEAR. I'M SURE WE CAN HELP WITH THAT.
MUCH OBLIGED, BUT I THINK I AM GOING TO DO THINGS ON MY OWN FOR A WHILE.
IT DOESN'T FEEL LIKE A WIN.
BUT IT IS A WIN. I'VE FINALLY GOT SOMEONE IN THE GAME THAT UNDERSTANDS THINGS FROM MY PERSPECTIVE.
WOULD YOU LIKE ME TO PLAY APPROPRIATELY THEMED MUSIC FOR THIS MOMENT?
NO!
END

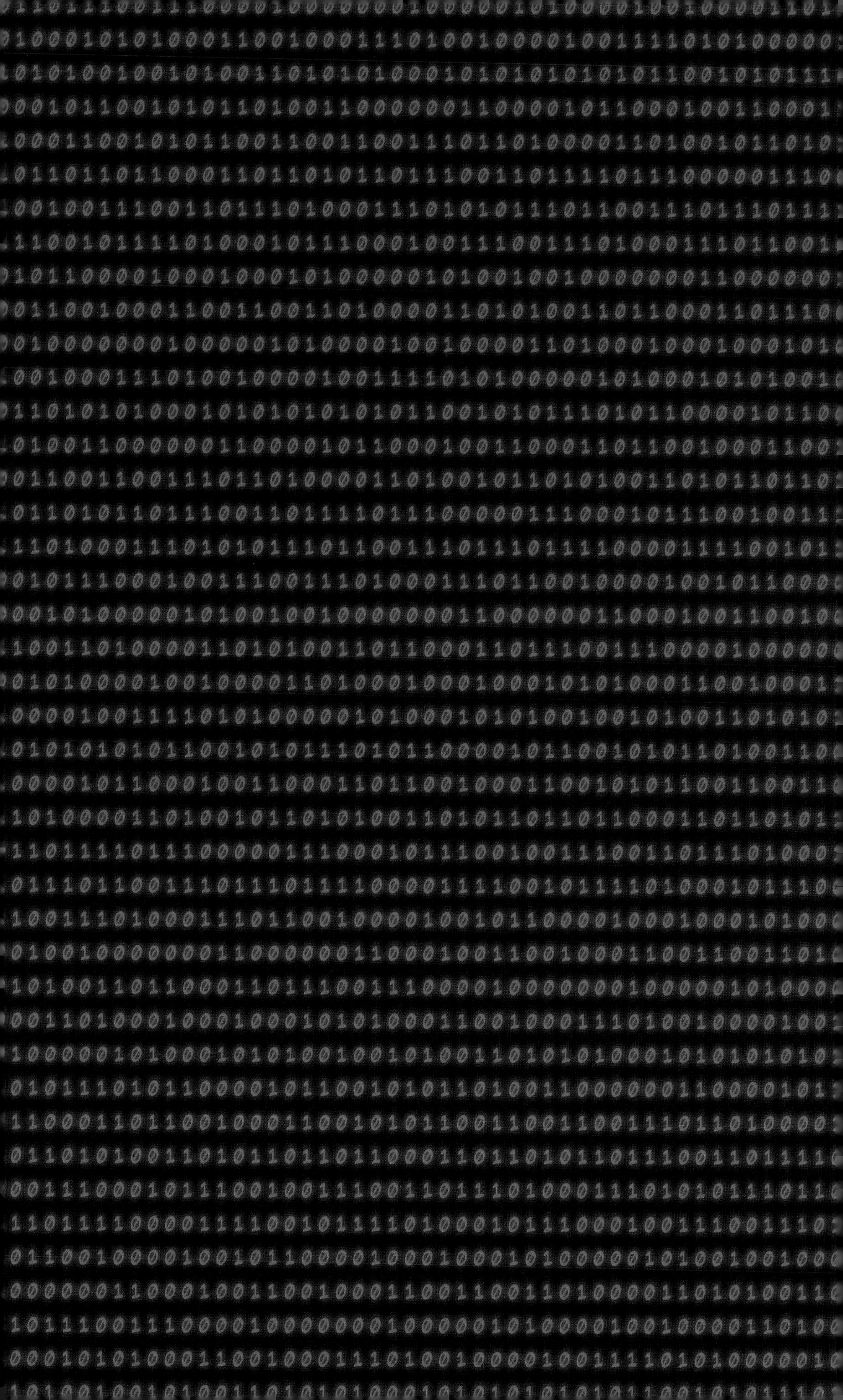

ROLE MODELS

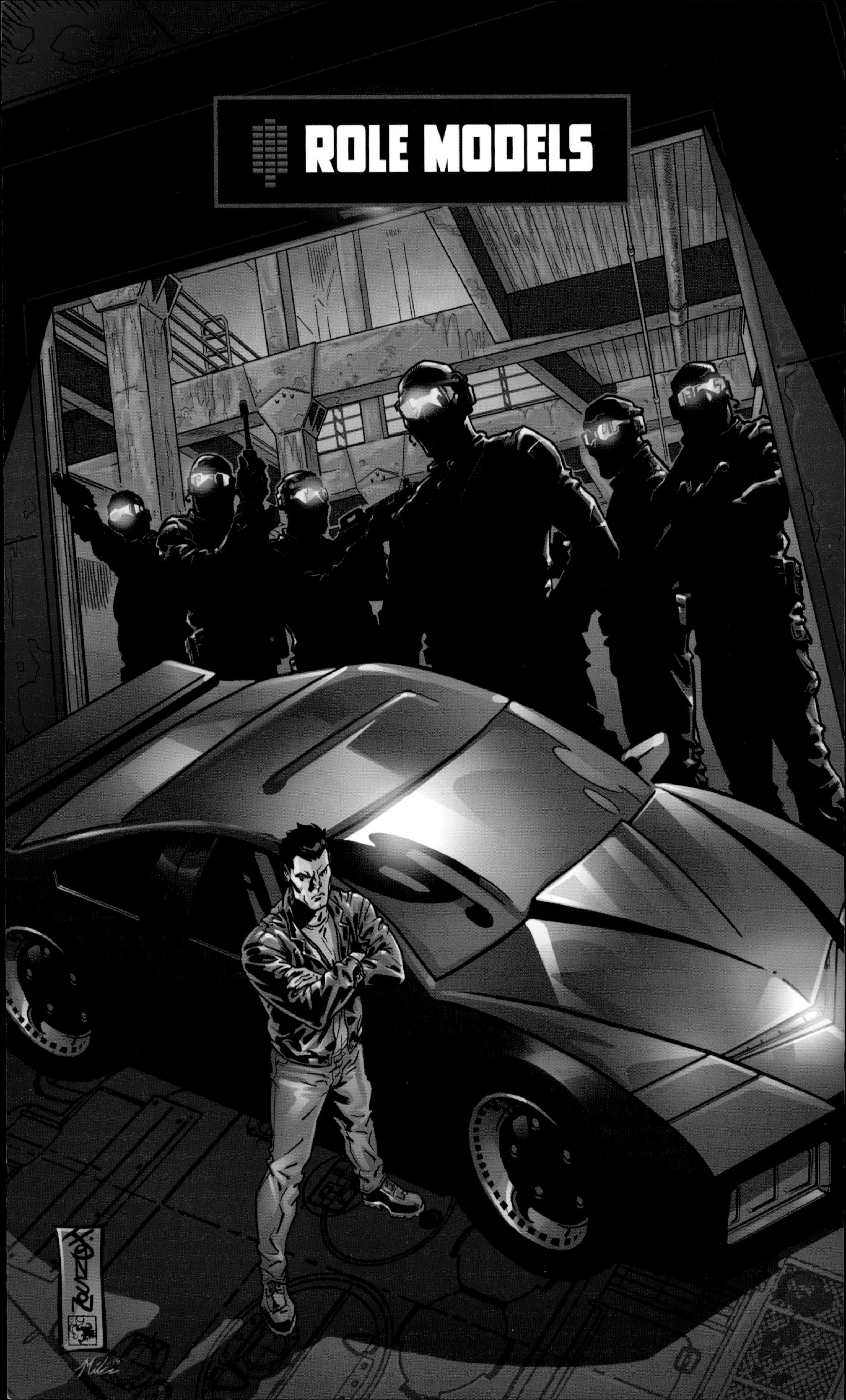

KNIGHT RIDER
KNIGHTSTRIKES

WRITTEN BY
JOE PRUETT

ILLUSTRATED BY
JASON JOHNSON

COLORED BY
SAI STUDIO

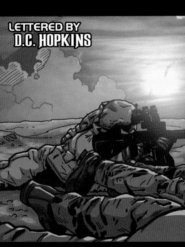

LETTERED BY
D.C. HOPKINS

EDITED BY
SHANNON ERIC DENTON

FRONT COVER BY
JASON JOHNSON

KNIGHT RIDER CREATED BY
GLEN A. LARSON

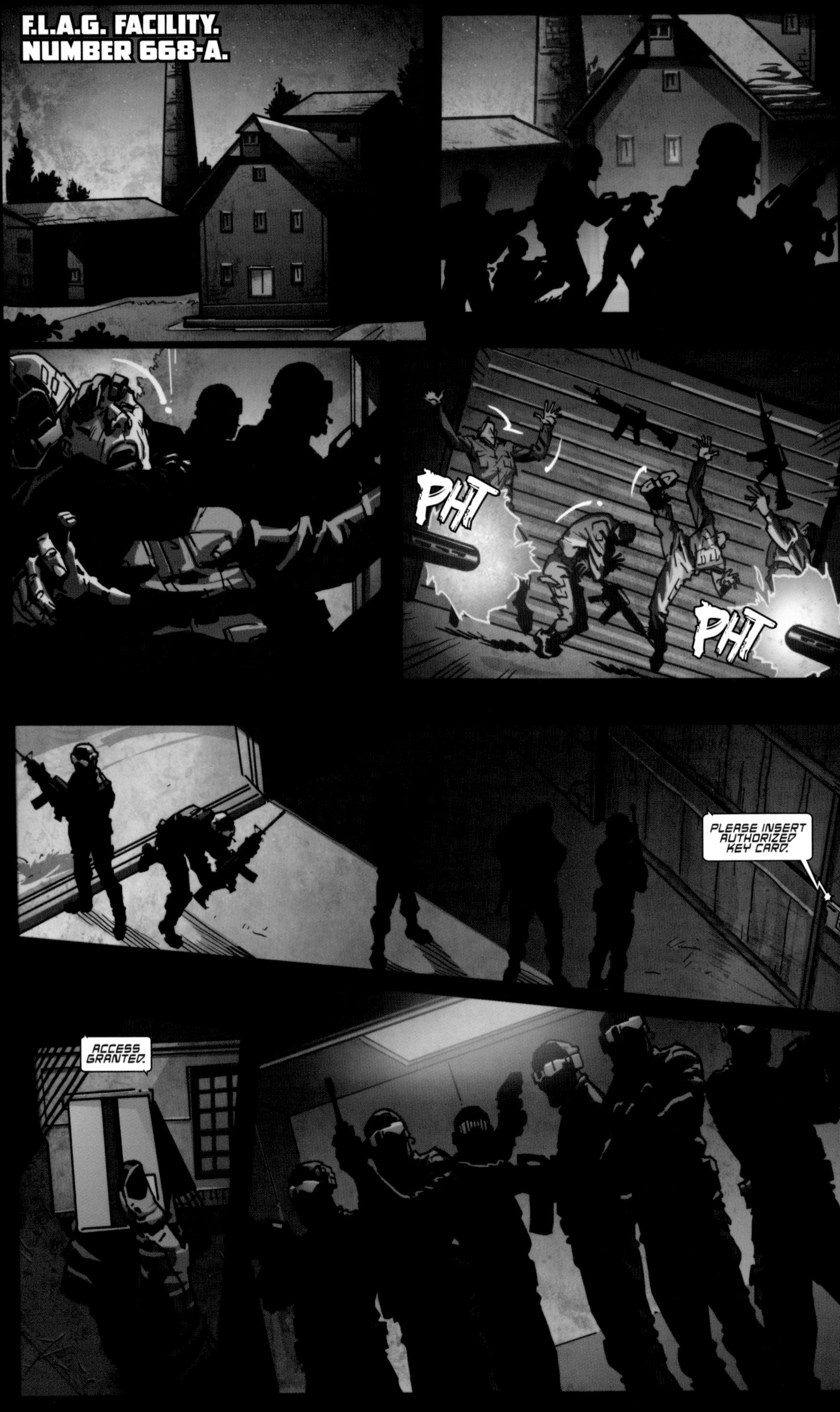
F.L.A.G. FACILITY.
NUMBER 668-A.
PHT
PHT
PLEASE INSERT AUTHORIZED KEY CARD.
ACCESS GRANTED.

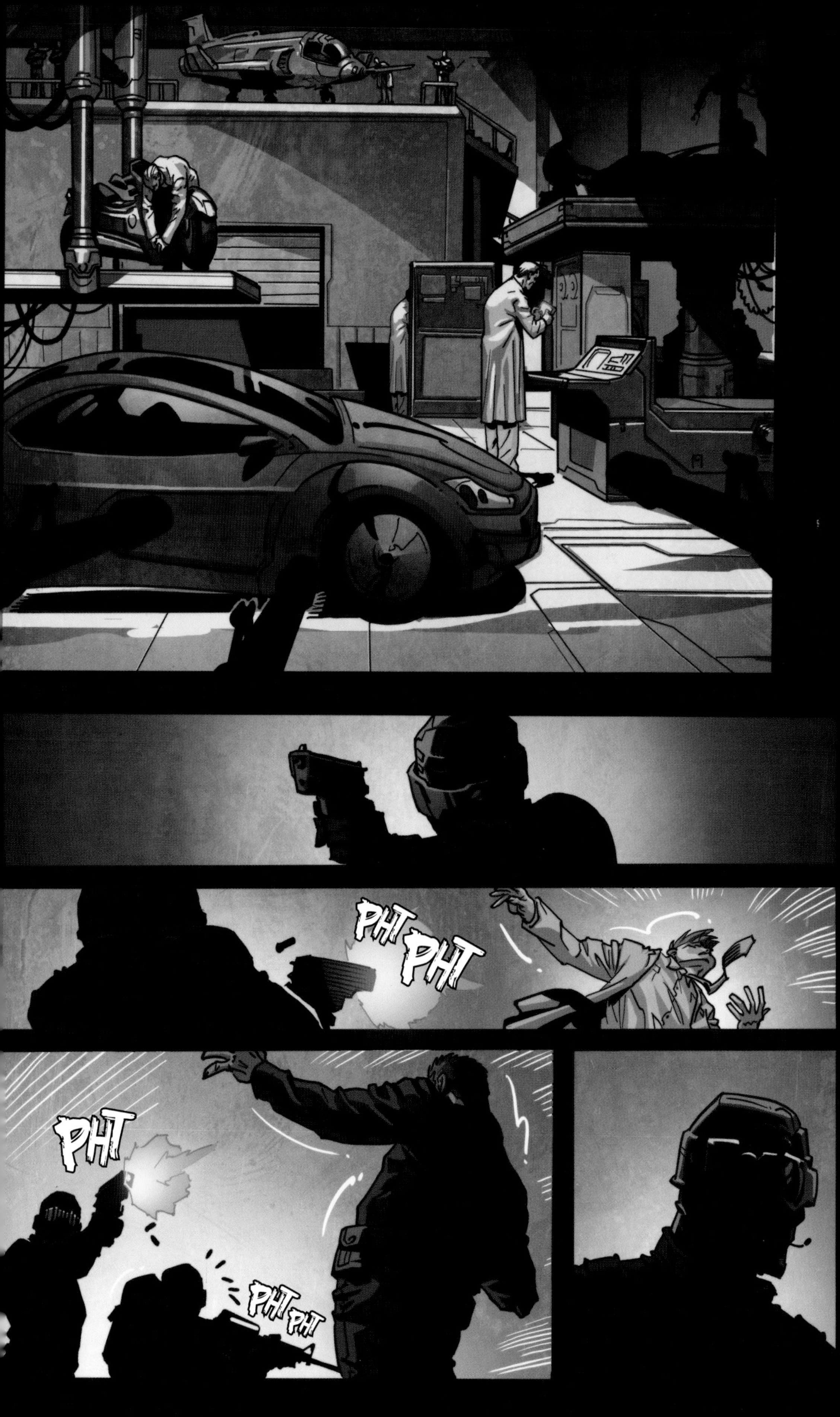
PHT PHT
PHT
PHT PHT

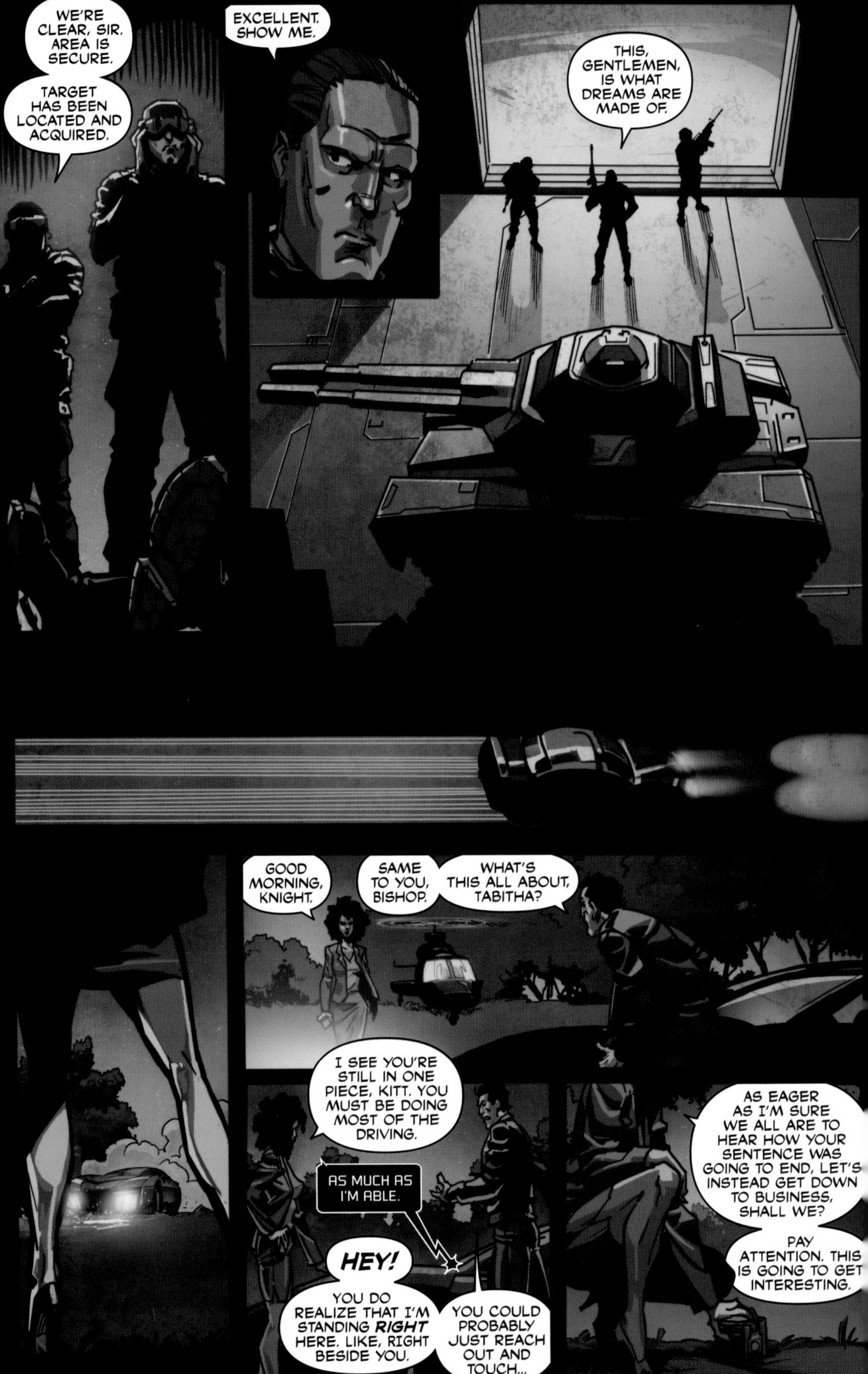
WE'RE CLEAR, SIR. AREA IS SECURE.
TARGET HAS BEEN LOCATED AND ACQUIRED.
EXCELLENT. SHOW ME.
THIS, GENTLEMEN, IS WHAT DREAMS ARE MADE OF.
GOOD MORNING, KNIGHT.
SAME TO YOU, BISHOP.
WHAT'S THIS ALL ABOUT, TABITHA?
I SEE YOU'RE STILL IN ONE PIECE, KITT. YOU MUST BE DOING MOST OF THE DRIVING.
AS MUCH AS I'M ABLE.
HEY!
YOU DO REALIZE THAT I'M STANDING *RIGHT* HERE. LIKE, RIGHT BESIDE YOU.
YOU COULD PROBABLY JUST REACH OUT AND TOUCH...
AS EAGER AS I'M SURE WE ALL ARE TO HEAR HOW YOUR SENTENCE WAS GOING TO END, LET'S INSTEAD GET DOWN TO BUSINESS, SHALL WE?
PAY ATTENTION. THIS IS GOING TO GET INTERESTING.

THIS IS F.L.A.G. FACILITY NUMBER 668-A. THIS PARTICULAR ONE HOUSED ONE OF OUR RESEARCH AND DEVELOPMENT LABORATORIES.

A *VERY* IMPORTANT R&D LAB, I MIGHT ADD.

SEVEN HOURS AGO IT WAS BREACHED.

BY WHOM?

WE'LL GET TO THAT. I SAID PAY ATTENTION.

WE HAD A TEAM ON SITE WITHIN SEVENTEEN MINUTES, AMPLE TIME FOR THE INTRUDERS TO LOCATE, SECURE, AND RETRACT THEIR PRIME OBJECTIVE, THE LG-23 PROTOTYPE.

THE LG-23 IS A 30,000-POUND ALL-TERRAIN, ARMORED VEHICLE CAPABLE OF SPEEDS IN EXCESS OF 70 MILES PER HOUR AND EQUIPPED WITH THE FIREPOWER OF A F-22 FIGHTER PLANE.

FAST, MOBILE, AND DEADLY. NOTHING SHORT OF A HELLFIRE MISSILE CAN CRACK ITS ARMOR. IT'S NOT SOMETHING THAT SHOULD BE IN THE WRONG HANDS.

IGNORING THE OBVIOUS QUESTION ABOUT WHY WE WOULD BE DEVELOPING SOMETHING LIKE THIS IN THE FIRST PLACE, LET'S JUST GET TO THE BASICS.

WHO HAS IT? WHAT ARE THEY GOING TO DO WITH IT? WHERE ARE THEY NOW?

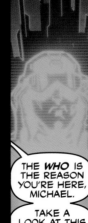

THE *WHO* IS THE REASON YOU'RE HERE, MICHAEL.

TAKE A LOOK AT THIS SURVEILLANCE VIDEO.

THIS MAN APPEARS TO BE THEIR LEADER.

WE'RE LUCKY ENOUGH TO GET A CLEAN IMAGE OF HIS FACE RIGHT... *HERE.*

STEPHEN TRAVIS.

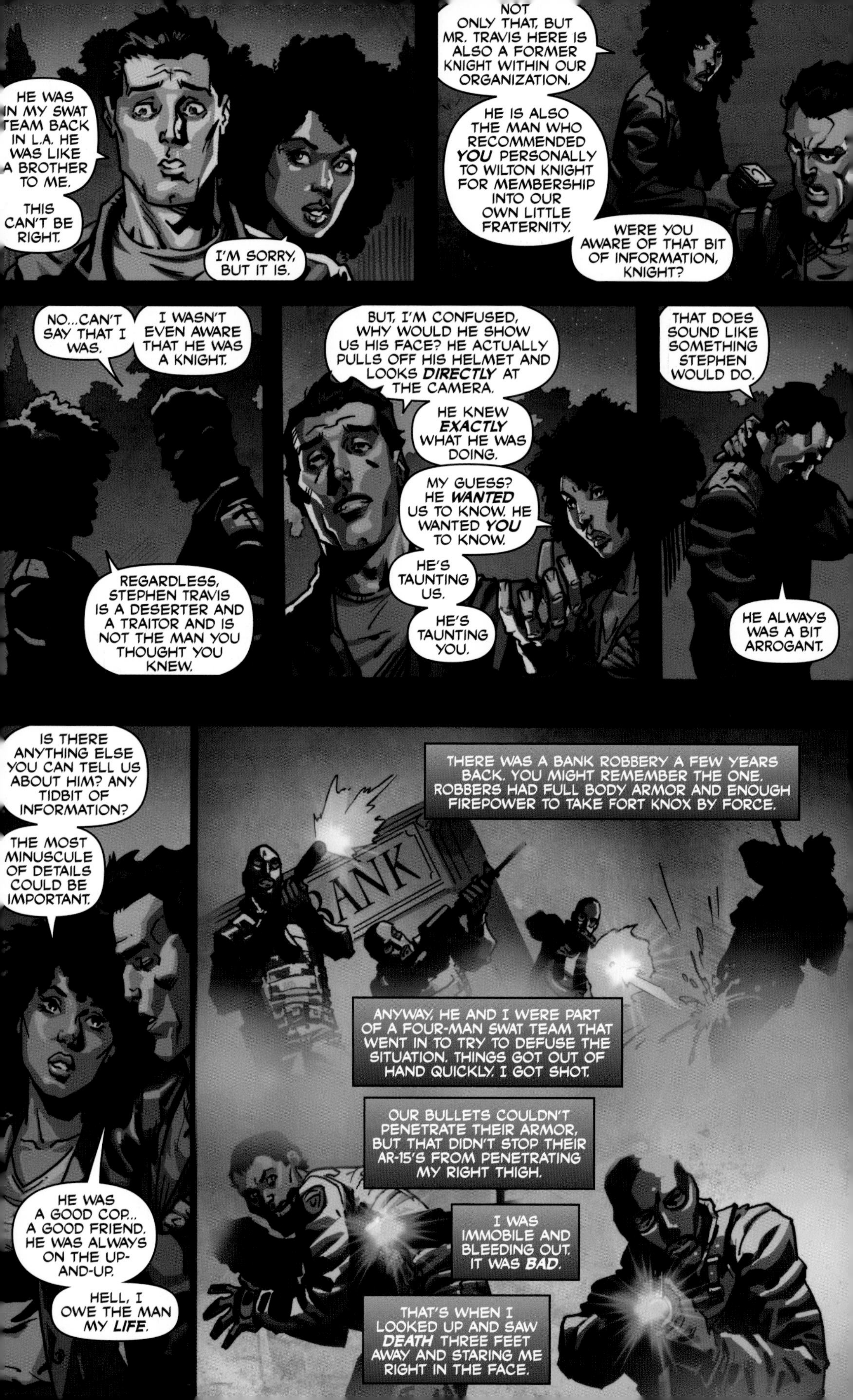
HE WAS IN MY SWAT TEAM BACK IN L.A. HE WAS LIKE A BROTHER TO ME.
THIS CAN'T BE RIGHT.
I'M SORRY, BUT IT IS.
NOT ONLY THAT, BUT MR. TRAVIS HERE IS ALSO A FORMER KNIGHT WITHIN OUR ORGANIZATION.
HE IS ALSO THE MAN WHO RECOMMENDED YOU PERSONALLY TO WILTON KNIGHT FOR MEMBERSHIP INTO OUR OWN LITTLE FRATERNITY.
WERE YOU AWARE OF THAT BIT OF INFORMATION, KNIGHT?
NO...CAN'T SAY THAT I WAS.
I WASN'T EVEN AWARE THAT HE WAS A KNIGHT.
REGARDLESS, STEPHEN TRAVIS IS A DESERTER AND A TRAITOR AND IS NOT THE MAN YOU THOUGHT YOU KNEW.
BUT, I'M CONFUSED, WHY WOULD HE SHOW US HIS FACE? HE ACTUALLY PULLS OFF HIS HELMET AND LOOKS DIRECTLY AT THE CAMERA.
HE KNEW EXACTLY WHAT HE WAS DOING.
MY GUESS? HE WANTED US TO KNOW. HE WANTED YOU TO KNOW.
HE'S TAUNTING US.
HE'S TAUNTING YOU.
THAT DOES SOUND LIKE SOMETHING STEPHEN WOULD DO.
HE ALWAYS WAS A BIT ARROGANT.
IS THERE ANYTHING ELSE YOU CAN TELL US ABOUT HIM? ANY TIDBIT OF INFORMATION?
THE MOST MINUSCULE OF DETAILS COULD BE IMPORTANT.
HE WAS A GOOD COP... A GOOD FRIEND. HE WAS ALWAYS ON THE UP-AND-UP.
HELL, I OWE THE MAN MY LIFE.
THERE WAS A BANK ROBBERY A FEW YEARS BACK. YOU MIGHT REMEMBER THE ONE. ROBBERS HAD FULL BODY ARMOR AND ENOUGH FIREPOWER TO TAKE FORT KNOX BY FORCE.
BANK
ANYWAY, HE AND I WERE PART OF A FOUR-MAN SWAT TEAM THAT WENT IN TO TRY TO DEFUSE THE SITUATION. THINGS GOT OUT OF HAND QUICKLY. I GOT SHOT.
OUR BULLETS COULDN'T PENETRATE THEIR ARMOR, BUT THAT DIDN'T STOP THEIR AR-15'S FROM PENETRATING MY RIGHT THIGH.
I WAS IMMOBILE AND BLEEDING OUT. IT WAS BAD.
THAT'S WHEN I LOOKED UP AND SAW DEATH THREE FEET AWAY AND STARING ME RIGHT IN THE FACE.

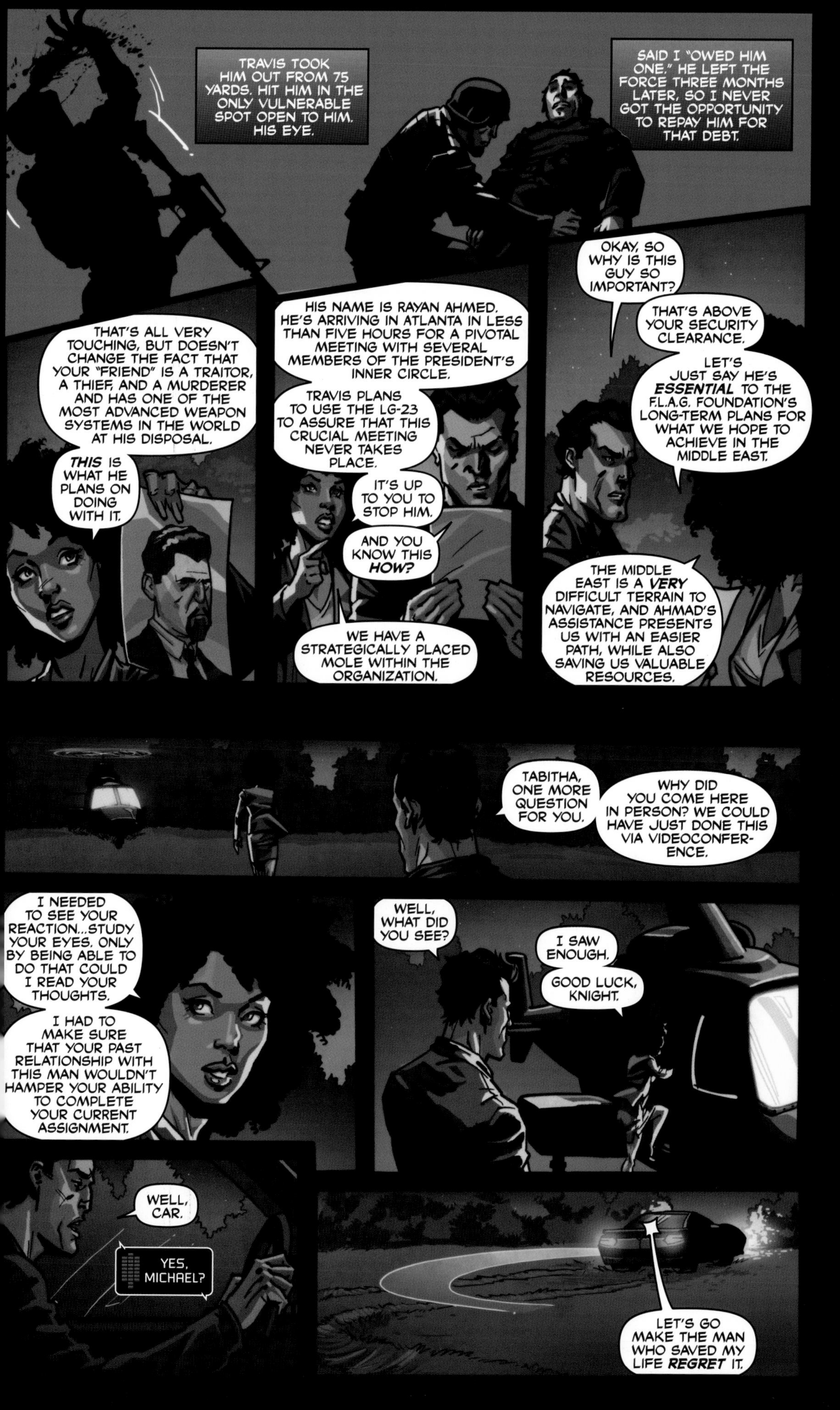

TRAVIS TOOK HIM OUT FROM 75 YARDS. HIT HIM IN THE ONLY VULNERABLE SPOT OPEN TO HIM. HIS EYE.
SAID I "OWED HIM ONE." HE LEFT THE FORCE THREE MONTHS LATER, SO I NEVER GOT THE OPPORTUNITY TO REPAY HIM FOR THAT DEBT.
THAT'S ALL VERY TOUCHING, BUT DOESN'T CHANGE THE FACT THAT YOUR "FRIEND" IS A TRAITOR, A THIEF, AND A MURDERER AND HAS ONE OF THE MOST ADVANCED WEAPON SYSTEMS IN THE WORLD AT HIS DISPOSAL.
THIS IS WHAT HE PLANS ON DOING WITH IT.
HIS NAME IS RAYAN AHMED. HE'S ARRIVING IN ATLANTA IN LESS THAN FIVE HOURS FOR A PIVOTAL MEETING WITH SEVERAL MEMBERS OF THE PRESIDENT'S INNER CIRCLE.
TRAVIS PLANS TO USE THE LG-23 TO ASSURE THAT THIS CRUCIAL MEETING NEVER TAKES PLACE.
IT'S UP TO YOU TO STOP HIM.
AND YOU KNOW THIS *HOW?*
WE HAVE A STRATEGICALLY PLACED MOLE WITHIN THE ORGANIZATION.
OKAY, SO WHY IS THIS GUY SO IMPORTANT?
THAT'S ABOVE YOUR SECURITY CLEARANCE.
LET'S JUST SAY HE'S ***ESSENTIAL*** TO THE F.L.A.G. FOUNDATION'S LONG-TERM PLANS FOR WHAT WE HOPE TO ACHIEVE IN THE MIDDLE EAST.
THE MIDDLE EAST IS A *VERY* DIFFICULT TERRAIN TO NAVIGATE, AND AHMAD'S ASSISTANCE PRESENTS US WITH AN EASIER PATH, WHILE ALSO SAVING US VALUABLE RESOURCES.
TABITHA, ONE MORE QUESTION FOR YOU.
WHY DID YOU COME HERE IN PERSON? WE COULD HAVE JUST DONE THIS VIA VIDEOCONFERENCE.
I NEEDED TO SEE YOUR REACTION...STUDY YOUR EYES. ONLY BY BEING ABLE TO DO THAT COULD I READ YOUR THOUGHTS.
I HAD TO MAKE SURE THAT YOUR PAST RELATIONSHIP WITH THIS MAN WOULDN'T HAMPER YOUR ABILITY TO COMPLETE YOUR CURRENT ASSIGNMENT.
WELL, WHAT DID YOU SEE?
I SAW ENOUGH.
GOOD LUCK, KNIGHT.
WELL, CAR.
YES, MICHAEL?
LET'S GO MAKE THE MAN WHO SAVED MY LIFE *REGRET* IT.

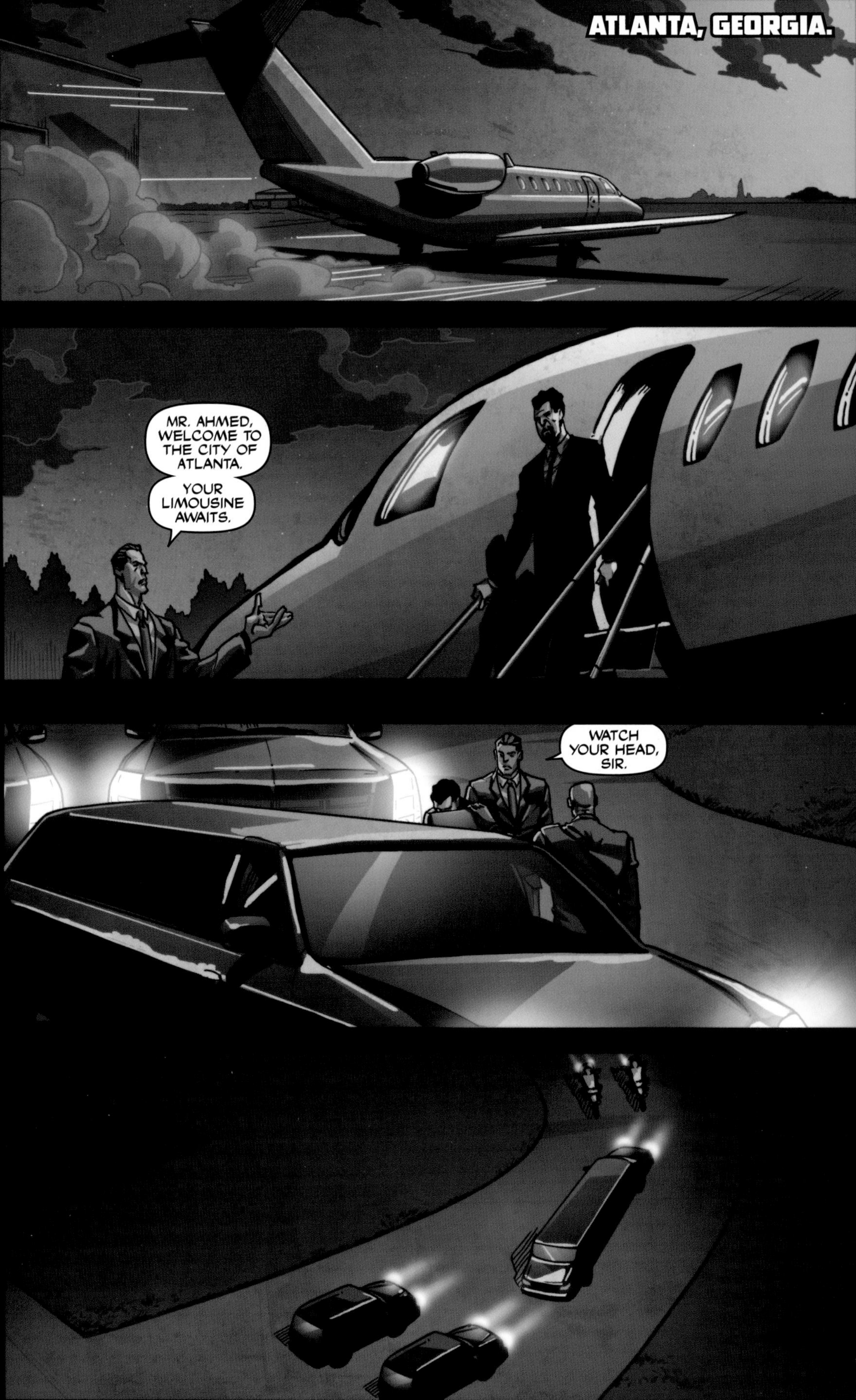
ATLANTA, GEORGIA.
MR. AHMED, WELCOME TO THE CITY OF ATLANTA.
YOUR LIMOUSINE AWAITS.
WATCH YOUR HEAD, SIR.

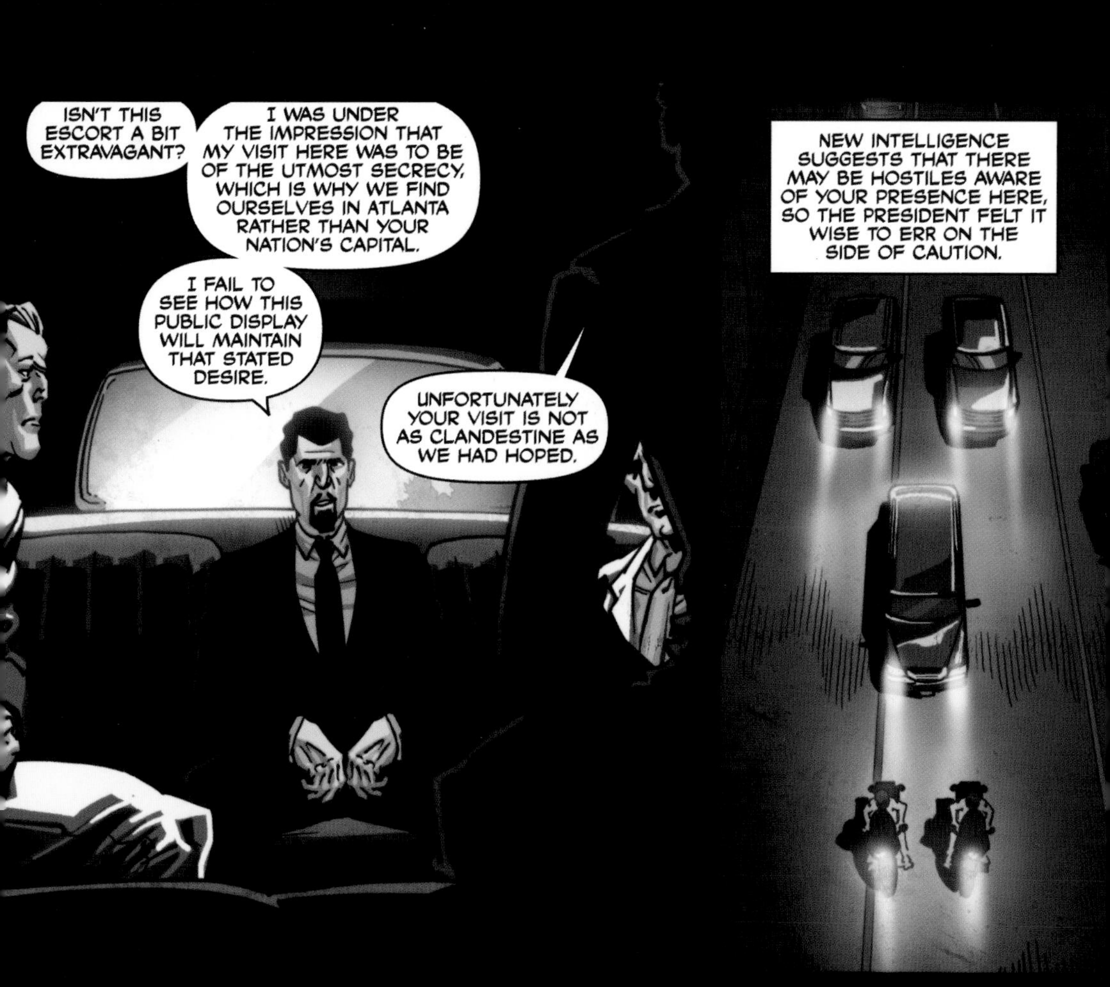
ISN'T THIS ESCORT A BIT EXTRAVAGANT?
I WAS UNDER THE IMPRESSION THAT MY VISIT HERE WAS TO BE OF THE UTMOST SECRECY, WHICH IS WHY WE FIND OURSELVES IN ATLANTA RATHER THAN YOUR NATION'S CAPITAL.
I FAIL TO SEE HOW THIS PUBLIC DISPLAY WILL MAINTAIN THAT STATED DESIRE.
UNFORTUNATELY YOUR VISIT IS NOT AS CLANDESTINE AS WE HAD HOPED.
NEW INTELLIGENCE SUGGESTS THAT THERE MAY BE HOSTILES AWARE OF YOUR PRESENCE HERE, SO THE PRESIDENT FELT IT WISE TO ERR ON THE SIDE OF CAUTION.
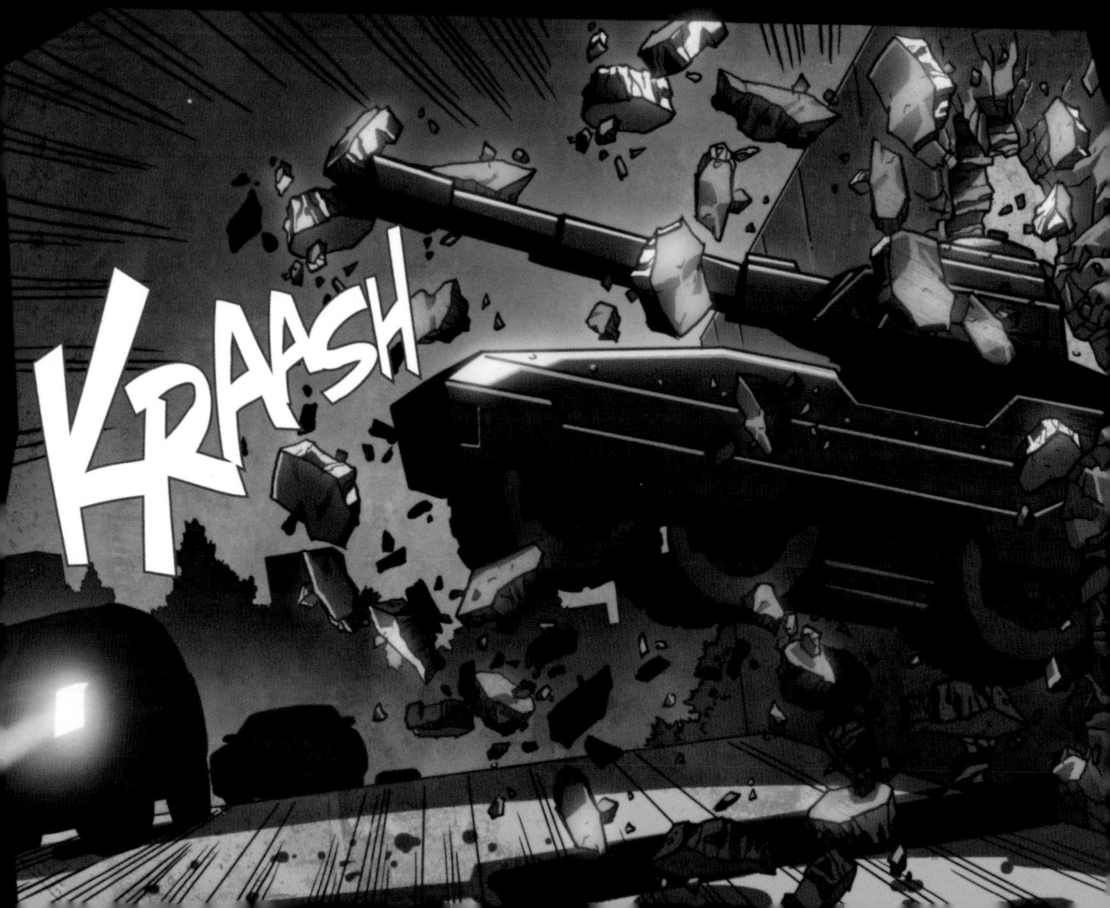
KRAASH

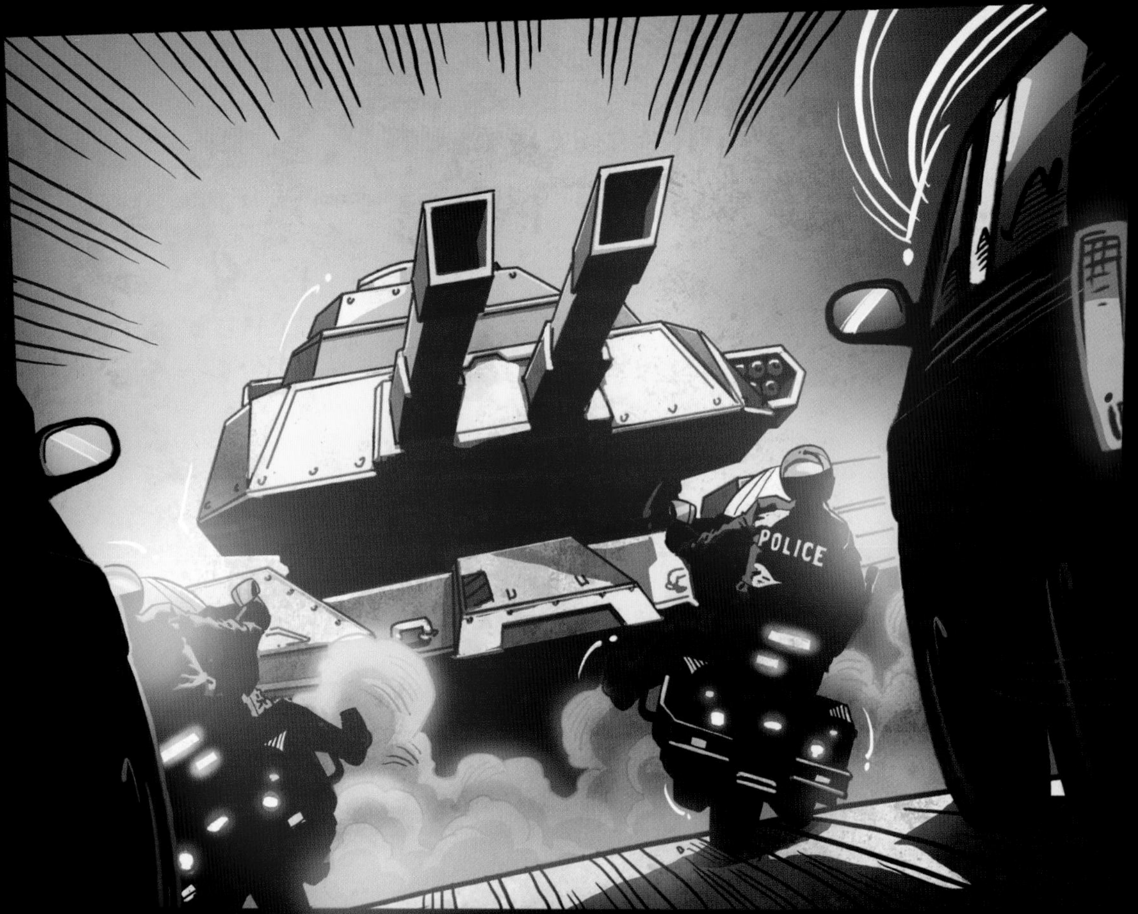
POLICE

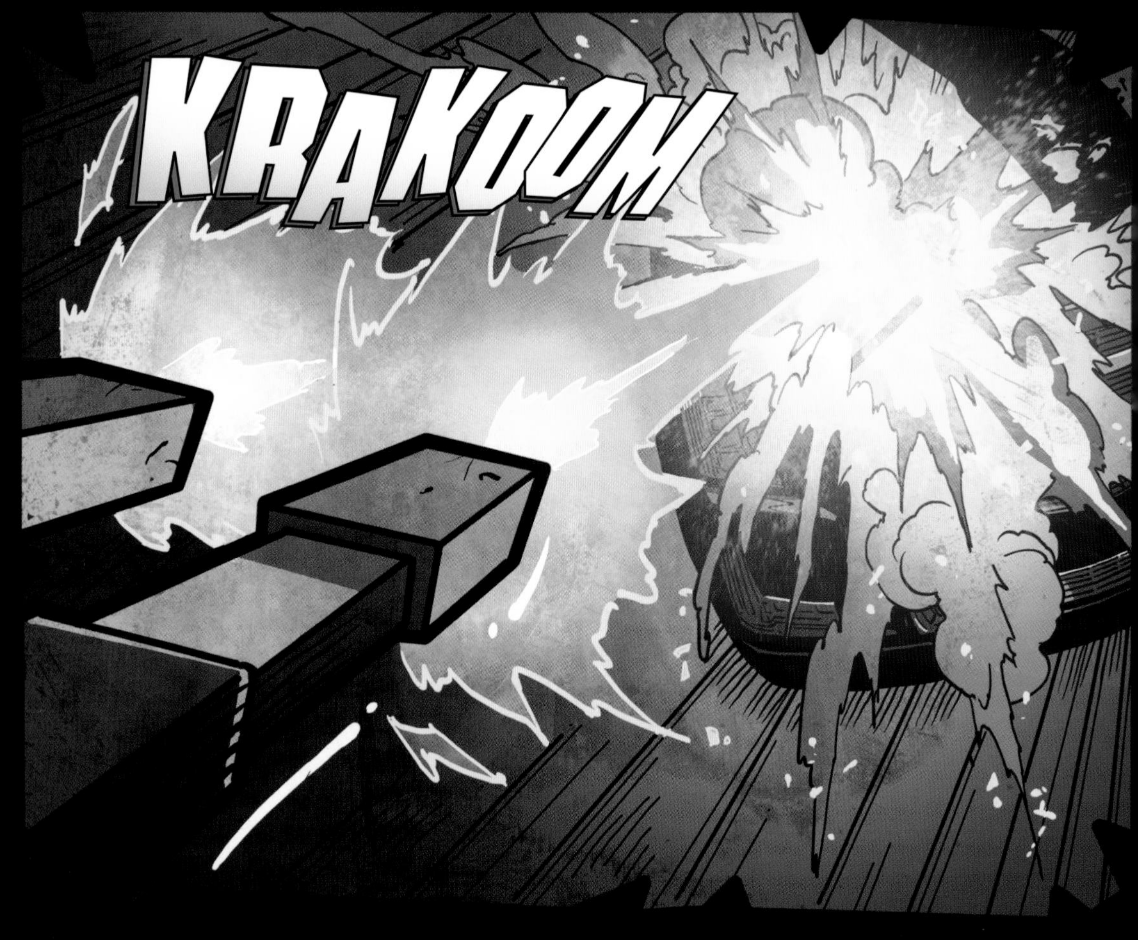
KRAKOOM

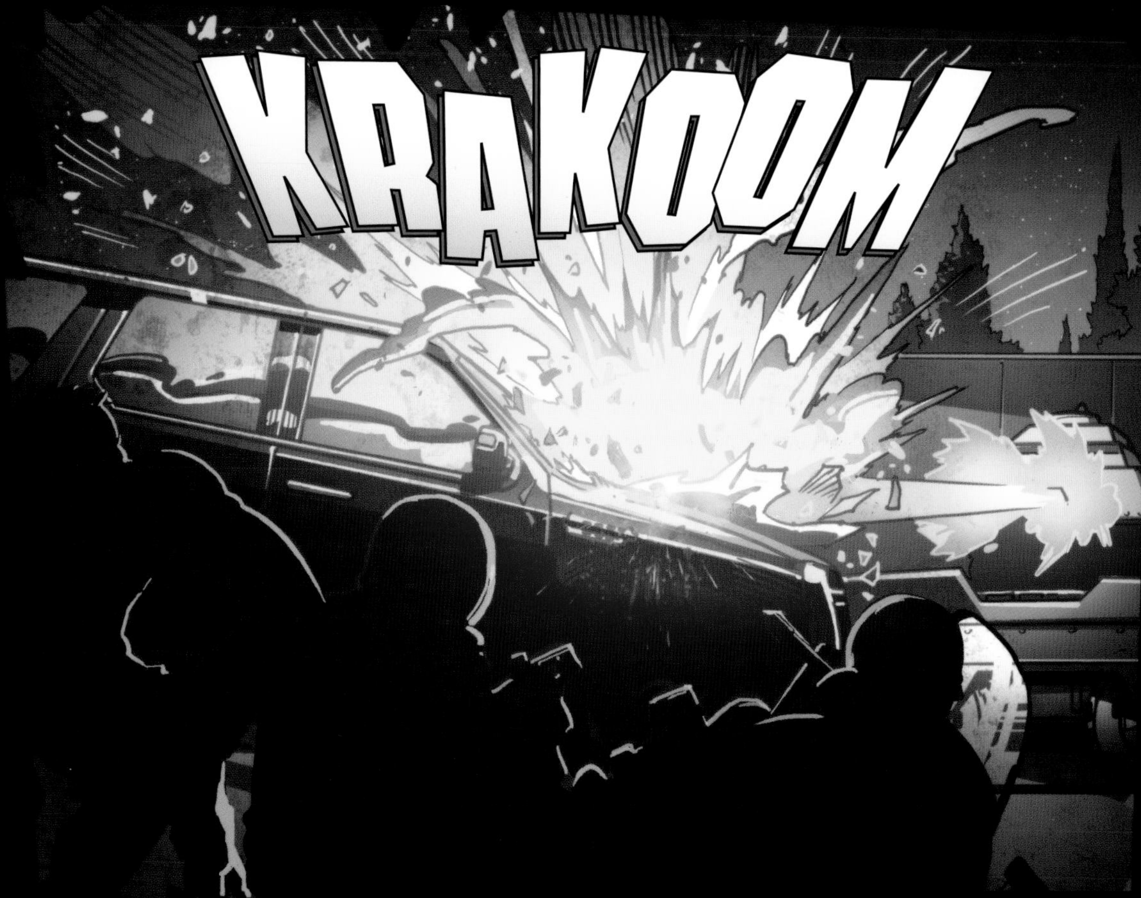
KRAKOOM
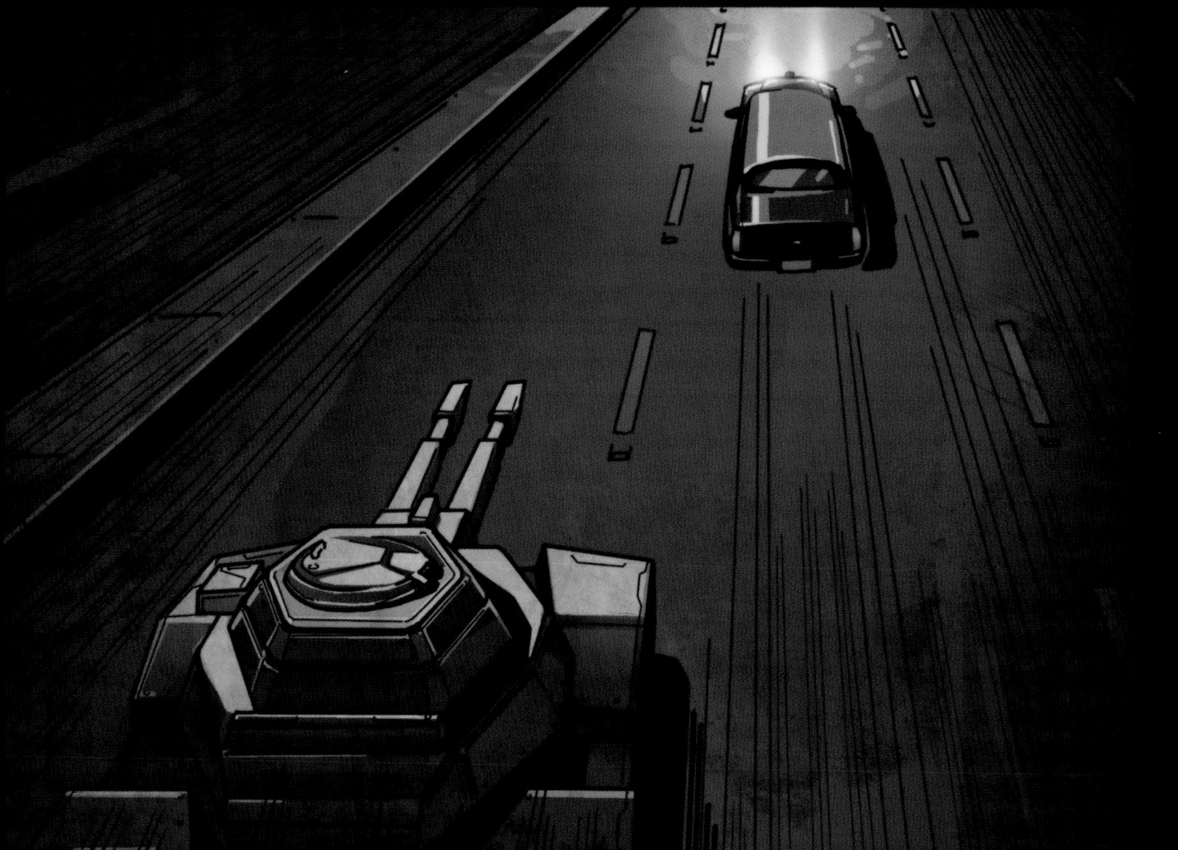

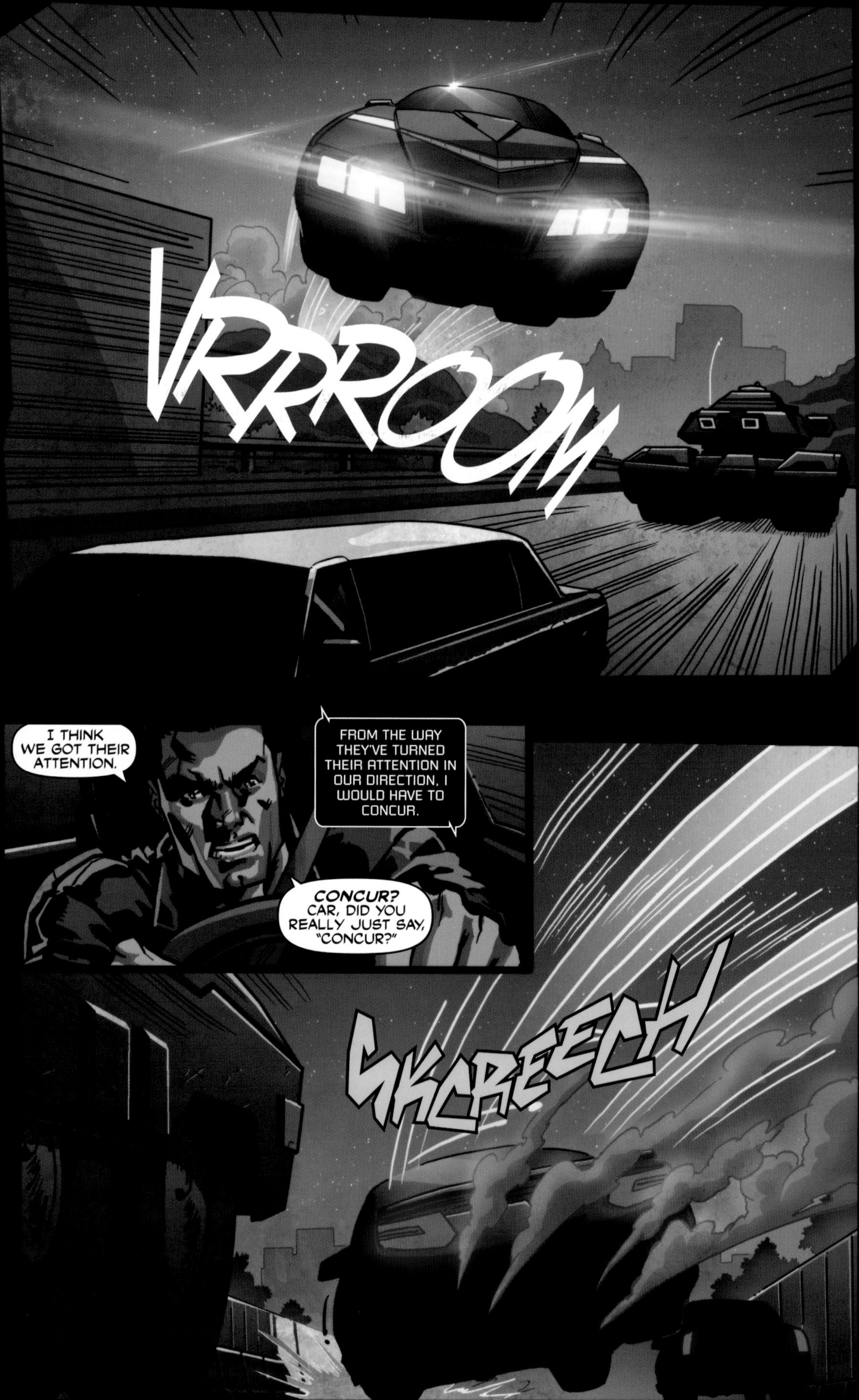
VRRROOM
I THINK WE GOT THEIR ATTENTION.
FROM THE WAY THEY'VE TURNED THEIR ATTENTION IN OUR DIRECTION, I WOULD HAVE TO CONCUR.
CONCUR? CAR, DID YOU REALLY JUST SAY, "CONCUR?"
SKCREECH

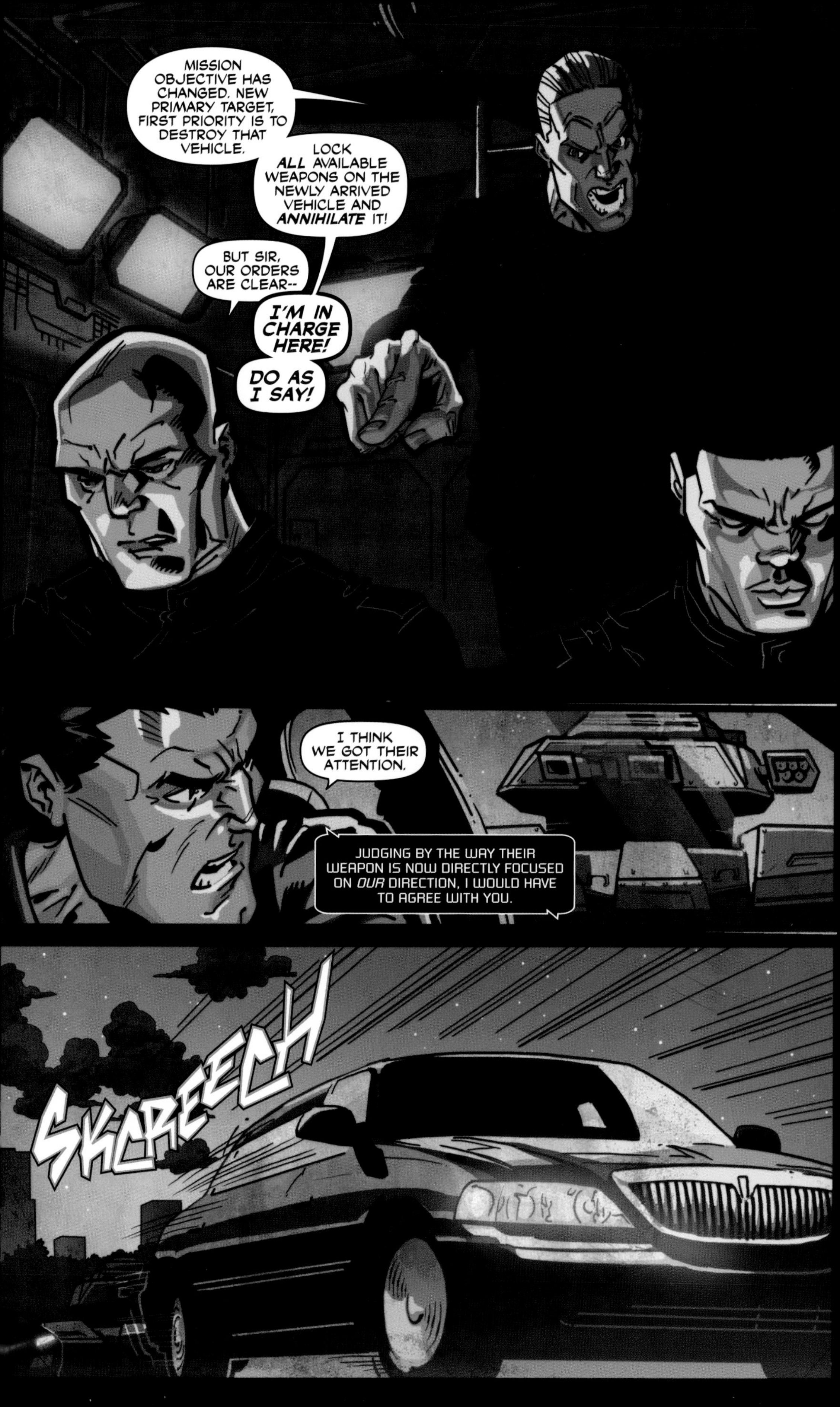
MISSION OBJECTIVE HAS CHANGED. NEW PRIMARY TARGET, FIRST PRIORITY IS TO DESTROY THAT VEHICLE.
LOCK ALL AVAILABLE WEAPONS ON THE NEWLY ARRIVED VEHICLE AND ANNIHILATE IT!
BUT SIR, OUR ORDERS ARE CLEAR--
I'M IN CHARGE HERE!
DO AS I SAY!
I THINK WE GOT THEIR ATTENTION.
JUDGING BY THE WAY THEIR WEAPON IS NOW DIRECTLY FOCUSED ON OUR DIRECTION, I WOULD HAVE TO AGREE WITH YOU.
SKREEECH

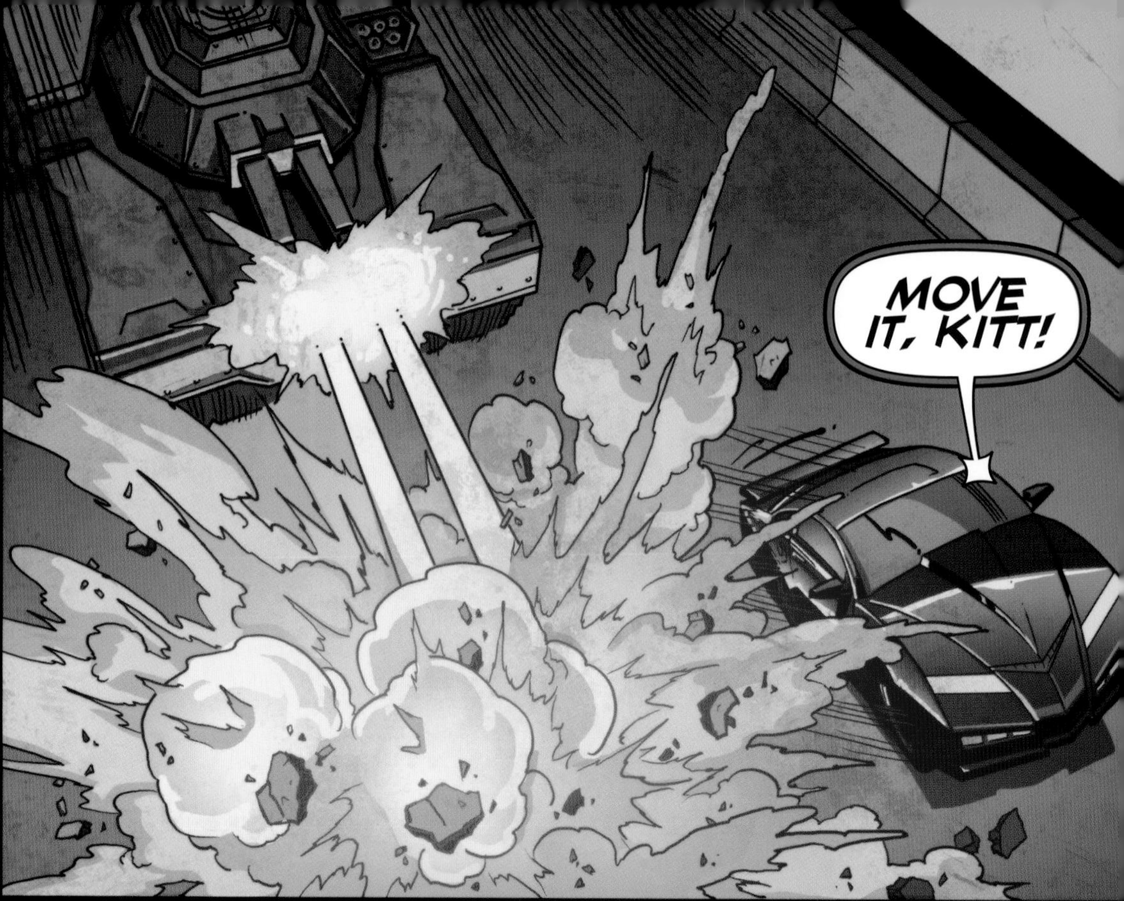
MOVE IT, KITT!

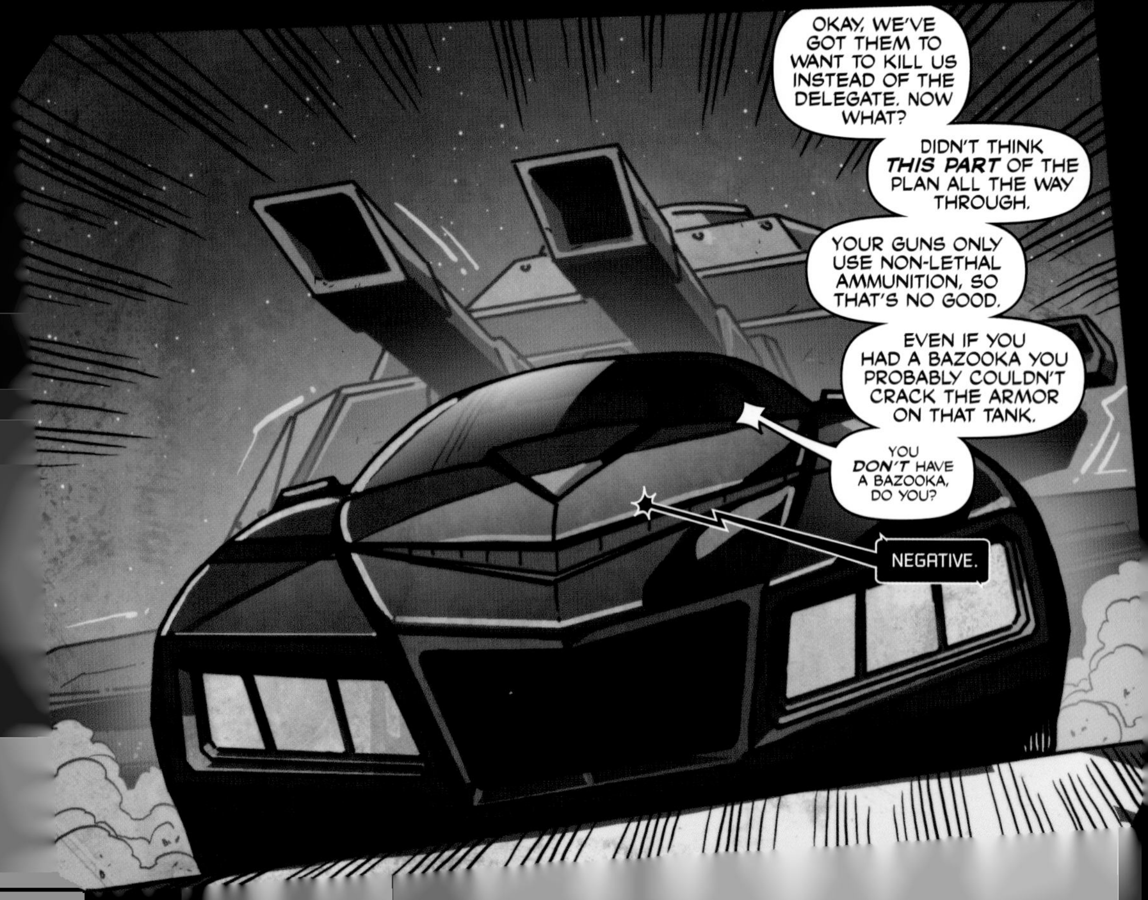
OKAY, WE'VE GOT THEM TO WANT TO KILL US INSTEAD OF THE DELEGATE. NOW WHAT?
DIDN'T THINK ***THIS PART*** OF THE PLAN ALL THE WAY THROUGH.
YOUR GUNS ONLY USE NON-LETHAL AMMUNITION, SO THAT'S NO GOOD.
EVEN IF YOU HAD A BAZOOKA YOU PROBABLY COULDN'T CRACK THE ARMOR ON THAT TANK.
YOU ***DON'T*** HAVE A BAZOOKA, DO YOU?
NEGATIVE.

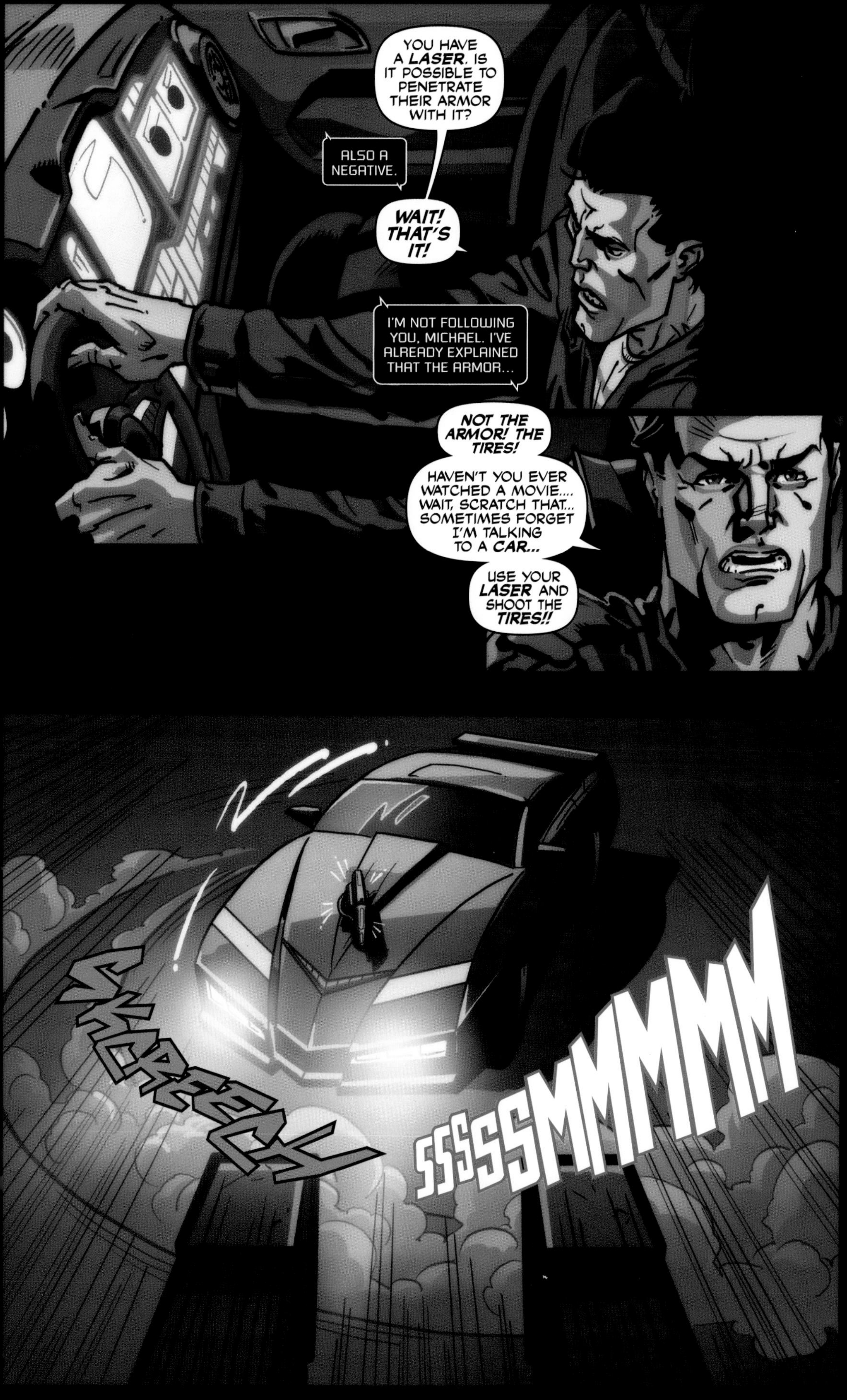
YOU HAVE A LASER. IS IT POSSIBLE TO PENETRATE THEIR ARMOR WITH IT?
ALSO A NEGATIVE.
WAIT! THAT'S IT!
I'M NOT FOLLOWING YOU, MICHAEL. I'VE ALREADY EXPLAINED THAT THE ARMOR...
NOT THE ARMOR! THE TIRES!
HAVEN'T YOU EVER WATCHED A MOVIE.... WAIT, SCRATCH THAT... SOMETIMES FORGET I'M TALKING TO A CAR...
USE YOUR LASER AND SHOOT THE TIRES!!
SKREECH
SSSSSMMMMMM

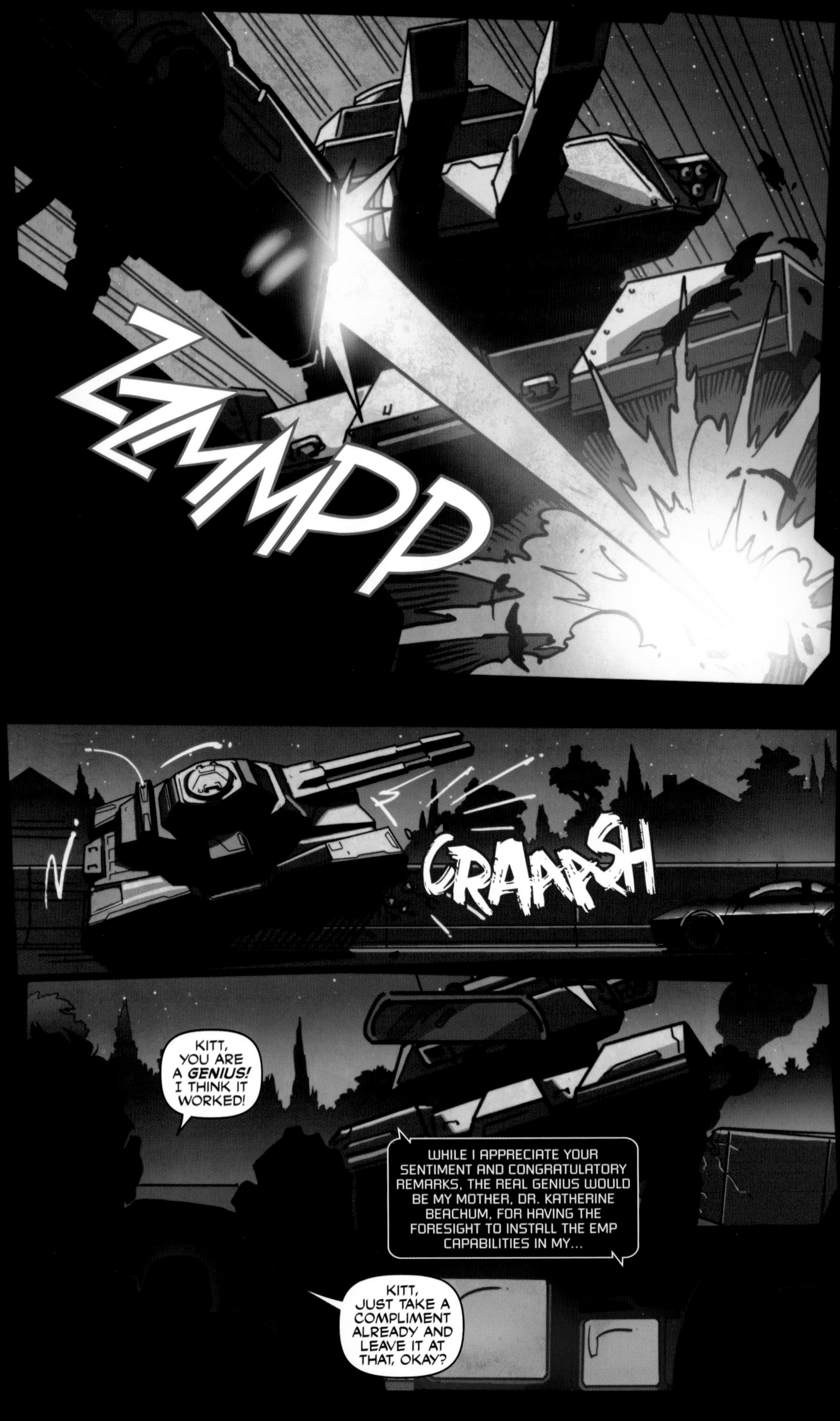
ZZMMPP
CRAAASH
KITT, YOU ARE A *GENIUS!* I THINK IT WORKED!
WHILE I APPRECIATE YOUR SENTIMENT AND CONGRATULATORY REMARKS, THE REAL GENIUS WOULD BE MY MOTHER, DR. KATHERINE BEACHUM, FOR HAVING THE FORESIGHT TO INSTALL THE EMP CAPABILITIES IN MY...
KITT, JUST TAKE A COMPLIMENT ALREADY AND LEAVE IT AT THAT, OKAY?

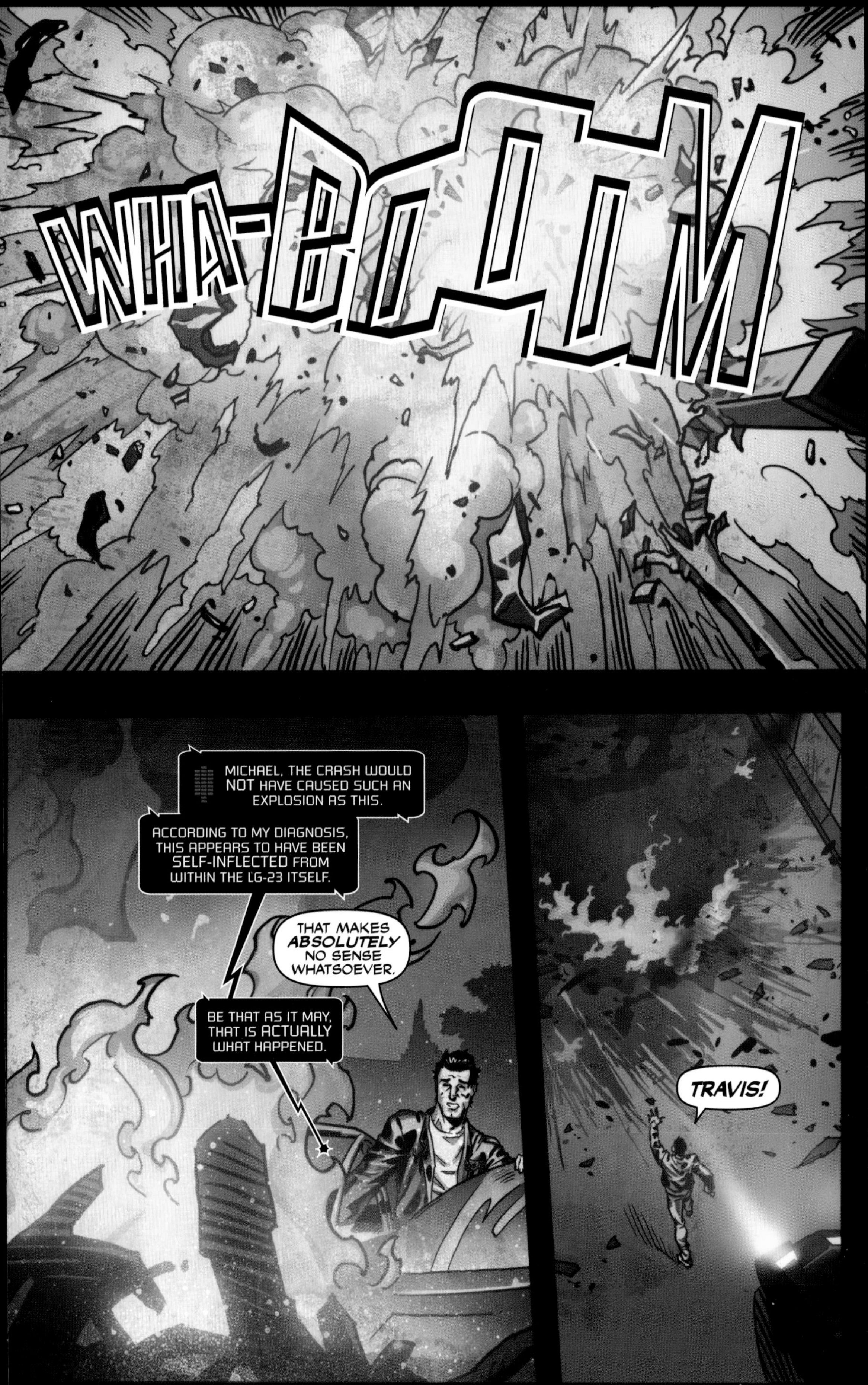
WHA-BOOM
MICHAEL, THE CRASH WOULD NOT HAVE CAUSED SUCH AN EXPLOSION AS THIS.
ACCORDING TO MY DIAGNOSIS, THIS APPEARS TO HAVE BEEN SELF-INFLECTED FROM WITHIN THE LG-23 ITSELF.
THAT MAKES ABSOLUTELY NO SENSE WHATSOEVER.
BE THAT AS IT MAY, THAT IS ACTUALLY WHAT HAPPENED.
TRAVIS!

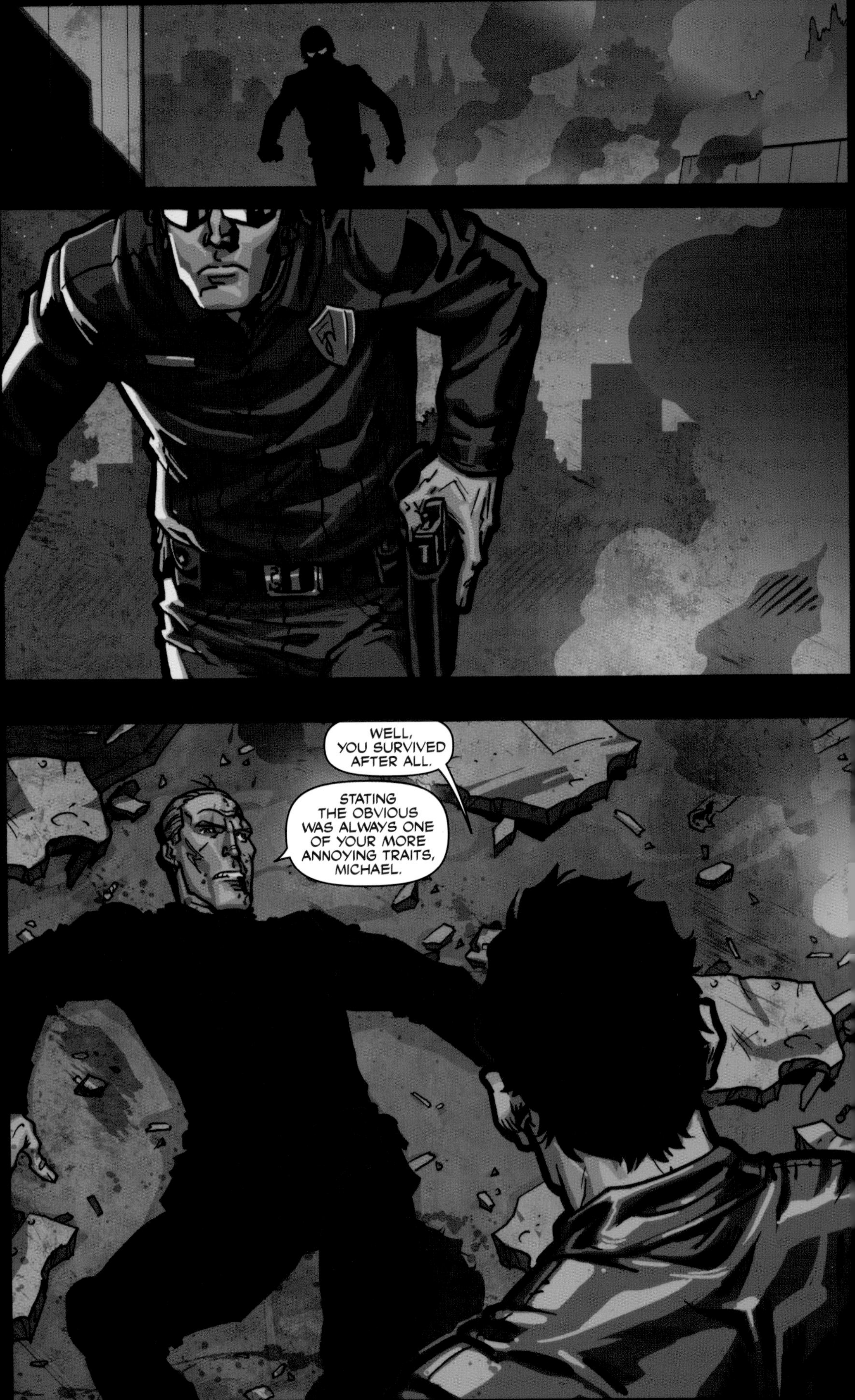
WELL, YOU SURVIVED AFTER ALL.
STATING THE OBVIOUS WAS ALWAYS ONE OF YOUR MORE ANNOYING TRAITS, MICHAEL.

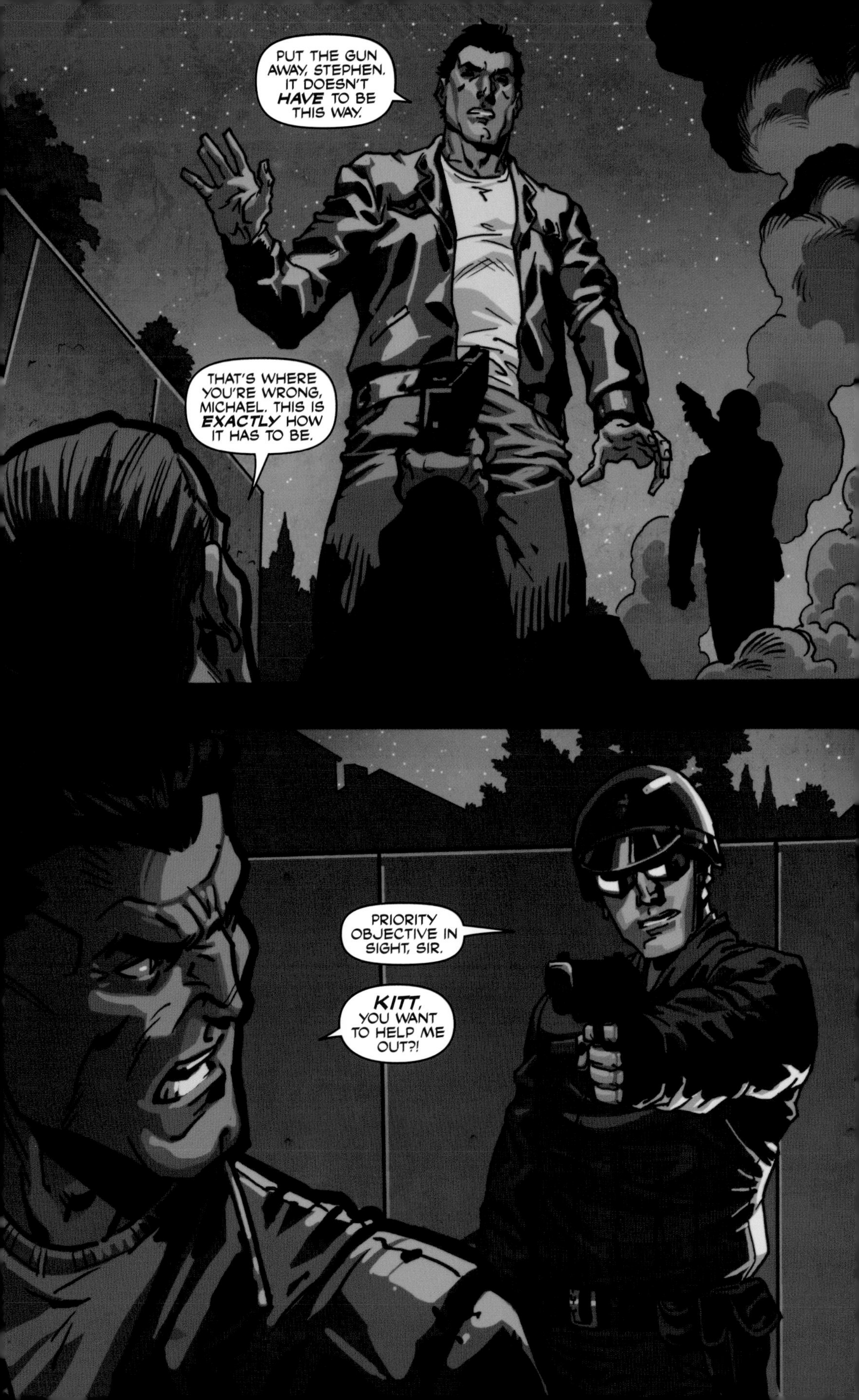
PUT THE GUN AWAY, STEPHEN. IT DOESN'T *HAVE* TO BE THIS WAY.
THAT'S WHERE YOU'RE WRONG, MICHAEL. THIS IS *EXACTLY* HOW IT HAS TO BE.
PRIORITY OBJECTIVE IN SIGHT, SIR.
KITT, YOU WANT TO HELP ME OUT?!

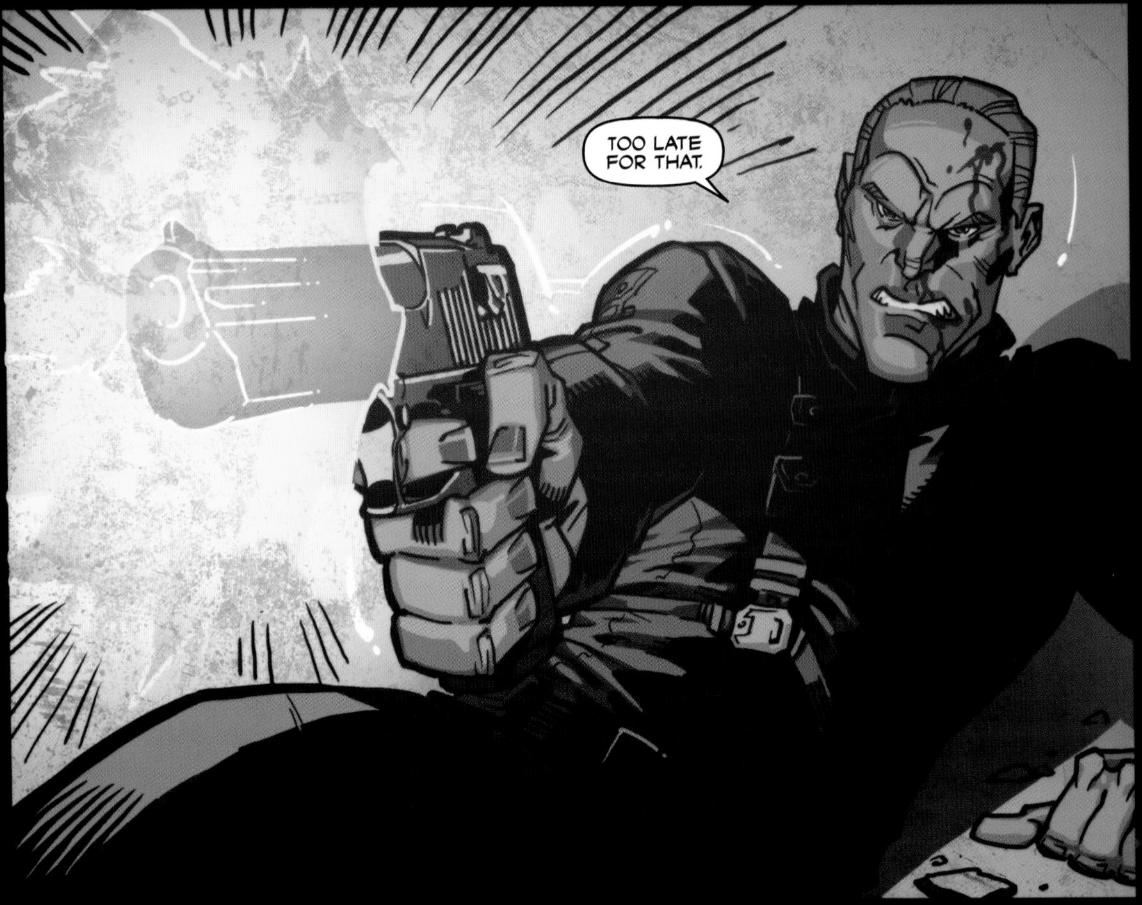
TOO LATE FOR THAT.

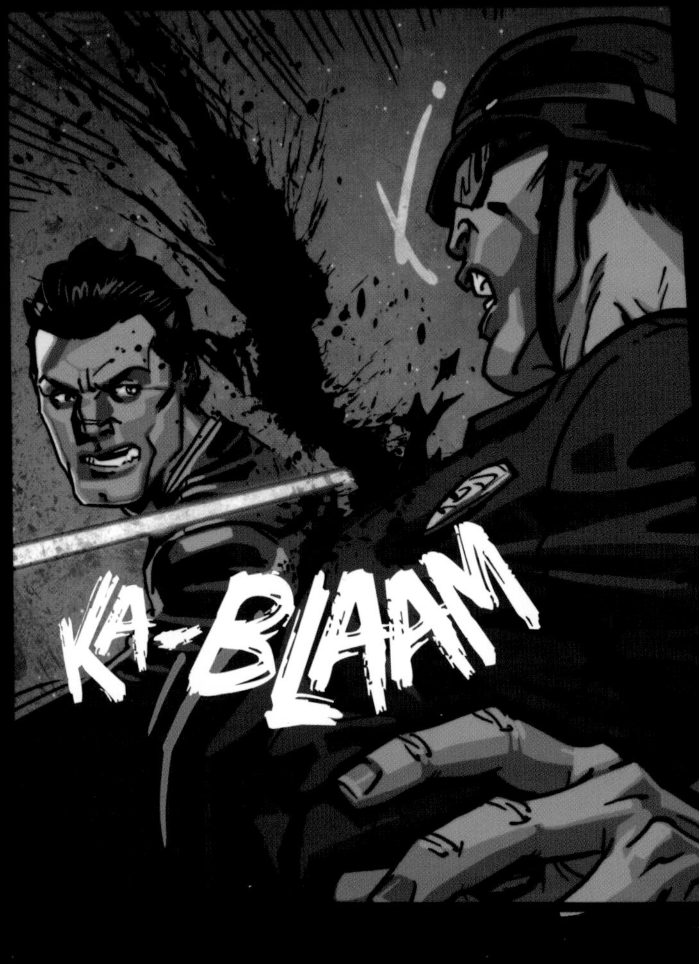
KA-BLAAM

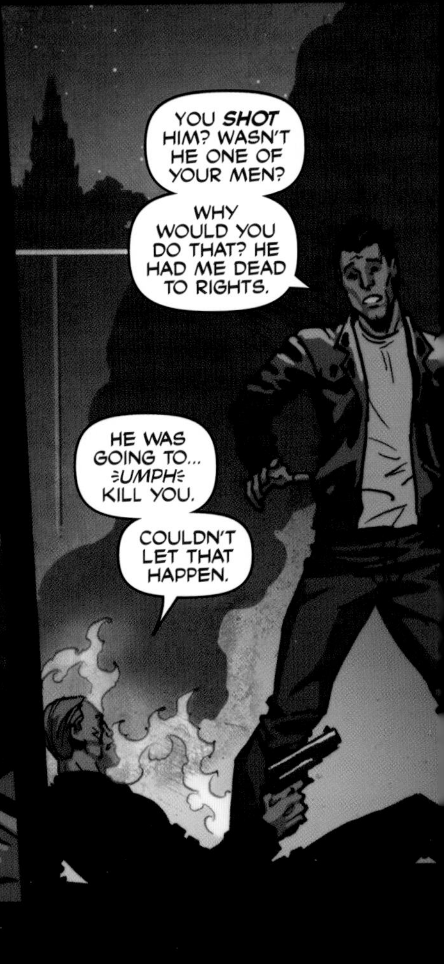
YOU SHOT HIM? WASN'T HE ONE OF YOUR MEN?
WHY WOULD YOU DO THAT? HE HAD ME DEAD TO RIGHTS.
HE WAS GOING TO... =UMPH= KILL YOU.
COULDN'T LET THAT HAPPEN.

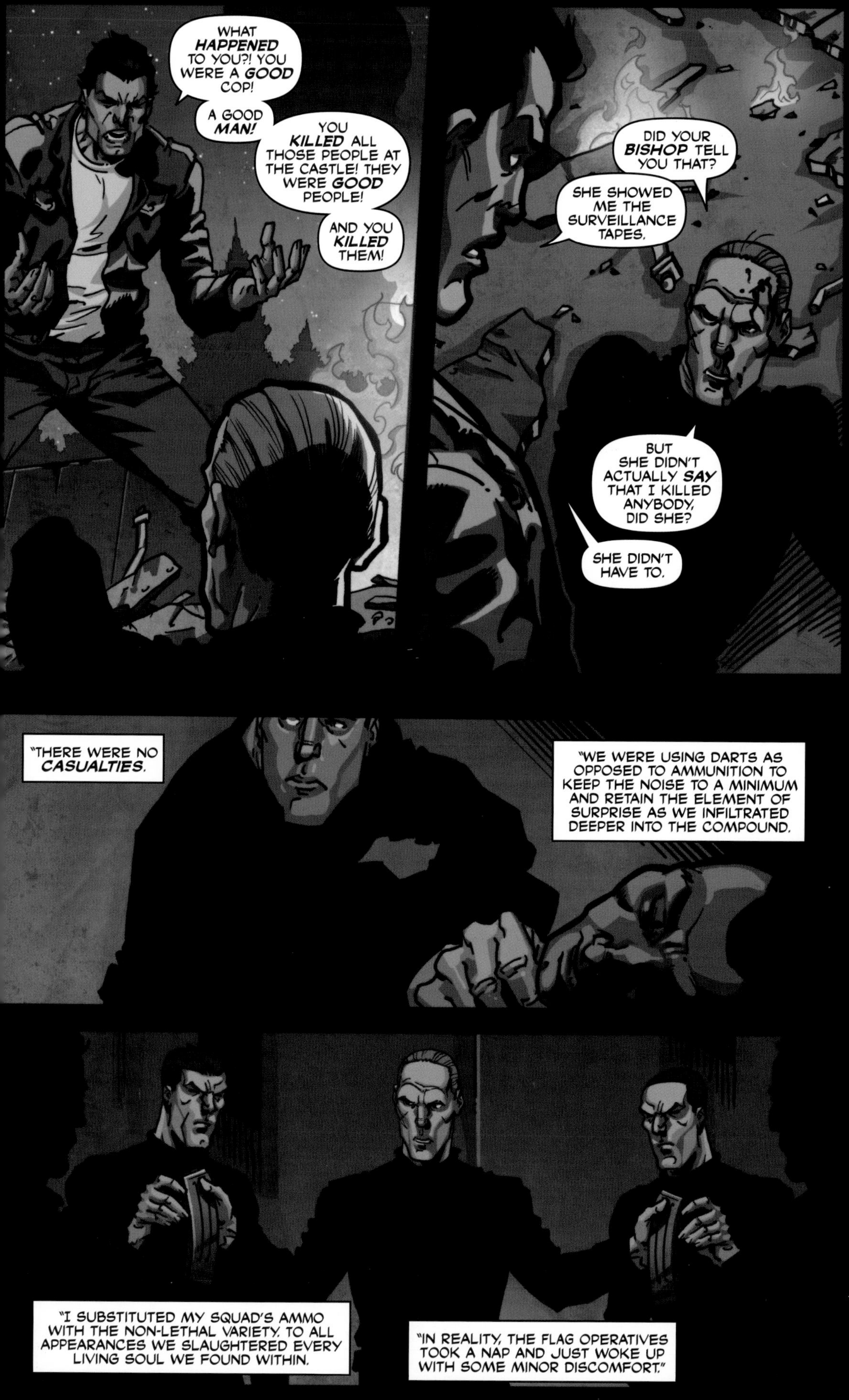
WHAT HAPPENED TO YOU?! YOU WERE A GOOD COP!
A GOOD MAN!
YOU KILLED ALL THOSE PEOPLE AT THE CASTLE! THEY WERE GOOD PEOPLE!
AND YOU KILLED THEM!
DID YOUR BISHOP TELL YOU THAT?
SHE SHOWED ME THE SURVEILLANCE TAPES.
BUT SHE DIDN'T ACTUALLY SAY THAT I KILLED ANYBODY, DID SHE?
SHE DIDN'T HAVE TO.
"THERE WERE NO CASUALTIES.
"WE WERE USING DARTS AS OPPOSED TO AMMUNITION TO KEEP THE NOISE TO A MINIMUM AND RETAIN THE ELEMENT OF SURPRISE AS WE INFILTRATED DEEPER INTO THE COMPOUND.
"I SUBSTITUTED MY SQUAD'S AMMO WITH THE NON-LETHAL VARIETY. TO ALL APPEARANCES WE SLAUGHTERED EVERY LIVING SOUL WE FOUND WITHIN.
"IN REALITY, THE FLAG OPERATIVES TOOK A NAP AND JUST WOKE UP WITH SOME MINOR DISCOMFORT."

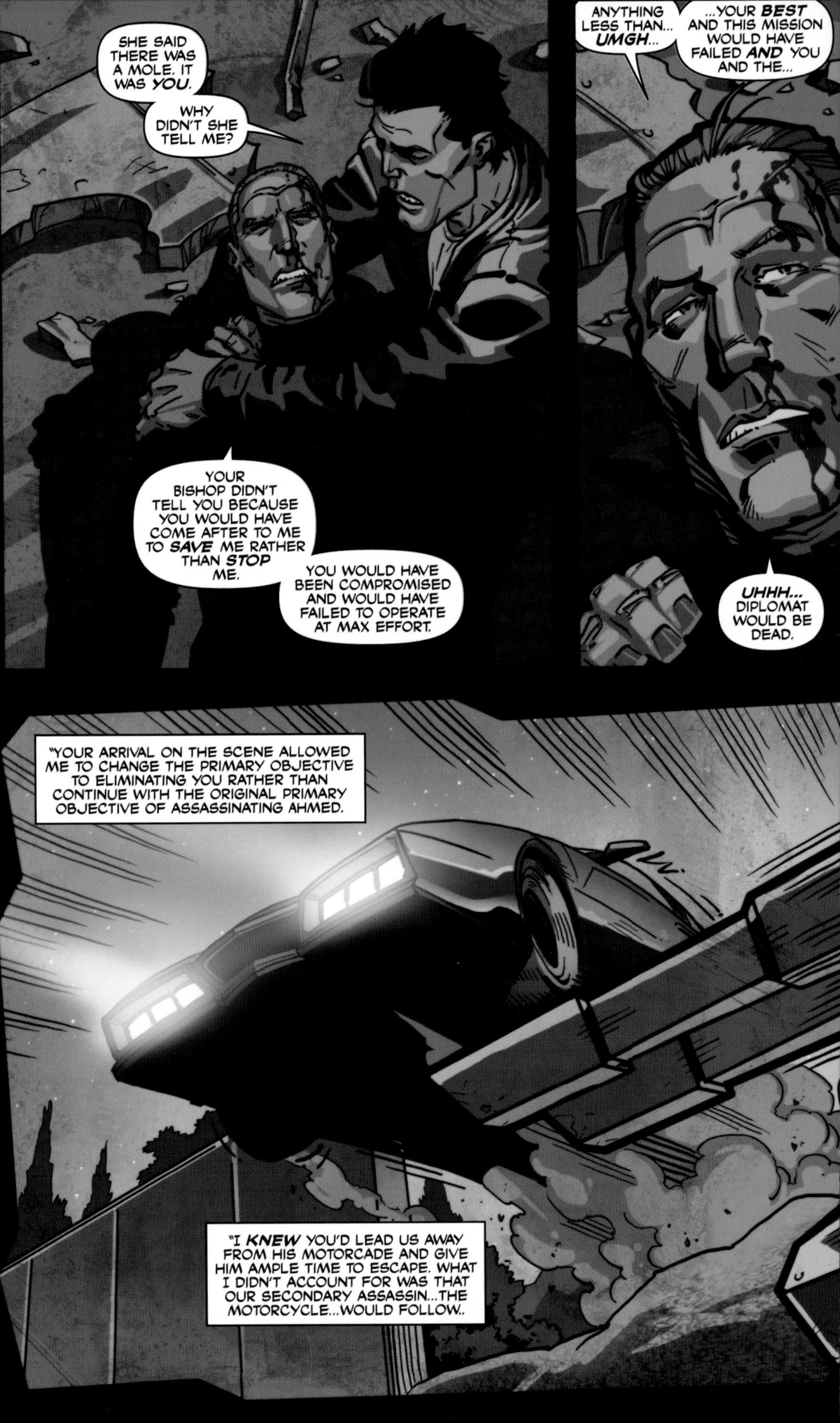
SHE SAID THERE WAS A MOLE. IT WAS YOU.
WHY DIDN'T SHE TELL ME?
YOUR BISHOP DIDN'T TELL YOU BECAUSE YOU WOULD HAVE COME AFTER TO ME TO SAVE ME RATHER THAN STOP ME.
YOU WOULD HAVE BEEN COMPROMISED AND WOULD HAVE FAILED TO OPERATE AT MAX EFFORT.
ANYTHING LESS THAN... UMGH...
...YOUR BEST AND THIS MISSION WOULD HAVE FAILED AND YOU AND THE...
UHHH... DIPLOMAT WOULD BE DEAD.
"YOUR ARRIVAL ON THE SCENE ALLOWED ME TO CHANGE THE PRIMARY OBJECTIVE TO ELIMINATING YOU RATHER THAN CONTINUE WITH THE ORIGINAL PRIMARY OBJECTIVE OF ASSASSINATING AHMED.
"I KNEW YOU'D LEAD US AWAY FROM HIS MOTORCADE AND GIVE HIM AMPLE TIME TO ESCAPE. WHAT I DIDN'T ACCOUNT FOR WAS THAT OUR SECONDARY ASSASSIN...THE MOTORCYCLE...WOULD FOLLOW..

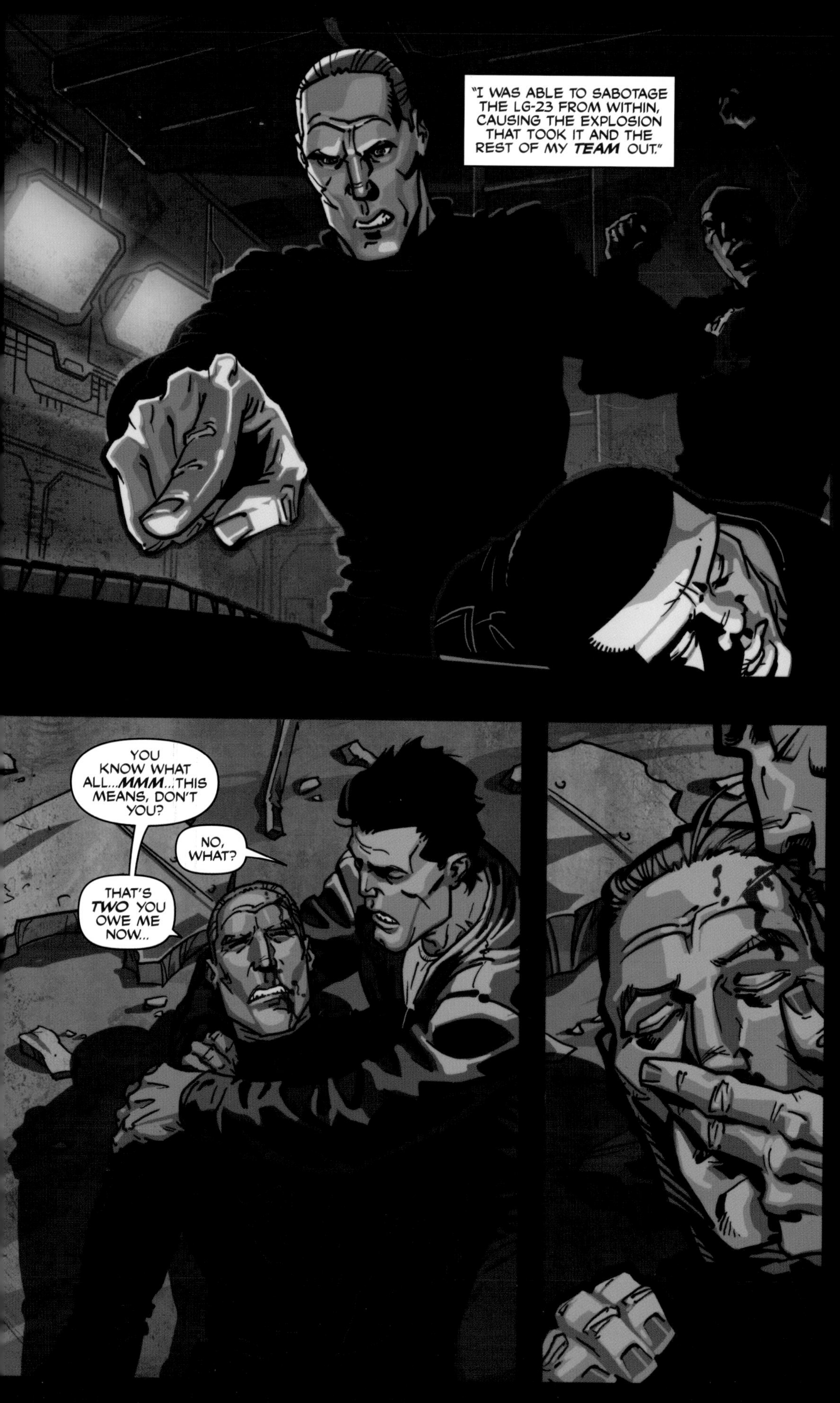
"I WAS ABLE TO SABOTAGE THE LG-23 FROM WITHIN, CAUSING THE EXPLOSION THAT TOOK IT AND THE REST OF MY *TEAM* OUT."
YOU KNOW WHAT ALL...*MMM*...THIS MEANS, DON'T YOU?
NO, WHAT?
THAT'S *TWO* YOU OWE ME NOW...

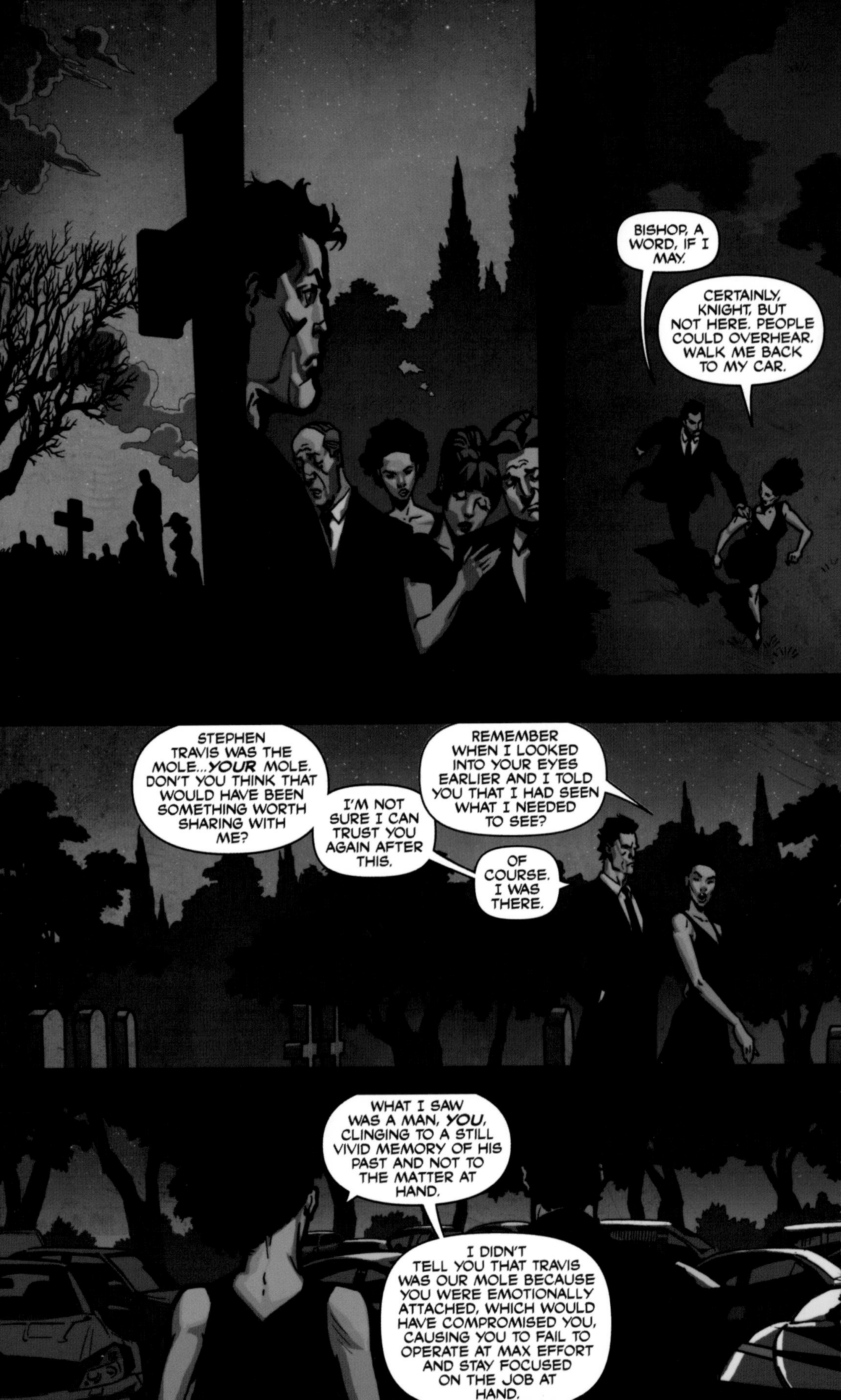
BISHOP, A WORD, IF I MAY.
CERTAINLY, KNIGHT, BUT NOT HERE. PEOPLE COULD OVERHEAR. WALK ME BACK TO MY CAR.
STEPHEN TRAVIS WAS THE MOLE...*YOUR* MOLE. DON'T YOU THINK THAT WOULD HAVE BEEN SOMETHING WORTH SHARING WITH ME?
I'M NOT SURE I CAN TRUST YOU AGAIN AFTER THIS.
REMEMBER WHEN I LOOKED INTO YOUR EYES EARLIER AND I TOLD YOU THAT I HAD SEEN WHAT I NEEDED TO SEE?
OF COURSE. I WAS THERE.
WHAT I SAW WAS A MAN, *YOU*, CLINGING TO A STILL VIVID MEMORY OF HIS PAST AND NOT TO THE MATTER AT HAND.
I DIDN'T TELL YOU THAT TRAVIS WAS OUR MOLE BECAUSE YOU WERE EMOTIONALLY ATTACHED, WHICH WOULD HAVE COMPROMISED YOU, CAUSING YOU TO FAIL TO OPERATE AT MAX EFFORT AND STAY FOCUSED ON THE JOB AT HAND.

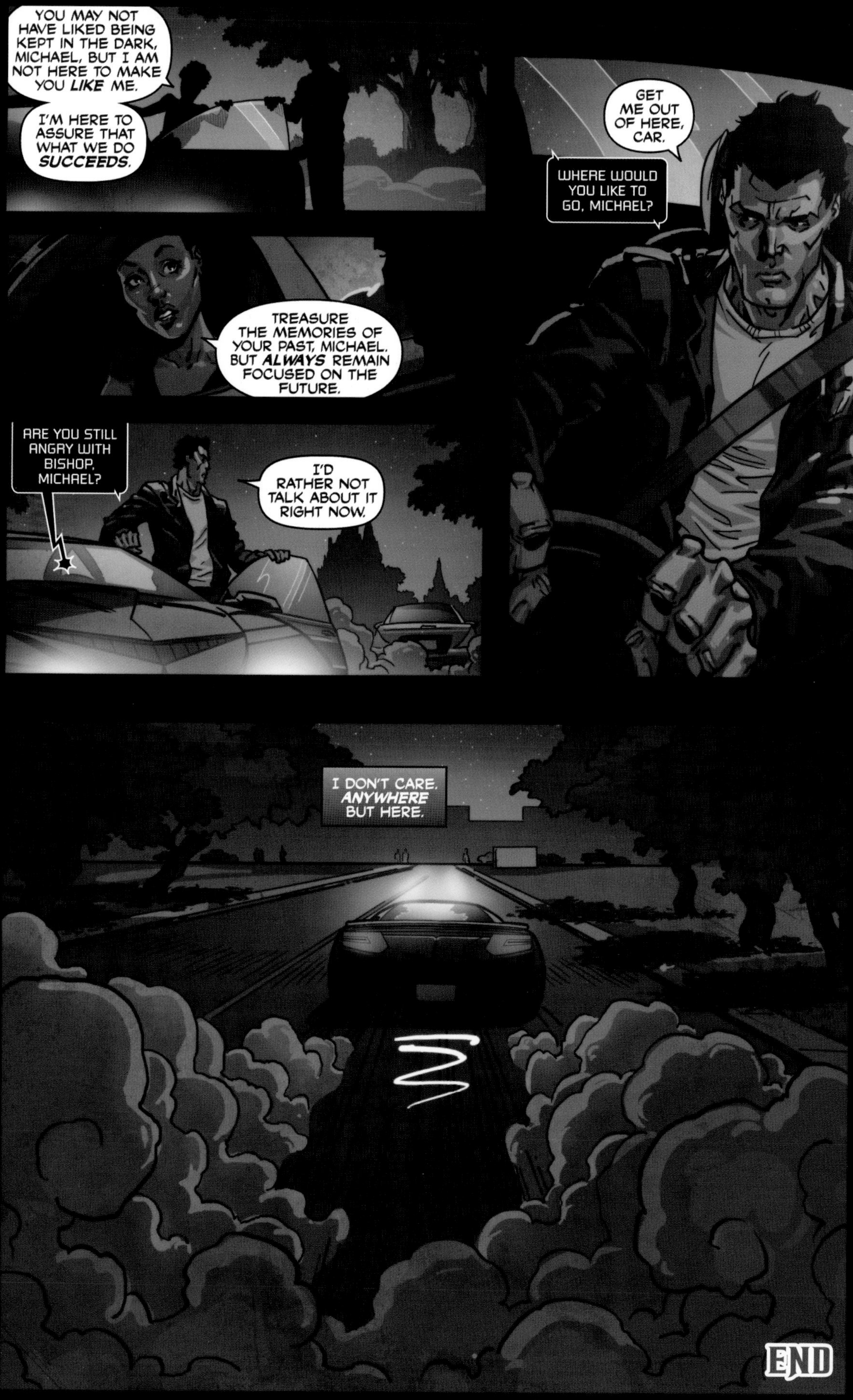
YOU MAY NOT HAVE LIKED BEING KEPT IN THE DARK, MICHAEL, BUT I AM NOT HERE TO MAKE YOU *LIKE* ME.
I'M HERE TO ASSURE THAT WHAT WE DO *SUCCEEDS*.
TREASURE THE MEMORIES OF YOUR PAST, MICHAEL. BUT *ALWAYS* REMAIN FOCUSED ON THE FUTURE.
ARE YOU STILL ANGRY WITH BISHOP, MICHAEL?
I'D RATHER NOT TALK ABOUT IT RIGHT NOW.
GET ME OUT OF HERE, CAR.
WHERE WOULD YOU LIKE TO GO, MICHAEL?
I DON'T CARE. *ANYWHERE* BUT HERE.
END

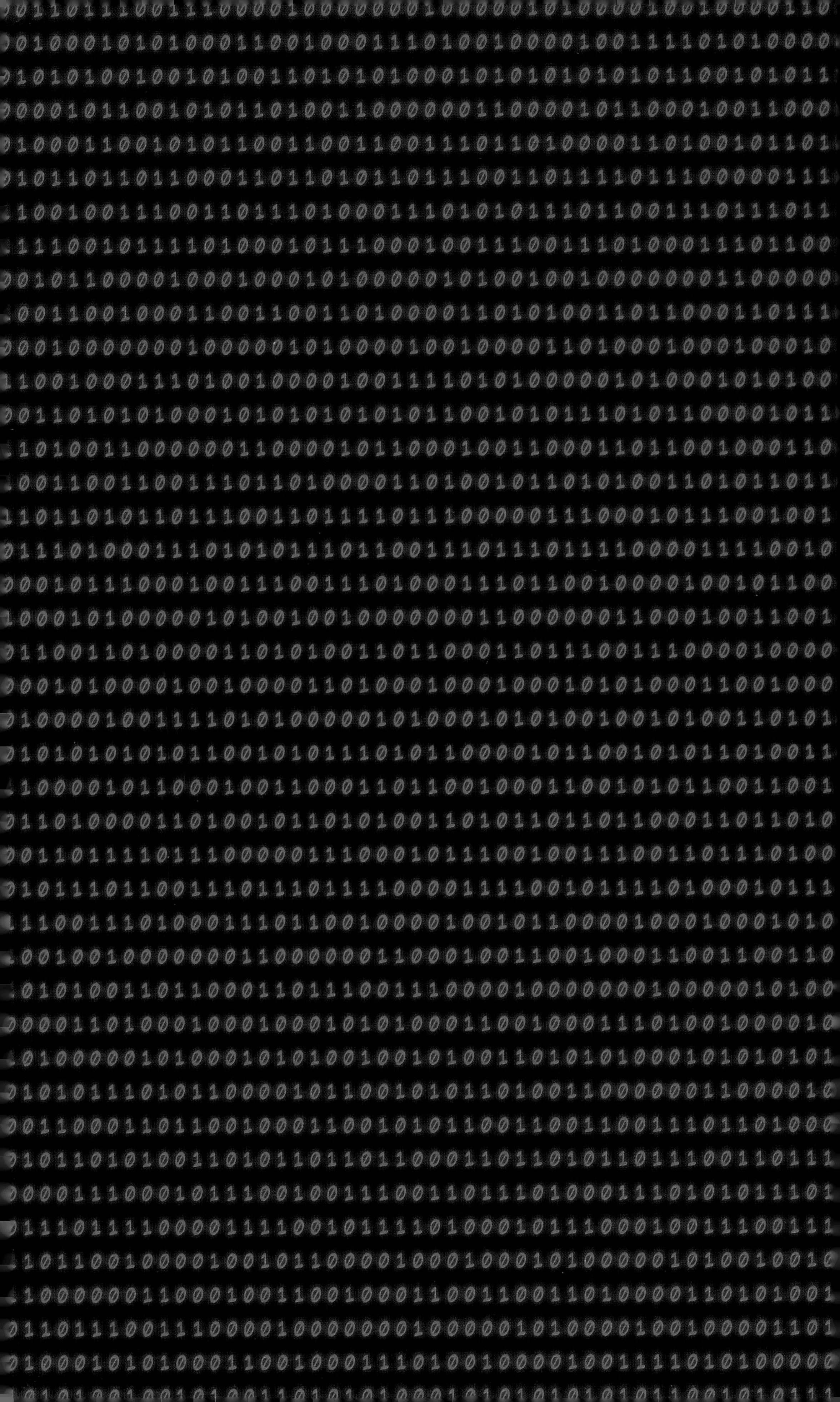

MILITARY INDUSTRIAL COMPLEXITY

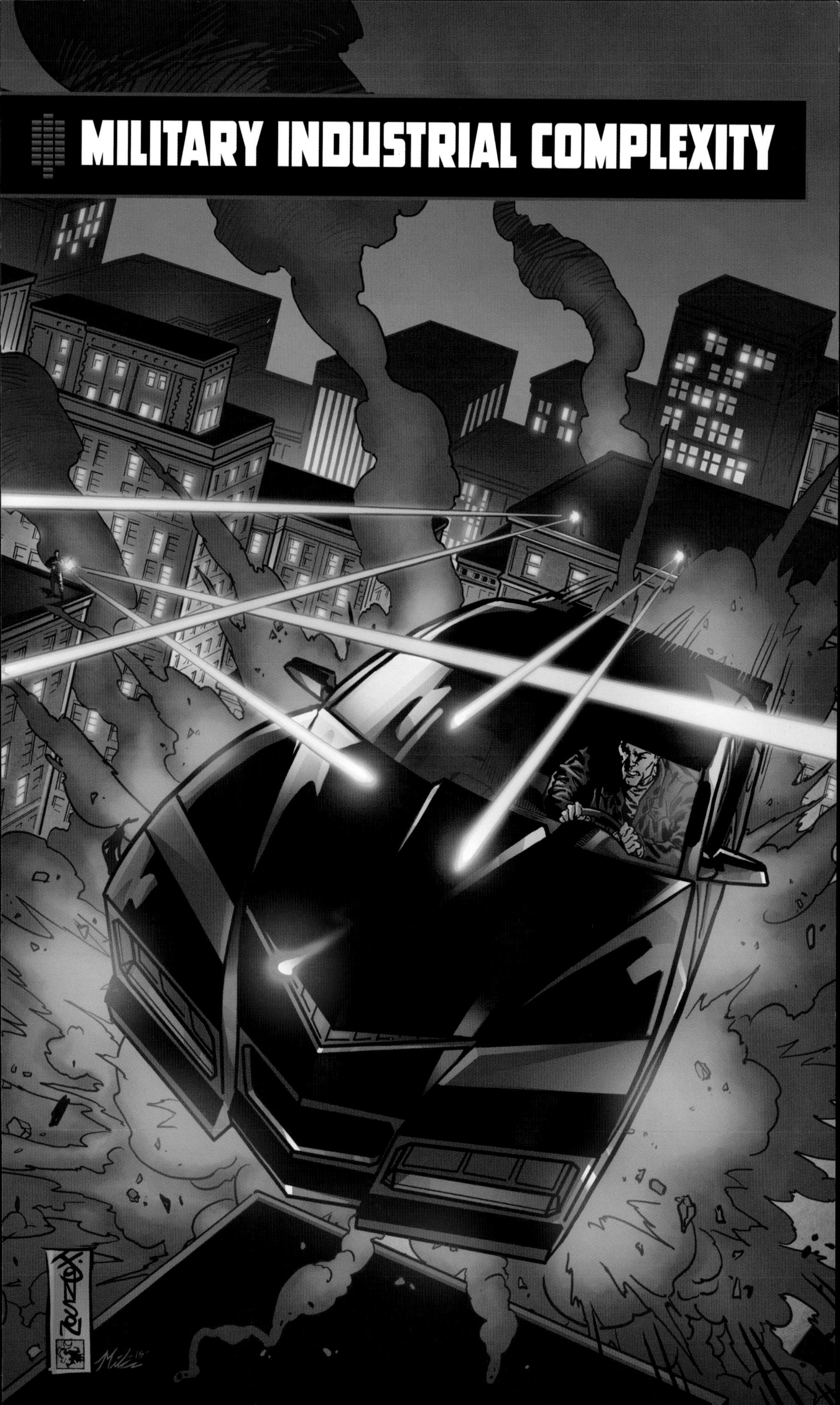

KNIGHT RIDER
KNIGHTSTRIKES

WRITTEN BY
B. CLAY MOORE

ILLUSTRATED BY
JASON JOHNSON

COLORED BY
MILEN PARVANOV

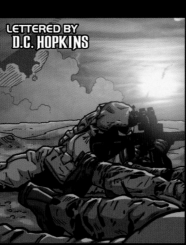

LETTERED BY
D.C. HOPKINS

EDITED BY
SHANNON ERIC DENTON

FRONT COVER BY
JASON JOHNSON

KNIGHT RIDER CREATED BY
GLEN A. LARSON

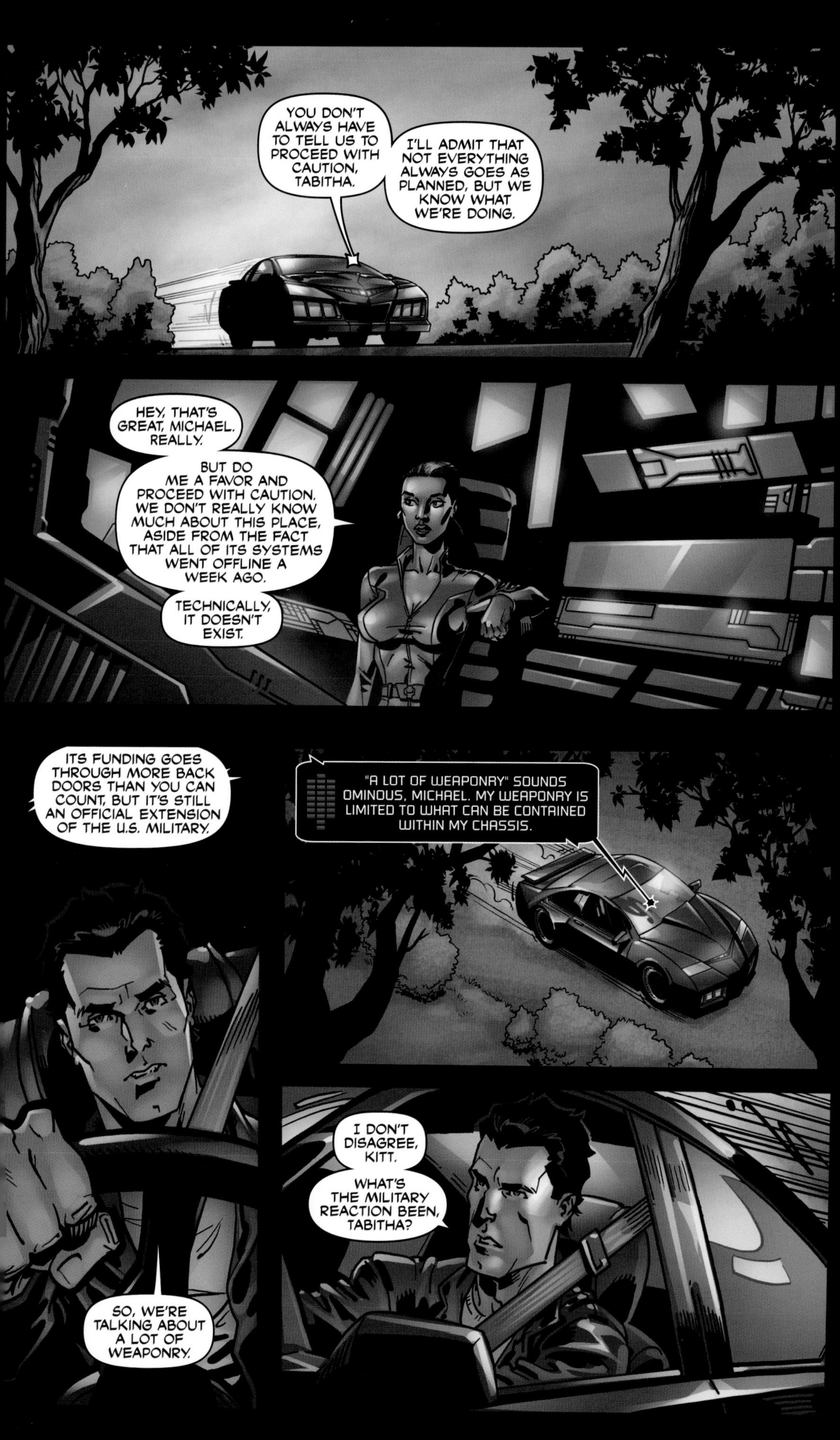
YOU DON'T ALWAYS HAVE TO TELL US TO PROCEED WITH CAUTION, TABITHA.
I'LL ADMIT THAT NOT EVERYTHING ALWAYS GOES AS PLANNED, BUT WE KNOW WHAT WE'RE DOING.
HEY, THAT'S GREAT, MICHAEL. REALLY.
BUT DO ME A FAVOR AND PROCEED WITH CAUTION. WE DON'T REALLY KNOW MUCH ABOUT THIS PLACE, ASIDE FROM THE FACT THAT ALL OF ITS SYSTEMS WENT OFFLINE A WEEK AGO.
TECHNICALLY, IT DOESN'T EXIST.
ITS FUNDING GOES THROUGH MORE BACK DOORS THAN YOU CAN COUNT, BUT IT'S STILL AN OFFICIAL EXTENSION OF THE U.S. MILITARY.
SO, WE'RE TALKING ABOUT A LOT OF WEAPONRY.
"A LOT OF WEAPONRY" SOUNDS OMINOUS, MICHAEL. MY WEAPONRY IS LIMITED TO WHAT CAN BE CONTAINED WITHIN MY CHASSIS.
I DON'T DISAGREE, KITT.
WHAT'S THE MILITARY REACTION BEEN, TABITHA?

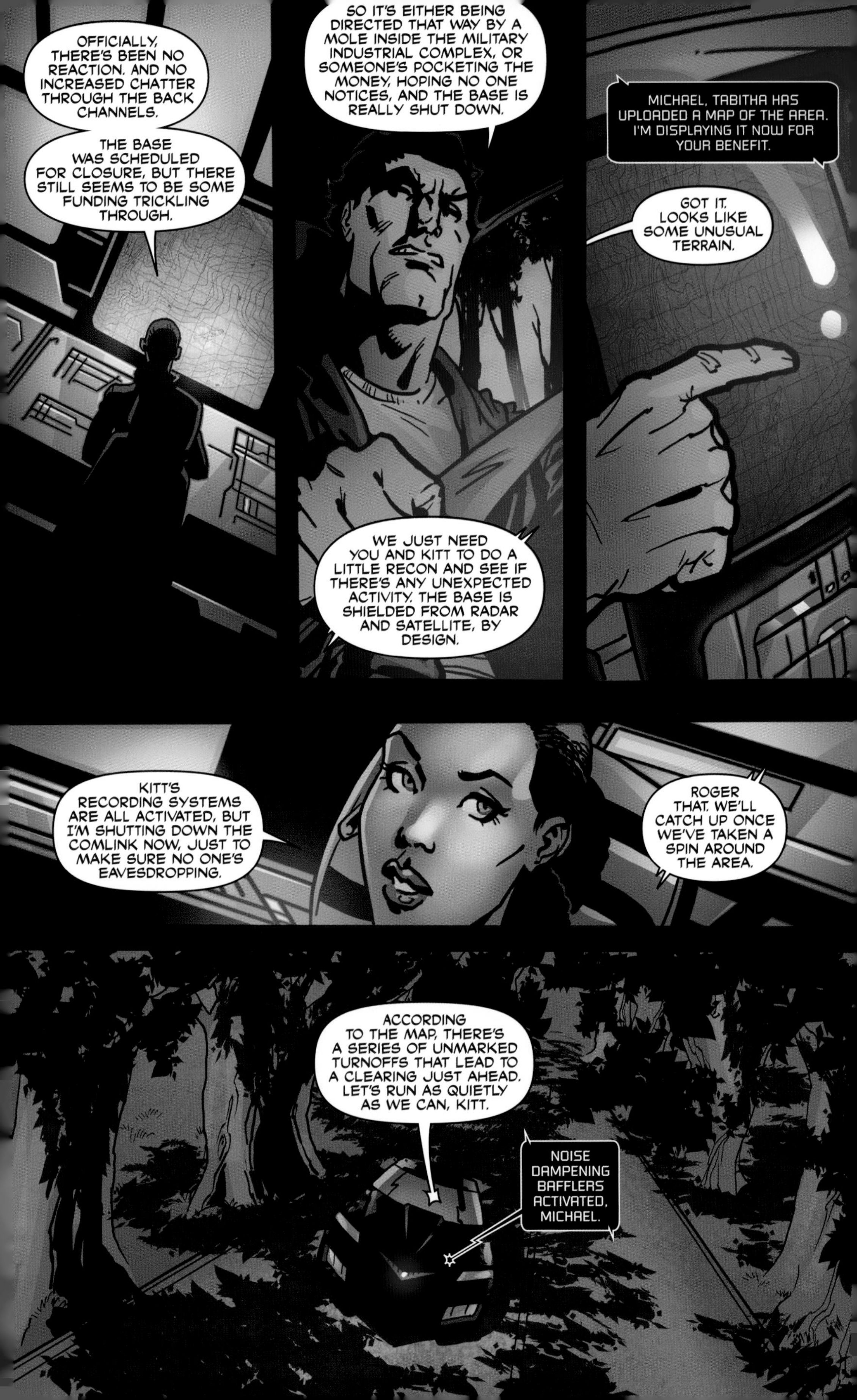
OFFICIALLY, THERE'S BEEN NO REACTION, AND NO INCREASED CHATTER THROUGH THE BACK CHANNELS.
THE BASE WAS SCHEDULED FOR CLOSURE, BUT THERE STILL SEEMS TO BE SOME FUNDING TRICKLING THROUGH.
SO IT'S EITHER BEING DIRECTED THAT WAY BY A MOLE INSIDE THE MILITARY INDUSTRIAL COMPLEX, OR SOMEONE'S POCKETING THE MONEY, HOPING NO ONE NOTICES, AND THE BASE IS REALLY SHUT DOWN.
WE JUST NEED YOU AND KITT TO DO A LITTLE RECON AND SEE IF THERE'S ANY UNEXPECTED ACTIVITY. THE BASE IS SHIELDED FROM RADAR AND SATELLITE, BY DESIGN.
MICHAEL, TABITHA HAS UPLOADED A MAP OF THE AREA. I'M DISPLAYING IT NOW FOR YOUR BENEFIT.
GOT IT. LOOKS LIKE SOME UNUSUAL TERRAIN.
KITT'S RECORDING SYSTEMS ARE ALL ACTIVATED, BUT I'M SHUTTING DOWN THE COMLINK NOW, JUST TO MAKE SURE NO ONE'S EAVESDROPPING.
ROGER THAT. WE'LL CATCH UP ONCE WE'VE TAKEN A SPIN AROUND THE AREA.
ACCORDING TO THE MAP, THERE'S A SERIES OF UNMARKED TURNOFFS THAT LEAD TO A CLEARING JUST AHEAD. LET'S RUN AS QUIETLY AS WE CAN, KITT.
NOISE DAMPENING BAFFLERS ACTIVATED, MICHAEL.

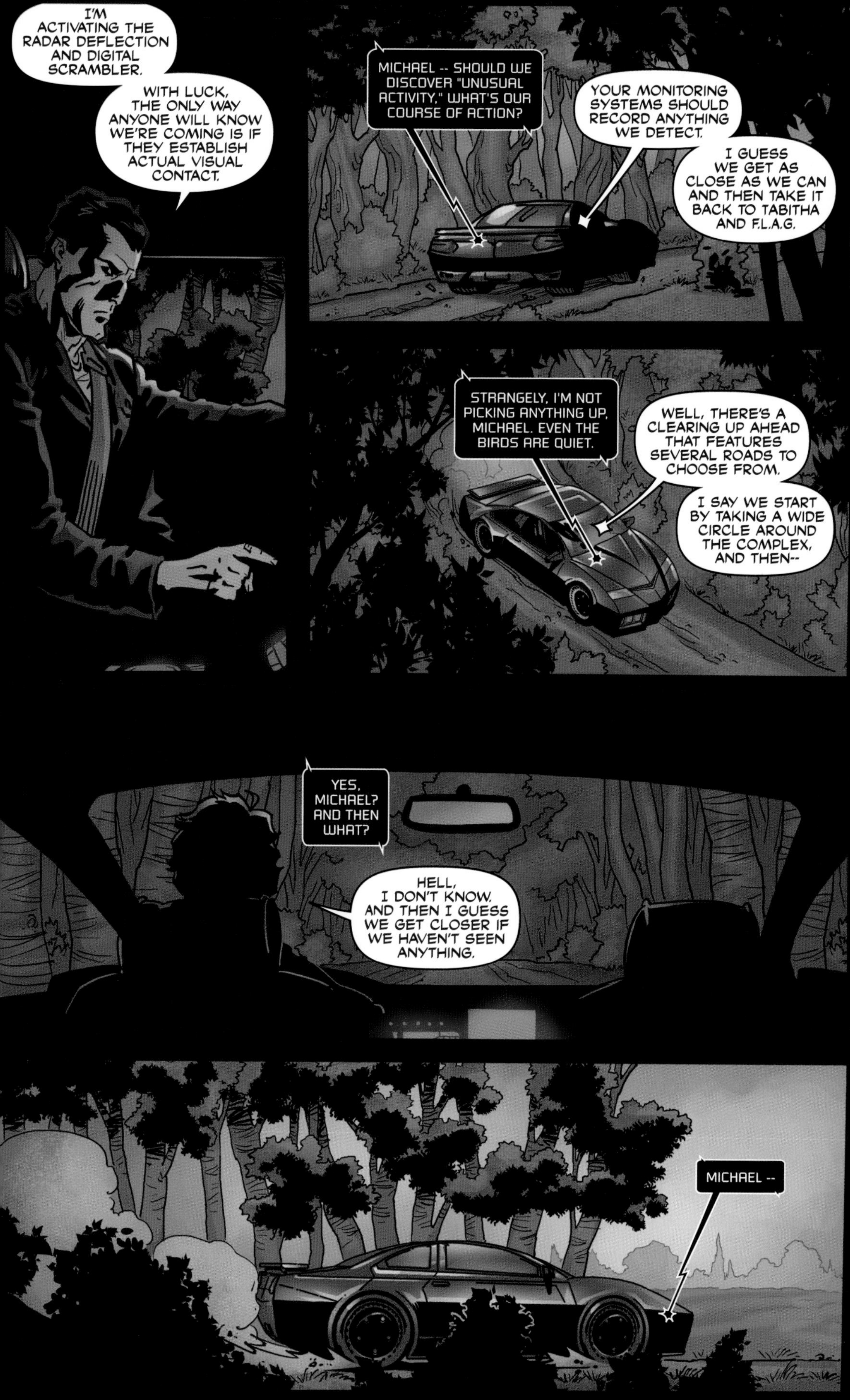
I'M ACTIVATING THE RADAR DEFLECTION AND DIGITAL SCRAMBLER.
WITH LUCK, THE ONLY WAY ANYONE WILL KNOW WE'RE COMING IS IF THEY ESTABLISH ACTUAL VISUAL CONTACT.
MICHAEL -- SHOULD WE DISCOVER "UNUSUAL ACTIVITY," WHAT'S OUR COURSE OF ACTION?
YOUR MONITORING SYSTEMS SHOULD RECORD ANYTHING WE DETECT.
I GUESS WE GET AS CLOSE AS WE CAN AND THEN TAKE IT BACK TO TABITHA AND F.L.A.G.
STRANGELY, I'M NOT PICKING ANYTHING UP, MICHAEL. EVEN THE BIRDS ARE QUIET.
WELL, THERE'S A CLEARING UP AHEAD THAT FEATURES SEVERAL ROADS TO CHOOSE FROM.
I SAY WE START BY TAKING A WIDE CIRCLE AROUND THE COMPLEX, AND THEN--
YES, MICHAEL? AND THEN WHAT?
HELL, I DON'T KNOW. AND THEN I GUESS WE GET CLOSER IF WE HAVEN'T SEEN ANYTHING.
MICHAEL --

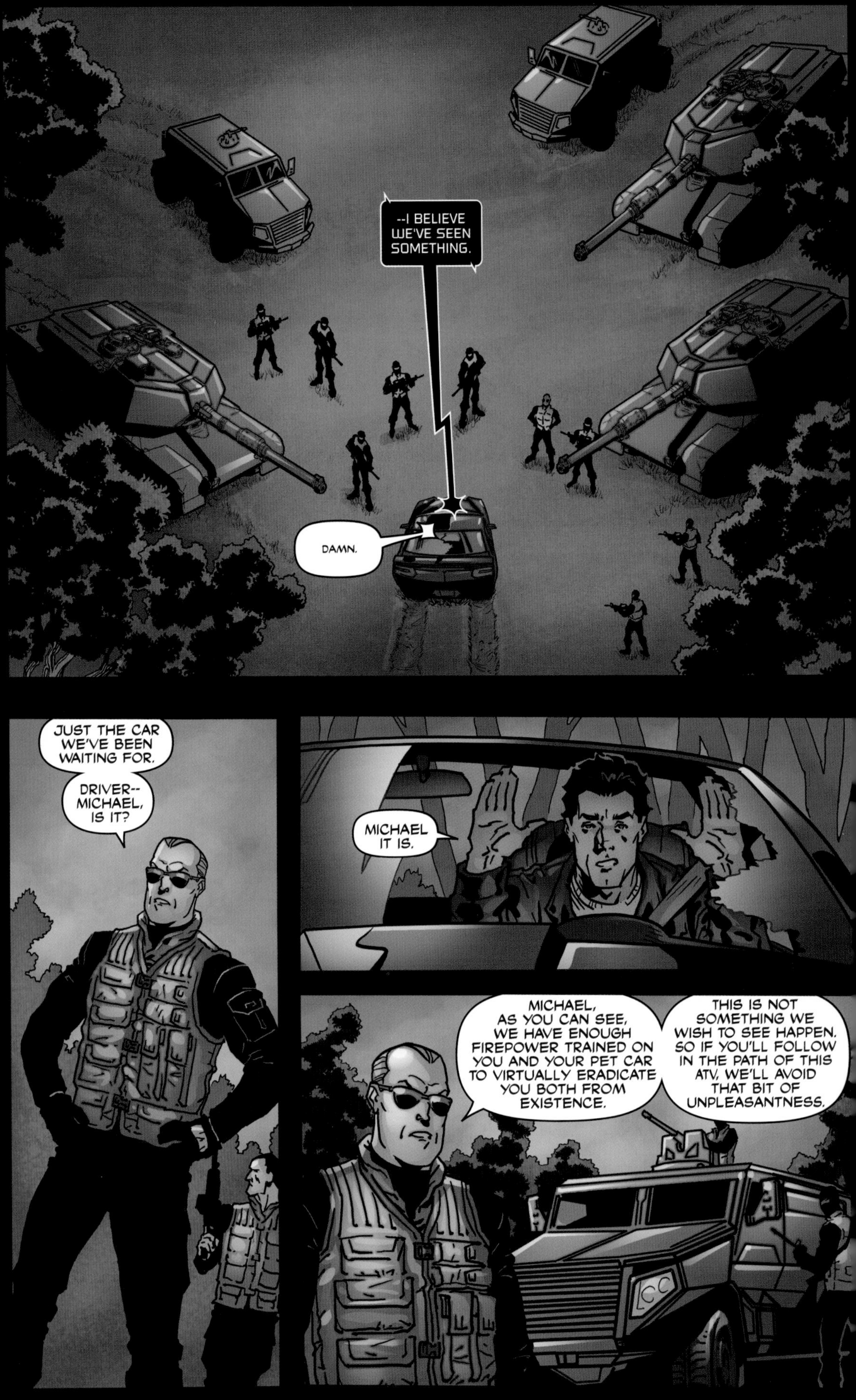
--I BELIEVE WE'VE SEEN SOMETHING.
DAMN.
JUST THE CAR WE'VE BEEN WAITING FOR.
DRIVER-- MICHAEL, IS IT?
MICHAEL IT IS.
MICHAEL, AS YOU CAN SEE, WE HAVE ENOUGH FIREPOWER TRAINED ON YOU AND YOUR PET CAR TO VIRTUALLY ERADICATE YOU BOTH FROM EXISTENCE.
THIS IS NOT SOMETHING WE WISH TO SEE HAPPEN. SO IF YOU'LL FOLLOW IN THE PATH OF THIS ATV, WE'LL AVOID THAT BIT OF UNPLEASANTNESS.

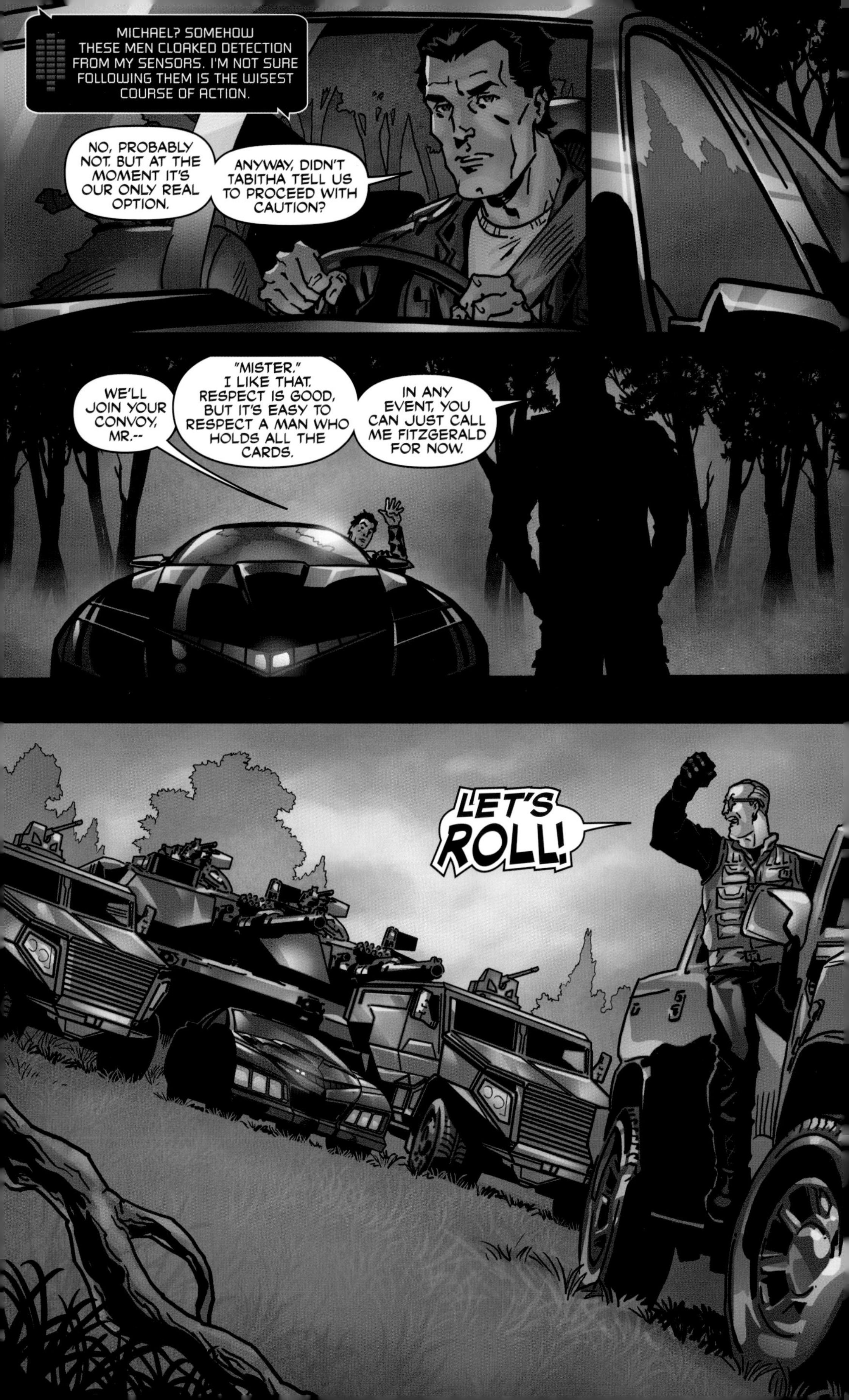

MICHAEL? SOMEHOW THESE MEN CLOAKED DETECTION FROM MY SENSORS. I'M NOT SURE FOLLOWING THEM IS THE WISEST COURSE OF ACTION.
NO, PROBABLY NOT. BUT AT THE MOMENT IT'S OUR ONLY REAL OPTION.
ANYWAY, DIDN'T TABITHA TELL US TO PROCEED WITH CAUTION?
WE'LL JOIN YOUR CONVOY, MR.--
"MISTER." I LIKE THAT. RESPECT IS GOOD, BUT IT'S EASY TO RESPECT A MAN WHO HOLDS ALL THE CARDS.
IN ANY EVENT, YOU CAN JUST CALL ME FITZGERALD FOR NOW.
LET'S ROLL!

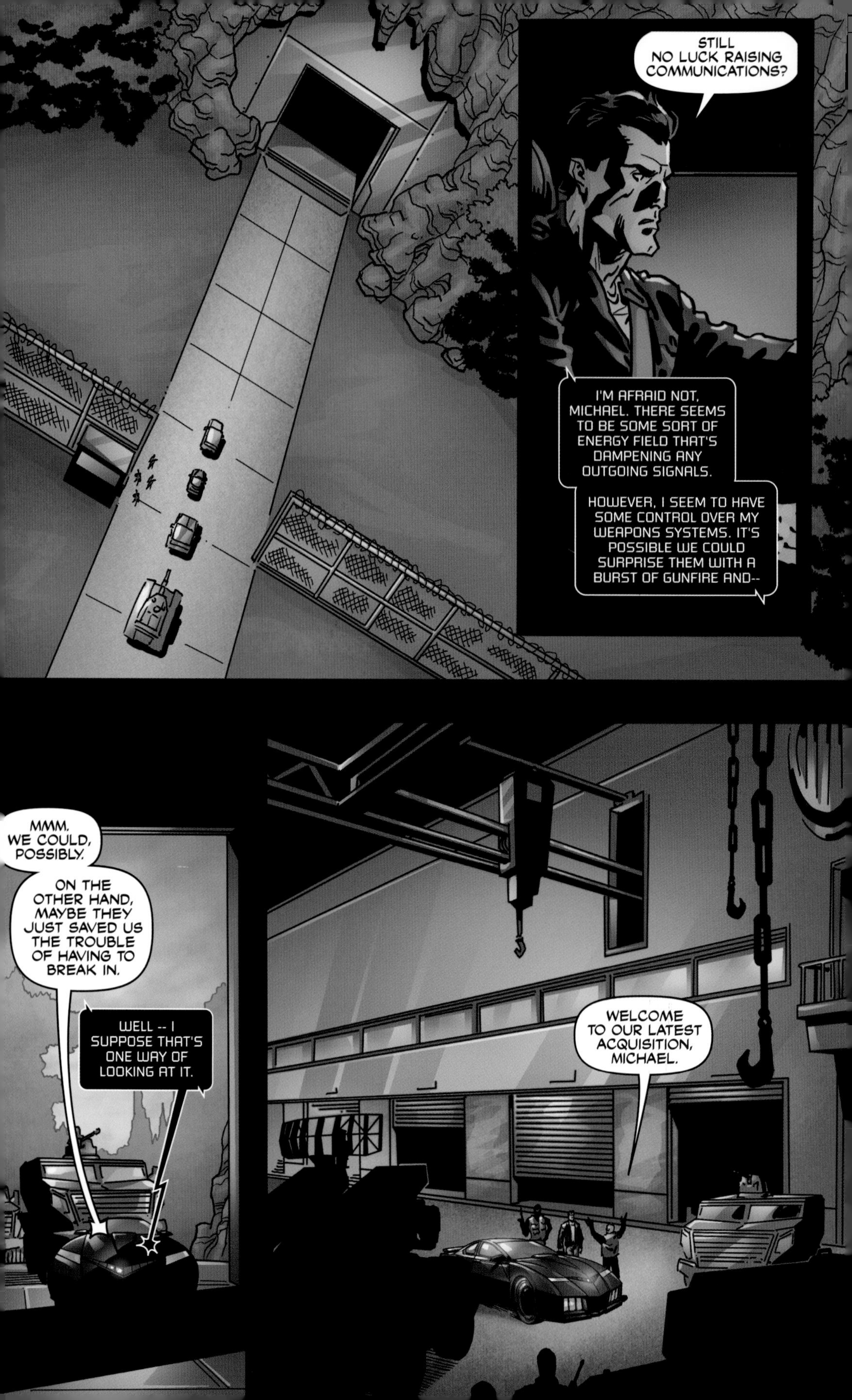
STILL NO LUCK RAISING COMMUNICATIONS?
I'M AFRAID NOT, MICHAEL. THERE SEEMS TO BE SOME SORT OF ENERGY FIELD THAT'S DAMPENING ANY OUTGOING SIGNALS.
HOWEVER, I SEEM TO HAVE SOME CONTROL OVER MY WEAPONS SYSTEMS. IT'S POSSIBLE WE COULD SURPRISE THEM WITH A BURST OF GUNFIRE AND--
MMM. WE COULD, POSSIBLY.
ON THE OTHER HAND, MAYBE THEY JUST SAVED US THE TROUBLE OF HAVING TO BREAK IN.
WELL -- I SUPPOSE THAT'S ONE WAY OF LOOKING AT IT.
WELCOME TO OUR LATEST ACQUISITION, MICHAEL.

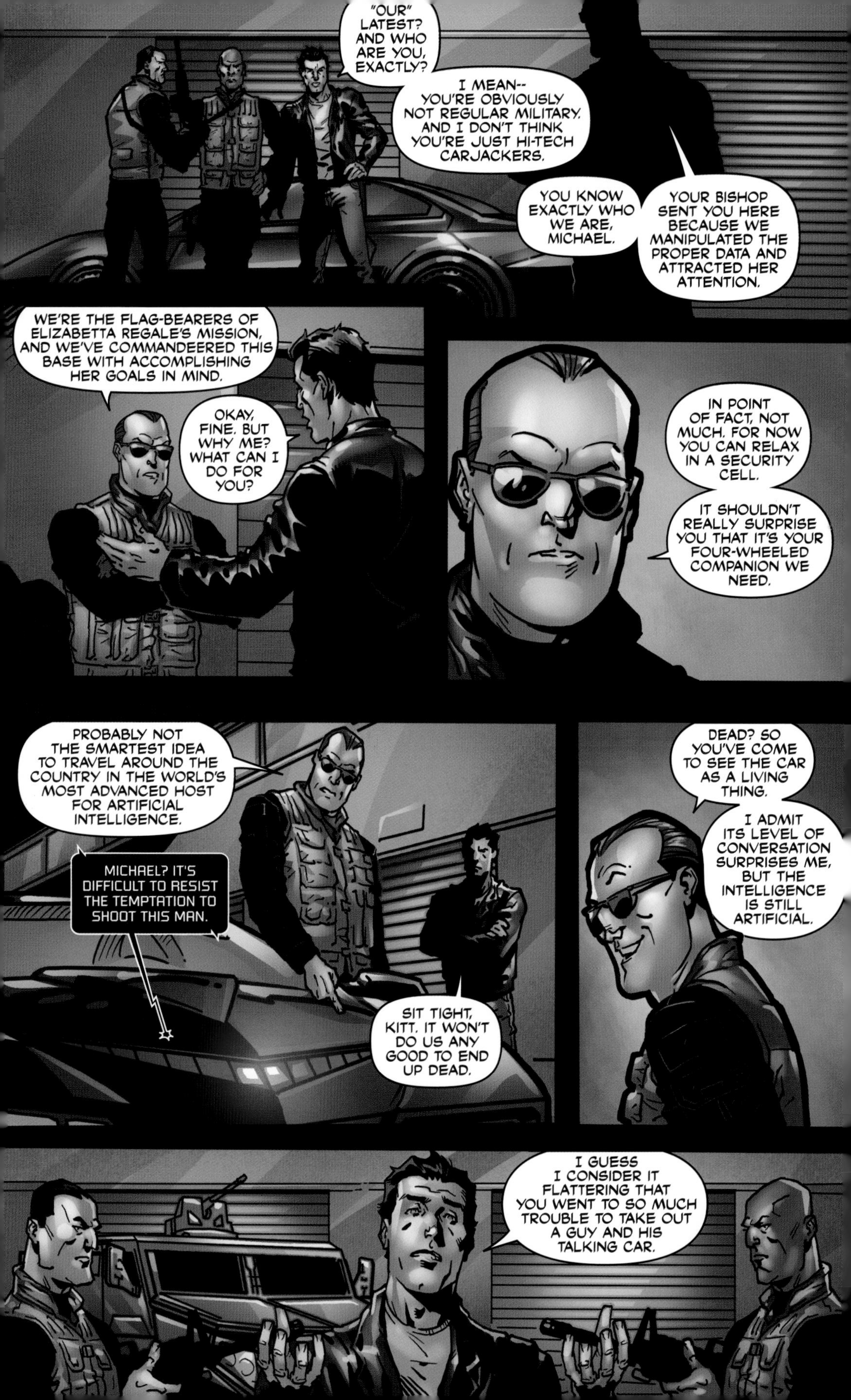
"OUR" LATEST? AND WHO ARE YOU, EXACTLY?
I MEAN-- YOU'RE OBVIOUSLY NOT REGULAR MILITARY. AND I DON'T THINK YOU'RE JUST HI-TECH CARJACKERS.
YOU KNOW EXACTLY WHO WE ARE, MICHAEL.
YOUR BISHOP SENT YOU HERE BECAUSE WE MANIPULATED THE PROPER DATA AND ATTRACTED HER ATTENTION.
WE'RE THE FLAG-BEARERS OF ELIZABETTA REGALE'S MISSION, AND WE'VE COMMANDEERED THIS BASE WITH ACCOMPLISHING HER GOALS IN MIND.
OKAY, FINE. BUT WHY ME? WHAT CAN I DO FOR YOU?
IN POINT OF FACT, NOT MUCH. FOR NOW YOU CAN RELAX IN A SECURITY CELL.
IT SHOULDN'T REALLY SURPRISE YOU THAT IT'S YOUR FOUR-WHEELED COMPANION WE NEED.
PROBABLY NOT THE SMARTEST IDEA TO TRAVEL AROUND THE COUNTRY IN THE WORLD'S MOST ADVANCED HOST FOR ARTIFICIAL INTELLIGENCE.
MICHAEL? IT'S DIFFICULT TO RESIST THE TEMPTATION TO SHOOT THIS MAN.
SIT TIGHT, KITT. IT WON'T DO US ANY GOOD TO END UP DEAD.
DEAD? SO YOU'VE COME TO SEE THE CAR AS A LIVING THING.
I ADMIT ITS LEVEL OF CONVERSATION SURPRISES ME, BUT THE INTELLIGENCE IS STILL ARTIFICIAL.
I GUESS I CONSIDER IT FLATTERING THAT YOU WENT TO SO MUCH TROUBLE TO TAKE OUT A GUY AND HIS TALKING CAR.

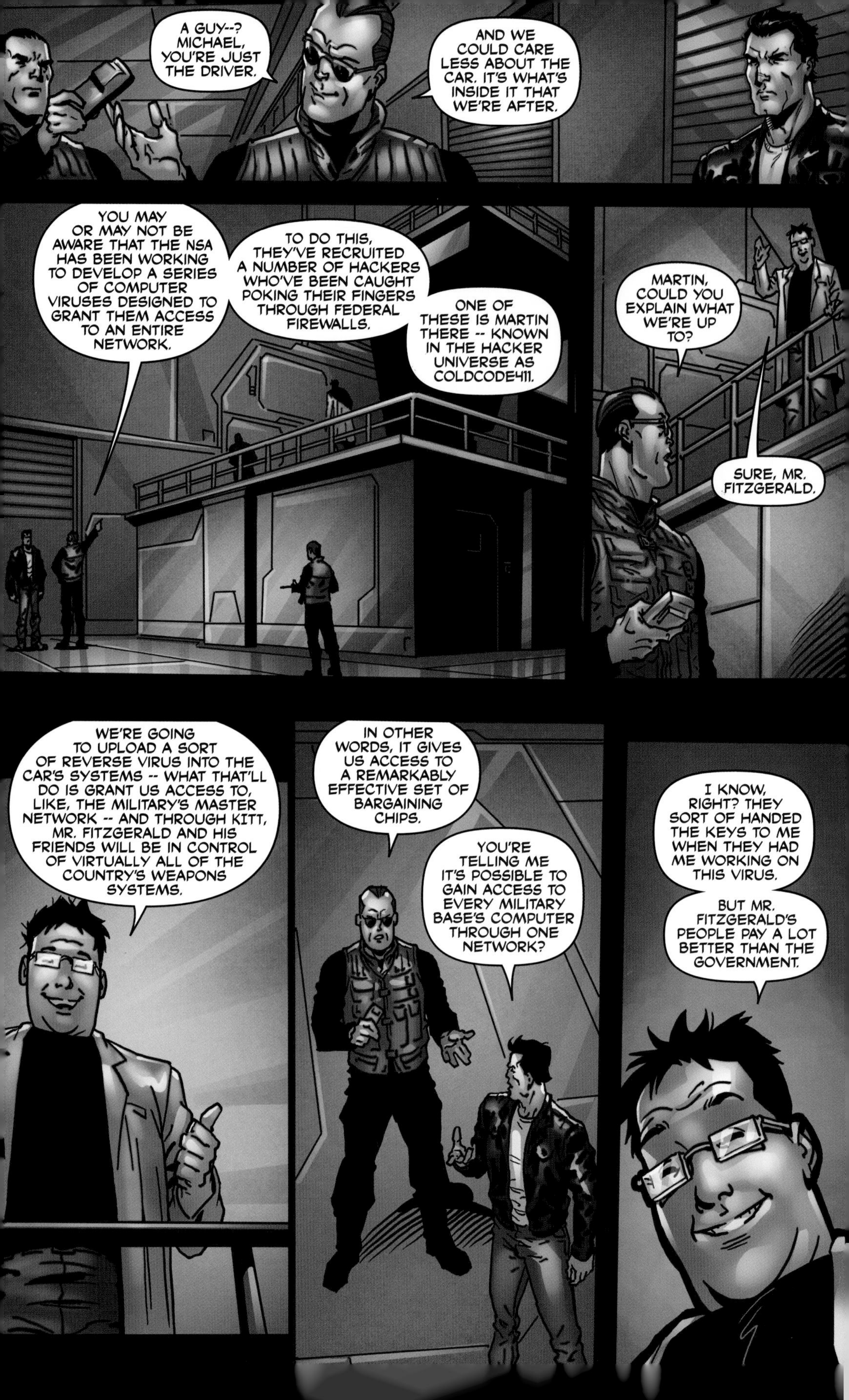
A GUY--? MICHAEL, YOU'RE JUST THE DRIVER.
AND WE COULD CARE LESS ABOUT THE CAR. IT'S WHAT'S INSIDE IT THAT WE'RE AFTER.
YOU MAY OR MAY NOT BE AWARE THAT THE NSA HAS BEEN WORKING TO DEVELOP A SERIES OF COMPUTER VIRUSES DESIGNED TO GRANT THEM ACCESS TO AN ENTIRE NETWORK.
TO DO THIS, THEY'VE RECRUITED A NUMBER OF HACKERS WHO'VE BEEN CAUGHT POKING THEIR FINGERS THROUGH FEDERAL FIREWALLS.
ONE OF THESE IS MARTIN THERE -- KNOWN IN THE HACKER UNIVERSE AS COLDCODE411.
MARTIN, COULD YOU EXPLAIN WHAT WE'RE UP TO?
SURE, MR. FITZGERALD.
WE'RE GOING TO UPLOAD A SORT OF REVERSE VIRUS INTO THE CAR'S SYSTEMS -- WHAT THAT'LL DO IS GRANT US ACCESS TO, LIKE, THE MILITARY'S MASTER NETWORK -- AND THROUGH KITT, MR. FITZGERALD AND HIS FRIENDS WILL BE IN CONTROL OF VIRTUALLY ALL OF THE COUNTRY'S WEAPONS SYSTEMS.
IN OTHER WORDS, IT GIVES US ACCESS TO A REMARKABLY EFFECTIVE SET OF BARGAINING CHIPS.
YOU'RE TELLING ME IT'S POSSIBLE TO GAIN ACCESS TO EVERY MILITARY BASE'S COMPUTER THROUGH ONE NETWORK?
I KNOW, RIGHT? THEY SORT OF HANDED THE KEYS TO ME WHEN THEY HAD ME WORKING ON THIS VIRUS.
BUT MR. FITZGERALD'S PEOPLE PAY A LOT BETTER THAN THE GOVERNMENT.

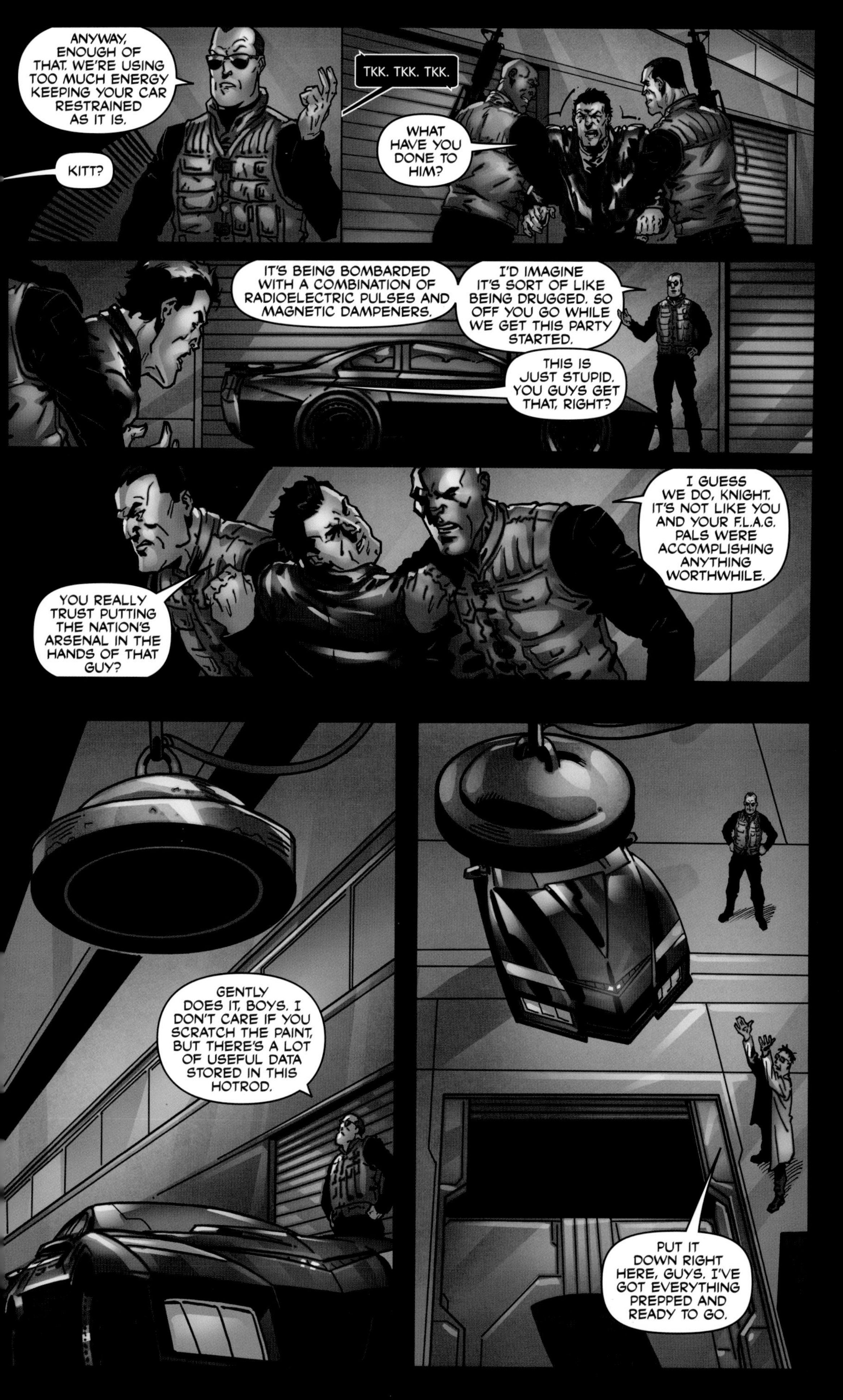

ANYWAY, ENOUGH OF THAT. WE'RE USING TOO MUCH ENERGY KEEPING YOUR CAR RESTRAINED AS IT IS.
KITT?
TKK. TKK. TKK.
WHAT HAVE YOU DONE TO HIM?
IT'S BEING BOMBARDED WITH A COMBINATION OF RADIOELECTRIC PULSES AND MAGNETIC DAMPENERS.
I'D IMAGINE IT'S SORT OF LIKE BEING DRUGGED. SO OFF YOU GO WHILE WE GET THIS PARTY STARTED.
THIS IS JUST STUPID. YOU GUYS GET THAT, RIGHT?
I GUESS WE DO, KNIGHT. IT'S NOT LIKE YOU AND YOUR F.L.A.G. PALS WERE ACCOMPLISHING ANYTHING WORTHWHILE.
YOU REALLY TRUST PUTTING THE NATION'S ARSENAL IN THE HANDS OF THAT GUY?
GENTLY DOES IT, BOYS. I DON'T CARE IF YOU SCRATCH THE PAINT, BUT THERE'S A LOT OF USEFUL DATA STORED IN THIS HOTROD.
PUT IT DOWN RIGHT HERE, GUYS. I'VE GOT EVERYTHING PREPPED AND READY TO GO.

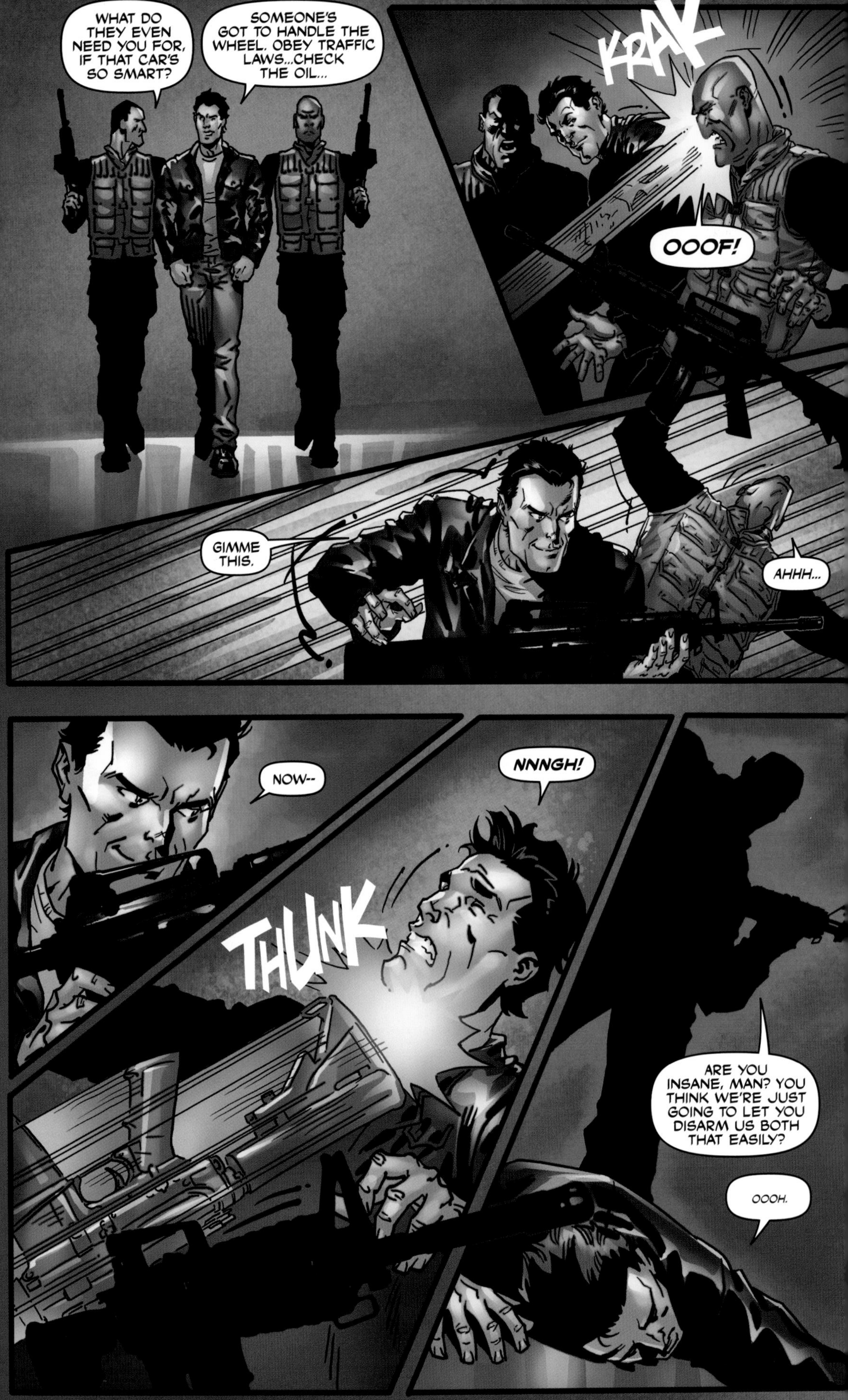
WHAT DO THEY EVEN NEED YOU FOR, IF THAT CAR'S SO SMART?
SOMEONE'S GOT TO HANDLE THE WHEEL. OBEY TRAFFIC LAWS...CHECK THE OIL...
KRAK
OOOF!
GIMME THIS.
AHHH...
NOW--
NNNGH!
THUNK
ARE YOU INSANE, MAN? YOU THINK WE'RE JUST GOING TO LET YOU DISARM US BOTH THAT EASILY?
OOOH.

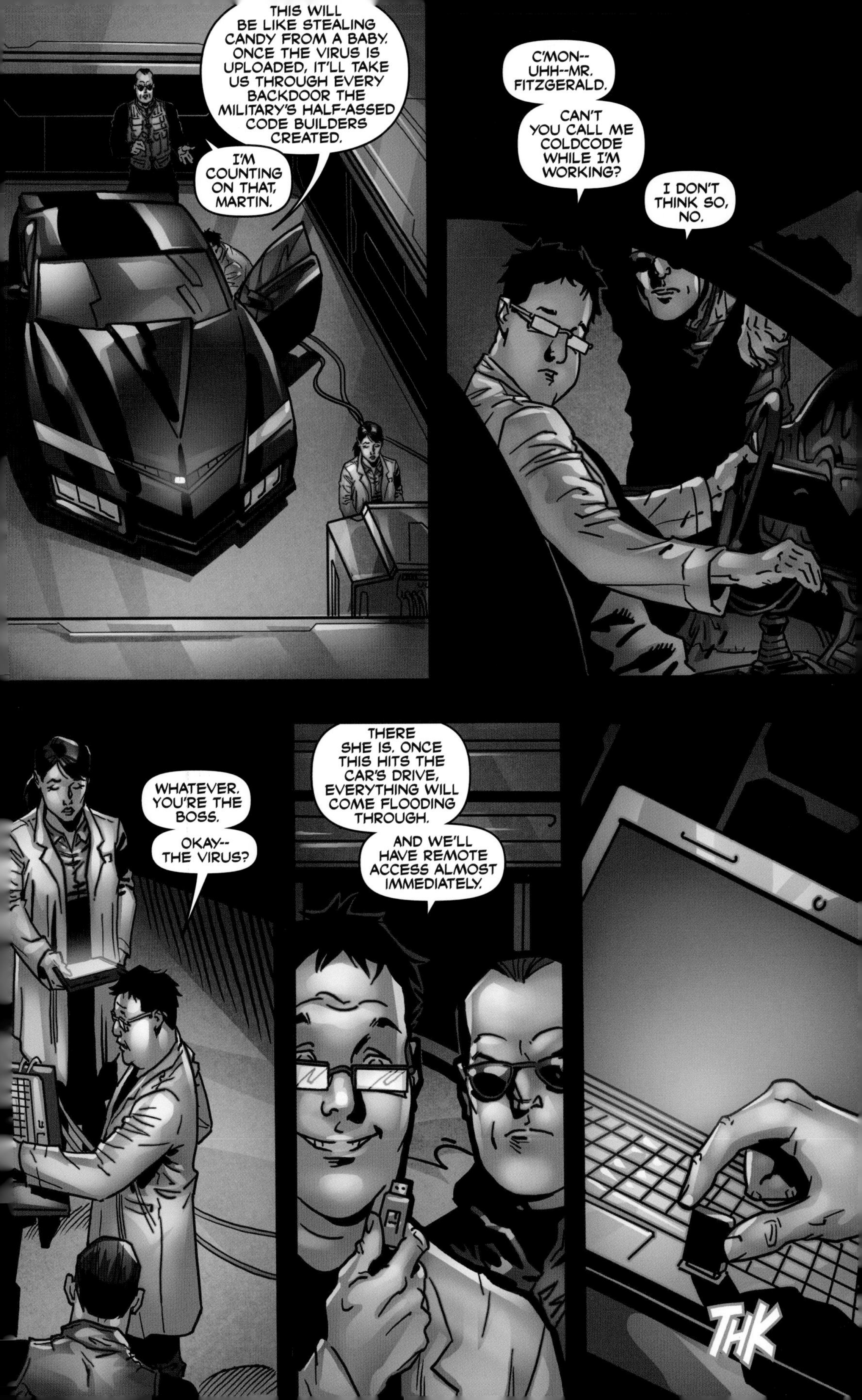
THIS WILL BE LIKE STEALING CANDY FROM A BABY. ONCE THE VIRUS IS UPLOADED, IT'LL TAKE US THROUGH EVERY BACKDOOR THE MILITARY'S HALF-ASSED CODE BUILDERS CREATED.
I'M COUNTING ON THAT, MARTIN.
C'MON-- UHH--MR. FITZGERALD.
CAN'T YOU CALL ME COLDCODE WHILE I'M WORKING?
I DON'T THINK SO, NO.
WHATEVER. YOU'RE THE BOSS.
OKAY-- THE VIRUS?
THERE SHE IS. ONCE THIS HITS THE CAR'S DRIVE, EVERYTHING WILL COME FLOODING THROUGH.
AND WE'LL HAVE REMOTE ACCESS ALMOST IMMEDIATELY.
THK

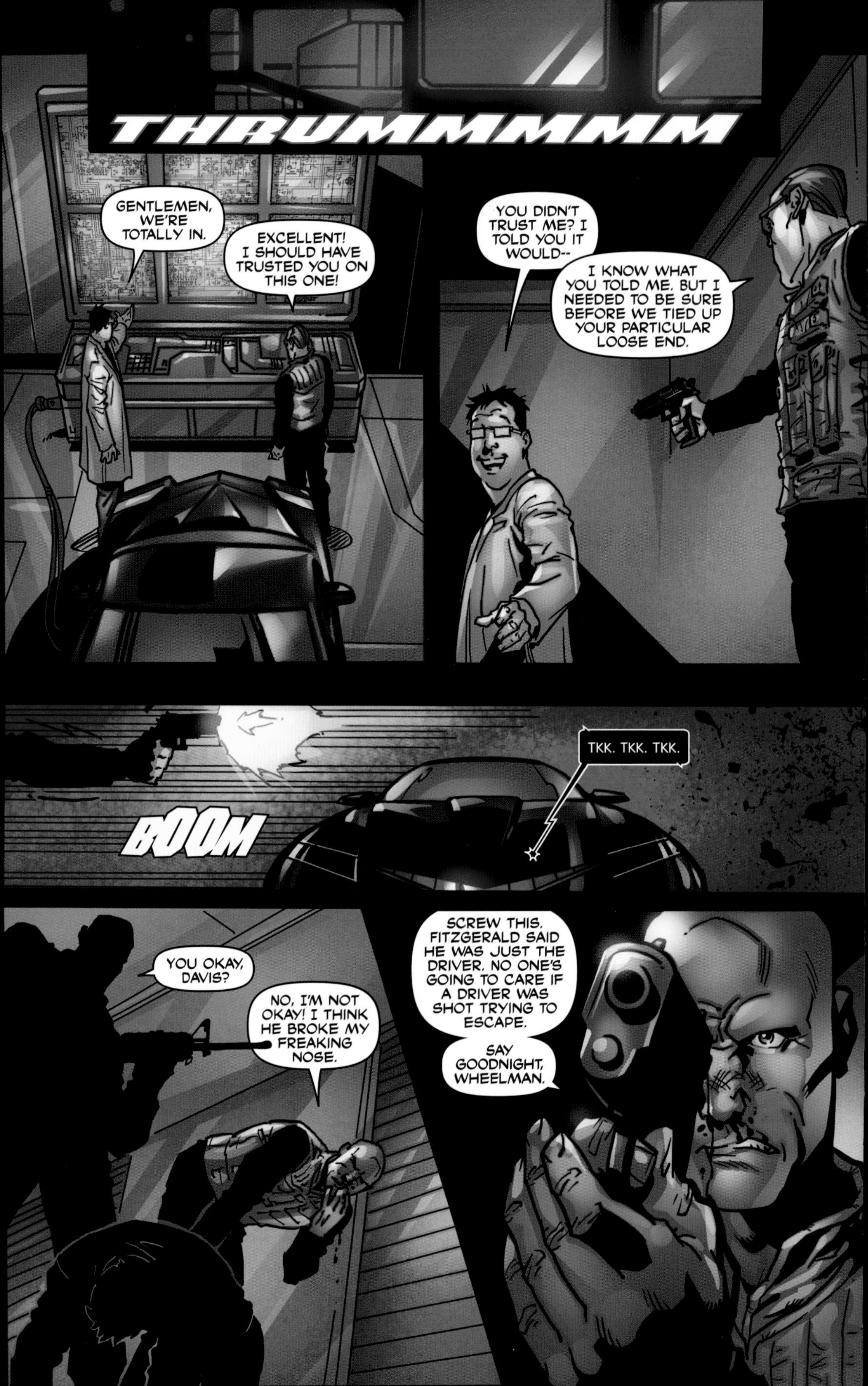
THRUMMMMMM
GENTLEMEN, WE'RE TOTALLY IN.
EXCELLENT! I SHOULD HAVE TRUSTED YOU ON THIS ONE!
YOU DIDN'T TRUST ME? I TOLD YOU IT WOULD--
I KNOW WHAT YOU TOLD ME. BUT I NEEDED TO BE SURE BEFORE WE TIED UP YOUR PARTICULAR LOOSE END.
BOOM
TKK. TKK. TKK.
YOU OKAY, DAVIS?
NO, I'M NOT OKAY! I THINK HE BROKE MY FREAKING NOSE.
SCREW THIS. FITZGERALD SAID HE WAS JUST THE DRIVER. NO ONE'S GOING TO CARE IF A DRIVER WAS SHOT TRYING TO ESCAPE.
SAY GOODNIGHT, WHEELMAN.

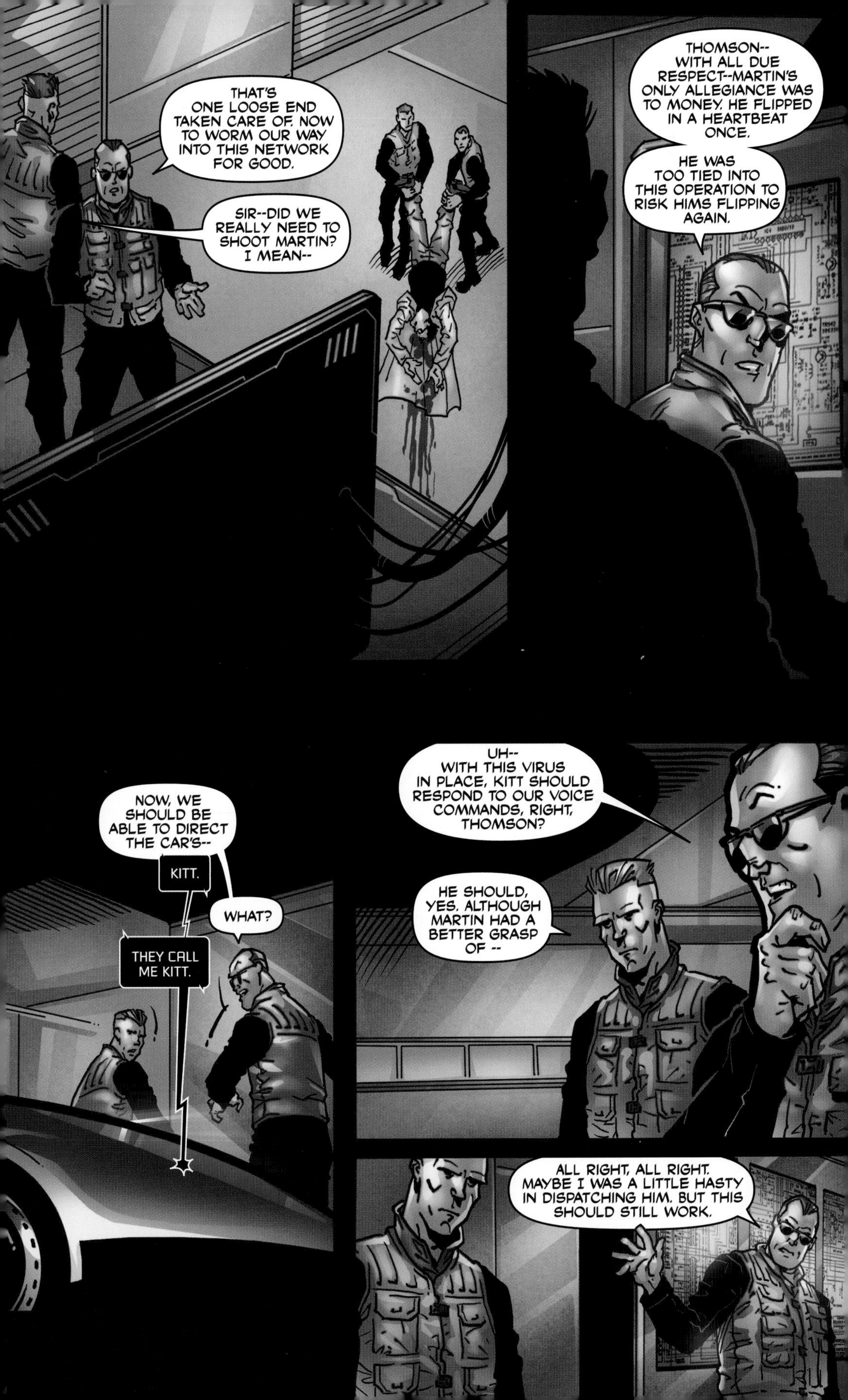
THAT'S ONE LOOSE END TAKEN CARE OF. NOW TO WORM OUR WAY INTO THIS NETWORK FOR GOOD.
SIR--DID WE REALLY NEED TO SHOOT MARTIN? I MEAN--
THOMSON-- WITH ALL DUE RESPECT--MARTIN'S ONLY ALLEGIANCE WAS TO MONEY. HE FLIPPED IN A HEARTBEAT ONCE.
HE WAS TOO TIED INTO THIS OPERATION TO RISK HIMS FLIPPING AGAIN.
NOW, WE SHOULD BE ABLE TO DIRECT THE CAR'S--
KITT.
WHAT?
THEY CALL ME KITT.
UH-- WITH THIS VIRUS IN PLACE, KITT SHOULD RESPOND TO OUR VOICE COMMANDS, RIGHT, THOMSON?
HE SHOULD, YES. ALTHOUGH MARTIN HAD A BETTER GRASP OF --
ALL RIGHT, ALL RIGHT. MAYBE I WAS A LITTLE HASTY IN DISPATCHING HIM. BUT THIS SHOULD STILL WORK.

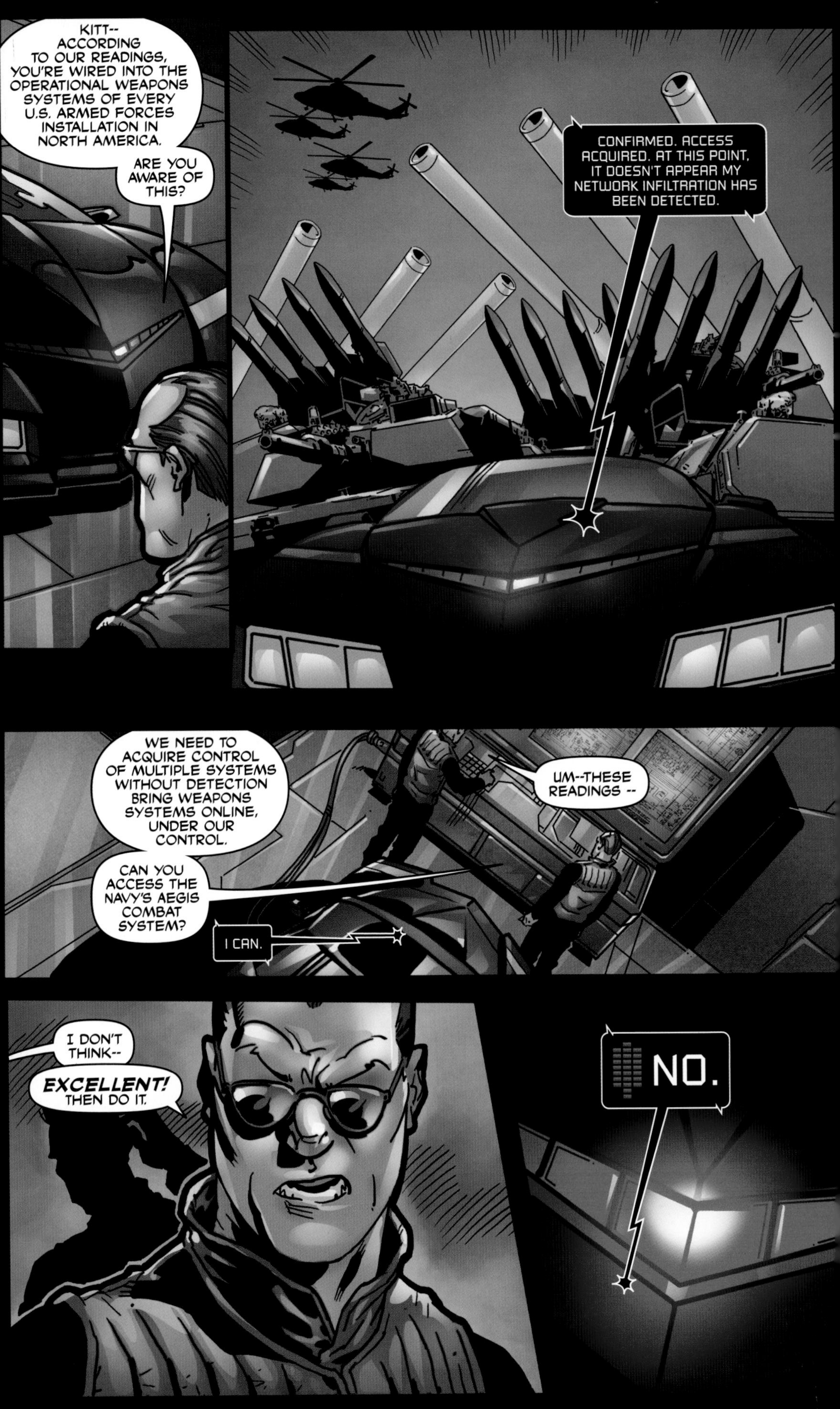

KITT-- ACCORDING TO OUR READINGS, YOU'RE WIRED INTO THE OPERATIONAL WEAPONS SYSTEMS OF EVERY U.S. ARMED FORCES INSTALLATION IN NORTH AMERICA.
ARE YOU AWARE OF THIS?
CONFIRMED. ACCESS ACQUIRED. AT THIS POINT, IT DOESN'T APPEAR MY NETWORK INFILTRATION HAS BEEN DETECTED.
WE NEED TO ACQUIRE CONTROL OF MULTIPLE SYSTEMS WITHOUT DETECTION BRING WEAPONS SYSTEMS ONLINE, UNDER OUR CONTROL.
UM--THESE READINGS --
CAN YOU ACCESS THE NAVY'S AEGIS COMBAT SYSTEM?
I CAN.
I DON'T THINK--
EXCELLENT! THEN DO IT.
NO.

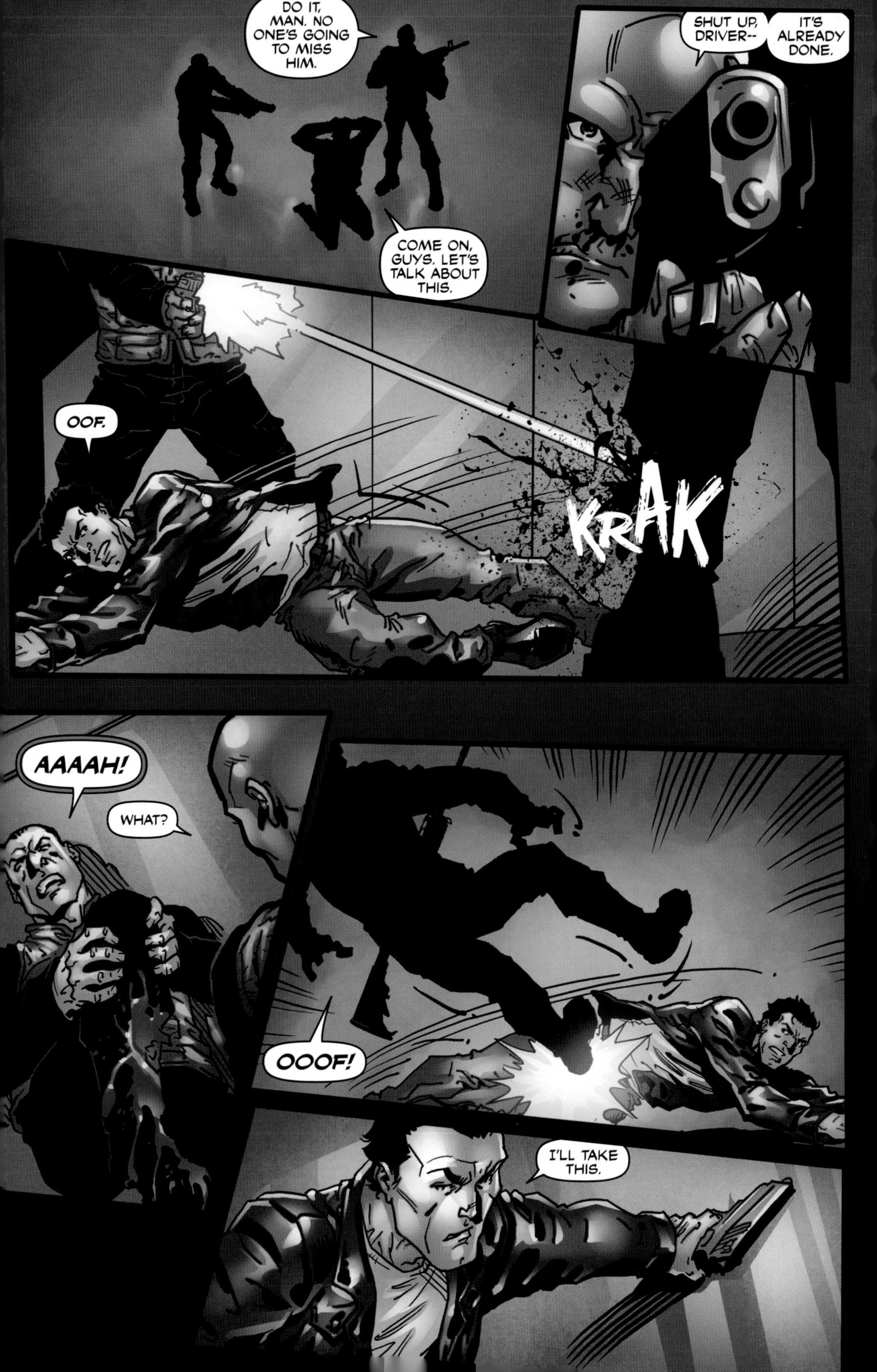
DO IT, MAN. NO ONE'S GOING TO MISS HIM.
COME ON, GUYS. LET'S TALK ABOUT THIS.
SHUT UP, DRIVER--
IT'S ALREADY DONE.
OOF.
KRAK
AAAAH!
WHAT?
OOOF!
I'LL TAKE THIS.

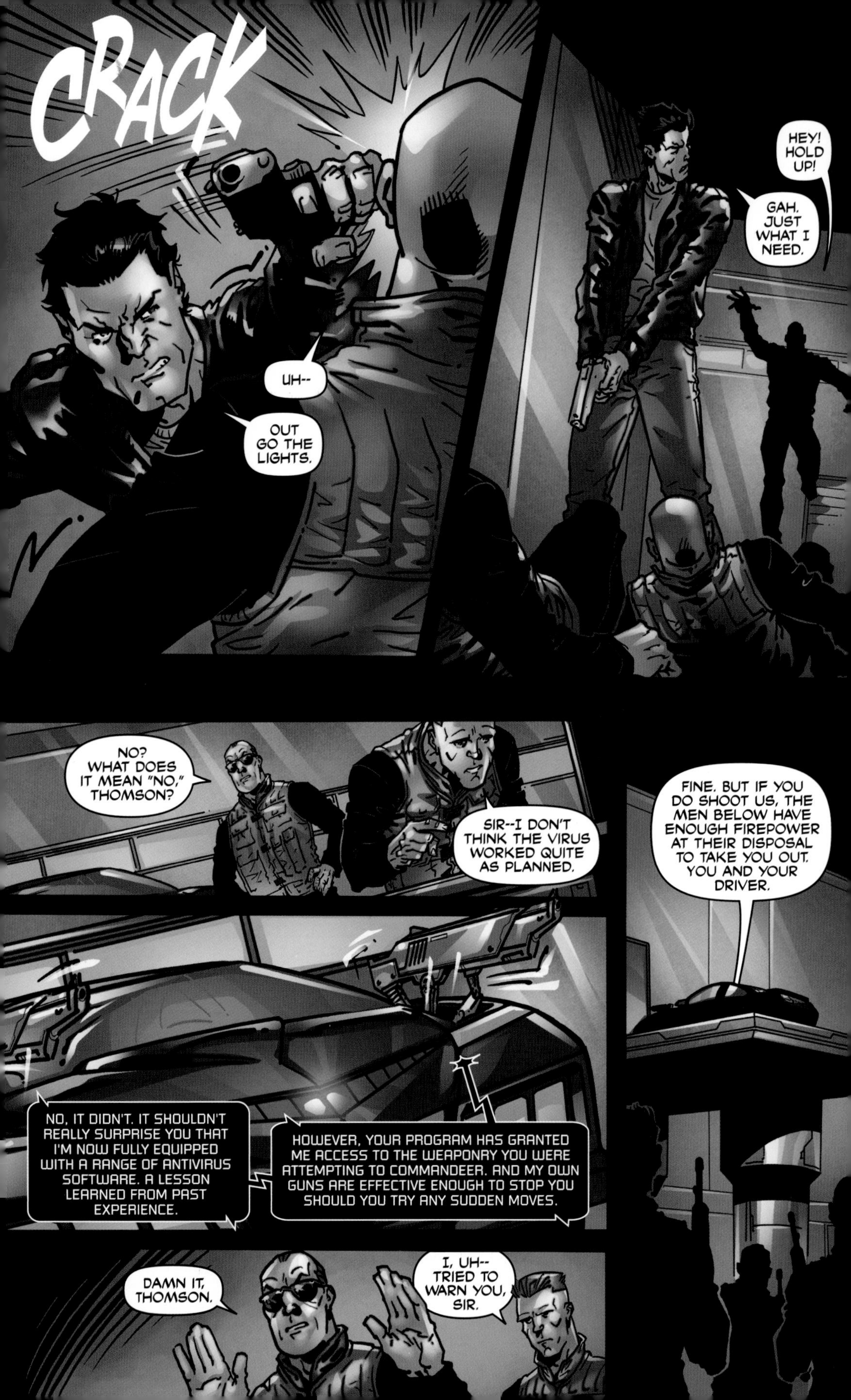
CRACK
UH--
OUT GO THE LIGHTS.
HEY! HOLD UP!
GAH. JUST WHAT I NEED.
NO? WHAT DOES IT MEAN "NO," THOMSON?
SIR--I DON'T THINK THE VIRUS WORKED QUITE AS PLANNED.
FINE. BUT IF YOU DO SHOOT US, THE MEN BELOW HAVE ENOUGH FIREPOWER AT THEIR DISPOSAL TO TAKE YOU OUT. YOU AND YOUR DRIVER.
NO, IT DIDN'T. IT SHOULDN'T REALLY SURPRISE YOU THAT I'M NOW FULLY EQUIPPED WITH A RANGE OF ANTIVIRUS SOFTWARE. A LESSON LEARNED FROM PAST EXPERIENCE.
HOWEVER, YOUR PROGRAM HAS GRANTED ME ACCESS TO THE WEAPONRY YOU WERE ATTEMPTING TO COMMANDEER. AND MY OWN GUNS ARE EFFECTIVE ENOUGH TO STOP YOU SHOULD YOU TRY ANY SUDDEN MOVES.
DAMN IT, THOMSON.
I, UH-- TRIED TO WARN YOU, SIR.

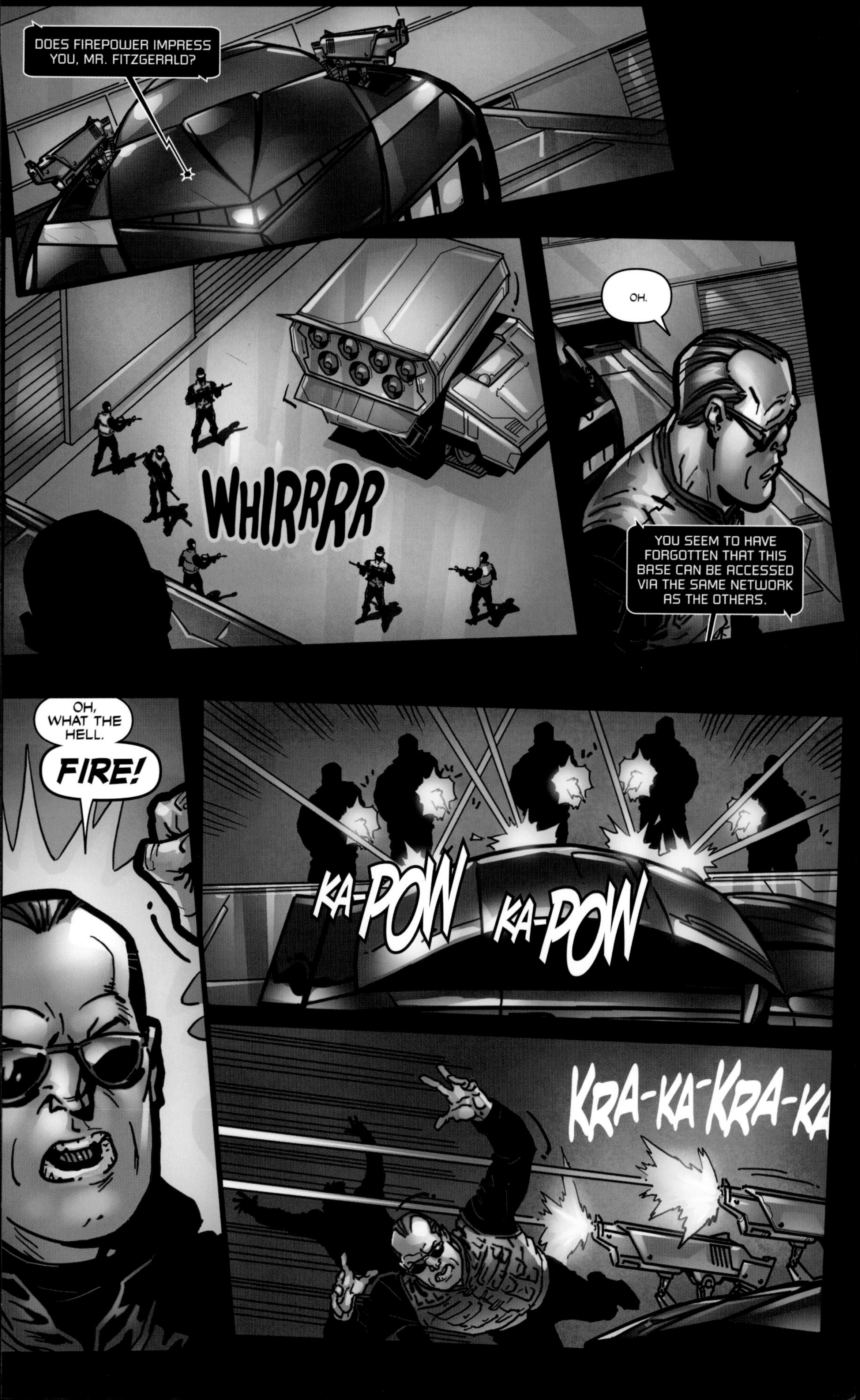

DOES FIREPOWER IMPRESS YOU, MR. FITZGERALD?
OH.
WHIRRRRR
YOU SEEM TO HAVE FORGOTTEN THAT THIS BASE CAN BE ACCESSED VIA THE SAME NETWORK AS THE OTHERS.
OH, WHAT THE HELL.
FIRE!
KA-POW
KA-POW
KRA-KA-KRA-KA

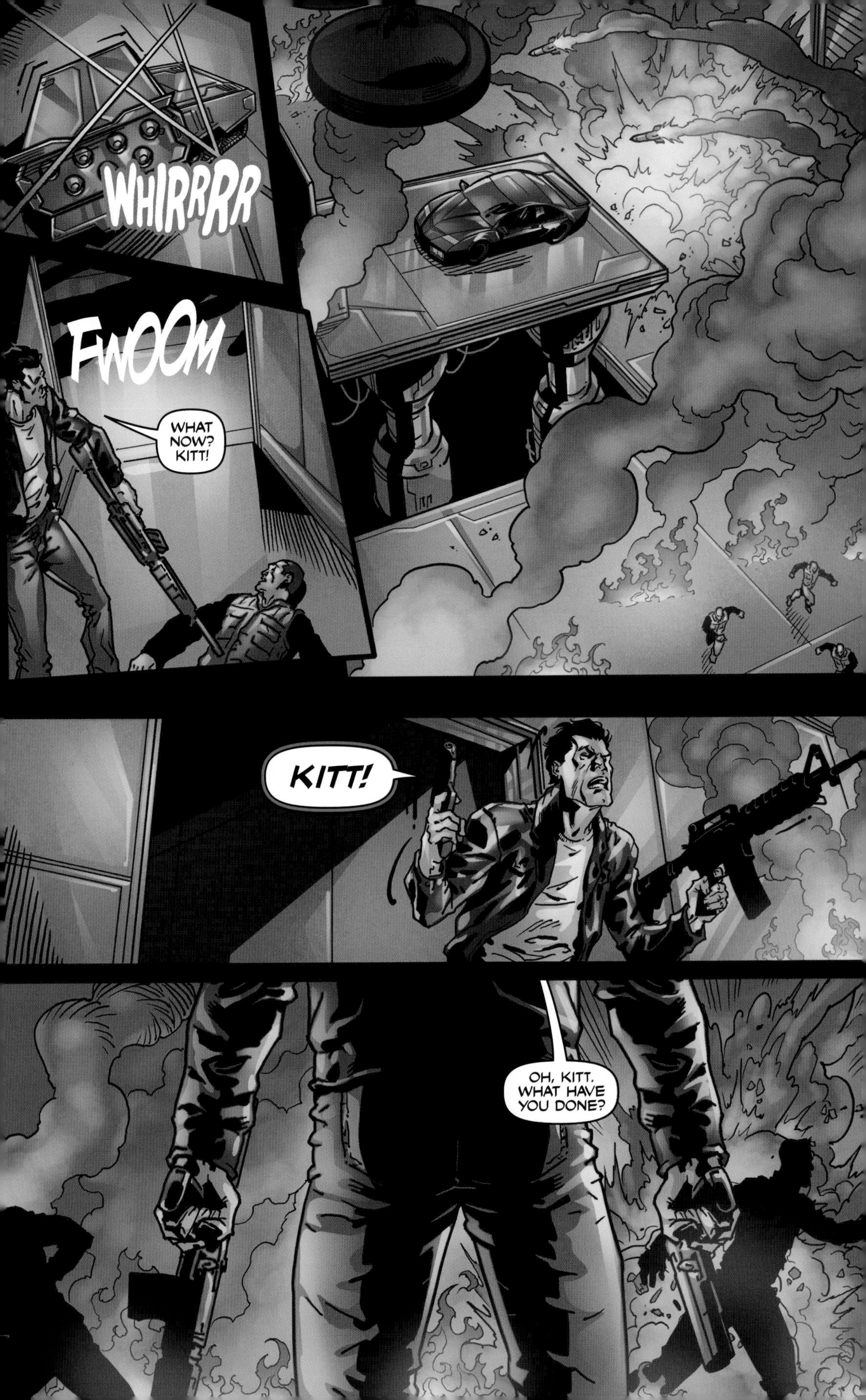
WHIRRRR
FWOOM
WHAT NOW? KITT!
KITT!
OH, KITT. WHAT HAVE YOU DONE?

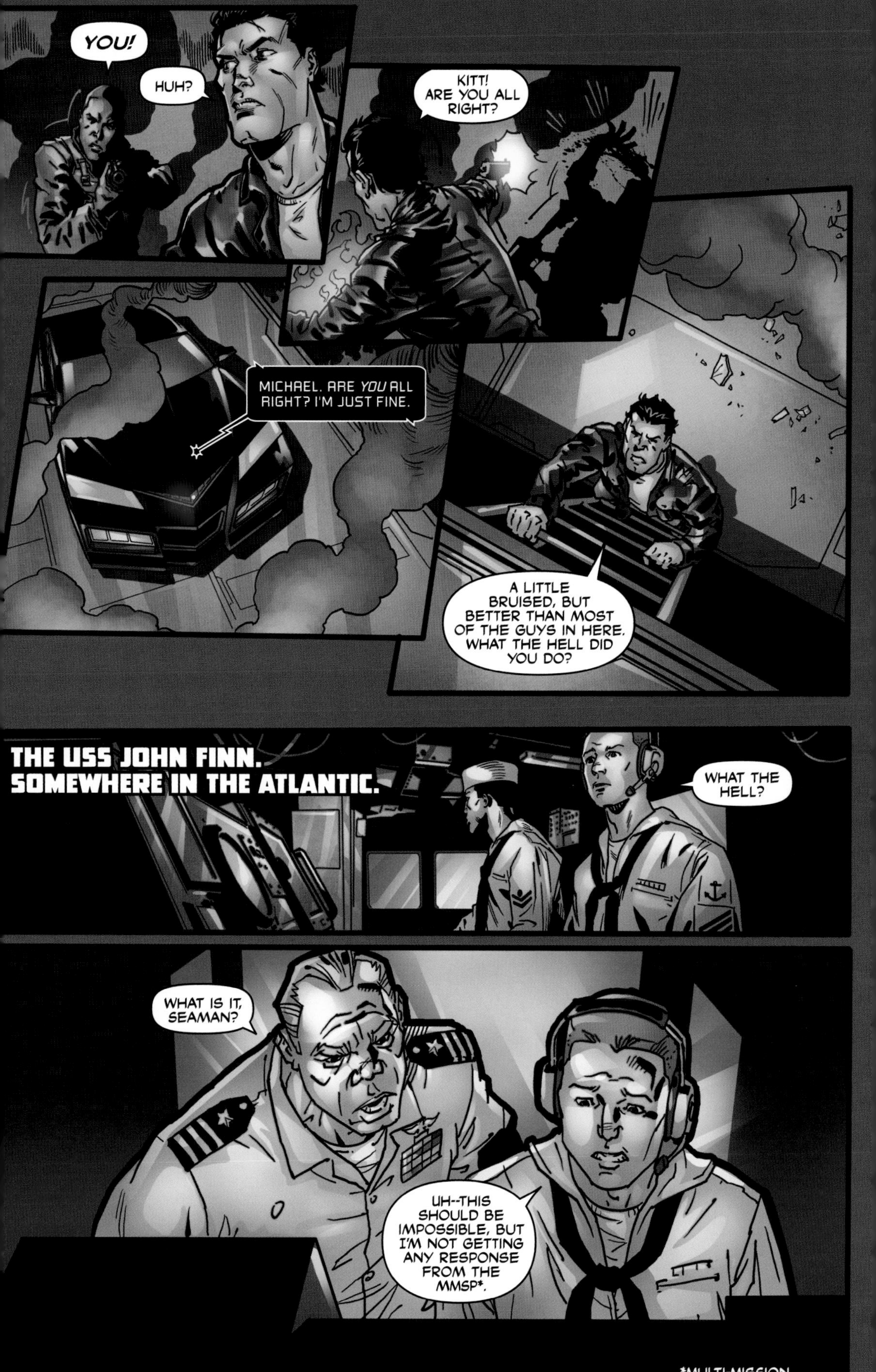

YOU!
HUH?
KITT! ARE YOU ALL RIGHT?
MICHAEL. ARE *YOU* ALL RIGHT? I'M JUST FINE.
A LITTLE BRUISED, BUT BETTER THAN MOST OF THE GUYS IN HERE. WHAT THE HELL DID YOU DO?
THE USS JOHN FINN. SOMEWHERE IN THE ATLANTIC.
WHAT THE HELL?
WHAT IS IT, SEAMAN?
UH--THIS SHOULD BE IMPOSSIBLE, BUT I'M NOT GETTING ANY RESPONSE FROM THE MMSP*.
*MULTI-MISSION SIGNAL PROCESSOR

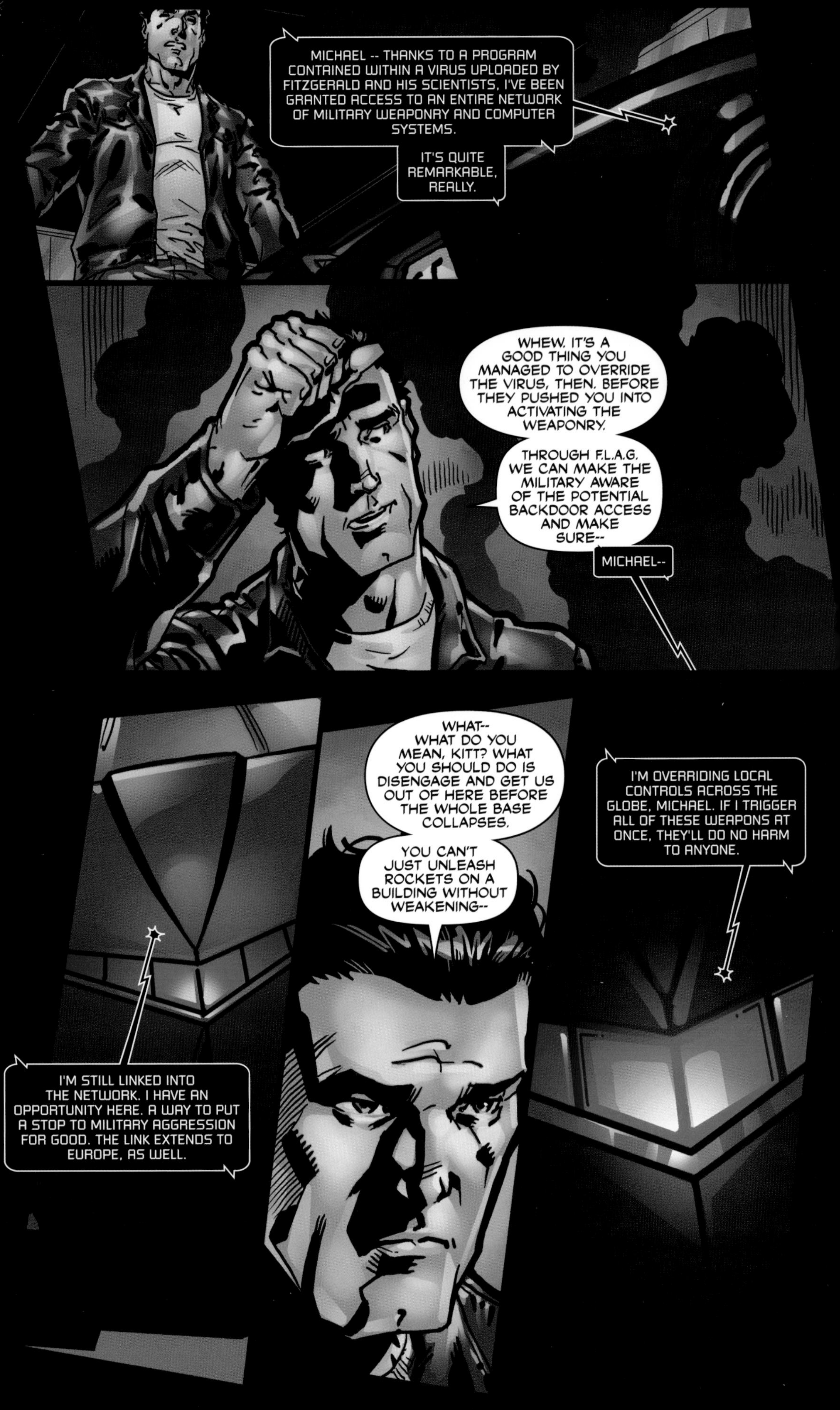

MICHAEL -- THANKS TO A PROGRAM CONTAINED WITHIN A VIRUS UPLOADED BY FITZGERALD AND HIS SCIENTISTS, I'VE BEEN GRANTED ACCESS TO AN ENTIRE NETWORK OF MILITARY WEAPONRY AND COMPUTER SYSTEMS.
IT'S QUITE REMARKABLE, REALLY.
WHEW. IT'S A GOOD THING YOU MANAGED TO OVERRIDE THE VIRUS, THEN. BEFORE THEY PUSHED YOU INTO ACTIVATING THE WEAPONRY.
THROUGH F.L.A.G. WE CAN MAKE THE MILITARY AWARE OF THE POTENTIAL BACKDOOR ACCESS AND MAKE SURE--
MICHAEL--
I'M STILL LINKED INTO THE NETWORK. I HAVE AN OPPORTUNITY HERE. A WAY TO PUT A STOP TO MILITARY AGGRESSION FOR GOOD. THE LINK EXTENDS TO EUROPE, AS WELL.
WHAT-- WHAT DO YOU MEAN, KITT? WHAT YOU SHOULD DO IS DISENGAGE AND GET US OUT OF HERE BEFORE THE WHOLE BASE COLLAPSES.
YOU CAN'T JUST UNLEASH ROCKETS ON A BUILDING WITHOUT WEAKENING--
I'M OVERRIDING LOCAL CONTROLS ACROSS THE GLOBE, MICHAEL. IF I TRIGGER ALL OF THESE WEAPONS AT ONCE, THEY'LL DO NO HARM TO ANYONE.

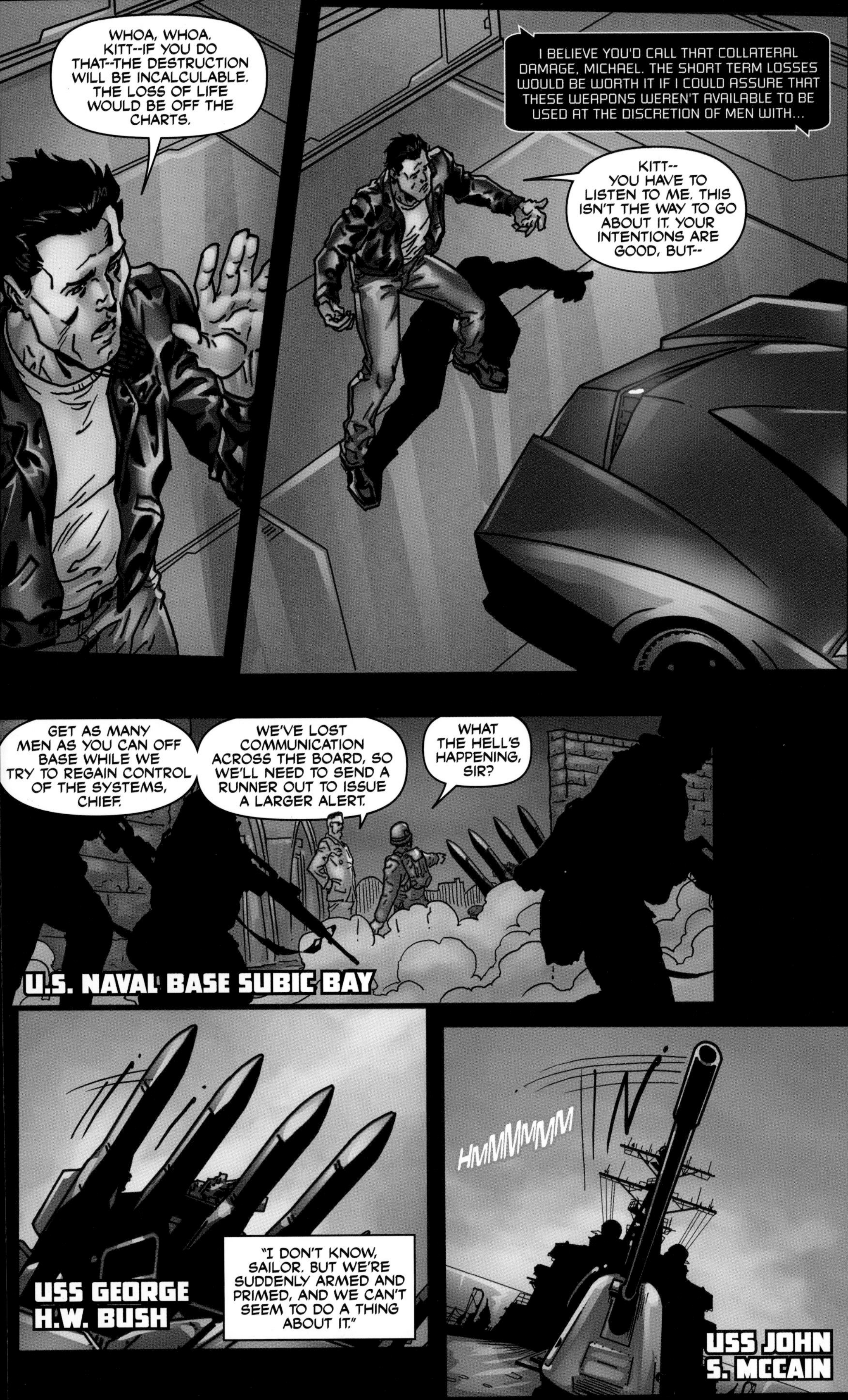
WHOA, WHOA, KITT--IF YOU DO THAT--THE DESTRUCTION WILL BE INCALCULABLE. THE LOSS OF LIFE WOULD BE OFF THE CHARTS.
I BELIEVE YOU'D CALL THAT COLLATERAL DAMAGE, MICHAEL. THE SHORT TERM LOSSES WOULD BE WORTH IT IF I COULD ASSURE THAT THESE WEAPONS WEREN'T AVAILABLE TO BE USED AT THE DISCRETION OF MEN WITH...
KITT-- YOU HAVE TO LISTEN TO ME. THIS ISN'T THE WAY TO GO ABOUT IT. YOUR INTENTIONS ARE GOOD, BUT--
U.S. NAVAL BASE SUBIC BAY
GET AS MANY MEN AS YOU CAN OFF BASE WHILE WE TRY TO REGAIN CONTROL OF THE SYSTEMS, CHIEF.
WE'VE LOST COMMUNICATION ACROSS THE BOARD, SO WE'LL NEED TO SEND A RUNNER OUT TO ISSUE A LARGER ALERT.
WHAT THE HELL'S HAPPENING, SIR?
USS GEORGE H.W. BUSH
"I DON'T KNOW, SAILOR. BUT WE'RE SUDDENLY ARMED AND PRIMED, AND WE CAN'T SEEM TO DO A THING ABOUT IT."
HMMMMMM
USS JOHN S. MCCAIN

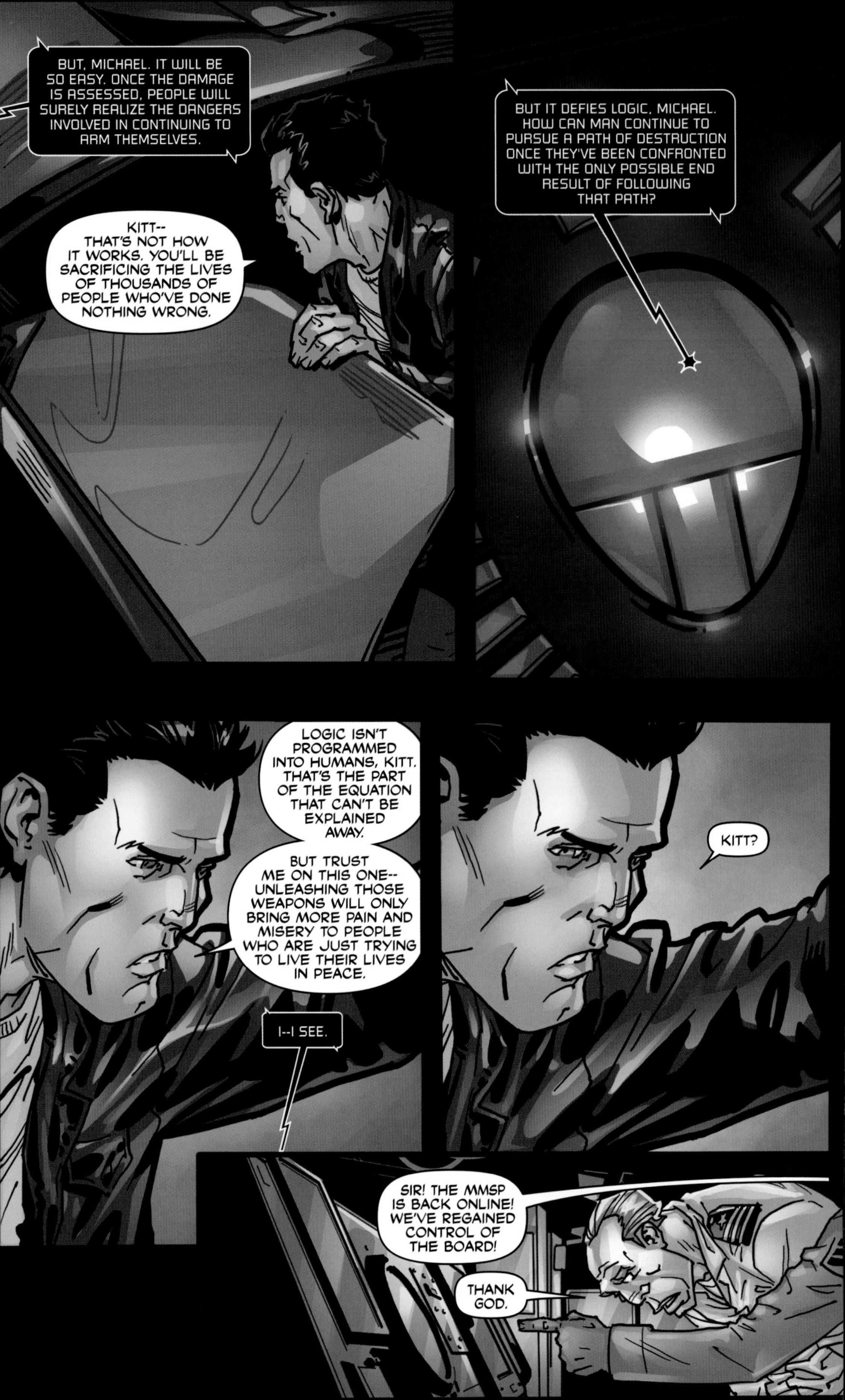
BUT, MICHAEL. IT WILL BE SO EASY. ONCE THE DAMAGE IS ASSESSED, PEOPLE WILL SURELY REALIZE THE DANGERS INVOLVED IN CONTINUING TO ARM THEMSELVES.
KITT-- THAT'S NOT HOW IT WORKS. YOU'LL BE SACRIFICING THE LIVES OF THOUSANDS OF PEOPLE WHO'VE DONE NOTHING WRONG.
BUT IT DEFIES LOGIC, MICHAEL. HOW CAN MAN CONTINUE TO PURSUE A PATH OF DESTRUCTION ONCE THEY'VE BEEN CONFRONTED WITH THE ONLY POSSIBLE END RESULT OF FOLLOWING THAT PATH?
LOGIC ISN'T PROGRAMMED INTO HUMANS, KITT. THAT'S THE PART OF THE EQUATION THAT CAN'T BE EXPLAINED AWAY.
BUT TRUST ME ON THIS ONE-- UNLEASHING THOSE WEAPONS WILL ONLY BRING MORE PAIN AND MISERY TO PEOPLE WHO ARE JUST TRYING TO LIVE THEIR LIVES IN PEACE.
I--I SEE.
KITT?
SIR! THE MMSP IS BACK ONLINE! WE'VE REGAINED CONTROL OF THE BOARD!
THANK GOD.

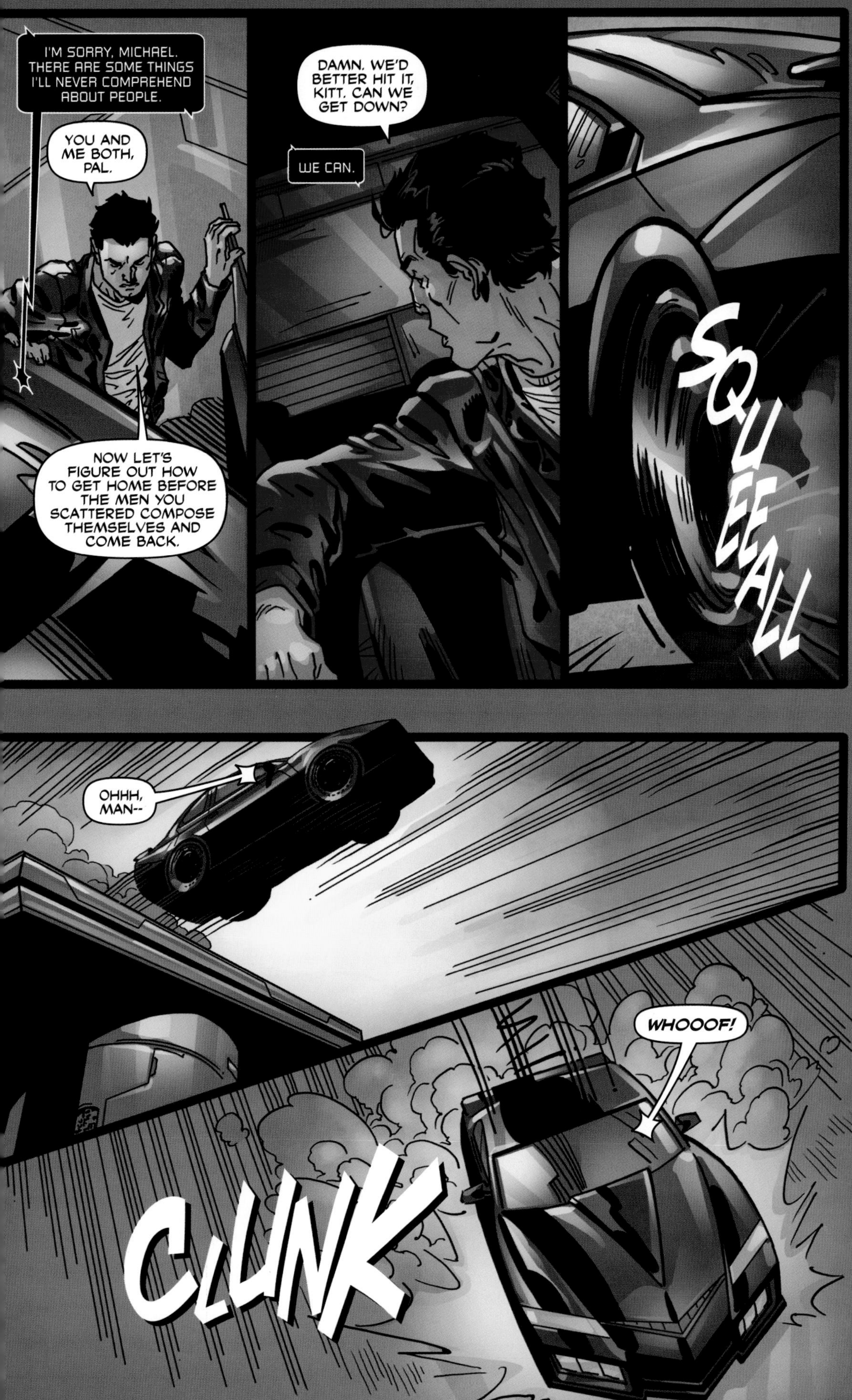
I'M SORRY, MICHAEL. THERE ARE SOME THINGS I'LL NEVER COMPREHEND ABOUT PEOPLE.
YOU AND ME BOTH, PAL.
NOW LET'S FIGURE OUT HOW TO GET HOME BEFORE THE MEN YOU SCATTERED COMPOSE THEMSELVES AND COME BACK.
DAMN. WE'D BETTER HIT IT, KITT. CAN WE GET DOWN?
WE CAN.
SQUEEEALL
OHHH, MAN--
WHOOOF!
CLUNK

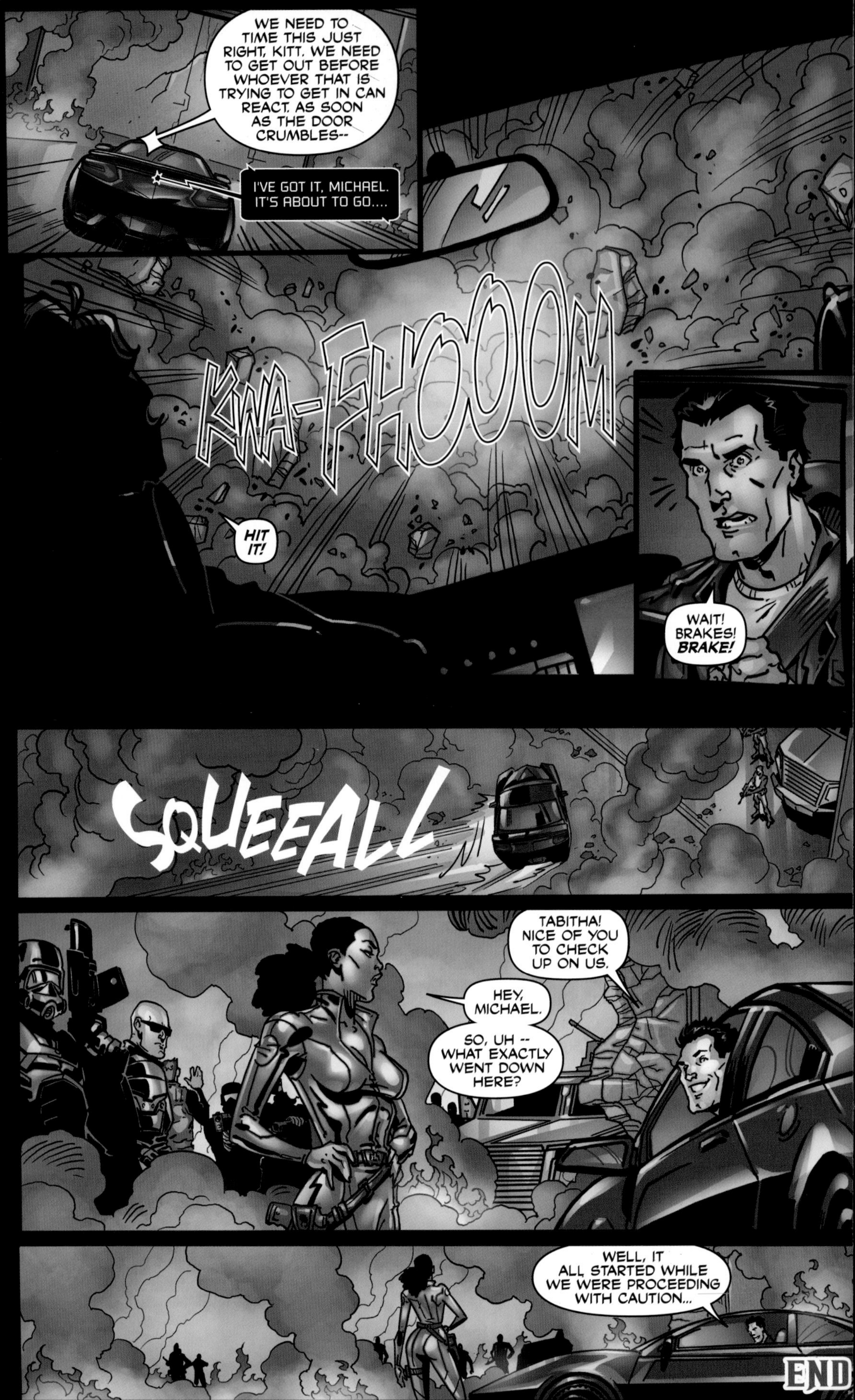
WE NEED TO TIME THIS JUST RIGHT, KITT. WE NEED TO GET OUT BEFORE WHOEVER THAT IS TRYING TO GET IN CAN REACT. AS SOON AS THE DOOR CRUMBLES--
I'VE GOT IT, MICHAEL. IT'S ABOUT TO GO....
KWA-FHOOOM
HIT IT!
WAIT! BRAKES! BRAKE!
SQUEEALL
TABITHA! NICE OF YOU TO CHECK UP ON US.
HEY, MICHAEL.
SO, UH -- WHAT EXACTLY WENT DOWN HERE?
WELL, IT ALL STARTED WHILE WE WERE PROCEEDING WITH CAUTION...
END

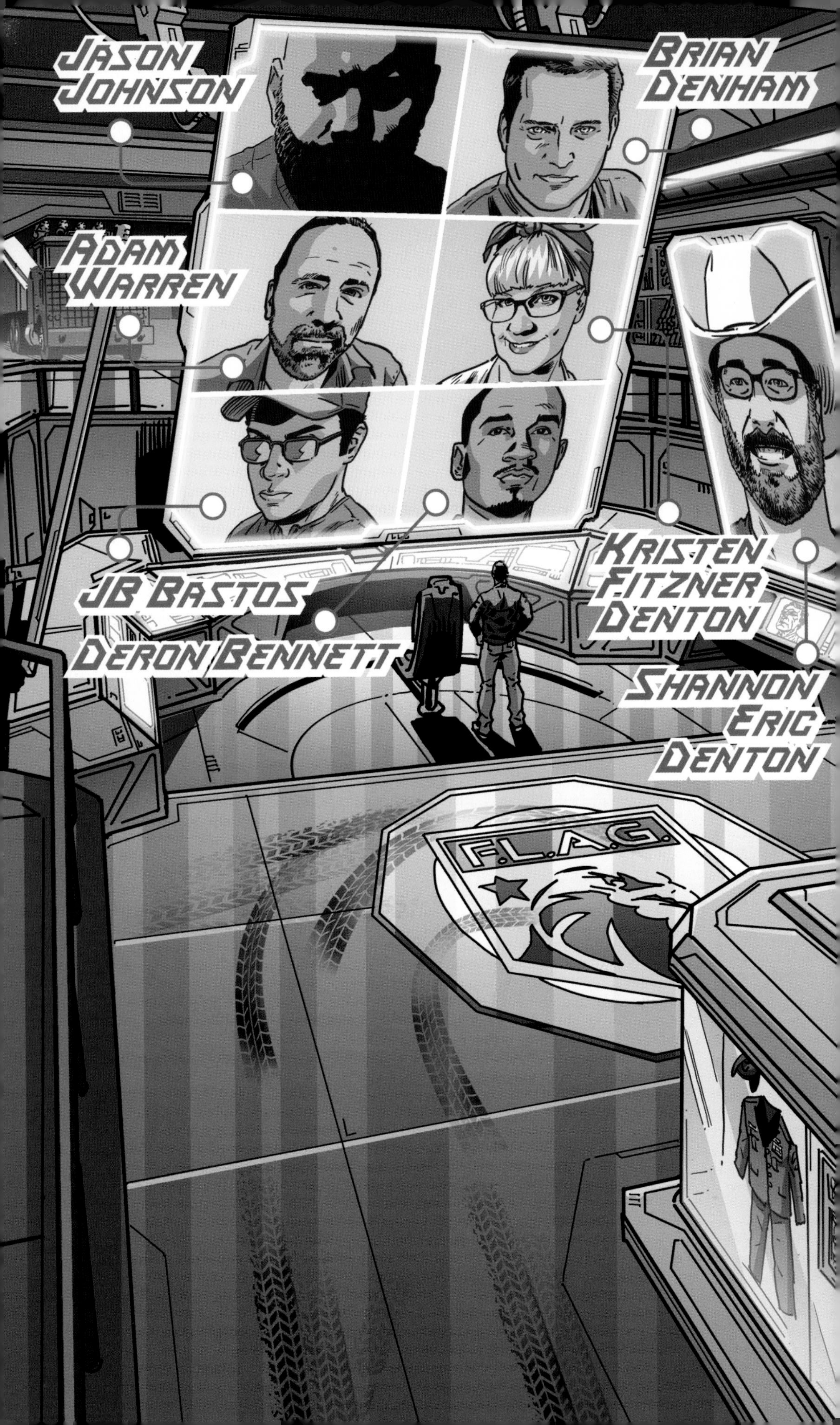

Jason Johnson
Brian Denham
Adam Warren
JB Bastos
Deron Bennett
Kristen Fitzner Denton
Shannon Eric Denton
F.L.A.G.

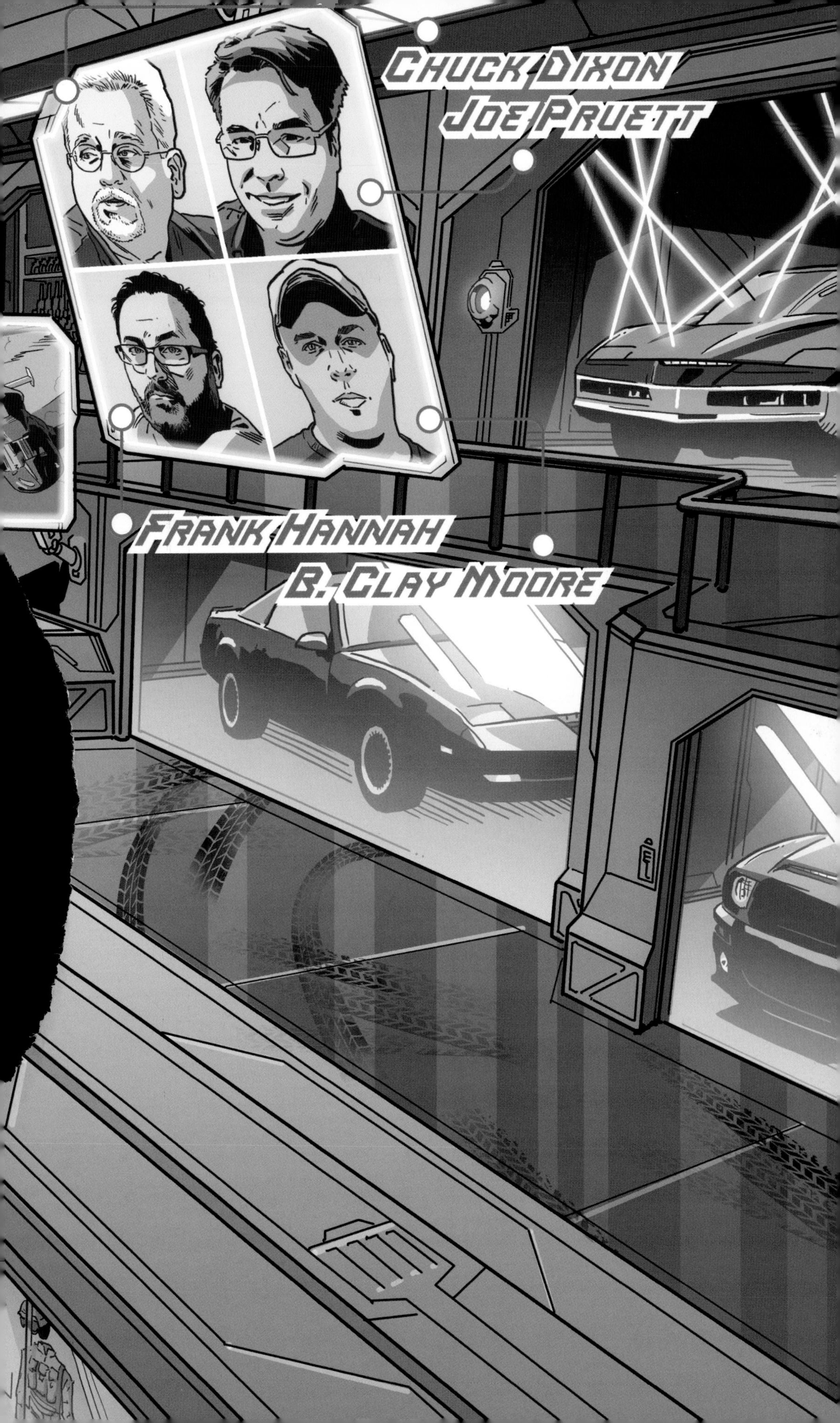
CHUCK DIXON
JOE PRUETT
FRANK HANNAH
B. CLAY MOORE

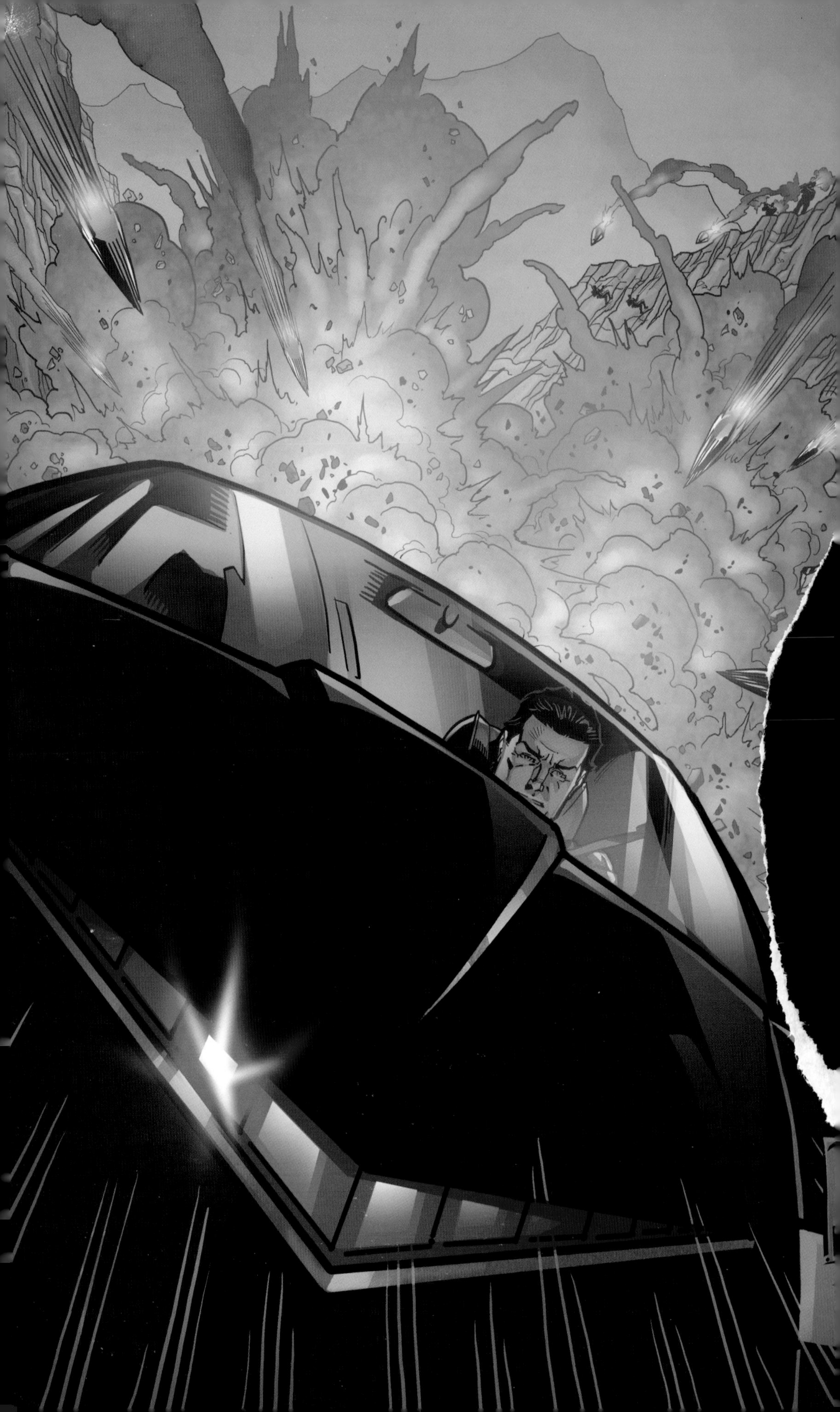